ENGLISH LAW

The Judicial Contribution

ENGLISH LAW
The Judicial Contribution

GEORGE W. KEETON

DAVID & CHARLES
NEWTON ABBOT

0 7153 6410 3

Set in 11 on 13-point Plantin
and printed in Great Britain
by W J Holman Limited Dawlish
for David & Charles (Holdings) Limited
South Devon House Newton Abbot Devon

CONTENTS

I

Anglo-Saxon Law

Maitland once remarked that a legal historian was not a special sort of person. The study of legal history assumes a knowledge of the societies in which the law of an earlier age functioned. As the late Miss Helen Cam emphasised in the perceptive introduction to her collection of Maitland's *Historical Essays*,[1] Maitland's researches into legal history led him inevitably into political and social history. In her concise phrase, he 'brought law to bear on history, and history to bear on law'.[2] Above all, he was at all times conscious that law exists for people, and therefore the habits of the people to whom laws were applicable must be familiar to the historian who writes about law.

It is always necessary to avoid the trap of considering legal rules from past ages out of context, and of attributing to them a significance unknown to those for whom the rules were framed; one must resist the impulse to see a system where there is none.

Tout in his lectures on *The Place of the Reign of Edward II in English History*[3] gives the same warning. He emphasises the 'unhistorical way of looking at history to which ordinary practical lawyers have at all ages been exceptionally prone', and he adds:

> They look at the past as a plane surface which has never been altered. They have imperfect appreciation of the idea of development. They assume that the modern categories have existed from all time, and persist in reading them back into an age which knew nothing of them. Take as an ancient example of this mental habit, the attitude of the seventeenth century lawyers of the school of Coke to mediaeval antiquities, which led them to read into history the ideas of their own age and profession.[4]

One is compelled to admit that the charge has been justified only too often, and it is characteristic of Maitland's genius that in his work he was always aware of this legal shortcoming. Perhaps the most striking illustration of this is to be found in the persistent attribution to William the Conqueror of the introduction of 'the feudal system' into England in the year 1066. In an incisive passage in his lectures on constitutional history, Maitland says:

> Coke in his voluminous works has summed up for us the law of the later Middle Ages, but in all his books, unless I am mistaken, there is no word about the feudal system. If we may say, he expounds that system in full detail, so far as that system was English, he is quite unconscious that he is doing anything of the kind: he has no thought of a system common to the nations of Europe, he is speaking of our insular law. No, for a 'feudal system' we must turn from Coke to a contemporary of his, that learned and laborious antiquary, Sir Henry Spelman. . . . Now were an examiner to ask 'who introduced the feudal system into England?' one very good answer if properly explained, would be Henry Spelman, and if there followed the question, 'what was the feudal system?' a good answer to that would be, an early essay in comparative jurisprudence. Spelman reading continental books saw that English law, for all its insularity, was a member of a great European family, a family between all members of which there were strong family likenesses. This was for Englishmen a grand and striking discovery; much that had seemed quite arbitrary in their old laws and now seemed explicable. They learned of feudal law as of mediaeval *jus gentium*, a system common to all the nations of the West. The new learning was propagated among English lawyers by Sir Martin Wright; it was popularized and made orthodox by Blackstone in his easy and attractive manner. If my examiner went on with his questions and asked me 'when did the feudal system attain its most perfect development?' I should answer, about the middle of the last century. It was then I should add that the notion of one grand idea and a few

> simple principles underlying the mass of mediaeval law, English and continental, was firmly grasped and used as a means of explaining all that seemed to need explanation in the old English law.[5]

Maitland's lectures were written in 1888, when the massive work of Bishop Stubbs still dominated English thinking on medieval law and politics, but his insight has been strongly reinforced by the work of later historians. Recently Richardson and Sayles, in their too little known work upon *The Governance of Mediaeval England*, have written:

> If we are to attempt a rational account of the settlement that followed the Norman Conquest, we must begin by dissipating a myth, the myth that almost immediately after his coronation King William introduced 'feudalism' into England and that he did this by alloting quotas of knight service to the estates of his tenants-in-chief. So rapid was his work, we are assured, that it was accomplished before the end of 1070. The details of this remarkable feat are unfortunately wrapped in almost complete obscurity, and the belief that it was performed at all rests, not upon contemporary authority, but solely upon an obviously erroneous assertion, more than a century later, by Roger of Wendover and the assumptions of J. H. Round—

which in fact, were founded upon a questionable interpretation of Wendover's works.[6]

Historians, one might observe, are often combative. Even normally pacific historians frequently belabour colleagues who persist in rival theories. Lawyers should understand this, for much of their professional life is spent in judicial combat. So far as our own particular theme is concerned, for something like a half-century the historians of this age have again been fighting over the Battle of Hastings. One school attributes a higher degree of civilisation, and even political organisation, to the Saxons. Richardson and Sayles, in fact, come close to denying a single vital idea, either in law or government, to the Normans. Others adhere firmly to the belief that civilisation and legal development like the chronology of our kings began on the morning after Saxon power fell forever at Hastings.

By the middle of the eleventh century, England had, with difficulty, achieved both unity and stability. This was the more remarkable since, from the time when the Romans finally withdrew early in the fifth century, the country had rarely been free of invasions, or threatened invasions. Angles, Saxons, Jutes, Frisians, Danes and Scandinavians, had all descended upon her shores, first to plunder and lay waste and later to settle. Naturally, since the eastern seaboard lay nearest the continent, was low-lying, and was punctuated by navigable estuaries, it was the eastern and north-eastern counties which bore the brunt of these invasions; but the Scandinavians, living further to the north, sailed round the Orkneys and the Shetlands (where they also settled) to reach Ireland (where they established a colony in the vicinity of Dublin), the Isle of Man, and finally, Lancashire and Westmorland. While all these peoples had a common, but remote Teutonic ancestry, they differed widely in their civilisation and customs. For example, the Jutes whose settlements were confined to Kent, the Isle of Wight and parts of Hampshire, had a distinct body of customs in which may perhaps be found the origin of gavelkind tenure, with its special incidents and equal descent to sons on death. This remained as a local variation to the general rule of primogeniture until 1926, when it was abolished by the Law of Property Act. Although Plucknett suggests that this tenure may have been at one time more widespread, the suggestion does not explain its peculiar tenacity in Kent.

One of the most striking features of English law (if such a term is permissible with respect to Saxon England) is the abundance of local customs. There were customs common to areas as large as counties. For example, the customs of Kent were claimed and recognised before the Justices in Eyre, and were reduced to writing to give them permanence; and so were the extremely important and numerous customs of London, which still formed a separate and comprehensive body of law, distinct from the Common Law, as late as the reign of Edward II. Every town of any size claimed its customs, and so did many manors. The supremacy of the Common Law was neither easily nor quickly achieved, and so long as General Eyres were held, the king's justices were watchful lest ground won with difficulty for the Common Law should again be overrun by local customs. By the fourteenth century the justices were saying that a local custom which is unreasonable cannot prevail against the Common Law. This left scope for the exercise of judicial discretion, yet it was necessary for the judges to proceed with caution, since all lawyers were aware that many of these customs antedated the Norman Conquest. For example, in speaking of the customs of the counties and cities Bracton says that 'one must always enquire what is the custom of the place and how it is used'. So far as the unfree tenures were concerned, the copyholder did not obtain the protection of the king's courts until the fifteenth century, and by that time, manorial custom was so firmly entrenched that, once again, it survived until the Law of Property Act, 1925. By this time it had become a formidable obstacle to the swift transfer of land.

While Saxon England showed a great richness and variety of local customs, they could nevertheless be grouped into three great divisions, having their roots deep in the history of Saxon England. The customs of the historic kingdoms of Northumbria, Mercia and Wessex showed important variations, derived from their separate development and former rivalry, and also from their different racial structure, although Wessex and Mercia showed fewer differences between themselves than they together did in respect of Northumbria. There was an important reason for this. Mercia and Wessex, covering west central England, the south and the south west, were overwhelmingly Saxon, and had been preserved for Saxon civilisation by the efforts of Alfred (whose mother was of Jutish descent) and his family, in holding back the tidal wave of Danish invasions, which had their origins in the north and the east. This area, known as the Danelaw, was preserved by Alfred's settlement with the Danish leader, Guthrum, as an area of Danish settlement, in which Danish customs should prevail. Even today this distinction between the inhabitants of north and south has not been finally extinguished, although the mobility of the present century has greatly reduced its significance. Place names, however, are more resistant to change, and those of Lincolnshire, Yorkshire and Lancashire show innumerable instances of their Scandinavian origin. The Danelaw was, in fact, a separate world in which Danish law prevailed, even though the settlement made by Alfred in 886, and the wise statesmanship of Canute in the first half of the eleventh century, had given rise to a feeling of greater security, in which a good deal of intermarriage and intermixture of the two races had taken place. Another factor promoting this fusion of races was the evolution of a Danish aristocracy in England (produced by more settled conditions and increasing prosperity), which, by a familiar pattern, found itself linked by mutual interest, habits and interests with its Saxon counterparts. Canute, in particular, employed Saxons and Danes impartially in his armies and in his rapidly developing administration.

Nevertheless, the inhabitants of the old historic kingdoms, which in the time of Edward the Confessor had been transformed into the three vast territorial earldoms, owned and, in important measure, governed by the foremost Anglo–Danish families, still remained conscious of differences. In the first half-century after the Norman Conquest there was continuing interest in those three distinct bodies of law, for a variety of reasons. The Norman conquerors were anxious to discover and apply the laws of the subject people who so greatly outnumbered them. The Saxons and Danes, whether secular or religious landowners, clung tenaciously to these same customs, which protected their remaining rights. We therefore have a number of compilations, probably from the hand of clerics, with titles such as the *Laws of Edward the Confessor*, the *Laws of William*, or the *Laws of Henry I*, compilations which are self-evident forgeries—for none of these kings ever enacted such a body of legislation—and in which the bias of the compiler is often in evidence. For example, in the so-called *Laws of Edward the Confessor*, forged sometime early in the twelfth century, in the reign of Henry I, the anti-Danish bias of the author is as evident as his admiration for the laws of Wessex. Inferentially, too, in

exhibiting the laws of pre-Conquest days as those of a lost Golden Age, the author equally showed anti-Norman bias. The author of the *Laws of Henry I*, written at approximately the same time, is very clearly conscious of the existence of different bodies of law in Wessex, Mercia and the Danelaw, and in order to harmonise them, he appeals also to Roman, canon, and even Frankish law—a process which would have been inconceivable in a pre-Conquest writer. One striking feature of these earliest legal text-books is that they are often concerned with matters of procedure—a hint that they were seen as guides to the conduct of pleas in county courts where the laws differed greatly, even half a century after the Battle of Hastings. Their existence should serve as a warning against any assumption that the habits of Saxons and Danes suffered any revolutionary change under Norman rule, or that the kingdom could be described as a unified whole.

At the same time, national unity had increased greatly in the last century of Saxon England, and in a number of important particulars, England at that time was in advance of other parts of Western Europe, and more particularly, of Normandy. This was partly the product of more settled conditions, and partly the result of the cautiously progressive governments. The Saxon and Danish rulers were ardent legislators. Practically every king of any consequence, except Edward the Confessor, issued laws from time to time, and the laws of Canute (who had an ambitious, but unfulfilled project for an extensive codification of his laws) were far in advance of anything else produced in Europe at about this time. They stand in marked contrast to the legislative poverty of William the Conqueror's reign. In the laws of these kings one can perceive an increasing attention to administration, to the regulation of procedure, and to the question of central control. Of these, one of the most interesting is that of Ethelred II, issued at Wantage in Berkshire at the beginning of the eleventh century. Its interest derives from many causes. First, Ethelred is usually styled 'the Unready', which really is a rather ponderous Saxon pun. Ethelred means 'noble counsel', so that 'unraed'—which was the equivalent of our modern 'unready'—meant 'lacking in counsel'. Nevertheless, Ethelred was a cultivated king, who married Emma of Normandy, great-aunt of William the Conqueror and second wife of King Canute. At this date the dynastic complications of the English, Norman and Scandinavian royal houses were considerable. Two other points, however, are of great interest. The first is that Ethelred, though a king of West Saxon stock, produced in these laws a compilation which was overwhelmingly Scandinavian in character. The second point is that these laws were not only promulgated, but applied, under a weak king, thus supplying evidence that the royal administration continued to function in times of difficulty.

These laws have very many points which merit discussion, but only one can be selected for attention here. They introduced the system by which twelve leading thegns in each wapentake (the Scandinavian equivalent of the hundred) go out from the court of the wapentake and swear on relics that they will not accuse any innocent person nor protect a guilty one. They are also commanded to arrest all men of bad repute who are in conflict with the reeve, the King's officer in the wapentake. Here we have an instance of the interest of the royal administration in the conduct of the affairs of the hundred, as well as a suggestion of a Scandinavian origin for the jury of presentment. Finally, in the leading thegns upon whom these responsibilities are cast we may perhaps discern the predecessors of the mysterious buzones, or leading men, with whom medieval Justices in Eyre were directed to confer at the opening of each visitation. The hundred, or wapentake, was a vigorous institution in later Saxon times. Edgar the Elder, in the tenth century, directed that it should meet as a corporate body every four weeks, and the legislation of Canute also dealt with its activities. The origin of the hundred is much disputed, and the two names, hundred and wapentake, both suggest that it might have been the unit from which a hundred men might be raised for the fyrd. Its governmental business included the trial of local offenders, and in it, until the Conquest, the bishops transacted ecclesiastical business. Subsequently, the Normans used it as the most convenient of the smaller units of local government.

In middle Saxon times, the vill, or township, still possessed governmental functions. Its size varied, and possibly depended upon the numbers and distribution of population. In some cases, the vill was coterminous with the manor of a local landowner; but several manors might be included in a single vill, or the vill itself might be no more than part of a manor. There was, in fact, nothing formal in the size and distribution of manors in Saxon times. What is clear, however, is that the vill, like the post-Conquest manor, was an agricultural unit, in which freemen tilled their land in common on the open-field system. It might also be an ecclesiastical parish. Representatives of the vill presented offenders to the hundred, reported on the occurrence of crimes (after the Conquest, to the coroner), raised the hue and cry in respect of cattle-thieves, and were responsible for the safe-custody of prisoners. Vestigial remains of these functions remained in the existence of the village pound and stocks until modern times, and all lovers of Shakespeare will remember the drollness of the watch (and especially of Dogberry and Verges in *Much Ado About Nothing*) who, as local constables, were appointed by the parish, as the successor of the vill, until the emergence of the modern police force at the beginning of the nineteenth century.

It would be quite wrong to regard Saxon England as possessing a hierarchy, either of governmental agencies or of courts, on the present-day pattern. Before all the separate kingdoms coalesced, men governed and administered locally, and they continued to do so afterwards. Until the emergence of royal officers in later Saxon times, there was little, if any, desire to centralise government, and wherever possible, men transacted public business in the area in which they lived. One cannot therefore differentiate the activities of the vill, the hundred and the county in accordance with any formal scheme. Everyone knew the sort of business which the moots of these three areas transacted. Equally, it is quite impossible to say who, as a matter of right, attended them. Possibly to the end of its effective life, the tungemot preserved the characteristics of a town meeting, attended by all those inhabitants who felt sufficiently involved to attend. Similarly, one cannot establish any date at which the gemots of the hundred and the county ceased in theory to include all freemen. Again, one cannot say that after that date they became representative. The idea of representation in the modern sense was as yet unborn. The hundred reeve was directed to bring four (or sometimes more) men of the hundred to sessions of the county court. These were sometimes *selected*—they were in no sense elected (one thinks of the selectmen of New England). Quite probably they were men of rather greater standing or wealth than their neighbours. The idea of social pre-eminence as a qualification for local office had a thousand years of English history behind it, when it was swept away this century.

Both Saxons and Danes, nevertheless, attached the very greatest importance to the affairs of the shire court, and there were many reasons for this. While any idea that in later times it comprised all the freemen of the shire must be discarded, it still remained a numerous body. When, in 1314, the Justices in Eyre met the representatives of the county of Kent at Canterbury something like four thousand people assembled, thereby doubling the population, and putting a great strain upon accommodation and supplies. With a smaller population and less royal pressure in Saxon times, the assemblies in the county capital would not be so great, but they would nevertheless be numerous, for the activities of the county court touched the lives of freeholders at innumerable points. Besides the ever-present question of crime, and local responsibility for it (for even in Saxon times, neighbours were bound together in tithings and frank pledge), there were questions of land tenure, taxation, and fyrd-service. Moreover, one may confidently assume that it was in the shire-moot that the progress of national policy was communicated and discussed. Many shire-moots were simply the continuation of the governing moots of old independent kingdoms. Others had been established when new counties were established in an era of increasing prosperity and administrative development. In all shire-moots, the proceedings were presided over by the Earl or Alderman, who in some cases would be a descendant of the former kings; and honour and special responsibilities were assigned to the great ones, in whom once again the predecessors of the medieval buzones may be detected. It was they who declared the customs of the shire in court, and again, who claimed them before the General Eyre in medieval times. In Fleta's expressive phrase, it was they who swayed the judgements, the rest following like sheep. The rest were the representatives of the hundreds and vills, who usually regarded service in the county court as an onerous duty, which they would escape if they could. It was because such service was regarded as a burden (and not, as now, a right) that at a rather later date suit of court was made one of the obligations of landholdings.

As we approach the Norman Conquest, another official steadily grows in importance in the business of the shire court at the expense of the alderman. Since the latter was frequently the descendant of the old line of local kings, now reduced to the status of territorial earls, and since also in numerous cases they would also be the most considerable landowners in the county, it was inevitable that such influence that they still exercised should be derived from their standing among local landowners. They were in no sense representatives of the central authority. To extend their control over local affairs, the later Saxon kings intruded into the direction of business in the shires, a king's representative, or reeve, who by a normal process of development, became known as the shire-reeve, or sheriff. The king's government resisted all efforts to make the office hereditary, although a number of shire-reeves founded landowning families. While it is true that the sheriff achieved his most considerable importance shortly after the Conquest, in part because the Normans identified him with the *vicomte* of Normandy, upon whom the dukes, and especially William, relied, as a check upon the powers and separatist aspirations of their barons, the sheriff in later Saxon times was not only a powerful local official, but also the representative of the king in the shire, through whom taxation was channelled to the royal treasury, and who represented and maintained the king's rights in the shires. The sheriff was no more popular in Saxon days than he was after the Conquest, and complaints of extortion and oppression by him are continuous—though as yet untinged by racial animosities. The sheriff combined all governmental functions in his own person. He collected taxes and royal dues, he shared with the alderman and the bishop the direction of public business in the shire gemot, he directed the apprehension and trial of lawbreakers, and finally after the Conquest he called out, and often led, the fyrd in times of danger, in this case once again taking over duties which formerly belonged to the alderman.

Normandy had nothing corresponding to the Saxon fyrd. For the defence of his duchy, William relied upon the obligations of his tenants-in-chief to render knight-service. This did not extend to adventures outside the borders of the duchy, and accordingly, the invasion of England was undertaken by a polyglot force, which included Normans, Bretons, Germans, men of the Low Countries, and even Italians. They were raised by contract, and they looked to William to reward them well with English land for their efforts. So far as the Normans were concerned, they were for the most part either personal companions or relations of the Conqueror himself with their followers, or younger members of baronial families, seeking their fortunes in foreign adventure. The money to pay them was raised by William from his own resources, by levies of a semi-voluntary character from his chief tenants (including the Church), from voluntary contributions from individuals and towns (some of which provided him with ships, men and provisions), and finally, from loans. William's Duchess, for example, provided him with a fine and well-equipped flagship. After the Conquest, as will be seen, William provided for the maintenance and retention of his newly won kingdom by the imposition of a heavy burden of knight-service upon those companions whom he had rewarded with land, but he was equally resolved to maintain the Saxon organisation of the fyrd, which was called out on a number of occasions when invasion threatened, either from Scandinavia or Scotland.

The classic theory of the fyrd, as stated by Stubbs and Freeman (and, following them, by many later historians), was that it was the assembly of able-bodied freemen, on whom rested the obligation to bear arms for national defence, in fact, a kind of early militia, or *levee en masse*, summoned locally, and serving under one of the great territorial earls. For example, we are told that the dilatoriness in assembling the Northumbrian fyrd by those enigmatic northern earls, Edwin and Morcar, to assist Harold in his two decisive battles of Stamford Bridge and Hastings, contributed in important measure to the destruction of the Saxon cause in 1066. There are difficulties, however, which have recently been analysed by Richardson and Sayles in an illuminating chapter in their *Governance of Mediaeval England.*[7] An imperfectly organised and ill-trained assembly in mass would not be an efficient fighting unit, and some of the Saxon kings from Alfred onwards were able commanders. There was also the problem of supplying and equipping very large assemblies of men, especially if they were required to cover considerable distances to meet the enemy, not to mention the question of who paid for their support and equipment, and by what machinery. These authors also stress that discipline could only be established by the existence of some continuing tie between commander and men. This existed in the town levies, of which we hear frequently in Saxon times, and between the landowner and his tenants. Apart from this, they conclude that fyrd-service was an obligation which Saxon law imposed on landowners in respect of a holding, possibly of five hides. In a charter as early as the year 800, Cenwulf of Mercia agreed that an estate of thirty hides should furnish only five men when the fyrd was called out,[8] and it is conjectured that the clause reflects a recent change from an obligation to provide one warrior for every six hides to one requiring one man from every five—and that the charter was securing the recognition of the lighter burden. Saxon land-holding, especially in later times, carried very many burdens, as Domesday shows. One object of a number of early landowners was to secure immunity from all burdens except the three customary ones—burhbot, brigbot and fyrdfare, ie the liability for maintaining fortresses and bridges, and military service.

The hide, the basis of Saxon social organisation, was a unit of variable extent. In Wiltshire, it amounted to approximately forty acres, but in Cambridgeshire it extended to one hundred and twenty acres. Once this is appreciated, the importance of the hide as a unit of social organisation becomes apparent. It was that unit which could be worked in common by the peasant tenantry; and five hides therefore could be regarded as a knight's fee, in which the lord exercised rights of jurisdiction, with unmistakable

Saxon names, such as Sake and Soke, toll and team, infangthief and (less frequently) outfangthief—rights which are still claimed in respect of local land holdings in the General Eyres of the fourteenth century. From this point of view, fyrd service becomes the obligation to serve in the fyrd with one or more tenants, when the alderman or, after the Conquest, the sheriff, calls upon the landowner.

The manorial system was spreading rapidly in England in later Saxon times and, as Stenton points out, for many generations before the Conquest the country had been moving towards the evolution of a manorial economy.[9] Indeed, so characteristic of English society had the manor become that William's Domesday Survey records the nature of manorial holdings with remarkable detail. At this point it is perhaps justifiable to ask whether the lord of the manor was the person upon whom had devolved the obligation for fyrd service, with one or more of his men. Of course, the manor was not always, nor perhaps often, a territorial holding of five hides. *Manerium* before the Conquest, like many other terms in common use, was a vague word, with a variable significance. It might mean a holding almost as large as a small county, with numerous villages, hamlets and farms, especially where the population was thin, or it might be a much smaller holding. Something also depended upon the nature of the land. Much of the north of England was outside the manorial system altogether, as the Domesday Survey showed. In other areas, the size of a manor might be inflated by the inclusion of forest or waste land. Manors tended to be small and compact where the population was thickest; but this pattern might again be disturbed by reason of a special grant, for example, to a religious foundation. The chief characteristic of a manor was the existence of the lord's hall, or manor-house, and it requires no effort of the imagination to realise that the summons of the alderman or sheriff, on the threat of an invasion, would be sent to this dwelling, in order that its lord might take appropriate action.

If this is so, we must investigate the classic story that after the Conquest there existed side by side the feudal levy of Norman ancestry, and the Saxon fyrd which, we are told, played a decisive part in the disastrous defeat of the Scots at the Battle of the Standard in 1138. The Battle of the Standard is so called because the men who rallied to the defence of the kingdom did so under the standards of their towns, so that there is here an important element of a national army, which could not be summoned under the normal obligations of land tenure. Such bodies of men were, by the standards of the day, well-armed and disciplined, for it was the practice of the towns to ensure this, for the defence of the towns themselves. At any moment (especially in the north) invaders might appear over the hills, and it would be necessary to man the walls.

However, if the classic theory of two armies is accepted the problem of how they were welded into an effective fighting force still remains. A further complication is that a tenant might be summoned to follow his lord (after the Conquest, a Norman) in the feudal levy, and by the sheriff to serve in the fyrd. If he were a Saxon, his situation would be unenviable. Plainly, a good many adjustments have to be made, especially when one remembers the legendary oath which William the Conqueror is alleged to have extracted from all freemen to serve him. The picture is at best a confused one. It is perhaps possible that this double military organisation never existed, except in the minds of later chroniclers, and the historians who have followed them. It is also possible that the territorial liability to furnish one man for the fyrd, imposed on five hides of land in Saxon times, was transformed into the *servitium debitum* of the knights' fees in post-Conquest days. This idea is pursued, with a wealth of suggestive detail, by Richardson and Sayles, and one may perhaps add that when the chroniclers speak of a fyrd being called out to resist invasion, they are referring to the full feudal levy, reinforced by the town levies, and possibly also by fortress guards, and even by the mercenaries, who, as we know, every king from William the Conqueror onwards (as well as some of his Saxon predecessors) frequently employed. Everyone knows that Ethelred the Unready raised the Danegeld to pay off Danish invaders. Fewer people are aware that he also used the Danegeld to pay for Danish ships and men to patrol the narrow seas against a renewed attack.

For the lawyer, these apparently remote topics have a vital interest. They should be sufficient to dispel forever the myth that there was a vital and fundamental break and a fresh beginning at the Norman Conquest. The Saxon manor continues and becomes increasingly standardised after the Conquest, but in essence it is Saxon, and not Norman. Military service for knights' fees becomes more onerous and is also standardised into a normal obligation between a man and his lord, but the essence of the relationship was already there before the Conquest. Saxons and Normans were apt to face similar problems in similar fashion, but because the Normans were more recent invaders of Normandy than the Saxons and Danes were of England, they were harder, and, in England at least, more oppressive. But innovators they were not, except in extreme necessity, as will shortly be explained.

To round off this sketch of the legal and administrative organisation of Saxon England, something must be added about Saxon kingship and the central government. Looking back into the misty hinterland of Saxon England, one is struck by the number of great names in the list of pre-Conquest kings. They include Alfred, of course, and also Canute the Dane, whose reign is in some ways more enlightened and more significant than that of William the Conqueror. Canute's empire, which stretched from Scandinavia across the North Sea to England and Wales and touched Ireland, and which had close social and cultural connections with the continent, was based upon a free flow of subjects irrespective of race, from one part to another, and upon an administration which drew able men from all. His peace was so firmly established that Canute was able to leave his wide-spread dominions (directly comparable in extent with the later Angevin Empire) in order to undertake a two-year pilgrimage to Rome. There is little in his reign which compares with the almost continual internal strife which characterised the Conqueror's, and it is ironic that the fable of Canute at the water's edge (used by a chronicler as an example of Canute's wisdom in rebuking the flatteries of courtiers) should have been perverted to serve as an illustration of his vanity and folly. But besides Alfred and Canute there are other kings whose names should be remembered. Edmund Ironside, Canute's great adversary, and Harold the last of the Saxons, were famous leaders. Only William compared with Harold, and but for the Scandinavian invasion which Harold destroyed, the entire future history of England might have taken a different course. Edward the Elder, Alfred's valiant elder brother, Ethelred the First, Athelstan, and even Edward the Confessor also were men of mark. Whatever may be the Confessor's personal shortcomings, long after the Conquest Englishmen looked back on his reign with nostalgia as a time in which England prospered and lived at peace. The picture may be overdrawn, but the substance is there. It is certain that during the quarter of a century during which he ruled, standards of living improved markedly and England prospered, commerce expanded, and Saxons became familiar with the sight of Norman merchants in their cities, and Norman bishops and abbots in their churches. There was no isolation from the continent. Saxon clerics had long enjoyed a high reputation for learning, while examples of English craftsmanship were known as far afield as Constantinople. In spite of internal feuds, England had evolved a satisfying concept of monarchy, some features of which still survive. Kingship had a sacerdotal character, as the coronation service indicated. The connection between Crown and Church was close, and it is seen at its highest in the Confessor's reign. Stenton points out that while kings and archbishops have often co-operated in a programme of ecclesiastical reform, there are few parallels in any country with the enthusiasm with which Edgar, in the second half of the tenth century, brought the entire power of the state to the furtherance of the far-reaching religious policy of that great Archbishop of Canterbury, Dunstan.[10] Edgar, too, was a peacemaker and Stenton adds that 'It is a sign of Edgar's competence as a ruler that his reign is singularly devoid of recorded incident.'[11]

Happy indeed is that nation which has no history, and this was England's lot during Edgar's reign. The amity between Church and State which was deliberately fostered by the greatest Saxon kings was never approached in the reign of any king after the Conquest, even though one of the professed aims of the Conqueror had been to reorganise the Church in England.

It would be difficult to express in precise terms the mode by which the Saxon kings were elected. There was a tradition that the choice was to be made from the descendants of Cerdic, a West Saxon chieftain who, with his son Cymric, traditionally came to England, and defeated the Britons in 494 or 495. There are also traditions that Alfred's mother, the Jutish princess, was descended from one or two nephews of Cerdic, the children of a sister who had married a Jutish chief. These traditions, though resting on exceedingly slender historical evidence, were nevertheless extremely valuable, not only in perpetuating veneration for the most illustrious leaders of the first Saxon invaders, but also for localising the question of the succession within a narrow class. Beyond that, one can say little. There was no rule of primogeniture. Personal qualities, and especially abilities as a leader in war, may frequently have influenced selection. It certainly did on the death of Edward the Confessor, when the notables felt that only a leader of the calibre of Harold, the son of the great Earl Godwine, but possessing connections with both the English and Danish royal houses, could preserve the country from invasion. At other times, the approval of the Church, as evidenced by its leading member, may have played a part, as it did while Dunstan was Archbishop of Canterbury; or again, the national situation may have prompted the setting aside of the royal line altogether, in favour of a foreigner, as it did in the election of Canute and William the Conqueror. Where the last king left several young sons, there was scope for palace intrigue, leading to the selection of one who was not the natural successor in blood. Besides all these particular interests, the Witan, the grand council of the nation, played its part on a number of occasions, although it would be wrong to suggest, as some historians have done, that kingship was elective within the House of Cerdic, and that it was the Witan which did the electing. Erroneous hypotheses such as these were propagated in later ages, after the emergence of Parliament, to justify the deposition of kings who were considered to have violated their coronation oaths by consistent misgovernment.

It has been suggested that one of the greatest achievements of Englishmen in the middle ages was the elaboration of an impersonal monarchy. By this it is implied that the essential structure of government could be carried on by the royal administration, in spite of the absence, minority, or incapacity of its kings. Richard I, for example, was absent from the country for almost the whole of his reign. His brother and successor, John, lost the whole of his French possessions, quarrelled with the Pope, misgoverned the kingdom, provoked Magna Carta and, finally, drove the majority of his barons into the arms of a French invader. His son, Henry III, succeeded at the age of nine years, to a divided kingdom and an empty treasury, and the middle years of his long reign were occupied in a life-and-death struggle with Simon de Montfort and the nation. During this period of a hundred years, from the death of Henry II to the accession of Edward I, the national government not only survived, but showed very marked development, and the essential structure of government—a national monarchy—remained secure, although not unchanged. The vitality of English institutions, resilient even during this period, is attributable to the fact that there had been established, at an amazingly early date, an administration which was proof against disruptive shocks, and against swift changes in the political outlook. It is a matter of deep interest that even at this period the trained men of the royal administration—the professional civil servants—remain at their posts, no matter whether kings or barons are in control. Writs continue to be issued in the king's name, the king's courts of justice continue to function, and the king's treasury continues to collect taxes.

The traditional answer to the question of how this had come about—so much in advance of what was happening elsewhere—is that the fortunate accident of the Norman Conquest gave England a strong central administration under energetic and national-minded kings at an early date. But not all the kings after the Conquest were strong, while others were far from wise. It may be added that preoccupations with the affairs of Normandy could well have weakened the administration of England—as, in fact, they did in John's reign, and as they had threatened to do even in the Conqueror's. For the explanation of the continuing vitality of English constitutional and legal institutions, it is necessary to look elsewhere than to the Norman Conquest. All the evidence suggests that during the six centuries of Saxon settlement and rule, Englishmen—whether Saxons, Danes or Scandinavians—had been slowly welded into a unified people, and that the process was stimulated under the constant threat of further invasions from across the North Sea. Further, the country's institutions reflected the temper of its people. Lady Stenton, and her late husband, point out that it was a remarkable feature of pre-Conquest legal procedure in England that so many people, after initiating a suit in court, thereupon proceeded to settle it by compromise rather than by the decision of the court. This habit of compromise pervades every area of life in later Saxon times, and has often been mistaken for vagueness or weakness. For example, the outstanding fact of government in the reign of Edward the Confessor was the existence of the three great super-earldoms of Northumbria, Mercia and Wessex with wide governmental functions. One of them lay dangerously near to Scotland. Nevertheless, there are few signs of fissiparous tendencies, in spite of the feuds of the great baronial houses. The contrast with France, where Normandy, Brittany, Anjou, Aquitaine, Toulouse, Burgundy, and even Boulogne were almost independent states, is striking. The Saxon kings were constantly extending the central authority, but the process was cautious and unspectacular. Finally, it should be noticed that Saxon England alone among Western countries possessed a state treasury and a national system of taxation, and it is significant that as soon as possible after Hastings William made his way, not to London, but to the Saxon capital, Winchester, to take possession, not only of the existing treasure, but of the records upon which future taxation would be based. After the Conquest, the national property-tax of geld continued to be levied in precisely the same way as before, as Domesday Book bears witness.[12] It was, concludes Sir Frank Stenton, 'the first system of national taxation to appear in Western Europe', adding that the Conqueror never attempted to set up anything in its place.

Of the Witan, as the supreme governing council of the nation, we hear a good deal in *The Anglo-Saxon Chronicle*. Modern historians, from Stubbs onwards, have sought to trace the evolution in William's reign, of this body from an assembly of the wise (implied by the name) and great in power and wealth, to an assembly of tenants-in-chief. That there was a change in composition and function after the Conquest was apparent, but its extent and significance can be exaggerated. The composition of the Witan differed from time to time as did that of the Duke's Council in Normandy. If the queen and the Atheling sometimes attended in England, so did Queen Matilda and Robert, the Conqueror's heir, in Normandy. The great clerics appeared on both bodies, and so did the greatest landowners who, in Saxon times, were not known as tenants-in-chief, but often held by charters conferring extensive liberties and grants of jurisdiction. The Witan showed no anxiety to overrule the autonomy of the shires, although it controlled the sheriffs, and through them, regulated the proceedings of the shire courts. The Duke's Council had little more formal authority, although William's forceful character might cause it, upon occasion, to encroach on local autonomy. What is apparent is that William regarded the two councils in England and Normandy as fulfilling almost identical functions, and since he had never heard of the feudal system, he failed to consider whether either conformed to a feudal pattern or not. Only writers of a much later age have conceived the possibility of a contrast between them.

Finally, if we were to ask by what means English administration and English justice after the Conquest were brought into operation, we should at once answer, by the writ. And the writ, as the normal instrument of government, was invented, not by the Normans, but by the Saxon administration of the tenth century.

2

Norman England

The Norman Conquest, like Saxon England, is enveloped by myths and legend, which it is difficult to penetrate—legends, moreover, which have been so continuously propagated that they are not easy to dissipate. One of them has been discussed already; ie that something called 'feudalism' was introduced into England in 1066. This chapter will begin with a consideration of two more —the first, that the Conquest decisively settled the fate of Saxon England, and profoundly changed the course of development of English institutions; the second, that in rewarding his followers, William avoided the errors which he had seen in Normandy, and scattered the possessions of his principal followers throughout the country, so that they could not effectively rise in arms against him. Strangely, in accepting the second myth, numerous followers of Stubbs have also recorded, as he did, that William and his son frequently called out the fyrd (whose nature has already been discussed) to put down the risings of his rebellious Norman barons. The spectacle of William relying apparently on a predominantly Saxon fyrd (of mythical origin) to put down his Norman barons, while pleasing, seems to suggest that something had gone wrong with his original plan. It is possible, indeed, that scattering the holdings of his major Norman subjects would have increased his problems rather than diminished them, for presumably they would have had a larger number of local contacts. Further, there would necessarily have been delay in complying with William's requests for service. However this will be considered later, it is sufficient at this point to note the evident inconsistency.

Consideration of this question makes it necessary to discover the condition of Normandy, and the nature of William's rule there before the Conquest. The Normans were, in origin, close kinsfolk of the Vikings who harried England in the ninth, tenth and eleventh centuries. They settled in Normandy in the ninth and tenth centuries, and their first duke, Rollo, received Normandy as a fief from the French king in the tenth century. Relatively small in numbers, they resembled their kinsmen who settled in England at approximately the same time in firmly establishing themselves and in assimilating some of the civilisation of the Franks amongst whom they now lived. They were converted to Christianity, and they adopted French as their kinsfolk had adopted English, as their medium of communication. Gradually, the particular dialect which they spoke became distinct from that language of the rest of France. It was harder in sound but it proved a remarkably convenient medium in which to express legal concepts. This was the tongue which they brought to England, and which they made the language of official life. In the law courts, Norman–French was spoken in the king's courts, Latin in the spiritual courts, and Anglo–Saxon and Norman–French competed in the local courts, where, naturally, many of the litigants and suitors were Saxons. As the king's courts gradually extended their jurisdiction, Norman–French became the recognised language of those courts, with the result that a very high proportion of the legal terms which we use today are Norman–French. The Year Books, too, stretching to the opening of the sixteenth century, are written in Norman–French, though it had long since ceased to be the language of ordinary conversation, even among persons of consequence. The Statute Book for a time showed a certain lack of consistency. The early statutes, including Magna Carta, are in Latin. Later some of them were written in Norman–French, and the exact meaning of passages of the Norman–French text of the Statute of Treasons of 1351 created some difficulties for the judges who tried Casement for treason in 1916. But Edward III's reign marked a decisive change. In spite of the fact that it was the language of a conquered people, English (as Anglo–Saxon had now become) continued to develop, and to flourish. It was producing a literature, of which Chaucer's works were outstanding examples. Even the Norman–French of the lawyers was becoming artificial. Edward III therefore directed that official transactions should be recorded in English. Thereafter, Norman–French was simply the special language of lawyers.

Until the eleventh century, the civilisation of Normandy lagged far behind that of England. There was no Norman craftsmanship to compare with that of the Saxons. There was no comparable literary output, and no comparable elaboration of local and governmental institutions. Monastic life was primitive, until it was transformed by the monastic revival of the tenth century, and it is doubtful whether the Norman knight, Herluin, who founded the great Abbey of Bec—which so greatly influenced the religious life of Normandy and later of England—could read, when, about the year 1035, he decided to renounce the world and become a monk. Right down to the Norman Conquest of England, the Normans have the appearance of a military caste, close knit by family ties and by personal loyalties, existing among an alien peasantry with whom they had little in common. This outlook they imported into England after 1066, and it only crumbled slowly.

Examination of the structure of Normandy before the Conquest reveals that the holders of virtually all the great fiefs were either cadets of the ducal family or were related to them by marriage. This was particularly true where the fief touched the frontier. The dukes even took the precaution of ensuring that the Archbishop of Rouen, the head of the Norman Church, was a member of the ducal family. From 989 to 1037 the archbishop was Robert, brother of Duke Richard II and of Emma, wife of Ethelred and Canute. On his death, he was succeeded, until his death in 1054, by Mauger, half-brother of Dukes Richard III and Robert I. When he died, there was no son of William the Conqueror old enough to be considered, and William's clerical half-brother was already Bishop of Bayeux. Had William's second son, Richard, lived longer, he too was destined for the Church, and it is probable that he would have become Archbishop, either of Rouen or Canterbury. Although William had followed the papal policy of separating ecclesiastical from lay affairs, and of establishing Courts Christian for matters of canon law, he was as resolved as his predecessors to prevent the Norman Church from pursuing any policy which would impair the duke's authority. He presided regularly at ecclesiastical synods, as he did in England after the Conquest.

Although a great deal in the character and the achievements of the Conqueror have long been a matter of controversy, some things are beyond doubt. That he was able, and a fine leader in war, even the hostile tribute of the monkish scribe in *The Anglo-Saxon Chronicle* bears witness. He was by any standards an exceptional man, capable of dominating others and recovering from temporary reverses. It is almost unbelievable that his father, Duke Robert I, should have left his duchy to one who was not only an infant, but a bastard. It is possibly even more remarkable that by tenacity, guile and force of character William should have retained it in the face of external aggression and internal revolt, extending over many years. William had the capacity for understanding the age in which he lived. The papacy was leading a great spiritual revival in western Europe, one aspect of which was a spread of monasticism. William not only encouraged this, but guided its growth in Normandy (as he did later in England), and by so doing, gained the support of the papacy for his invasion of England, where the independence of the Church from Rome, and its identification with the national life, had caused it to incur disfavour. It was a symptom of this disfavour, and for this reason, that when Robert of Jumieges, a Norman, was expelled from the see of Canterbury, in Edward the Confessor's reign, his place was filled by Stigand, a supporter of Earl Godwine. Both of them were opposed to the papal movement for reforms in the Church, which must necessarily have extended papal authority in England. Stigand, in fact, achieved the distinction of being declared deposed, and also excommunicated, by no less than five successive popes. Harold when he succeeded Edward the Confessor naturally inherited the disfavour which his father, Godwine, had incurred, and it was intensified by the mutual support of himself and Stigand. William was therefore able to represent the invasion of England as a crusade for which papal support was freely offered. When to this is added the close association of William's principal councillor, Lanfranc, with Pope Alexander II, the weight of opinion adverse to England following Edward the Confessor's death can be estimated.

William displayed the same statesmanship in respect of his barons as he did with the Church. Many of the older baronial houses, descendants of the Companions of Rollo, had perished or had been dispossessed during the civil wars. Newer men had replaced them, and these were bound to William by close ties. In due course, a number of them would manifest the same turbulence as their predecessors, but in 1066 there was unity, and little threat of external complications. Even Brittany, so long Normandy's rival, was quiescent. Alan of Brittany led the Breton contingent in William's invasion, and was rewarded with over four hundred manors in Yorkshire, Lincolnshire and East Anglia, which constituted the honour and earldom of Richmond—a great fief in which there is little sign of William's alleged determination to scatter the possessions of his principal supporters. Indeed, it seems probable that in giving the Breton such extensive possessions in the midlands and the north, William was relying upon him to act as a barrier to Scottish invasion at a time when the Conqueror's hold on the north was tenuous.

It is scarcely surprising that William made no effort to perpetuate the three historic earldoms of Northumbria, Mercia and Wessex, for these were not only the successors of independent kingdoms, but also the sources of strength of the greatest of the Saxon noble houses, which had frequently shown defiance to the pre-Conquest kings. The heads of these houses, Godwine and Harold in Wessex, Tostig in Northumbria, Leofric, Edwin and Morcar in Mercia, had frequently raised forces which threatened the throne itself. It is in their day that one hears of a Wessex, Mercian or Northumbrian fyrd, and however each was recruited, it constituted a powerful fighting force. The abolition of these earldoms after the Conquest was not only a normal measure of prudence, but an important factor in hastening the unification of the country. But where there was danger from abroad, William was prepared to create earldoms with palatine powers, so that effective and prompt resistance to the invader would be forthcoming. Kent was given to William's half-brother Odo, the fighting Bishop of Bayeux. Cornwall, with extensive lands in the west of England, was given to William's other half-brother and trusted lieutenant, Robert, Count of Mortain. Durham, a key region for defence both against Scotland and Scandinavia, became a palatinate under its bishops. The great Earldom of Hereford, with palatine jurisdiction, was created at this period to hold back the Welsh, and there was also an Earldom of East Anglia, again to keep watch on Scandinavian invasions. All these were extensive jurisdictions, paralleling those which existed on the borders of Normandy, and once again William gave them to close relations and trusted companions.

Failure to appreciate the nature of these grants has been responsible for attributing to Lanfranc a sophistry of which he was not guilty. In 1084 the adventurous spirit of Odo, Bishop of Bayeux and Earl of Kent, led him to aspire to the papacy, and he persuaded a number of leading barons to join him in an expedition to Rome to advance his claims (although Pope Gregory VII was still alive). When William learned of it, he ordered the arrest of his half-brother, and brought him to trial before Lanfranc and other leading members of his council. Since one of William's early administrative changes had been to separate the lay and the ecclesiastical jurisdictions, Odo claimed that as a prelate, he was exempt from lay jurisdiction. To this Lanfranc replied that it was not the Bishop of Bayeux, but the Earl of Kent, who was on trial. Odo was therefore condemned and sent a prisoner to Normandy where, in spite of papal protests, he remained for the rest of the reign.

Lanfranc adopted precisely the same attitude towards William, Bishop of Durham, in 1088, in the reign of William Rufus. William had been implicated in a league of disaffected barons against the new king, and the last public act of Lanfranc was to preside at the trial which followed the king's forfeiture of the lands of the bishop. When he disputed the forfeiture, a special court was assembled at Salisbury where the bishop, as Odo had earlier done, claimed that a lay court had no jurisdiction over him as he was a cleric. Once again Lanfranc stressed that the bishop was subject to the jurisdiction, not as an ecclesiastic, but as a tenant-in-chief of the Crown, and, he might have added, one to whom palatine powers had been committed. The upshot of the trial was that the bishop was allowed to go into exile; and Lanfranc's two great cases go no further than to establish that clerics who hold palatine earldoms were subject to the king's secular jurisdiction in respect of their secular office. As the Common Law developed in the king's court, however, it became settled law that clerics answered in the king's courts in respect of their temporalities. In the reign of Richard I, Hugh de Nunat, Bishop of Coventry, was cited to answer for acting against his fealty. *Curia Regis* held that if he should not appear within forty days, he should be subject to the judgment of the bishops in respect of matters spiritual, and to the judgment of laymen in respect of his acts as the king's sheriff. Bracton states clearly that the king has power to direct process against bishops in respect of their baronies. In the reign of Edward I, a dispute between the Archbishop of York and Antony Bek, Bishop of Durham, was heard in the king's court because it concerned the acts of the bishop as a palatine earl, and the archbishop did not dispute the fact that, besides his spiritual office, the bishop was a secular ruler, and therefore in that respect, within the king's secular jurisdiction. At the opening of Edward II's reign, Walter Langton, Bishop of Coventry and Lichfield, treasurer of Edward I, was arrested, condemned and imprisoned for abuses committed whilst acting as treasurer. Few principles are more clearly established at such an early date than the double capacity of bishops and prelates.

At no time did the tenants-in-chief in England ever accept that suits relating to land could be heard in Courts Christian. The greater part of Church land in England was held by normal feudal tenures, as the Year Books abundantly testify, and this was so whether the Church originally acquired the land by grant from the Crown or by gift from a tenant-in-chief in knight-service; and in respect of such land, the Church performed the normal feudal services. Even Anselm, Lanfranc's equally great (and saintly) successor as Archbishop of Canterbury, was sternly rebuked by William Rufus, for furnishing ill-equipped knights for service against the Welsh. Not unnaturally, the Church was ready to accept at an early date the alternative of a payment of scutage in exchange for knight-service.

While it is easy to see that such matters must necessarily come before the king's courts (where complaints of the incidence of knight-service from both lay and ecclesiastical tenants were very numerous), it is less obvious that frankalmoign should be similarly treated. By this tenure religious foundations held on spiritual, as contrasted with knightly, services. Originally, the Church argued that as the land had been given to God in 'free alms' in perpetuity, disputes relating to it should be heard in the Courts Christian, but as the doctrine of tenure established itself the church courts were compelled to give ground. If one reads the classic account of frankalmoign which appears in the first volume of Pollock and Maitland's *History of English Law*, one must necessarily accept the fact that such grants were conceived entirely in terms appropriate for a spiritual court to consider. Normally, the gift was made, not to an abbey alone but to God, the abbey, its abbot and monks, and these grants usually contained clauses invoking excommunication on those who should seek to disturb the quiet possession of the grantees. Even Henry II, the greatest of England's medieval kings, was compelled to concede in the Constitutions of Clarendon, that if a dispute arose between a clerk and a layman concerning any land claimed to be held on spiritual tenure, a jury of twelve men should be summoned to discover whether (*utrum*) the tenement were lay or spiritual. If it were held on spiritual tenure, then the matter should go forward in the ecclesiastical court. This, it will be seen, provided for the famous Assize of *Utrum*, which was treated in the king's courts as a normal possessory assize, by virtue of which claims to ecclesiastical lands were established. It was, in fact, the parson's writ of right, establishing his claim to his freehold, and the fact that it was originally only a preliminary step in the proceedings was completely forgotten. The courts spiritual, it would appear, had no wish to prolong a losing battle, more especially as, by the thirteenth century, the king's courts had already held that some of the major tenants in frankalmoign—the bishops and major abbots

—could avail themselves if they chose of the ordinary lay remedies for land, such as the writ of right, and therefore, by gradual steps, the Assize of *Utrum* ceased to be available to them. The whole of this at times obscure process illustrates the way in which the jurisdiction of the king's courts gradually extended. Because it came to be regarded as more efficient, and remedies given were more effective, the Church, like many other orders in the community, sought the king's courts, and the application of the coherent system of law which it gradually developed. Had the central administration remained weak, and had not the Common Law been created, this tendency would not have existed.

This, however, is to look a long way ahead. Earlier mention was made of two fallacies, which are, in fact, linked. The first was that the Conquest, ie William's victory at Hastings and his coronation at Westminster on Christmas day, settled the fate of Saxon England. William did not see it in that light at the time, and the whole of the rest of his reign was to prove how wise he was to be cautious. He was fortunate in that Godwine's sons were dead, Tostig had been slain at Stamford Bridge, and Harold's brothers except Gurth had died with him at Hastings. Edwin and Morcar, of the house of Leofric of Mercia, had never commanded the respect which was given to Godwine and his family. They had hesitated when, if they had rallied to Harold, they could have turned the scale. No one suggested that either should succeed him. They quickly made their peace with William, and they were allowed to retain most of their lands. Later they conspired and ultimately were dispossessed and slain. There were, however, other contenders. The Scandinavian royal house had claims through Canute, and throughout William's reign they threatened the east coast, and fermented internal rebellions. More immediately, William's circuitous march on London, by way of Winchester and Wallingford, allowed the remnants of Saxon power to rally at Berkhampsted to elect Edgar Atheling, the lineal descendant of the line of English kings, as Harold's successor, but his election was swept aside when William entered London. The Atheling, indeed, adhered to William, and outlived him by nearly forty years. But although the English lost their natural leaders, they long remained unsubdued, more especially in the north, where William spread devastation and sullen resentment in a desperate effort to secure its submission.

Broadly, William can be regarded as continuing the work of conquest throughout his reign, and this had important consequences, both in law and administration. Being a politic king, his intention was to leave as much as possible undisturbed. He claimed the crown, not as conqueror, but as Edward's lawful successor. He promised to preserve the English laws as they had been in the Confessor's time. He promised also to uphold the customs of London. Accordingly, in the early years, apart from distributing to his followers the estates of those who had been in arms against him, he left many Saxon landowners undisturbed, at least for the time being. Constant rebellions nevertheless made the redistribution of land a continuing process, and by the end of the reign all the major Saxon nobles had been replaced by Normans or other continental followers of William. Precisely the same occurred in the Church after Lanfranc was called to Canterbury. Saxon bishops and abbots made way for Norman prelates. Nevertheless, in relation to the native Saxon cultivators, the Normans remained a small minority, stretched thinly through the country, and William expected them to remain in a state of constant readiness to aid him in the event of trouble. For that reason, knight-service was imposed as a heavy burden. It was estimated to be approximately five times as heavy as in Normandy, and it is surely no coincidence that it could yield for mutual defence approximately 4,000 men, that is to say, about as many as fought under William at Hastings. With that number he gained a kingdom, and with that number he successfully retained it. But even in William's time, scutage was not unknown, although as a result of the extent of knight-service demanded, it could be a heavy financial burden, as even large abbeys complained from time to time.

It would be an interesting, though time-consuming, exercise to trace the influence of the Conquest in the land law which the lawyers practising in the king's courts ultimately elaborated, and which, in turn, reacted upon land law in Normandy. There is the fundamental distinction between the military and non-military tenures, whether free or unfree. There is the great characteristic of the military tenures, until the reign of Henry II, when the two races were merging, that title to land held in knight-service was vindicated by trial by battle. There were the incidents of wardship and marriage, and the burden of suit of court. There was the tacit acceptance of primogeniture, which greatly simplified the task of the overlord in ensuring that the obligations of knight-service were performed. While some of these could have evolved independently of the Conquest, there can be no doubt that the Norman conquerors attached the very greatest importance to them, as instruments aiding them in the difficult task of holding down a vastly more numerous population.

On the other hand, neither William nor his successors had any wish to see his followers enlarge their powers except where, on the borders, this was an inescapable necessity. Further, as many historians have pointed out, there was never, at any one time, any general resumption of land by the king, and a re-grant on new terms. This, as will be shown, would have produced economic and governmental chaos which William and his councillors would have been quite unable to resolve. It followed therefore that when land was available for distribution, William re-granted it on the terms on which it had been held before. His followers were rewarded by grants, not of fiefs, but of manors. His half-brother, Count Robert of Mortain, received the largest single grant, amounting to approximately six hundred and forty manors, scattered over many counties. It is true that a substantial number of these were in Devon and Cornwall, where Robert, as Earl, had extensive rights of jurisdiction, as William's lieutenant. But Domesday Book on almost every page shows Norman grantees receiving lands on exactly the same terms as those of their Saxon predecessors. This is true whether the grantees are barons or religious foundations. It was not many years after the Conquest before the new order of landowners found themselves involved in innumerable disputes concerning the extent of their rights, and also of their burdens. This is one of the matters which Domesday Book endeavoured to solve by establishing a national record, though it was only partially successful in this, for the land-tenures of extensive parts of England, especially in the north, are omitted altogether. In other areas, rights and duties are uncertain or disputed. Contemporary accounts of the process of its compilation seem to suggest that after the recording commissioners had returned, the king sent out other commissioners to settle disputed claims. Even these were not entirely successful, for some disputes dragged on until the reign of Henry I.

The policy underlying William's grants becomes plainer if we examine the still surviving records of some of the most famous disputes of the reign, and the manner in which they were resolved. The importance which William attached to their proper settlement in accordance with Saxon law is shown by the fact that he appointed some of the ablest members of his court to preside over the hearings, which were sometimes protracted. Lanfranc himself, though archbishop and virtually prime minister (and sometimes even William's deputy when the king was in Normandy), often sat through long disputes. Originally trained in Italy in the study of law, he enjoyed a reputation for learning in Roman and Lombard law before he entered the Church. Later, he was even more highly regarded for his learning in canon law. Nevertheless, although well turned sixty when he followed William to England, he set to work patiently to master the intricacies of Saxon law (meaning in this case the law of the West Saxons), as well as its strange vocabulary. Almost equally eminent in their administration of a system which must have seemed very strange to them were Geoffrey, Bishop of Coutances, and Odo of Bayeux. Both were reputedly learned in the canon law. Both, like Lanfranc, were of outstanding ability, and both, again like Lanfranc, acquired a knowledge of Saxon law more extensive than is attributed to any pre-Conquest Saxon administrator.

This is the more considerable achievement since at this date there were no surviving law-books, and in any event, the tradition of Saxon law was an oral one. The trials of land disputes of William's reign have not often received the attention from lawyers which they deserve,[1] for they supply valuable clues to much that happened later. In the first place, even as early as William's reign the royal administration was sending justices into the shires to sit in the county court. This was a necessary measure, not only to ensure that the king's dues were paid, but also to limit the powers of the Norman sheriffs, to whom much governmental activity was unavoidably delegated. The same system also reminds us that William from the outset perceived the importance of the shire court as the centre of local governmental activity, and that he was ready—even eager—not only to preserve it, but to extend the functions of the county court. These of course were governmental, and the decision of cases and the trial of offenders were only one aspect of them. For the transaction of their business, the county required the attendance of all men of consequence, together with representatives of the hundreds and townships, as in Saxon times, and it is from the great trials of William's reign that the continued vitality of this institution can be estimated. Yet again, one can detect in them the remarkable care which William's administration took, not only to establish titles, but also to preserve continuity with Saxon England.

By no means all the justices whom William sent out were clerics. Some were barons, and some were sheriffs. The record of the case often states that the trial was held before some distinguished judge 'and in the presence of my barons'. This gave a salutary reminder to the litigants that the justice for which they prayed was the king's justice, but the fact that the traditional suitors of the county court were also present emphasised that the king was also upholding the ancient laws and customs of the English.

One or two examples may make this even plainer. Between 1071 and 1074, there was a succession of disputes concerning lands of which the abbey of Ely claimed it had been wrongfully deprived. They were heard by the united courts of the neighbouring counties before Geoffrey of Coutances, the Bishop of Lincoln, the Saxon Earl Waltheof (not yet dispossessed and killed) and two sheriffs, Picot and Ilbert. A good deal of the time was occupied with discussions of evidence relating to Saxon custom. Eventually judgment was given for the abbey, but much still remained unsettled, for a second case, extending over the four years between

1080 and 1084, was heard at Hertford, where Geoffrey of Coutances again presided over a court consisting of a number of tenants-in-chief, and a combined assembly of the county courts of the three adjacent shires.

Geoffrey is once again found presiding over a session of combined county courts and in the presence of the tenants-in-chief, in a dispute between two Saxon prelates—Wulfstan, Bishop of Worcester, and Walter, Abbot of Evesham—concerning the extent of their rights in the manors of Bengeworth and Great Hampton. Odo presided in similar fashion over another land dispute in which the complainant was the Abbot of Evesham, and also in a dispute between Gundulf, Bishop of Rochester, and the sheriff Picot concerning land at Freckenham in Norfolk, where there was an assembly of no less than four county courts.

In all these assemblies, we are told, the members of the county courts included both French (ie Normans) and English. But this was not all. The litigants in all these cases were permitted to bring forward Saxon witnesses, to testify to the existence of the rights which they claimed, and which had been recognised long before 1066.

Perhaps the most important, and the most interesting of this series of trials is that which occurred at Pennenden Heath in Kent, sometime between 1072 and 1076. Once again the king's presiding justice was Geoffrey of Coutances, and piquancy is added to the account by the fact that the principal litigants were Lanfranc, in his capacity of Archbishop of Canterbury, and Odo of Bayeux as Earl of Kent, both of whom at other times presided over exactly this kind of trial. The case concerned lands which Lanfranc claimed were part of the see of Canterbury, and which he alleged Odo had wrongfully withheld. The record of the case expressly mentioned that in the Kent county court there were assembled, not only all the Frenchmen of the shire (who were presumably landowners), but also, and more especially, those English who were well acquainted with the laws and customs of the land, and picturesquely it continues that there came to the trial Aethelric, a dispossessed Bishop of Selsey, 'a man of great age, and very wise in the law of the land, who by the King's command was brought to the trial in a waggon in order that he might declare and expound the ancient practice of the laws'. The customs which he declared won the case for Lanfranc.

The concern of William and his ablest counsellors for these laws is one of the most striking features of the years which immediately followed the Conquest. Another point should also be made, when those who were considered learned in the laws had explained them, the presiding judge directed a group of men appointed by the court to give a collective statement upon them on oath. In this we have the germ of the later assize of freeholders, and later still, of the jury. Stenton suggests that something like it may have existed even in Saxon times, and as he also points out,[2] before William's death Englishmen in all but the remotest parts of the land had become familiar with it through its employment in the Domesday Inquest. In the fourteenth century, it is well to remember, the county was still meeting the king's Justices in Eyre in the shire courts and was claiming the customs of the county.

It is perhaps difficult in cases such as those just mentioned, where Norman courts patiently elucidate the Saxon system of landholding, usually for the benefit of the Norman newcomers, to determine where the concepts of tenancy-in-chief and knight-service fit in. A further problem is the relation of the knightly to the non-knightly tenures. These questions tend to remain unanswered in medieval text-books of the law of property, written at a time when tenures had ceased to reflect social realities. For example, in the time of Littleton, in the fifteenth century, a baron might hold land in copyhold, which was in origin an unfree tenure, and earlier still the holding of a villein.

In order to make the development of the land law in later times comprehensible, it is necessary to look at the situation as it was in the first half-century after the Conquest. It has already been pointed out, and Domesday Book together with the trials mentioned above abundantly confirm it, that the Norman invaders stepped into the shoes of the dispossessed Saxons. With exceptions that will be mentioned shortly, what they received were manors, held with the same rights and burdens that existed before the Conquest. No other solution was possible. The Normans were few, and their principal preoccupations were fighting (or holding themselves in readiness to fight) and governing, either nationally or locally. Although England's agricultural economy suffered severely from the disruption of the Conquest, it recovered as William's reign progressed. It was carried on by Saxon cultivators within the manors, who continued to operate the open-field system precisely as if the Conquest had never occurred. Within most manors, there were both free and unfree tenants. The free tenants held in socage which, significantly, was a non-knightly tenure, the services for which were discharged either in rent or in kind. Their disputes arising out of the occupation of land were settled in the lord's court, and the lord's steward exercised a regulatory jurisdiction over them.

The varieties of socage were very numerous, and some of them shade off into villeinage, but the tenure was very old. The term by which it is described is Saxon, and it is not found in Normandy. Bracton derived it from the French word, *soc*; meaning a ploughshare. This is now generally agreed to be erroneous, but the fact that Bracton gave it strongly suggests the connection between the tenure and agriculture; and very much the same significance exists if the truer derivation from the Saxon *sokeman* is adopted. Socage, therefore, is the appropriate tenure for the cultivator of the soil. It was not subjected to any liability for knight-service, either because the cultivator, not being a Norman, was not encouraged to follow knightly pursuits, or because the interruption of his farming would have seriously prejudiced the agricultural economy upon which all depended.

However, it is possible that the socagers were extra men summoned for the defence of the kingdom after the Conquest, when the fyrd was called out. As knight-service did not exist in Saxon times this explanation seems to be the most likely one, and if it is, the puzzle arising from a possible conflict of duty is resolved. The lord provided the specified number of knights as required by his knightly tenure. The sheriff assembled the socagers to whom knight-service had no application. It is at any rate certain that, on these occasions of national emergency after the Conquest when the fyrd *was* assembled, there were numbers of Saxons present, and only exceptionally would this be a consequence of the obligations of tenure in chivalry. Finally, it can be stated that such Saxons would not be villeins. These were considered unfit to bear arms at all. Villeinage is a status of a semi-servile kind; but very early after the Conquest it comes also to denote a tenure, one in which the incidents are unfree, and in which the tenants are not protected by the king's courts—at any rate before the fifteenth century—but must necessarily go to the court of their lord. There is, however, a paradox. A villein would hold any land which he occupied in villeinage, although it should be added that there were many landless villeins, usually part of the labour force of the manor. But certainly by Bracton's time freemen were holding in villeinage.

The process of distinguishing the tenure from the status began early. It should be added that villeinage as a status was practically obsolete by Tudor times, the serf's labour having been replaced by services derived from contract. From one point of view, it can be said that there was a tacit conspiracy to get rid of it. If a villein escaped from the land of his lord, and remained at liberty for a year and a day, he automatically became a free man. As the Middle Ages progressed, enquiries into the past of an able-bodied stranger were not pursued—particularly in the towns. And the Common Law always leaned slightly in favour of freedom. Thus Fleta, writing about thirty years after Bracton, says:

> Freedom, indeed is the natural power of every man to do what he pleases, unless it is forbidden by law or force. In another fashion it is said that freedom is the purging way of bondage because they are clear contrary the one to the other[3]

and he points out that a temporary reduction in status of a freeman into servitude 'takes away nothing of his freedom from him who is free'.

To turn to the other end of the social scale, William rewarded his adherents of suitable status with grants of land in return for which knight-service was exacted, and that amount of land which bore the service of one knight was termed a knight's fee. These varied so much in extent that it is virtually impossible to make any general statement about them. Some fees might be as small as a single hide of land. Others, especially in the north, were very much larger. The productivity and situation of land might have influenced computations, but it is not easy to decide. Once again, we should beware of the idea of a 'system' where there was none. Nor did a number of the incidents of knight-service, other than the obligation to furnish knights, become free from doubt until after much conflict between the king and his tenants-in-chief. On these and allied matters, Pollock and Maitland give a warning which must be heeded:

> Soon after the Conquest a process begins whereby the duty of service in the army becomes rooted in the tenure of land. This goes on for a century; but before it is finished, before the system of knight's fees has been well ordered and arranged, the kings are already discovering that the force thus created is not what they want, or is not all they want. It may serve to defend a border, or to harry Wales or Scotland for a few weeks in the summer, but for continuous wars in France it will not serve; the King would rather have money; he begins to take scutages. This practically alters the whole nature of the institution. Another century goes by and scutage itself has become antiquated and unprofitable; another, and scutage is no longer taken. Speaking roughly we may say that there is one century (1066-1166) in which the military tenures are really military, though as yet there is little law about them; that there is another century (1166-1266) during which these tenures still supply an army, though chiefly by supplying its pay; and that when Edward I is on the throne the military organisation which we call feudal has already broken down and will no longer provide either soldiers or money save in very inadequate amounts. However, just while it is becoming little better than a misnomer to speak of military tenure, the law about military tenure is being evolved, but as a part rather of our private than our public law. The tenant will really neither fight nor pay scutage, but there will be harsh and intricate law for him about

the reliefs and wardships and marriages that his lord can claim because the tenure is military. Thus in speaking of tenure by knight service as it was before the days of Edward I, we have to speak not of a stable, but of a very unstable institution, and if of necessity we describe it in general terms, this should not be done without a preliminary protest that our generalities will be but approximately true.[4]

The harsh and intricate law of which the authors speak was only elaborated after much wrangling between king and tenants-in-chief, the result of it being frequently embodied, as a species of compact, in legislation. Its existence, and enforcement, was one of the instruments by means of which Charles I was able to rule for eleven years without a Parliament; and by an ironic twist, the remote descendants of these Norman tenants-in-chief came to regard military tenures as an intolerable burden, and socage, the originally despised tenure, as the most desirable form of land-holding. One of the first acts of the Restoration Parliament in 1660 was the final abolition of military tenures, all of them, except for purely ceremonial incidents, being converted into 'free and common socage'.

It has been mentioned that the king's grants of land, by way of so many manors, were normally scattered, and the tenant-in-chief might well find, not only that the administration of them was difficult, expensive and time-consuming, but also that he had difficulties in furnishing the required number of knights when called upon. For over two centuries after the Conquest, the tenant-in-chief could not only not rid himself of the feudal burdens on the land—he could not rid himself of the land itself. In the eyes of the royal administration he remained liable for the burdens of the land, whatever he did with it. It therefore came about that he sub-feudated, that is to say, he granted out part of the land for an estate of one of various possible interests, in exchange for services due to him. In this way, he could farm out either part or the whole of his obligation to furnish knights, so that when the king called on him, he in turn could call upon his undertenants. Sub-infeudation was already taking place before the Conqueror died in 1087. By the thirteenth century, instances of derivative sub-infeudation six and seven deep appear in the records. Once Edward I, by the Statute *Quia Emptores* in 1290 permitted sale as an alternative to sub-infeudation, with the substitution of the purchaser as the person responsible to the Crown for an apportioned part of the services, sub-infeudation declined rapidly in importance, and with the decay of the seignorial courts, a presumption arose that all land in military tenure was held in chief of the Crown.

It will be apparent that this elaborate structure based on tenure by military service was something quite distinct from the traditional Saxon landholding, though the two systems were linked by the manor and the lord of the manor. Such a lord would normally hold in knight-service from his overlord, and so on upwards to the tenant-in-chief, who held of the king. Since the ancient laws of the English could not encompass this structure, matters relating to military tenure could not be heard in the shire court. Further, one of its unvarying characteristics was suit of court, ie the duty to attend upon the immediate overlord, to give him counsel, and to adjudicate upon disputes relating to land arising from tenure. At the apex of the system, the king held his court for his tenants-in-chief. Each such tenant, irrespective of the size of his holding, was jealous of the privileges of his order, although at an early date a distinction becomes apparent between the *majores barones*, who attended on the king in person, and the *minores barones*, who are excused from frequent attendance and, when they are summoned, receive their summons (and incidentally pay their taxes) through the sheriff of the county in which their land is situated. After Magna Carta, these latter gradually become distinguishable as the knights of the shire and, later still, the earls, bishops, barons and abbots can be recognised as the House of Lords—but this is a long way ahead.

But in spite of such distinctions, all the tenants-in-chief share a common characteristic. Their land disputes must be tried by the king's judges, in accordance with rules which are based upon the customs of men such as themselves, except insofar as these have been modified by measures for which their consent has been obtained. In this principle, one may detect two concepts which are ultimately of very first importance in the development of English institutions. The first is the Common Law—a law which, in its first manifestation, is common only in the sense that it is common to all those who resort to the king's court, ie the tenants-in-chief. It was only by the steady expansion of the jurisdiction of the king's courts, until it came to comprehend the disputes of all free men, that the Common Law became the law of England, and that it progressively superseded or circumscribed all local laws.

The second concept is that of Parliament as the Grand Inquest, or deliberative body, of the nation. This, too, lay far ahead, and in Norman times all that had happened was that the Saxon Witan had been merged with the Norman Duke's Council which, as a body meeting regularly, comprised the officers of the king's household and the greater tenants-in-chief. Until the latter part of the thirteenth century, it is this body which claims to speak for the nation, but there are signs of change. The growth of trade gave increasing importance to the merchants, from whom kings who prosecuted foreign wars must seek resources. At first, the part played by the Commons in government is a purely subordinate one, and even as late as the reign of Edward II the name of Parliament is given to a number of assemblies which are purely baronial. But the tendency is too strong to be resisted, and during the long reign of Edward III something like a settled form for Parliament has been established, with the Commons as a necessary and increasingly active element. It is by no means impossible that, had the Conquest never occurred, the Witan would ultimately have evolved into Parliament; but it was the Norman Conquest which firmly established the position of the tenants-in-chief as a special order in the state.

3

The End of the Norman Conquest

One of the most striking facts of English history is the brevity of Norman rule. It began in 1066 and was over by 1154. In less than a century an alien aristocracy had landed, fought, taken over and gone some way towards merging with the Saxon and Danish population. The failure of the newcomers to establish their dynasty is shared by another alien and racially allied dynasty, that of the Danes, a century earlier. Just as before the Conquest the Danes mingled with the Saxons, giving an increased breadth and variety to Saxon life, so by the reign of Henry II the same process was already well advanced between the Normans and English. There was one important difference. The Danish aristocracy had never completely replaced the Saxon, although it was powerfully established in the north and the midlands, and assimilation was therefore easy. After the Norman Conquest, it was retarded by the paucity of Saxon heiresses.

The Conqueror had four sons and several (possibly six) daughters, and it might seem that the succession was secure. His eldest son, Robert, succeeded to Normandy, and the Conqueror seems always to have intended to keep his Norman and English dominions distinct. His second son, Richard, was killed hunting in the New Forest in 1075. He was unmarried. Thereafter, the English heir was William Rufus, who was also killed in the New Forest, in 1100, again unmarried. At various times Robert sought to acquire England, while William Rufus, and later his brother and successor, Henry I, sought to acquire Normandy. In this Henry was successful, and although Robert had at least two sons, they were unable to recover Normandy, and their line vanishes from

English history. Henry I had a son, William, and a daughter, Matilda, but the young William was drowned in *The White Ship*, in his father's lifetime. He, too, was unmarried. The daughter, Matilda, married first, the Emperor, and on his death, Geoffrey of Anjou. Although Henry made repeated efforts to secure the acceptance of his daughter as his successor, the barons and the City of London chose Stephen, a younger son of the Count of Blois, who had married the Conqueror's daughter, Adela, owing to their dislike of Matilda and her husband, Geoffrey of Anjou. The result was a civil war lasting throughout most of the reign, between the supporters of Stephen and the supporters of Matilda. It ended when Stephen died in 1154, and Matilda's son succeeded as Henry II.

There were thus four Norman kings if Stephen is included. In reality, Stephen was a member of a French baronial house, who possessed very extensive lands in England, and whom the English barons regarded as their natural leader. During the disorder of his reign, the administrative system which Henry I had laboriously created collapsed, and with it, the royal authority. At this date, it is plain, there existed no conception of 'impersonal monarchy' such as that which enabled England to survive the absence and imprisonment of Richard I; the loss of Normandy by civil war, and foreign invasion of John's reign; or the prolonged struggle between king and barons during the reigns of Henry III and Edward II. If, as we are frequently warned, we should resist the inclination to measure the breakdown of government in Stephen's reign with the conditions of a later age, it may perhaps be compared with the conditions which existed in the struggles between Saxon and Dane which led, first, to the establishment for a time of a Danish king, and then to the relatively peaceful transfer of kingship to the Saxon, Edward the Confessor. There was no collapse of royal power, even in this earlier age, comparable with that which characterised the reign of Stephen. This is the measure of the Norman failure. It stresses the fact, which will be more fully discussed later, that the true development of English institutions begins with Henry II, not with William the Conqueror, and it is for this reason that modern historians tend to regard Henry II as the greatest of our medieval kings.

It must also be appreciated that Henry II was not only not a Norman, but on the contrary, he was the descendant of the rulers of Anjou, who maintained a stubborn animosity to the Norman dukes. The Conqueror's most frequent enemies, prior to 1066, had been the Angevins, with whom he had fought long and bitterly for the possession of Maine, a key principality lying between the two duchies. There was no Viking blood in the Angevins. They were Franks—quick-thinking, adroit, self-seeking and unscrupulous. An Angevin was accustomed to despise the slower-witted Normans. When, therefore, Henry II succeeded to both Normandy and England, uniting them with Anjou and through his wife, Eleanor, with Aquitaine, it was a triumph of statecraft, achieved against all probability, and, so far as Normandy was concerned, against vindictive enemies. Under Henry's restless genius Normandy, like England, was to suffer a transformation in its institutions, and on both sides of the Channel they were to come closer together than they had ever done before. Six historic units—England, Ireland, Normandy, Maine, Anjou and Aquitaine—were in his reign united in what is sometimes called the Angevin Empire, although the units exhibited deep-rooted differences in racial stock, civilisation and institutions. The measure of Henry II's abilities is the rapidity with which this scattered empire fell to pieces in John's reign, thereby transforming the Anglo-Norman baronage of England into English barons whose energies, once their continental fiefs were lost, were concentrated upon English problems. Their changed outlook is evident in their reluctance to serve overseas in sporadic efforts to recover the king's lost French dominions, and in their unfaltering dislike of, and opposition to, 'foreigners' in the entourage of successive kings. Such foreigners were comprehensively classed as French, whether, like Piers Gaveston in the reign of Edward II, they came from noble Gascon families who had adhered to the English crown over several generations, or whether, like Henry III's 'French' counsellors, they came from Toulouse and Provence, areas which far from being within the English orbit in France, had usually been in conflict with the English rulers of Gascony.

Examples such as these, to which many others could be added, will emphasise that, while from the reign of Henry II onwards, English public life was open to much foreign influence, much of it emanating from France, it was certainly not a continuation of the Norman tradition. In many respects, it was opposed to that tradition, and, further, Normandy itself was exposed to similar influences. One illustration of this is that the harsh Norman-French of the English law courts was quite distinct from the French spoken at the royal court.

If one surveys the ninety years of Norman rule, it seems to divide naturally into three periods. The first is the period of the continuing Conquest, extending over the whole of the reigns of William I and William II, ie until 1100. During that period, the Saxon landowners were replaced by Normans, whose holdings depended upon their obligation to furnish the king with military aid in emergency. Secondly, the royal authority was recognised as paramount, and the king's administration exercised a firm control over local institutions—which continued with vigour after the Conquest—through the sheriffs, and the justices whom the king's council sent out at frequent intervals to ensure that justice was done, and the king's dues (of which the profits of justice were an important element) were regularly remitted to the royal exchequer. The Anglo-Saxon chronicles suggest that royal burdens lay heavily upon the people during the reigns of the first two Norman kings. To put it simply, England—a wealthy country by contemporary reckoning—was being efficiently exploited by its foreign kings; and their tenants-in-chief were not slow to follow their example. These are the natural consequences of conquest, and one cannot explain too much; but they should serve as a corrective to the picture of the Conqueror as an enlightened ruler, giving a fresh impulse to English civilisation. The celebrated character study of the Conqueror, written as the chronicler says 'by one who had often looked upon him, and lived some time in his court', while it gives full recognition to the fact that during his reign he had brought England to subjection and peace (even though in wide areas of the north it was the peace of death), at the same time mentions his covetousness and greed which, as a later part of the same entry shows, had caused him to amass considerable treasure at Winchester, which his son and successor promptly dissipated.

The Conqueror's most striking quality was his far-sightedness. He recognised from the outset that if his conquest was to endure, its continuity with Saxon England must be manifest. It was for this reason he not only promised to retain the laws as they existed in Saxon times, but actually did so. The laws of his own feudal tenants were a superstructure which left the pre-existing fabric largely unaltered. Both by temperament and policy, William was no innovator. What he sought to do, in legal matters, was to establish certainty and precision where, in Saxon times, these qualities had been rare. Even today, one is impressed by the size of the task which he set the Domesday Book Commissioners—and the speed with which they achieved it. The returns which they brought back to Winchester were monumental, and even in the digested form in which they appear in Domesday Book itself, their detail captures the imagination. We are told the extent of ploughland, the number of pigs and sheep, and in addition, we are told of mills and barns, and also the history of the taxation of the manorial unit. The detail is staggering. We are told that at Eckington, in the time of Edward the Confessor, two men held land on the terms that they mowed their lord's meadow one day a year. At Dinedor, 'no-one fishes in the river without leave'. It suggests that after the Conquest, some local customary rights were threatened, for at Nottingham, it is recorded, 'the burgesses were accustomed to fish in the water of the Trent, and now they make complaint that they are forbidden to fish'. The Book also records a wealth and variety of local customs, which long enriched English local life, and some of which are not yet obsolete.

Before one becomes too censorious of the Norman overlords who apparently had interfered with the fishing rights of the Nottingham burgesses, one should mention that in our own day they have been destroyed, not by feudal overlords, but by pollution created by local firms. In *Pride of Derby & Derbyshire Angling Association v British Celanese*,[1] the Court of Appeal granted the plaintiffs an injunction against the defendant company and several other defendants, including the Derby Corporation, all of whom had polluted the Trent by sewage, effluent and chemicals, and had thereby destroyed the fishing in the Trent and its tributary, the Derwent. It may do something to place some alleged medieval 'oppression' in perspective to cite a passage from the judgment of Lord Evershed,[2] Master of the Rolls, in that case—a passage which has additional significance today:

> But Sir Andrew Clark (for the Derby Corporation) went further. He went the length of arguing, if it were necessary, that no injunction ought ever to be granted against a local authority in any circumstances, at any rate in regard to sewerage works. He argued further that an injunction, though negative in form, being mandatory in substance was a means of bringing, as I understand him, some sort of improper pressure to bear upon the Minister in the exercise of his duties in granting licences and so forth, and further was a wrongful interference with the corporation's own right to deal with their own problems in such order as they thought fit.
>
> It is, of course, open to the corporation to submit all or any of these propositions, including the most extreme of them, to the court. But it is also open to the plaintiffs, whose rights, as it has been proved, have been seriously damaged, to come to Her Majesty's courts, and to ask for (and, if possible, obtain) redress for those wrongs. In the circumstances, it startled me that the corporation thought fit through their counsel to submit that it was not 'sensible'—that was the word used, according to my note—of the plaintiffs to sue the corporation in these courts; and not only that, but to make the extravagant suggestion that the action was one brought by the solicitors for the plaintiffs for the sole purpose of making for themselves a profit in the way of costs.

In this case the burgesses of Derby made their point, as one hopes the burgesses of neighbouring Nottingham did in respect of the same river in 1085; but one might ask whether we have really advanced so far in these matters in the intervening nine centuries.

The Conqueror, as has been mentioned earlier, made one fundamental change in legal administration in England. In the reorganisation of the English Church which he and Lanfranc carried out, the bishop ceased to be one of the presiding members of the shire court, as he had been in Saxon times, and the full hierarchy of ecclesiastical courts, with their wide jurisdiction over laymen, was introduced. It would be an extremely difficult task today to attempt to establish, even in outline, how far the canon law, as created in Italy and applied on the continent, was ever applied to England before the Conquest. There had been no period of Saxon history, when the church courts had been the layman's refuge against anarchy, as they were in western Europe during the Dark Ages, and indeed, although the English bishops exercised jurisdiction over their clergy, and possessed an uncertain degree of control over laymen, one symbol of which was their participation in the ordeals, the intimate connection between Church and State which was such a feature of Saxon England would have discouraged the establishment of any system of church courts.

For good or ill, the problem was solved during the reign of the Conqueror, and the consequences were far-reaching. William's attitude to the Church was a complex one. Personally devout, he was a loyal son of the Church, and was pledged to advance its interests. But so far as he was concerned this implied that the Church's interests should coincide with his own; and also that papal authority should only be exercised in England with the king's consent. This attitude, which he shared with other western European rulers, was to produce bitter conflict in the next hundred and fifty years. In England, it was to lead to the struggle between Henry II and his rebellious Archbishop, Thomas Becket and, ultimately, to the Constitutions of Clarendon, defining and regulating the respective spheres of Crown and Church.

In the legal sphere, the effects of this fundamental change were less obvious, but more enduring. Pollock and Maitland have shown that in legal matters, not of political importance, the contact between England and the Papal Curia was close and constant. They have also shown that a remarkable number of English clerics enjoyed a reputation for learning in the canon law. To look a long way ahead three great English prelates just before the Reformation—Warham, Morton and Wolsey—were all of the highest repute as canonists. Further, English legal scholarship was enriched by accretions of continental canonists. Very often learning in the canon law went hand in hand with learning in Roman law, usually termed, by way of contrast, the civil (ie the secular) law. Possibly English and American law students have forgotten that the letters LL.B stand for Bachelor of Both Laws, and the laws to which they refer are the canon and the civil law; and although the teaching of the canon law was prohibited at the Reformation, the universities continued to turn their backs on the teaching of English law until the second half of the eighteenth century.

It has sometimes been stated that until the Reformation, the church courts were a powerful obstacle to the final supremacy of the Common Law courts, and even Maitland spoke of the antagonism in the Middle Ages of the canonists and civilians on the one side, and the common lawyers on the other. One hesitates even today to demur from Maitland, but perusal of a number of Year Books reveals no such antagonism. Even as early as the reign of Edward II there is evidence of a clear working arrangement between the two jurisdictions, and the Common Law courts were quick to recognise matters which were appropriate to 'Courts Christian' and to send them there. Admittedly this had not always been so, but it is significant that even in the first quarter of the fourteenth century the royal courts were still drawing approximately half their judges from the ranks of the king's administration, all of whom were clerics. To take a single example. The outstanding two judges at this period, as the Year Books plainly show, were Bereford and Harvey de Stanton. Bereford came from the ranks of pleaders in the Common Law courts. Stanton had come directly from the royal secretariat, and was a cleric. More important, perhaps, there is no discernible difference in their outlook upon the Common Law or upon the canon law.

Antagonism between the two jurisdictions is a characteristic of an earlier period, and particularly of the reign of Henry II. During the confusion of Stephen's reign, the church courts, as a stable system in an uncertain world, had tended to extend their jurisdiction, and there were many unsettled questions. Who tried criminous clerks? Ought the church courts to hear ordinary pleas of debt? Were questions relating to advowsons a matter for the church courts or for the king's courts? And finally as has already been noticed, was frankalmoign a matter for the king's courts or the church courts?

The Constitutions of Clarendon purported to settle all these matters by way of compromise. So far as criminous clerks were concerned, the question whether a man was in orders or was not was to be tried in the king's courts (ultimately by the reading test or 'neck verse'). If it were established that the accused was a cleric, he was sent back to the church courts, where a royal officer would watch the proceedings. The church courts were not to hear pleas of debt, nor matters relating to advowsons which, curiously, were regarded as a matter of real property. Advowsons, at this date, it should be mentioned, were often appendages of manors. Frankalmoign, as we have seen, was in essence a spiritual matter, but once again it was assimilated to the law of real property through the extended use of the Assize of *Utrum*.

Even with these limitations, much jurisdiction remained to the church courts, and the influence of the canon law upon the developed fabric of English law has been more extended than is sometimes conceded. It included all questions of marriage, including nullity and separation, and it therefore elaborated rules governing legitimacy. The influence of the Church in establishing the principle that marriage was the monogamous union of lifelong duration can scarcely be overrated, and the elaborate rules relating to nullity and separation remained the basis of the English law of marriage for centuries after the Reformation. Even when, in 1857, Parliament established a special divorce court, with jurisdiction to grant divorces which permitted parties to marry again, the grounds for a petition still owed much to canon law principles. It is only in our own day that the law of marriage and divorce has freed itself from canon law influences, with the result that the law of marriage in England is today in a greater state of uncertainty than it has been at any time since the Norman Conquest.

The church courts also had jurisdiction over the administration of estates of moveables of persons deceased. To prevent their intrusion into the descent of real property, the Common Law courts established the principle that on a person's death, his freeholds passed directly to the heir—a doctrine which survived until the nineteenth century. But moveables were within the jurisdiction of the church courts, and were distributed by either an executor appointed by the will, or by an administrator appointed by the ecclesiastical court. This, too, remained a characteristic of English law until in the nineteenth century Parliament created a statutory Court of Probate; but in the intervening centuries the church courts had established and applied principles relating to wills and succession which differed widely from those which the Common Law courts had developed in respect of freeholds.

Other instances of the influences of the canon law upon the Common Law could be given—even in the criminal law, where the modern law of bigamy, incest and perjury owes something to this source. There was, however, an even more enduring influence which the canon law exercised upon the Common Law, which is evident in every writer from Bracton to Coke, and even beyond. It was explained by the late Richard O'Sullivan, KC, in a lecture entitled *The Philosophy of the Common Law*.[3] In it he stressed the intimate connection between the underlying principles of the Common Law, and the great Christian learning of the medieval philosophers. So many of the major conceptions of the Common Law—the conception of reasonableness and of personal freedom, of natural law and natural rights, of equity and natural justice—are derived, consciously or unconsciously, from the great stream of medieval Catholic teaching. Appreciation of this helps to explain why the antagonism between common lawyer and canonist, which Maitland suggested, is rarely apparent before the Reformation.

So far, only the first phase of Norman England has been

mentioned—the period of the continuing conquest. The second period, in which the Norman influence reached its culmination, was the reign of Henry I—a period of thirty-five years in which a strong king, and again a stern and covetous one, consolidated the work of his father, and developed some institutions of enduring importance. Although Henry could be both stern and cruel, he is not inappropriately termed 'the Lion of Justice', and the *Anglo-Saxon Chronicle* (in language strangely anticipatory of a 'Times' obituary) wrote: 'A good man he was and there was great awe of him. No man dared misdo against another in his time. He made peace for man and beast. Whoso bare his burden of gold and silver, no man durst say him aught but good.'

Henry nevertheless applied and extended the stern forest code to an even greater degree than his father. On the other side of the ledger, it can be recorded that, in association with the saintly Anselm, his Archbishop of Canterbury, he worked out a satisfactory compromise with the papacy which, during his reign, prevented the extension to England of the struggle between the papacy and the secular rulers of Europe which is known as the 'Investiture Contest'.

Henry I's reign is notable for important advances, both in the structure of government and in the development of English law. Henry had succeeded in ousting Robert from his Duchy of Normandy, as William Rufus had also done, and his reign was therefore devoted to the efficient administration of both realms. The researches of Richardson and Sayles have recently thrown much additional light on this question, and they necessitate a modification of the opinions expressed by Stubbs, Maitland and even Plucknett.

The central point of the researches of Richardson and Sayles is that Henry created an efficient administration both in Normandy and England by the development of an Exchequer on each side of the Channel, and also by the creation of the office of justiciar. In England, he appointed a man of quite outstanding ability in Roger de le Poer, better known as Roger of Salisbury (of which see he was bishop). This remarkable man was successively Chancellor, 'justice of all England', and then chief justiciar; and when the king was in Normandy, the administration of the kingdom was in his hands. The authors write:

> The problem with which Henry I was confronted when he had made good his hold upon Normandy was to provide for the ordered government of his duchy and his kingdom when he was perforce absent. He must divide his time between his two dominions, but all the while he must retain a firm hold on each. The device he adopted was to create the office of justiciar, a minister who was to act as his viceregent, was to issue writs and was to preside over a central, sedentary court, known both in Normandy and England as the exchequer. We must not credit Henry I with too great originality or too great foresight. Doubtless he used, even though he improved, instruments ready to his hand. There seems, however, to be no contemporary document to show that any great minister had borne the title of chief justiciar before it was conferred on Roger of Salisbury; nor has anyone yet found a reference to the exchequer in either England or Normandy before the year 1109, when, it would seem, the office of chief justiciar was created. But even if we could prove that some earlier minister had borne that title or that the exchequer had existed *eo nomine* on either side of the Channel at the beginning of the twelfth century, we should not have proved that the system which is in operation after 1109 was in operation before that date. For the essence of that system is that it was permanent and no temporary device. The apparatus of the system, as a whole, is found in England under Roger of Salisbury and not before; and, though the evidence is not so detailed or so clear, this is true also of Normandy at the same period and not earlier.[4]

Much patient research has shown that when Henry was in Normandy, the government of the kingdom was in Roger's hands, and further, that the entire administration of justice proceeded from him. Further, the Barons of the Exchequer, whether lay or clerical, not only controlled taxation and assisted the justiciar in the administration of the king's justice in the Exchequer, but also went out to sit in the shire courts representing the royal administration in the despatch of cases there.

The importance of Henry's changes can be in part assessed by the events which followed his death. Roger of Salisbury was deprived of his office of justiciar in 1139, and thereafter, no one seems to have been appointed to succeed him. As Stephen lost Normandy to his Angevin rival in 1145, and thereafter his energies were concentrated upon his unsuccessful struggle to maintain his position in England, the main purpose in appointing a justiciar lapsed. Once Stephen had been succeeded by Henry II, the need for a justiciar was immediately experienced again. For a time, the office was divided between two lay justiciars until at length, in 1180, the survivor was replaced by another layman, Ranulf Glanville, the reputed author of the first recognisable text-book of English law,[5] whilst a few years earlier Richard fitzNigel, Bishop of London, great-nephew of Roger of Salisbury, wrote a full account of the working of the Exchequer, under the title *Dialogue of the Exchequer*. With these two works, which in different ways reflect the immense creative activity of Henry II's reign, the true literature of the Common Law begins. Significantly, Glanville's work expounds the writ system, upon which the expansion of the Common Law was beginning to depend, while fitzNigel's examines the work of the Exchequer, as the power-house of the administration, both fiscal and legal. Although it is not yet a court, a great many matters of importance are decided there. There is little surviving evidence of this from the reigns of Henry I and Henry II, but as Richardson and Sayles point out, since the Barons of the Exchequer were regularly sent out to the shires as itinerant justices, it is inconceivable that they should not also have decided similar actions in the central court of the Exchequer.

Historians are wont to pass somewhat quickly over the dismal record of Stephen's reign, in which the limitations of the Norman conception of government, even as developed by a king as able as Henry I, were demonstrated. So long as Roger of Salisbury remained, the weaknesses were not too apparent. Beside him were his son, Roger, who was Chancellor, and two nephews, Nigel,

Bishop of Ely and Alexander, Bishop of Lincoln. As Stubbs remarks, the entire administration of the kingdom depended upon the Exchequer which, for thirty years, had been in the hands of this able family. When they went, the mechanism of the state crumbled. Stubbs sums up:

> The arrest of Bishop Roger (in 1139) was perhaps the most important constitutional event that had taken place since the Conquest; the whole administration of the country ceased to work, and the whole power of the clergy was arrayed in opposition to the King. It was also the signal for the civil war, which lasted with more or less activity for fourteen years.[6]

It is possible to go a step further. The arrest of Roger of Salisbury marks, more than any other single event, the end of the Norman Conquest of England, and with it, the limits of the Norman impact upon England and English law. It cannot be asserted with confidence that England in 1135 was more prosperous, or more fully in contact with the continent than she would have been had there been no Conquest. Her local institutions were as yet largely unchanged, and so was her system of taxation, for which Domesday Book was still the starting point. Long after Henry I's reign we are told that the clerks of the Exchequer took the Book with them whenever they attended the king on his royal progresses. The Conqueror found English law divided into three great customary systems, with innumerable local variations tenaciously maintained. These customary laws still existed in the reign of Henry I, and they were still Saxon and Danish. As yet the Common Law was scarcely glimpsed. There is a law of the king's court by which alone the king's tenants-in-chief are bound in their disputes relating to land, and something closely resembling it is reproduced in the courts of the great honours and baronies in which the tenants-in-chief administer justice to their under-tenants. The king's court is now a good deal more active than the Witan, and (if the word is to be used) it is more feudal in character. But it does many more things than the Witan attempted. It supervises local justice, and sends out justices to the shires from the ranks of the royal officials, and the lay and clerical barons of the king's council. Again, the clergy have become a separate estate and, as the comment of Stubbs which has just been mentioned shows, they could upon occasion exercise a dominating influence upon public affairs. In the reign of Henry II they were to be responsible for the most serious constitutional struggle of the reign, and one from which even that powerful king did not emerge victorious. Henry I, as we have seen, created the office of justiciar, and also the Exchequer as later kings were to know and use it. Beyond these things, the contribution of the Normans in the legal or administrative sphere is negligible. It was, in fact, a fortunate thing for England that the Conqueror's line died out with his grandson, Stephen. For the Norman system to work, it was necessary that it should be controlled by a firm, even a ruthless, hand. When it was removed, the barons, who owed their existence in England to the Conquest, did not hesitate to destroy it.

Once these factors are weighed, it is apparent that the true starting-point of English legal and constitutional development is not 1066 but 1154, when Henry II succeeded to Stephen. Whilst it is true that Henry II owed something to the work of his grandfather, Henry I, this is only true to the extent that all medieval kings owed something to their predecessors—as, for example, William the Conqueror owed much to Edward the Confessor, and even something to Canute. There is also a circumstance of great importance to remember in considering the work of Henry II. His Empire, so called, was a personal union of several quite distinct elements, each administered separately, and each with its own customs and institutions. He could not introduce a unified administration nor a common system of law. Being the unwearying ruler he was, he sought to introduce changes in Anjou, Maine and Aquitaine, exactly as he sought to do in Normandy and England, but they were distinct changes, and the dominions other than Normandy and England into which they were introduced were less developed and more resistant to change than those two great dominions.

Only between England and Normandy was there any considerable interchange of administrative personnel, and only between

England and Normandy was there any considerable similarity in institutions. Here Henry II almost certainly profited from the work of his grandfather, who had created the Exchequer in both countries and had placed a chief justiciar or seneschal at the head of it. Further, the fact that until the reign of John, many English and Norman barons held estates on both sides of the Channel meant that the feudal customs of England and Normandy tended to show many resemblances. This is by no means always the result of introducing Norman customs into England. The Norman barons frequently complained that their dukes were arbitrarily introducing English customs into Normandy. This was the more resented since from 1154 onwards their dukes were Angevins.

It is only necessary to think of the incessant administrative and legal activity of Henry II's reign to realise that we are in a different world, and that the conservatism of Norman rule is far behind. Henry II's reign has many links with our modern law. It saw the introduction of practices that have been of enduring importance, some of them recreated out of the ruins of Norman administration. At its centre, as has been mentioned, was the justiciar, presiding over the constantly expanding work of the Exchequer. The restoration of its functions was one of Henry's first tasks, and it is evident from the *Dialogue of the Exchequer* that it was discharged with characteristic thoroughness, and was recognised as the key to the Angevin government. It was because such great authority was committed to the justiciar, from almost the beginning of Henry's reign, that government continued to function, and justice continued to be administered promptly and efficiently during the reign of Henry's two successors. This was the essence of the impersonal monarchy which could survive political upheavals, and which permitted and facilitated, not only continuous constitutional growth, but also the inexorable advance of the jurisdiction of the king's courts.

In the judicial sphere Henry II built upon, extended and adapted the system which his grandfather had established. Richardson and Sayles have reconstructed for us the activities of the itinerant justices sitting in General Eyres in the reign of Henry I.[7] They closely resemble in composition and function the General

Eyres of the reign of Henry II, and whilst the practice of sending them out is Norman (there are indeed examples to be found in the reign of William the Conqueror), the shire courts in which they sat, and the lawmen who attended them, and who presented the findings of the hundreds to the justices[8] were of Saxon origin and antedated the Conquest. In the twelfth century the Justices in Eyre are not yet necessarily professional lawyers. They are barons and clerics from the king's household, or even sheriffs, and when they are not sitting in the shires, some of them are sitting as Barons of the Exchequer.

Until commissions of General Eyre ceased to be issued in the reign of Edward III, the General Eyre was the supreme manifestation of royal authority in the shires. The justices were appointed to hear all pleas, and when the Justices in Eyre came into the county, the work of all other courts was suspended. Even cases from that shire before the Court of Common Pleas (when that court achieved a separate identity in the reign of Henry III) were transferred to them. But the work which the justices did went far beyond adjudication. It was their function to inquire into all misdeeds and abuses of authority since the last visitation, and the close connection of the justices with the Exchequer is evidenced by the unremitting attention which they paid to royal dues and amercements. Receipts from General Eyres were an important item in the royal budget.

Such an institution, impressive and greatly feared as it was, is essentially a product of the early Middle Ages, characterised by an assumption that the king's justices are competent to discharge all governmental functions, as the justiciar in the Exchequer does nationally. With increasing specialisation, they must necessarily make way for professionals—whether in administration or justice. The first steps towards this important change came when, early in his reign, Henry decided to send out justices from the central administration on regular circuits several times a year, but with limited commissions. In the civil sphere, they were appointed primarily to try by assize, the new actions for the protection of seizing of land which Henry had elaborated, and which were progressively bringing all freeholders into the king's courts. On the criminal side, these Justices of Assize, as they were termed, tried serious crime, ie felonies which the county presented before them, and for the trial of which the local courts, with their antiquated procedure and reliance upon the ordeals, had gradually proved inadequate. In this way, the most characteristic feature of English superior justice was introduced, ie the formal concentration of the king's courts in London, and the regular circuits of Justices of Assize. In essence, the assize system, so popular in the Middle Ages, remained a peculiar feature of the English judicial system for eight hundred years.

Henry II's changes in the land law place the creative vigour of his administration in striking contrast with the static and primitive Norman system, and it would be interesting to speculate how the land law might have evolved had the line of Norman kings stretched into the thirteenth and fourteenth centuries. Their major contribution, it has been shown, was the introduction of knight-service, accompanied by heavy burdens, and the introduction of trial by battle for the protection of title to a military tenure. The transition to the possessory assizes and the Grand Assize in the reign of Henry II is usually attributed to a softening of manners; but there had been no indication of this in Stephen's reign. The collapse of the central authority facilitated innumerable quasi-legal dispossessions by force of arms, and it is a sign of Henry's greatness that he faced this promptly, making forcible dispossession a criminal offence, offering the Grand Assize, or jury of neighbouring landowners as an alternative to trial by battle, and protecting seizin itself by the invention of the possessory assizes, which played so dominating a part in the establishment of peaceable possession, and which were still the normal recourse of landowners before the Justices in Eyre in the fourteenth century. This revolution in the land law, by virtue of which all important actions relating to freehold tenure in land were progressively brought before the king's justices, followed the pattern of the changes which Henry's father, Geoffrey, had introduced into Anjou, and his control of the new system was secured by his decree that none need answer for his free tenement without royal writ, and by his further decree that if, in an action begun in the court of a lord, the tenant of the land (ie the freeholder in possession) claimed the assize, the trial must forthwith be transferred to the king's court. Such as ordinance, necessarily involving the collapse of seignorial jurisdiction, would not have been capable of enforcement had not the freeholders of England recognised the very great superiority of the royal justice. From this point of view, it is not without significance that Richardson and Sayles[9] directly connect the introduction of the principal possessory assize, the Assize of Novel Disseisin, with the disorders of Stephen's reign, and the general desire to put an end to the uncertainties of title and the possibility of private wars.

One more point may be made, before mentioning the crowning achievement of Henry's legal activities. During his reign both the ordeals and trials by battle were superseded by the gradual extension of the jury or inquest to legal procedure of all kinds. It was used, as we have seen, to elicit the evidence demanded by the Domesday Book inquisitors. Something very like a jury was used in proceedings before the Conqueror's justices in trying disputed land-suits, and again, something like it was used in proceedings before the Justices in Eyre. The coroner also used a jury in the investigation of deaths by homicide. Henry extended it to all matters relating to the seisin of land by his possessory assizes, and by his reform of the criminal law, he established both the jury of presentment, which later became known as the Grand Jury, and the petty jury, or trial jury. The former was abolished as recently as 1933, the latter is still used, although the area of its operation in criminal trials is today circumscribed by the activities of magistrates' courts. It could be argued that here we have an example of Norman influence. For many years, the traditional view was that the Duchy of Normandy adopted the jury from the decaying Carolingian Empire, that it was in use before the Conquest, and that the Normans brought it to England with them.[10] This theory, derived from the researches of an industrious German, Brunner, was accepted, though with some hesitation by Pollock and Maitland, who nevertheless conceded that 'there seems to be good reasons for believing that some of the Scandinavian nations came by route of their own to something that was very like a jury', although they hazard the view that 'it seems unlikely that any new discovery will disturb the derivation of our English from the Frankish inquests'.[11]

This prediction is a good deal less happy than many of those made by these great historians. There has been much research since their *History of English Law* appeared, and today the tide of opinion, led by Stenton, Richardson, Sayles and others, favours a native origin, dating from the reign of that same Ethelred the Unready mentioned earlier. So far from the Norman origin being plain, there is no record of a Norman jury before 1133, and even at that date, it was held before an English earl, the Earl of Gloucester, who had had plenty of experience of them in England.[12] Once again the Normans fail to fulfil expectations. In any event, the word 'jury' implies an oath, and the Normans were not addicted to oaths. For this reason they had little liking for ordeals and compurgation, both Saxon institutions.

Whilst it is not possible to discuss many of the changes which Henry II introduced into every aspect of English political and legal institutions, it is necessary to state in general terms the effect of what he did for the development of English law. To quote Pollock and Maitland again

> If we try to sum up in a few words those results of Henry's reign which are to be the most durable and the most fruitful, we may say that the whole of English law is centralised and unified by the institution of a permanent court of professional judges, by the frequent mission of itinerant judges throughout the land, by the introduction of the 'inquest' or 'recognition', and the 'original writ' as normal parts of the machinery of justice.[13]

This is the root of the matter, and every one of the points which these authors mention emphasises the degree of control which he exercised over the legal system, in which his interest was unremitting. That interest often led him to sit in court to administer justice in spite of innumerable other activities awaiting his attention. It is in his reign that something recognisable as a Common

Law begins to emerge. It is an amalgam of Anglo-Saxon and Danish customs and Norman laws governing military tenures, both of which are about to be transformed by several mighty agencies—the ever-expanding body of original writs, of which Glanville wrote; the assizes which Henry introduced; and finally, by the activities of his judges, whether at Westminster or on circuit. It is significant that although for some centuries to come, English law was to remain remarkably rich in local customs, we no longer hear, after Henry's reign, of the laws of Mercia, Wessex and Northumbria, but of a Common Law of England—that is to say, the law of the king's courts, about which treatises of the calibre of Bracton and Fleta would be written almost exactly a century later, and as the concluding words of Pollock and Maitland's great work remind us, they and their judicial colleagues were building, not for England alone but 'for kingless commonwealths on the other shore of the Atlantic Ocean'—and now, one can perhaps add, for many other commonwealths, too. This we owe ultimately, not to a Norman Conqueror, nor even to a distinguished line of Saxon kings, but to a bow-legged and unprepossessing prince of Anjou, of restless energy and great constancy of purpose who built, perhaps, a good deal better than even he knew.

4
The Emergence of the Judiciary

The conception that the king is the 'fount of justice' is not older than the Norman Conquest. In all probability it is not older than the reign of Henry II. For the Anglo-Saxons justice was a local matter, administered chiefly in the shire courts, and was largely dependent upon local customs, preserved in the memory of those persons who declared the law in court. It is a curiosity of our jurisprudence that English law in the period before the Conquest has not been used to illustrate Savigny's conception of law as the product of the *Volksgeist*. Had Maine been aware of Savigny's theories at the time when he wrote *Ancient Law* it is possible that he might have drawn attention to this. But although Maine was familiar with Savigny's theories on possession he does not mention his wider juristic speculations. The principal change introduced by the Norman Conquest, so far as the central jurisdiction was concerned, was that the king's court now became, for the first time, the court in which disputes relating to land-tenure among the king's tenants-in-chief were regularly decided. As a consequence, there have been preserved accounts of some of the most celebrated trials of the Conqueror's reign, in which land titles and rights relating to land were established. As we should expect, there is no hint of any professional judiciary at this period. The trials were held locally in the presence of the county court or of several county courts by the king's representatives, sent out from *Curia Regis*, and the tenants-in-chief. The presiding officer was often a leading cleric, and those whose names most frequently appear are Lanfranc, Archbishop of Canterbury; the king's half-brother, Odo, Bishop of Bayeux and Earl of Kent; and finally

Geoffrey, Bishop of Coutances. All three seem to have taken pains to acquaint themselves, usually by oral evidence from neighbouring landowners, with the intricacies of pre-Conquest land holding; and they played an important part in establishing continuity between the Saxons who had held before the Conquest and the Normans, whether lay or clerical, who had dispossessed them.[1] There were in addition others who served as judges from time to time, both lay barons and sheriffs; but at this date the appointments were intermittent, being limited to the particular dispute. Nevertheless, these special judicial commissioners of William the Conqueror's reign played a part, albeit a limited one, in settling the guide lines for the future development of English law. The trials over which they presided show clearly the determination of the king, and his commissioners, who held a special place in his councils, to maintain the customary law of England as it had existed in late Saxon times. This attitude was of decisive importance, for without it, it is difficult to see how the importation of much Norman law into England could have been resisted.

These appointments of high officials of the central administration cannot be seen as the creation of a regular judiciary. Since we are told that they sat along with the tenants-in-chief, presumably of the area in which the dispute arose, they can be regarded as local sessions of the *Curia Regis*, and as such, part of the general administration of the country of which adjudication was an element, though not necessarily the most important element.

The work of Richardson and Sayles[2] has shown that the fundamental change in administration in England came, not at the Norman Conquest in 1066, but after the Conquest of Normandy by Henry I in 1109, following which there was established both in England and Normandy the office of chief justiciar, with a new court, the Exchequer, over which he presided. It was through the justiciar that the realm or duchy was administered when the king was on the other side of the channel. With the governmental consequences of their change we are only incidentally concerned, but the effect upon the judiciary and ultimately upon the development of English law were very great. Until the reign of Henry III, the justiciar was the most powerful official in the royal administration. When the king was abroad he fulfilled the function of a viceroy. When the king was at home, he was the head of his administration; and the place in which he exercised his wide and general powers was in the Exchequer, upon which the king's revenue depended. With the loss of Normandy during the reign of King John, the vice-regal side of the justiciar's functions lapsed, and primarily for this reason, the office itself died out during the reign of his son.

As we have seen the period of Norman rule in England lasted from 1066 until 1154. During that period Norman magnates had completely replaced the Saxon and Danish aristocracy, but the national life existing below this Norman façade remained largely unaffected. The Normans were always few in numbers, they remained a military aristocracy and they were not innovators. In the sphere of law they superimposed notions of feudal tenure upon an intricate, but well-settled system of local land-holding. What is more directly in point is that apart from the feudal law administered to the tenants-in-chief in the king's courts, the Norman judges sent out from the king's courts painstakingly attempted to elucidate what the pre-Conquest customs, whether in land tenure or in more general matters were, and then gave effect to them. These customs varied greatly from place to place, and could be generally grouped into three distinct systems—the Northumbrian, the Mercian and those of Wessex. In the reign of Henry I men still regarded them as living bodies of law.

Possibly the most significant innovation of Henry I's reign, and also of the entire Norman period, was the introduction of frequent judicial eyres. Their importance in the evolution of English law has, until recently, been very greatly underrated, although the labours of several modern historians have done something to correct this. The Selden Society, for example, has published three volumes of the proceedings of the Eyre of Kent in 1314–15, and more recently two volumes upon the Eyre of London in 1321, upon which the late Miss Helen Cam has, in her Introduction, thrown a good deal of new light. Unfortunately the proceedings of many of the earlier eyres have not survived, yet for over two centuries—from the reign of Henry I to the middle of the reign of Edward III—they were a unique institution, exercising a major influence upon the development of English law.

Richardson and Sayles in *The Governance of Mediaeval England*[3] have pointed out how extensive was the work performed by the General Eyres in the reign of Henry I, and entries upon the pipe rolls of that reign indicate that the essential features of the General Eyres of the thirteenth and fourteenth centuries are already apparent. The justices are sent out from the king's central court. They are appointed to hear *all* pleas, and at this date they are administrators—either lay or clerical—and not lawyers. Indeed at this early date there are no lawyers in the sense of professional English lawyers at all. They hold their sessions in the presence of the county court, still a most active body, dealing with many other matters than judicial proceedings. The king is actively concerned with the government of the counties for a variety of reasons, but the two principal ones are, first his determination to see that the shires are correctly governed, that the laws are observed and that all officials are properly discharging their functions: and second, that the king's rights and profits are fully accounted for. Amongst these latter are the fines, amercements and other dues arising from the administration of justice. These at the conclusion of the eyre are remitted to the Exchequer; with which each official must make a settlement and receive his discharge. Thus, in the beginning of English legal development, there is a close connection between royal administration, justice and revenue. From early in the reign of Richard I there have been preserved what are known as the 'chapters of the eyre', which in the late thirteenth century became increasingly detailed. These 'chapters of the eyre' set out, and classified the business which the Justices in Eyre were required to discharge. This is extremely comprehensive, and much of it is concerned with other things, besides the administration of justice. It includes, for example, inquiries into royal rights of wardship and marriage and escheats, wreck and treasure-trove, and even inquiries into the efficiency and regulation of the king's castles. But there are also included pleas of the Crown, such as murder, homicide and violent crime; and on the civil side there is provision for the trial of actions concerning the tenure of land. What is of particular importance is that the entries on the pipe rolls from the reign of Henry I which Richardson and Sayles have analysed show that the Justices in Eyre were already dealing with these matters in the reign of Henry I; and that as a result of their activities, the first steps towards the creation of a Common Law of England were already being taken. Further they show that in the judicial proceedings which the justices conducted there were present lawmen or *juratores*, who had already reached a decision in the local courts, and who were required to attend the session of the General Eyre to present their findings. These are regarded by the two distinguished authors as the forerunners of the juries of presentment.[4] Their task was not always an easy one. They were not infrequently punished by fines for deficiencies, and there was often a desire to avoid such service. Sometimes they offered to pay a fine to escape from further service. It is most probably one of the significant ways in which Norman rule was felt to be more oppressive than the pre-Conquest Saxon Government that the king's justices pressed so hardly on the *juratores*, for the same authors bring forward strong evidence from which it may be inferred that they are the successors of the lawmen who declared the law in the shire courts before the Norman Conquest.

During the disorders of Stephen's reign this royal control was greatly relaxed, and may have broken down completely. When order was restored, Henry II sent out the itinerant justices once again, and, as we have noted, they survived until the middle of the fourteenth century. But there were other, and more far reaching, developments in the sphere of law during the reign of this tireless and resourceful king, who was not a Norman but an Angevin, who ruled a collection of lands on both sides of the English Channel, each with its own distinctive culture, administration and system of laws. It is during his reign that the real development of the Common Law of England begins. The criminal law was reformed, and the responsibility for its enforcement, so far as serious crime was concerned, was placed predominantly in the hands of the king's justices. In the sphere of civil law, by the introduction of new remedies such as the writ or right and the possessory assizes (which substituted the decision of juries of neighbouring landowners for the more primitive trial by battle when there was a dispute concerning title to land), the decision of actions relating to freehold land was gradually transferred from the courts of feudal lords to the royal courts. This very large influx of judicial business was responsible in the thirteenth century for many major changes. In the first place it meant that judicial business was now so extensive that some members of the royal administration were occupied with it, progressively, to the exclusion of all other work. In other words, the administration of justice became separated from other kinds of administration and was placed in the hands of specialists. For some time to come, they were still regarded like other administrators as part of the royal household, accompanying the king on his progress through the country. As far as one group of justices —the Barons of the Exchequer—were concerned the physical difficulties of transporting Exchequer records about the country caused them to become established at Westminster, and this was the more easily achieved since, as Richardson and Sayles[5] point out (in this respect invalidating the views expressed by Stubbs in his *Constitutional History*), the Exchequer was not technically part of the household. It is for this reason that the Exchequer is recognisable in its judicial aspect as a separate court at an earlier date than the other two courts of Common Law—the King's Bench and the Common Pleas. These continued to accompany the king for some time to come, and the inconveniences were many.

The increase in the business of the king's courts, even apart from the work of the Exchequer, was so considerable during the reign of the early Plantagenets that they had already divided into two branches. One, the Court of Common Pleas, was particularly occupied with the civil actions relating to land which the reforms of Henry II had created. The other, the King's Bench, as its name implies, was concerned with matters, including administration, in which the king had a special interest. This court was most closely associated with the royal person, and most of our medieval kings sat at one time or another in the King's Bench. The association of the Crown with the Common Pleas was a good deal less close, but until the end of John's reign it is sometimes difficult to say there are two distinct courts. They are served by a common body of judges, and indeed for three years, from 1209, there was only a single court, the sittings of which were sometimes suspended during the troubled reign. When it did sit, it did so at Westminster,[6] and in the section of Magna Carta which deals with the desired reforms in the administration of justice, Chapter 17 provides that a Court of Common Pleas shall sit at some fixed place. So it came about that this court took its place beside the Exchequer at Westminster. For some time yet the King's Bench continued to follow the king's person, though in the later Middle Ages it, too, became established at Westminster.

The next two chapters of Magna Carta (Chapters 18 and 19) indirectly pay an impressive tribute to one of the judicial innovations of Henry II's reign. They provide that the possessory assizes which that king introduced should be held only in the county where the lands in question lie; and that the king, or in his absence the justiciar, shall send into each county four times a year, two justices who, with four knights chosen by the county court, shall hold the assizes. These provisions emphasise the enduring popularity of Henry II's major changes in the trial of actions relating to freehold land. They also point to another of Henry's innovations. The comprehensive inquiries of the General Eyres had never been popular. Moreover as the Middle Ages advanced, it was established that they should not visit a county more frequently than once in seven years, and in some cases the interval between visitations was a good deal longer. When the Eyre of London assembled in 1321, there had been no eyre for over forty years and the memory of officials and suitors of the correct procedure had grown dim. Seven years was not nearly often enough for the trial of actions relating to land; and even on the administrative side it was often difficult to satisfy the detailed inquisitions of the justices. With the very great increase of judicial work which Henry's changes in the trial of actions relating to land had introduced there was also established an entirely new system of itinerant justices—the Justices of Assize. These were either members of the king's central body of justices or practitioners or royal administrators (often clerks, and therefore usually in holy orders). The evolution of this body produced consequences of major importance for the development of English law. In the first place, it was responsible for a professional and corporate approach to English law. Gradually, judicial work became distinct from other kinds of administration, and it came to be handled in conformity with settled principles. It discouraged the continuance of localism and local custom in law to the detriment of the Common Law. Local customs had to be claimed and proved, and if they were in conflict with Common Law they were declared invalid. At the same time, this body of justices took an active part, not only in the process of building up the Common Law by a multiplicity of decisions in court, but in the preparation and promulgation of statutes by the king's council and by Parliament. Thus, Chief Justice Hengham in the reign of Edward I said in one case: 'We agreed in Parliament that the wife if not named in the writ should not be received.'[7]

A year or two later Chief Justice Hengham, possibly the most famous (and the greatest) of medieval judges, with the possible exception of his successor, Bereford, rebuked council with the words: 'Do not gloss the statute, for we know better than you; we made it.'[8]

In this environment, judges were conscious that the Common Law was a fluid and rapidly developing system, and in sharp contrast with their successors, they could speak with confidence and authority upon the intentions of the legislator. For example, in another case Bereford said of the statute *De Donis*,

> He that made the statute meant to bind the issue in fee tail, as well as the feoffees, until the tail had reached the fourth degree, and it was only through negligence that he omitted to insert express words to that effect in the statute, therefore we shall not abate this writ.[9]

It is of this double function that Fleta was thinking when he wrote at the end of the thirteenth century in the Prologue to his treatise:

> The laws and customs of the realm were, moreover, reasonable from the beginning and have long subsisted and, what is greatly to be praised, the King does not disdain the counsel of such men, albeit subjects, whom he knows, by witness of their wisdom and eloquence, to surpass others in soberness of conduct and in experience of the law and to be most learned in the customs of the realm, and whom he rightly deems to be most ready to determine actions and decide disputes by the dictates of justice, acting now with severity and now with lenience as it seems to them expedient on the circumstances of the case.

Plucknett has summed up the position in the fourteenth century in the following terms:

> We shall be getting nearest the truth it seems, when we remember that the fourteenth century was in urgent need of good law, firmly enforced, for then we shall understand that the judges' great preoccupation was to apply the best law they knew as courageously as they could, and that our modern difficulties, whether political or juridicial, to them would have seemed, if not unintelligible, at least irrelevant and pedantic.[10]

They would have appeared pedantic for the very good reason that the king was regarded as the fountain of justice in something more than a formal sense, and he manifested his interest in its administration in a variety of ways. Until the close of the Middle Ages kings sat regularly not only on the council, but in the court of King's Bench. In the reign of Edward II (and in other reigns) we find the king intervening by way of advice, and by the transfer of cases to the council, even from the proceedings of Justices in Eyre. In one case before the Eyre of Kent, Chief Justice Harvey de Stanton, a close colleague of Bereford, declared that he could not apply a statute because he had received instructions from the king about it. This may appear to negative the assertion of Fleta that the king had a strict regard for justice—but such interventions were usually prompted by the desire to bring to the attention of the judge some fact of which he would otherwise be ignorant;

it again stresses the close connection between the royal administration and the administration of justice by the king's judges.

There were other links. The intimate connection between the Common Law Bench and the Exchequer has already been noticed. Something more will be said of this later. There was also a close connection, punctuated by occasional rivalry, between the judges and the clerks in Chancery. These were a distinct body of clerks, under the general supervision of the Chancellor, through whom the royal commands were transmitted by way of formal communications. Prominent amongst those were the writs by means of which litigation in the king's courts was most frequently initiated. Upon occasion, there was consultation between the king's justices and the clerks in Chancery upon the scope or form of a writ. For example, during the hearing of the case of *Latimer v Thwing* included in cases heard before the Eyre of Kent in 1314 but decided in the reign of Edward I—a case upon the possessory assize of *mort d'ancestor*—a dispute arose concerning its proper form and Mutford, one of the counsel in the case, said:

> This writ was challenged in the term of St Hilary so that the complainant immediately came to us from Lincoln, and told us how his writ had been challenged. Whereupon Sir William[11] and I went to the Chancery and asked the Bishop's[12] clerks what form they used, and they said they sometimes used one and sometimes the other. But for reasons that were stated, a man may vouch to warranty under this writ and warranty goes to the right, and a warrantor ought to have a term day, and seeing that this writ touches the right more nearly than does a writ of novel disseisin. We agreed that the form of the writ was good; and I tell you that you will never get any other form out of the Chancery in future.[13]

There exists also from the reign of Edward II a letter written by William of Airmyn, who occupied an office in the Chancery roughly corresponding to that of the Master of the Rolls of later date. Addressed to the Chancellor, it reports that he has held conference with the chief justices of the King's Bench and the

Common Pleas, together with a Baron of the Exchequer and a justice of the Common Pleas, in a chamber in the Exchequer building at Westminster.[14] Such conferences were apparently not unusual and they indicate the degree of association maintained between the Chancery Clerks and the Common Law justices at this period, when the Common Law was developing rapidly.

The Chancery Clerks were a distinct body within the royal administration, and by the end of the reign of Edward I they were distinct from the clerks of the king's household. In spite of their close connection with the machinery of justice, they were rarely appointed to judicial office. This is the more noticeable since many other king's clerks, and more especially those connected with the work of the Exchequer, regularly received such promotion.

One hundred and twelve years separates the signing of Magna Carta by King John in 1215 from the murder of his great-grandson, Edward II, in 1327; and during that time very great changes took place both in the organisation and nature of the English judiciary. At the death of Edward II, the three Common Law courts were distinct, each with its own records, and whilst the King's Bench was still closely associated with the king's person (and was frequently presided over by the king), the Exchequer and the Common Pleas were permanently established at Westminster. Nominally, each had a distinct competence, although the work of both the Exchequer and the King's Bench in the sphere of ordinary civil business was showing a tendency to expand. So far as the Exchequer was concerned, its principal activity was financial, and the Barons of the Exchequer had always possessed a competence to hear cases connected with the revenue, but litigants were familiar with the Barons of the Exchequer as Justices in Eyre and as Justices of Assize, and although work in the Common Pleas continued to grow, it was not surprising that some litigants should wish to have their disputes settled in the Exchequer. A succession of ordinances in the latter part of the reign of Edward I and during the reign of Edward II sought to limit its jurisdiction to hear pleas to those connected with the revenue, not out of any tenderness for the justices of the Common

Pleas, but in order to confine the Barons of the Exchequer to revenue work which was becoming great in volume and complexity.[15]

Possibly the most important change during this century of progress was in the composition and method of recruitment to the bench. It has been mentioned that Henry I's itinerant justices were either clerks or lay barons. The work they did was of general governmental character, and accordingly the qualities which made them valuable in the king's council would also fit them for work in the General Eyre. By the reign of Henry III, however, the articles of the Eyre—ie the heads under which their activities could be classified—had become elaborate and increasingly technical, and it is easy to see from Fleta's account of them that they had become even more elaborate and still more technical by the end of the thirteenth century. That meant that the appointment of anyone but a royal administrator with special legal competence, or a justice of the Common Law courts, had become a rarity, and the same could be said in respect of the appointment of Justices of Assize or of justices appointed on other special commissions. Indeed, something like the modern practice was already being followed. In the first place Common Law justices were appointed, but if these were insufficient for circuit work, the royal administration would appoint either a clerk from the Exchequer, or a lawyer practising in the Common Law courts as an itinerant justice, and not a few of these eventually became full Common Law justices at a later date.

During the same period, the character and professional background of the king's judges shows a marked change. At the time of Magna Carta, clerics, very often drawn from the body of royal clerks, overwhelmingly predominated, and their predominance persisted during the reign of Henry III. So far, too, the literature of English law had been written by men who were clerics. Of these works, the most outstanding and the most long-lived in its influence, was Bracton's great treatise on English law written sometime round about the middle of the thirteenth century, at the time of the great struggle between the barons, led by Simon de Montfort, and the king. There is much that is significant from the standpoint of judicial development in his career and work. All who have written about him have remarked on the number of ecclesiastical appointments which he held, culminating in the Chancellorship of Exeter Cathedral, but this was the consequence of his career as a royal clerk. Plucknett[16] comments on the fact that although his active career was at its peak during the barons' war, he cannot be detected as a partisan of either king or barons; but that is not in the slightest degree remarkable. During the reign of Edward II, when a fresh struggle with the barons divided the country, the activities of the royal administration and the royal judges continued without interruption. At this period, in fact, the country had already secured the inestimable benefits of an impersonal royal administration and an impersonal bench of judges, both of which continued to function, though not without difficulty, whatever the political upheavals. There was never any suggestion that these two branches of government changed with changing political fortunes. The aim of each side was to capture the machine, not to destroy it.

Like many royal administrators, Bracton, although never a Judge of the Common Pleas, served from time to time as a Justice of Assize, and as a Justice in Eyre and, for a short time, as a Justice of the King's Bench. His was, indeed, a typical official career of the period for a royal clerk in holy orders, and it received the normal reward—ecclesiastical preferments. In other ways, too, his career was typical. As a clerk he seems to have studied civil and Common Law in Italy, and it is certain that he was influenced by the Italian jurist, Azo, and probably also by other contemporary civilians. These influences are reflected in his treatise. Sir William Holdsworth has said:

> We cannot say that all Bracton's law is English in substance, that the influence of Roman law is merely formal. No doubt there is a body of thoroughly English rules; and Bracton differs at very many points from the Roman texts. But it is clear that he has used Roman terms, Roman maxims, and Roman doctrines to construct upon native foundations a reasonable system out of comparatively meagre authorities.[17]

And Holdsworth continues that Bracton discusses with Roman law terminology, legal concepts, such as contract, fraud and negligence, about which at this date there were no Common Law rules.

It is of course true that Bracton was writing a treatise, not applying law in court, but in doing so, he was anticipating problems which Common Law judges would be called upon to face in the future, and he was using, possibly in bolder fashion, methods which the judges of his own day applied to the solution of problems which came before them. They never minimised their creative function, although it was necessarily restricted by the increasing formalism of the original writs. But the writ system was not the whole of the Common Law. There was a much more flexible procedure by bill. Bolland had already drawn attention to this, as a method by which equitable principles were applied in the General Eyre. More recently, Richardson and Sayles have emphasised that there is ample evidence of a general procedure by bill in the Common Law Courts in the thirteenth and fourteenth centuries, and very recently, in her Introduction to her fine edition of *The Eyre of London*,[18] the late Miss Helen Cam has discussed the extensive use of procedure by bill before the Eyre of London in 1321.

Notwithstanding this exercise in juristic speculation on which both Maitland and Holdsworth have commented, and which in our opinion represents the process of reasoning which a judge of his day would adopt when facing a novel problem, especially when acting as a Justice in Eyre, Bracton's work is firmly based upon Common Law materials, used in a way which was habitual, not only with the judges of his day, but with the judges of succeeding centuries.

This basic fact was most fortunately established by the discovery of what is now known as *Bracton's Note Book* by Sir Paul Vinogradoff, and which was edited by Maitland. The *Note Book* contains Bracton's transcripts of approximately two thousand cases from the plea rolls, and even this is not all, for the plea rolls themselves survive, and they contain the pencilled directions which Bracton himself wrote for the guidance of the copyist which he employed. Reproductions of some specimen extracts may be studied in Lady Stenton's edition of *The Eyre Rolls of Lincolnshire and Worcestershire.*[19] Such entries were not available to the lawyers of his day, so there can be no suggestion that Bracton was using what we would now regard as case law. He was using his special knowledge of the progressive development of English Common Law by the judges as the basis of his systematic exposition of a rapidly-growing system of law. But the *Note Book,* as Lady Stenton in her Introduction to these eyre rolls shows, can tell us a good deal more. A substantial part of our knowledge of the judicial eminence of Martin of Pattishull is derived from the frequent citation of his decisions by Bracton, who cites his decisions more frequently than those of any other justice. One of his contemporaries and close colleagues, upon whose decisions Bracton also relied, was William Raleigh who, like Bracton, was a Devon man. Lady Stenton traces their careers in detail, and shows that the careers of all three were similar, and closely linked. All three were clerics, whose legal careers began in the reign of King John and whose judicial activities reached their peak in the middle of the reign of his son, Henry III. In all probability Bracton, whilst still a king's clerk, served as a clerk in eyres conducted by one or other, or both, of his senior colleagues. Martin himself had served as a clerk to a still more famous judge, Simon of Pattishull, to whom he was not related, although they probably came from the same village. Maitland conjectured that Bracton's fondness for citing the decisions of Martin of Pattishull and William Raleigh was due to the fact that they headed a school of lawyers, but Lady Stenton more plausibly suggests that he began his legal apprenticeship as clerk to Pattishull until Pattishull's death, and thereafter to William Raleigh.[20] Raleigh in due course passed from the bench to a bishopric—a fitting reward for his judicial eminence in a troubled age. Bracton's ready access to the rolls recording these decisions suggests not only a close connection with these two great judges, but possibly also service as a clerk in the Exchequer, where the rolls were deposited. Wherever one looks in the reign of Henry III, one finds clerical justices, with an Exchequer connection and receiving ecclesiastical preferment.

At the very outset of his treatise, Bracton emphasises that he is writing a practical manual for justices and their clerks, and that it is based upon well-established judgements of just men in actual cases which have arisen for decision. Where he adds, as Maitland has noted, principles in areas of law not yet occupied by the king's judges, he is doing so with the intention that the materials he collects shall be used as guide-lines for further law making, and as such his work was long used.

If we look ahead approximately sixty years to the judiciary in the reign of Henry III's grandson, the unfortunate Edward II, we can discern that a major change is taking place. As the reign progresses the proportion of clerical to non-clerical judges decreases. Throughout the whole reign, the King's Bench and the Common Pleas were served by nineteen judges. Of these, eight (or possibly nine) were clerks, but no new clerical justice was appointed after 1316. One justice, John Benstead, who had been an important official under Edward I, and who accepted the less important office of justice under Edward II, did so, it has been suggested, because he wished to renounce his ecclesiastical orders and marry. In any event, he did so and founded a family. After the reign of Edward II, for reasons which will be discussed later, the clerical element rapidly disappeared from the bench.

The reign of Edward II is therefore transitional. It begins with a very distinguished Chief Justice of the Common Pleas, Ralph of Hengham, who was a cleric. When he retired he was succeeded in 1309 by a Chief Justice who is even more famous, Sir William Bereford, who had risen from the ranks of advocates in court. He served almost throughout the reign, until he was succeeded, in July 1326, by Harvey de Stanton, another cleric. On these and other appointments, Tout comments:[21]

> Our conclusions, then, are that judicial office was still freely open to clerks and other persons who were not professional lawyers. The increasing tendency was, however, to appoint as judges, lawyers who had made their mark as advocates.

The transitional nature of the reign can perhaps be best

appreciated by considering the careers of Bereford and Stanton. Bereford has been made familiar to us by Bolland's biography of him, and by the frequent references by Maitland, Holdsworth and others to his directness of speech, his learning, and his judicial courage. In the Common Pleas, the Year Books of Edward II show him sitting most frequently with Stanton, who lacks nothing of his learning, though Bereford's forcefulness is equated by Stanton's subtlety and courtesy. Professional lawyer and cleric appear to complement each other, and it seems appropriate that they died within a few months of one another.

If Bereford's career points the way to much that was to follow, even including its involvement with Edward II's unlucky favourite Piers Gaveston, Stanton's looks back to an age that was passing. Like many other king's clerks who rose to judicial eminence he served in the Exchequer, with which his connections remained very close. Towards the end of the reign, after many years of distinguished judicial service, he even served for a short time as Chancellor of the Exchequer. Before he received a regular appointment as a judge of the Common Law courts, he had already served as a Justice in Eyre, when his financial expertise, derived from Exchequer service, was doubtless of importance. Even after his appointment as a Common Law judge he served as Chief Justice in two long and very notable General Eyres—the Eyre of Kent in 1314 and the Eyre of London in 1321. The records of both, happily, have been edited and published by the Selden Society, and they give us a very full picture of this great medieval institution. But Stanton also achieved the unique distinction of serving as Chief Baron of the Exchequer, Chief Justice of the King's Bench briefly, during the king's temporary triumph in 1323–4, and finally as Chief Justice of the Common Pleas, until his death in the year of Edward II's murder. No cleric was ever to rise so far in the king's judicial service again, and no judge was ever to preside over the three Common Law courts in turn in the future. By any standards Stanton was a very remarkable man, and with his death one phase in the evolution of the English judiciary ended. The clerics were steadily giving place to the lawyers. As Turner has pointed out, if the bench had continued to recruit from the clerics, the influence of civil and canon law upon the Common Law might have been greater[22] although there is little indication of a bias in favour of either alien system in the judgements of most of the clerical justices. Being recruited from the body of the king's clerks, their allegiance to the Church was little greater than that of the laity.

5

The Medieval Judiciary and the Common Law

We are accustomed to regard the transition to a judicial bench composed of professional lawyers as a major advance in English legal development. It will be one of the objects of this chapter to consider how that conclusion is justified and what followed from the change. The reign of Edward II is something of a turning point. It has been pointed out that in this reign, clerical and lay judges, drawn from the royal secretariats (and particularly from the Exchequer), were almost equally balanced, not only in numbers, but in importance. There were clerical appointments which continued well into the reign of Edward III, but never again would a judge with a clerical background such as that of Harvey de Stanton occupy so prominent a place in the judiciary. Already the exposition of the law before the courts had passed into the hands of pleaders who were known sometimes as counteurs or 'narrators'. These are compendiously referred to as serjeants, and might legitimately expect elevation to the bench. The day when Bracton, Archdeacon of Barnstaple, Martin Pattishull, Dean of St Paul's and William Raleigh, Treasurer of Exeter, moulded the Common Law from the bench, belonged to a past that was already coming to appear remote, and it is not without significance that John Benstead, originally a clerk in the royal wardrobe and for a time Chancellor of the Exchequer, who was appointed a judge of the common bench in 1309, abandoned the minor orders in which he had hitherto been, was knighted, acquired land, and founded a family. Possibly at this date the ecclesiastical preferments with which the king had been accustomed to reward clerical judges were not as attractive as they had been; and in any case, they were not always given. There seem to have been other ways for a judge to make money, for salaries were very small. A chief justice received between £40 and £60 a year, and other judges had to be content with 40 marks. Their salaries were also frequently in arrears, and it seems to have been the practice, both then and for some time afterwards, for persons of consequence and great corporations, to make grants of pensions, rents or lands to the judges. Judicial salaries were improved during the reigns of Edward III and Henry IV, but even then they were only paid irregularly. This, however, is by no means the whole story. A considerable part of their income was derived from fees. It was only in 1826 that this source of judicial income was abolished, and that judicial salaries were more than doubled (to £5,500) to compensate for the loss.

The secularisation of the bench followed a good way behind the secularisation of the profession of pleader. At the beginning of the thirteenth century there were professional lawyers practising both in the king's courts and the church courts,[1] and it would seem that a number of these were in religious orders. However by the fifth Lateran council the clergy were forbidden to practise in secular courts, except in their own causes or on behalf of the poor. Already in the reign of Henry III, therefore, the secular pleaders in the royal courts were organising themselves into a fraternity, and in 1292 Edward I commanded the judges to provide a certain number of attorneys and apprentices to follow the court, adding that they would have the exclusive right of practising before it. About the same time there are indications that the training of apprentices to the law was in the hands of the senior members of the profession, and that it included as one element, attendance in court in *The Crib*, a place set aside for students where they were under the eyes of the judges. By the fifteenth century the legal profession had been organised into something like its modern form, and the principle had been adopted that the judges were selected by the king exclusively from the ranks of the serjeants-at-law. Well before this rule had become firmly established, clerical judges had disappeared from the bench.

From this change there emerged one of the most characteristic features of English law. Whilst the two universities ignored the constantly expanding body of law growing up in the royal courts, and continued to teach Roman and canon law, which long remained the principal avenue to royal service, the Inns of Court became in Coke's expressive phrase, 'the most famous University for the profession of law only, or of any one human science in the world', where students acquired, often painfully, a lengthy practical education in the Common Law, and from their strong corporate life, a common and distinctive outlook upon society, as a result of which they eventually became, as counsel, not learned only, but learned in the law.

When the Inns of Court were founded is not known with certainty, but it occurred in the age when many of the oldest colleges of Oxford and Cambridge came into existence, and the corporate life which flourished there had much in common with that of the universities. There were also clear resemblances to the guilds of craftsmen which protected the interests of their members, preserved the monopoly of their craft, and established and preserved professional standards of conduct. There is a reference in Chaucer to the Temple as a corporate body, in which young men were instructed in the law, and it would seem that the Inns of Court, with their subsidiary Inns of Chancery, were already in existence and were exercising their corporate function in respect of a numerous body of practitioners and students in the reign of Edward III, and that their government was already in the hands of judges and serjeants. Once the clerical element on the bench and in the practice of the law had gone, the way was open for the profession to develop a vigorous and self-sufficient life of its own. By the fifteenth century, references to Inns, and the part which they played in legal education are very frequent. Fortescue, for example, has a good deal to say about the Inns of Court, and he equated the serjeants with the doctors of the universities. Plucknett[2] suggests that this similarity may have been conscious.

Before the end of Edward I's reign the supply and education of entrants to the legal profession was already a matter of interest and importance to the royal administration. In 1272, a royal writ to Chief Justice Metingham and his judicial colleagues of the common bench directed that there should be chosen from every county some of the worthier and more promising students to follow the court and to take part in its business; 'and no others'. In this way, not only was there provision for the lawyer to learn his business, but there was also manifested a desire to exclude from the proceedings of the king's courts all those who were not properly trained.

Exclusion from the practice of the law in the king's courts of those who were untrained was a gradual process but when it was achieved, the monopoly of the Bar was rigorously enforced. The Inns of Court had an absolute control over admissions to membership. Only when the novice had satisfied the requirements of his Inn was he eligible for call to the Bar. The sovereign selected the serjeants from the ranks of eminent practitioners in the courts on the advice of the judges, and as the Middle Ages progressed, the serjeant left his Inn of Court, and joined his own separate guild, the Serjeants Inn, which included not only the serjeants, but the judges. By the same period too, it had been established that the only persons eligible for selection as a judge of the king's courts were serjeants.

The consequences of this were of the very first importance for the development of English law. Establishment of the principle that only serjeants were eligible for judgeships was responsible for that close and intimate partnership between bench and bar, which has for so long been an outstanding characteristic of English legal life. It has been a source of strength to both, and a guarantee of the independence of the legal profession from external—and especially from official—control. For this state of affairs to exist, it was necessary for the line of 'clerical' judges to come to an end, even though some of the greatest names in the early history of the Common Law are those of clerical judges. To regard these 'clerical' judges as outposts of Rome, or as adherents of the canon law, would be misleading. Many of them were clerics only in order that they might receive the ecclesiastical preferments which were the normal rewards for service in the royal administration. This was, in reality, the root of the matter. Clerical judges might be, and often were, eminent and learned, and they made great contributions to the earliest phase of the development of the Common Law, but they owed their office to royal selection, and they remained part of the royal administration. Had they continued to dominate the judiciary, or had they even remained an important element in it, the judiciary would have developed in England as it did on the continent, as a branch of the royal administration. It would have been an occupation in which both place and promotion depended upon royal favour—as indeed the Stuarts later came to look on it. It could not have possessed that independence of outlook which the English judiciary preserved so tenaciously, and which was derived from its close links with an independent legal profession.

Independence of outlook in turn depended upon impartiality and detachment from major political conflicts. Even in the troubled reign of Edward II, when the bench was still shared on equal terms between clerics and lay lawyers, and when its status as a branch of the royal administration was as yet unchanged, it is remarkable that the great and bitter conflict between king and barons should have had very little impact upon the judiciary. Ironically it was only one of the earliest, and greatest, lay judges, William de Bereford, who was deeply involved. As a friend and admirer of the king's favourite, Piers Gaveston, he incurred the wrath of the baronial opposition, who demanded that he should be banished. By the exercise of great dexterity, he was able to insinuate himself into their confidence without, apparently, losing that of the king. The result was that he retained his office of Chief Justice of the Common Pleas until the last years of the reign. Two factors affecting this are of interest. The first was his close association with Harvey de Stanton, a cleric who occupied the three chief judgeships in succession, who had reached the bench by way of the royal administration, and who remained closely associated with some of the principal members of the royal administration. The second is that Bereford's commanding position among the Common Law judges was quite unaffected by his unfortunate political associations in the early years of this troubled reign. In this respect, his career shows some resemblance to that of another great Common Law judge of the period, Ralph de Hengham, who was implicated in the allegations of corruption, investigated by Edward I's Chancellor, Burnell, in 1289. Unlike his fellow Chief Justice of the Common Pleas, who fled abroad, Hengham (who was Chief Justice of the King's Bench) remained to face the charges, paid a very large fine and shortly afterwards was restored to office as Chief Justice of the Common Pleas.

The close continuing association of the judges with the royal administration throughout the fourteenth century necessarily involved them from time to time in political crises, and because of their regular acceptance of presents and fees from private litigants, there was at such times a serious danger of charges of corruption being lodged against them, although nothing like Chancellor Burnell's great investigation of 1289 was ever initiated again. Nevertheless, allegations of corruption are recurrent, and in 1350, William Thorpe, Chief Justice of the King's Bench, was convicted of bribery. At a later date the judges were very deeply involved in the constitutional upheavals of Richard II's reign. In his struggle with the baronial opposition, which had established a commission of reform to regulate public business and the royal household, Richard induced some judges in 1387 to condemn violations of the royal prerogative. This body of judges was headed by the Chief Justice of the King's Bench, Tresillian. When a new Parliament assembled in 1388, the baronial party was strongly in the ascendent, and it was now their turn to draw up and present charges against the king and his supporters. Amongst these was Chief Justice Tresillian, who was found guilty of treason and, being captured during the course of the trial, was hanged. The other judges who had concurred in his opinion on the illegality of the commission were also found guilty, but on the intercession of the queen and the bishops, the death sentence was commuted to one of perpetual exile in Ireland.

Tresillian has the distinction of being the only English chief justice who was hanged for offences alleged to have been committed by him in his judicial capacity. The lesson was a harsh one, and English judges took note of it! The deposition of Richard II, and the accession of Henry IV, led to a dynastic conflict between the Houses of Lancaster and York which lasted until the accession of Henry VII in 1485. During that prolonged struggle, the judges as a body remained detached, with the result that they remained in office no matter which faction was temporarily supreme, even though the political sympathies of some of them are known. Gradually there evolved the doctrine of judicial neutrality, and with it, the principle of judicial independence. It is from this period that we have the first clear intimations that, in the view of the judges, justice must be administered without concern for political implications. This, in turn, required that the judges themselves should not become entangled in matters of high policy. This they stated in so many words when they were invited by the House of Lords in 1460 to pronounce judicially upon the validity of the Duke of York's claim to the throne, and they similarly declined in *Thorpe's Case* in 1454 to give an opinion upon the extent of Parliamentary privilege. This, they said, was a question which the legislature alone could determine.

It was this studied detachment which made it possible for some of the outstanding judges of the century to manifest a very high degree of independence from the king. The legend of Sir William Gascoigne and the wild Prince Hal may not be capable of direct proof, but there are other evidences of the independence of the chief justice. Two judges who held office during the Wars of the Roses, Chief Justice Markham and Sir John Fortescue, were renowned, both in their own time and subsequently for declining to bend the law to suit royal policy. Fortescue indeed wrote a treatise for the education of the unfortunate Prince Edward, the heir of Henry VI, who was killed at Tewkesbury in 1471. It not only contains Fortescue's celebrated description of England as a limited or constitutional monarchy, but also a strong assertion that the Common Law is supreme in England, so that even the sovereign must observe it.

The change in the outlook of the judiciary upon their function, and their progressive refusal to be involved in the determination of questions of high policy which was the consequence of their disassociation from the royal administration, was in turn linked with other changes in outlook. So long as judges were drawn from the various orders of clerks, they were always aware of the rules of two other systems of law—the civil law and the canon law; and some of them had enjoyed a legal education, if not at Oxford or Cambridge, then at a continental (usually an Italian) law school. Bracton's treatise is a classic illustration of this dualism in outlook. It also reflects Bracton's desire to present the Common Law as a complete and developed system, so that when native materials are lacking or unsatisfactory, he does not hesitate to interpolate rules drawn from the civil law. The outlook of the professional lawyers who replaced the clerics was narrower. For them the Common Law is a self-sufficient system, and its rules have in the past proved capable of adaptation to meet the needs of a vigorous and rapidly changing society. As a result the rules became steadily more complex, and they were developed by means of a specialised legal logic. It is seen possibly at its most developed stage in Littleton's *Tenures,* which Sir Edward Coke, who wrote an elaborate commentary upon it, describes as the most perfect and absolute work in any human science. Significantly it is the first great book upon the Common Law not written in Latin, and showing no trace of Roman law. Its learning is the learning of the Year Books, which in Littleton's day had been systematised into a tough and self-sufficient legal discipline, and like them, the *New Tenures* is written in Norman–French. Holdsworth's estimate of it shows how completely the Common Law, in the hands of the professional judges, had turned in upon itself by the second half of the fifteenth century. He says:[3]

> It summed up the results of the professional development of what was then the most important branch of the common law. It shows that the common law was not merely a collection of rules of pleading and practice which could be compendiously strung together in the short tracts which for the last century and a half had been the only law books which the legal profession had produced. It shows that it possessed principles and doctrines of its own which were scientifically exact and yet eminently practical, because they were founded upon the actual problem of daily life. The book was founded upon the Year Books, but it was no mere summary of decisions. The author

tries to get beyond the decisions to the 'arguments and reasons of the law', and thus to construct from the already vast number of decisions upon the various parts of his subject a coherent body of legal doctrines by which a man more sooner shall come to the certainty and knowledge of the law. It is the pioneer of a long series of text books upon various branches of the common law in its completed form. It has been, and it is, a model both in its methods and in its style to succeeding writers.

To this discerning analysis of Holdsworth two points may be added. Littleton's *Tenures* was written on the eve of the application of printing to the sphere of knowledge. It was one of the first books to be printed, and it was quickly followed by the Year Books, and by other legal works. Already, before Coke wrote his commentary upon it, Littleton's *Tenures* had passed through more than seventy editions, and had inspired the labours of an earlier commentator. These things emphasise the hold which the study of the Common Law had gained upon English society in the sixteenth century. They also made clear how complete and self-confident the discipline of the Common Law had now become. The study of it opened out an entirely new world to the inquiring mind, and its popularity serves to explain why the Inns of Court were in that century thronged with young men of position, many of whom had at no time entertained thoughts of a legal career.

The second point is that this great body of learning owed nothing at all to the two universities. It was the achievement of practitioners whose professional life was spent in and about the courts and the Inns of Court. In this respect it gained something, and it also lost something. One may conjecture how the Common Law could have developed had it engaged the attention of scholars at Oxford and Cambridge, as Justinian's *Digest* had captured the intellectual powers of the Italian law schools some centuries before. One result of this might have been that the influence of the jurist might have been greater, and that of the judge less. But this did not happen, and the Common Law gained in toughness and precision in consequence; and because it remained a thing apart from the learning of the universities, it preserved a rugged character and an independence of outlook which provided intellectual support to the claim of the judges to independence and security in the discharge of their office. This proved to be of the first importance, not only for the judges themselves, but for the future of the Common Law, when the testing time came under the Stuarts. Although all four kings who ruled from 1603 to 1689 exercised their prerogative right to dismiss judges at will, the tradition of judicial independence was strong enough to survive this period of stress, and to enable the lawyers to insist upon security of judicial tenure in the Revolution of 1688.

Another change of permanent significance in the function of the judge, which occurred in the later Middle Ages, was the separation of the judge from the legislature. When Parliament was taking shape in the reigns of the first three Edwards, the judges, as royal counsellors, were summoned as a matter of course and they were expected to attend. Harvey de Stanton, for example, was rebuked by the king for leaving a Parliament at Lincoln without royal permission. Although one or two of the judges can be detected taking part in the political conflicts of the reigns of the first two Edwards, this was not a general attitude, and as was pointed out earlier, their detachment was responsible for the fact that they remained in office, no matter which party was dominant. The principal parliamentary function of the judges was always to give advice upon the form and effect of legislation as they had done at an earlier period in council, before Parliament emerged, and the Year Books have many illustrations of the familiarity of the judges with the purpose and effect of statutory changes. It has already been mentioned that Chief Justice Hengham in a case in 1305[4] said to counsel: 'Do not gloss the statute, we know it better than you, for we made it', and Justice Brabazon in another case about the same time said that he would take counsel with his fellow judges on the meaning of 34 Edward I St I, as they were present when it had been made.[5] Even as late as the reign of Edward III, the Chancellor, the treasurer, and some of the judges protested against 15 Edw III St I, because they were not present when it was made.[6] By this date, however, such interventions had become exceptional, even though the judges still continued to be summoned to Parliament, and they occasionally attended. It was in consequence of the survival of this summons to Parliament that the right of the House of Lords to call on the judges for advice when the House was sitting as a court of final appeal was preserved. It was still exercised from time to time in the nineteenth century. The last occasion was the trial of Earl Russell for bigamy in 1901[7] 'and right uncomfortable they looked' as an eyewitness noted. A more significant example is possibly the summons of the judges to advise the House of Lords in the great trade union appeal, *Allen v Flood.*[8]

The rapid growth in the power of Parliament and the dissociation of the judges from the process of law making brought about important changes in the attitude of the judges to the development of the law. During the formative period they had actively assisted in making laws in council, and because of this close association, they had not hesitated to advise parties to litigation on remedies which were open to them. During the Eyre of London, Stanton suspended some proceedings before him so that they could be remitted to the council for fuller consideration, and on at least one occasion whilst sitting as a judge on the Common Pleas he was prepared to put aside the operation of a statute on a direct command from the king, regarding this as a normal incident of judicial administration. By the latter part of the reign of Edward III, all this is changed. The discretionary powers of the crown, with the exception of the dispensing power, were gone. All changes in the law must be brought about by legislation. The judge's function had been narrowed. Whilst he could, and did, develop the Common Law, it was no longer in his power to disregard the provisions of a statute, nor could he introduce a major development of a novel kind.

It was at one time thought that this change, both in outlook and function, was a direct product of the Statute of Westminster II in 1285. During the constitutional upheavals of the reign of Henry III the barons, in the Provisions of Oxford in 1258, had deprived the clerks of Chancery of the power of fashioning any new units, declaring this to be a matter for the council, in which, in their view, the voice of the barons should be predominant. This prohibition, it was suggested, was relaxed by clause 24 of the Statute of Westminster II 1285, which restored to the Chancery Clerks the power to fashion writs *in consimilu casu*, that is to say, in cases similar to those to which an existing writ applied; and it was suggested that by this means the clerks, with the co-operation of the judges, were able to bring about the very considerable extensions of the Common Law which took place in the period between 1285 and the end of the sixteenth century.

Since the energetic attack made upon this traditional attitude by the late Professor Plucknett, it is difficult to maintain this view, more especially if the words of clause 24 are considered. It provides that

> whensoever from henceforth it shall happen in the Chancery that there is to be found a writ in one case, but not in another case although involving the same remedy, the clerks of the Chancery shall agree in framing a writ, or else they shall adjourn the plaintiffs to the next Parliament, or else they shall write down the points upon which they cannot agree and refer them to the next Parliament, and so a writ shall be framed by the consent of the learned in the law, to the end that the court from thenceforth shall no longer fail those who seek justice.

Plucknett[9] points out that this clause provided a regular procedure for the steady expansion of the law by the enlargement of the writs in narrowly defined circumstances. He adds that very little use was actually made of this section, and that it was the general feeling that the writs should be increased by Parliament, possibly acting through a small group of administrators and lawyers. The core of his argument is that the expansion of the Common Law was proceeding by well-understood judicial processes, and that it remained substantially unaffected by the statute of 1285.

Judges and serjeants, in fact, had already evolved their own technique for the development of Common Law principles, and that technique is abundantly illustrated from the Year Books. In Plucknett's view it was being used before 1285 and it continued independently of the statute. Gradually, they were developing a complete system, drawing strength, coherence and an underlying philosophy, from the material which continued to accumulate in the Year Books, and in due course, it produced its own literature—first Bracton, Fleta, Britton and others, and later Littleton and Fortescue—all of it uninfluenced to any noticeable degree by the learning of the two universities, and (so far as Fortescue and Littleton are concerned) by Roman law. Indeed, as the Middle Ages drew to a close, the gap which had opened between the universities and the Inns of Court broadened, and this is nowhere more apparent than in the ponderous works of Sir Edward Coke, in whom Common Law learning reached its summit. Although he is capable of misinterpreting the learning of the medieval Common Law, it is quite apparent that he had found it to be a wholly satisfying discipline, developed not by the methods of the academic philosophers, but by the gritty logic of practising lawyers, whose active life was spent in argument before judges similarly trained. Even the language which they used differed from that employed at the universities, where Latin was to remain the medium of communication for some time to come. In the age of Bracton and Fleta—the age when clerical judges were still dominant—it had been accepted practice to write treatises upon the Common Law in Latin. Littleton's great treatise was characteristically written in professional law French, and by the time Coke wrote his *Institutes*, it had become customary to write legal works in English. At no time in their history did the Inns of Court seek to ape the two universities. The Common Law, with its tough fibre, its doctrinal complexities (especially in the land law), in its procedural affectations, and in its reverence for authority, was the product of legal experience in the courts. It owed very little to abstract speculation, and little to borrowing from Roman law.

At every point, it drew strength from its own inner resources. Today, it is no longer possible to believe that the Common Law courts imported the jury from Normandy, and that its remote origin is to be discovered in the administrative system created by the successors of Charlemagne. Maitland, Plucknett and others have given an authority to the researches of Brunner, and later of Hoskins which more recent research by Stenton, Lady Stenton, Richardson and Sayles has discounted. At the present moment the scales have tipped strongly in favour of a Saxon, and ultimately of a Scandinavian, origin for this most characteristic institution of the Common Law, but whichever view is the right one, it is not open to question that in the hands of the common lawyers the jury became an institution of cardinal importance. Introduced in criminal cases as an alternative to the ordeals and compurgation, when in 1215 the pope forbade any further participation by the clergy in these outmoded rituals, and at first viewed with suspicion by persons accused of crime, it came to be regarded as the chief protection of the innocent. In criminal trials with a political element, the jury was regarded as the subject's principal bulwark against arbitrary imprisonment and death at the hands of the executioner.

In civil cases, the part played by the jury in shaping the Common Law was even more fundamental. At first, the jurors who decided issues of fact in proceedings instituted by the Grand and Possessory Assizes were neighbours of equal degree to the parties, who decided the issue according to their own knowledge. By the close of the Middle Ages a clear distinction had been drawn between witnesses, through whose testimony matters of fact were established before a court which comprised judge and jury, and the jury themselves, to whom the decision upon matters of fact was committed. The inclusion of the jury in the machinery of the Common Law courts was, however, responsible for the rigid (and at times artificial) distinction between matters of fact, and questions of law which has accompanied the progressive development of the Common Law, and which had no counterpart in the development of the equitable jurisdiction of the chancellors. Because issues of fact were placed before juries, it became a settled rule that pleadings must be exchanged until the dispute between the parties had been narrowed to a single issue of fact, which could be placed before the jury for decision. Unencumbered by the presence of a jury, the Chancery judges were able to extend their inquiry to the conduct of the parties over long periods, and to give a decision upon the merits of their case in the light of that conduct.

But in the reign of Edward II, when clerical judges still shared the bench upon terms of equality with professional lawyers, pleadings had already become a matter of major importance in the prosecution of a suit. The development of the Common Law was confined strictly within the framework of the writ system. It was not sufficient to have suffered a wrong. The wrong must be capable of being pursued within the terms of a writ—either an original writ, or an action 'on the special case'. Each writ had its procedure, and in consequence, its own form of pleading, and it was because of the importance and progressive technicality of pleading that the Year Books concentrate to such an extent upon it, and that books containing precedents of writs and pleading appear at a comparatively early date. Holdsworth points out[10] that the object of the pleadings was to arrive at an issue of fact or law. In the Middle Ages, the pleadings were oral allegations made in court. It was only later that pleadings were exchanged before the parties came to court, and were entered upon the court roll. At an earlier date, the proceedings were livelier. The debate upon the pleadings were far ranging, and in it (in Holdsworth's words):

> the line between argument and decision will tend to become obliterated—serjeants or apprentices present, but not engaged in the case, will intervene with their advice, and what they say is naturally interesting to the profession. A judge will give information as to the proper course of procedure, or will even condescend to give a little lecture for the benefit of the student. Naturally, reports which record such proceedings will be discursive and conversational. In some of our older Reports the reasons given by the judges for their former decisions are styled arguments. The Year Books are really the reports of arguments—arguments used by the Bar and the Bench. It was the argument rather than the final decision which interested the profession, partly because there was then no such rigid theory as to the binding forces of decided cases as that to which

we are accustomed, partly because the discussion and the elucidation of legal principles were to be found in the argument rather than in the dry formal decision, and partly because decisions upon points of law were often not given, or, if given, were difficult for the preview reports to collect.

No other legal system has comparable records extending over so long a period, and presenting such a lively picture of law in action. Step by step, and reign by reign, it is possible to trace how the Common Law was built up, by daily discussions, in court, between the serjeants and the judges, free from the domination of the learning of the universities. In the history of English law, the separation, leading for long periods to actual antagonism, between the practitioners and the professors, has existed for centuries and even today is over-long in disappearing. It has led to the deeply entrenched exclusion of the professors from the bench —an exclusion which is peculiar to the English legal system, and is difficult to defend, now that the age of procedural dexterity is long past. The search today is no longer exclusively for underlying legal principles, but for solutions to problems which accord with the changing outlook of society in rapid transition.

The exclusion, however, had its origins in the conviction of the common lawyers that only a life-time spent in the application of the law in the courts qualified the practitioners for judicial office. In that sense, the law was a 'mystery' in the medieval meaning of the term. Its subtleties and overfine distinctions made little appeal to those trained in the universities. Thus Maitland has reminded us[11] that the great Francis Hotman, whom Elizabeth I invited to Oxford, wrote disparagingly of Littleton, thereby earning a characteristically blunt rebuke from Coke, whose extravagant praise will not be universally echoed today. Still, Littleton's great achievement was that he was able to demonstrate that the law of real property was a good deal more than a collection of rules of pleading and practice. From his exhaustive knowledge of the Year Books, he was able to construct a coherent and logical body of rules, upon which all later writers have built. In his first book he discussed the various estates in land which existed in the

Common Law. In his second, he discussed the incidents of tenure, and in the third, he explained the law of co-ownership and a number of special topics. In doing so, he formalised doctrines which had long ceased to represent social realities, and gave them permanence, at any rate until the reforms of the nineteenth and twentieth centuries. Some of these doctrines were much older than Littleton of course. For example, the theory that all freehold land was held ultimately by grant from the king because of the completeness of the Norman Conquest first appears in the reign of Henry I, and was a legal fiction invented to explain the basis of feudal dues which the crown exacted. Again the principle that in the creation of Common Law estates, the seizin must never be in abeyance, had relevance in an age when knight-service was still a means of national defence. It had become a metaphysical concept long before Littleton's day. Nevertheless, it remained to plague the law of real property until the Property Legislation of 1925. It was in the land law that the art of the medieval pleader reached the greatest subtlety, and after the appearance of Littleton's treatise all of that subtlety was transferred to the substantive law which Littleton had systemised. Its construction on a national basis had been made possible by the fact that the reforms of Henry II had been responsible for the progressive transfer of all actions relating to freehold land to the royal courts, and more particularly to the Court of Common Bench, in which alone the real actions (ie the actions leading to the recovery of the land itself) could be initiated.

All three Common Law courts took a share in the development of the law of contract and tort through the personal actions (ie actions for which the remedy was, not the restoration of a chattel, but the award of a sum of money by way of compensation or damages). This is a story which has often been told, and never more concisely than in Maitland's *Forms of Action.* It is probably in the development of the personal actions founded upon the original writs that one can perceive most clearly the strength and the weaknesses of the practical approach to legal development.

Plucknett[12] notices the remarkable fact that the Common Law of contract was created with so little outside influence. The

Church had developed a comprehensive theory of the binding force of obligations deliberately undertaken, and for some time the church courts were a serious rival to the Common Law courts in this branch of the law. So also were the mercantile courts, although the Common Law succeeded in confining their jurisdiction to merchants, whether English or foreign, and their transactions. So the Common Law of contract developed in remarkable isolation, and it was left to a later age to harmonise, so far as was possible, the Common Law, canon law and mercantile law rules governing contract.

At first sight conditions might have appeared favourable to an importation of Roman law concepts into this branch of the law. Bracton, who may have studied in Italy, and who was certainly familiar with the works of a number of Romanists and especially of Azo, appears at first sight to have borrowed substantially not only Roman terms, but Roman concepts of contract, but the predominant view today is that Bracton's treatment of contract, though Romanesque in form, is English in substance, and that some of it, at any rate, was based upon recent decisions of the Common Law courts.

What is perhaps of greater significance is the date from which substantial development can be traced. In the fourteenth century the Common Law courts had not advanced far beyond the position stated by Bracton, and a very great number of mercantile contracts were still being dealt with in local and manorial courts. When in the latter part of the century and during the fifteenth century the development of contract through the action of *assumpsit* was seriously undertaken, serjeants and judges were able to handle their materials with confidence, and without any consideration of what the church courts may have been doing, then or at an earlier period. The church courts attached great importance to good faith. They had developed the conception of *causa* as a basis for the legal enforceability of an agreement, and they had introduced a remedy which bears some resemblance to specific performance. The common lawyers were completely indifferent to these and allied conceptions. With caution and by the employment of their own special legal logic, they extended the remedy of *assumpsit* to wider and wider classes of obligation, and when at the end of the fifteenth century they were faced with the possibility that *assumpsit* might be applicable to all agreements deliberately undertaken, whether formal or informal, they invented the requirement of consideration, which was to be developed piecemeal, following the historic decision of the Court of Exchequer Chamber in *Slade's Case*[13] that

> every contract executory imports in itself an *assumpsit* for when one agrees to pay money or to deliver anything thereby he assumes or promises to pay or deliver it, and therefore when he sells any goods to another and agrees to deliver them at a day to some, and the other in consideration thereof agrees to pay so much money at such a day, both parties may have an action of debt or an action of the case on *assumpsit*, for the mutual executory agreement of both parties imports in itself actions upon the case as well as actions of debt.

To have proceeded so far by the beginning of the seventeenth century was a considerable achievement, more especially when it is remembered that the Common Law courts had developed the law of contract, as the spider spins its web, from materials contained inside itself.

Even more striking developments were achieved in the following two centuries, more particularly by the development of that variety of *assumpsit* which is known as *indebitatus assumpsit*. Its history has been traced by several distinguished legal historians and is well summarised by Lord Atkin in his speech in *United Australia Limited v Barclays Bank Limited*:[14]

> The story starts with the action of debt which was not necessarily based upon the existence of a contract for it covered claims to recover sums due for customary dues, penalties for breaches of bye-laws and the like. The action of debt had its drawbacks, the chief being that the defendant could wage his law.[15] There followed the application . . . of assumpsit to debt. 'The defendant being indebted then promised.' At first there

must be an express promise; then the courts implied a promise from an executory contract (*Slade's Case*). *Slade's Case* was not a claim in *indebitatus assumpsit*, but the principle was applied, and it became unnecessary to prove an express promise in these cases. Then the action was allowed in respect of cases where there was no contract executory or otherwise as in the cases where debt would have lain for customary fees and the like, and by a final and somewhat forced application to cases where the defendant had received money of the plaintiff to which he was not entitled. These included cases where the plaintiff had intentionally paid money to the defendant, for example, claims for money paid on a consideration that had wholly failed and money paid under a mistake; cases where the plaintiff had been deceived into paying money, cases where the money had been extorted from the plaintiff by threats or duress of goods. They also included cases where money had not been paid by the plaintiff at all but had been received from third persons, as when the defendant had received fees under colour of holding an office which in fact was held by the plaintiff, and finally cases like the present where the defendant had been wrongfully in possession of the plaintiff's goods, had sold them and was in possession of the proceeds. To find a basis for the actions in any actual contract, whether express or to be implied from the conduct of the parties, was in many of the instances given obviously impossible. The cheat or the blackmailer does not promise to repay the person he has wronged the money which he has unlawfully taken, nor does the thief promise to repay the owner of the goods stolen the money which he has gained from selling the goods. Nevertheless if a man so wronged was to recover the money in the hands of the wrong-doer, and it was obviously just that he should be able to do so, it was necessary to create a fictitious contract; for there was no action possible other than debt or *assumpsit* on the one side and action for damages for tort on the other. The action of *indebitatus assumpsit* for money had and received to the use of the plaintiff in the cases I have enumerated was therefore supported by the imputation by the court to the defendant of

> a promise to repay. The fiction was so obvious that in some cases the judge created a fanciful relation between the plaintiff and the defendant. Thus in cases where the defendant had wrongly sold the plaintiff's goods and received the proceeds it was suggested in some cases, not in all, that the plaintiff chose to treat the wrongdoer as having sold the goods as his agent and so being under an implied contract to his principal to repay ...
>
> But the fiction is too transparent. The alleged contract by the blackmailer and the robber never was made and never could be made. The law[16] in order to do justice, imputed to the wrongdoer a promise which alone, as forms of action then existed, could give the injured person a reasonable remedy ...
>
> These fantastic resemblances of contracts invented in order to meet requirements of the law, as to forms of action which have now disappeared, should not in these days be allowed to affect actual rights. When these ghosts of the past stand in the path of justice, clanking their medieval chains, the proper course for the judge is to pass through them undeterred.

Exactly the same kind of development had taken place in the law of tort, although here, adherence to the forms of action had produced, not a comprehensive general theory but a number of particular torts which only in the present century are being united by the development of general principles. As Plucknett has pointed out, the king's courts were not anxious to entertain personal actions, and even in the sixteenth and seventeenth centuries legislation unsuccessfully attempted to keep actions not involving title to land in the local courts.[17] It was only with the development of the action on the case for negligence which took place from 1800 onwards that the way was open for the massive extension of tortious liability, which is still rapidly proceeding. Plucknett has written:

> The field of tort was by no means extensive until the last century, and consequently its development had not reached a really advanced stage. Much of it was also annexed to neigh-

> bouring provinces within the approach of modern times. *Trespass de clauso fracto* and *de ejectione* became part of the law of property, and deceit, with its derivation *assumpsit*, became one of the roots of the law of contract. The great prominence and growth of the law of tort in the last few generations is clearly associated with the sudden mechanisation of contemporary life, and with the growth of large and wealthy businesses (necessarily carried on through fallible servants and agents) engaged in finance, insurance, transport and an endless variety of enterprises which are productive of torts and tort litigation. There can be no doubt that the universal practice of insurance has provided the superior courts with thousands of cases which would probably have escaped the reports if the parties had no other resources than their own in contesting them.[18]

Although Plucknett does not mention it specifically, the motor-car has contributed more to the law of torts than any other single agency, and its modern development has also been greatly influenced by the growth of a feeling of social responsibility, and also by the transformation from a predominantly rural to an increasingly urban society.

6

The Making of Modern Equity

In the course of his judgement in the Court of Appeal in *Re Hallett's Estate*,[1] Sir George Jessel, MR, said:

> The rules of the Courts of Equity are not like the rules of common law, supposed to have been established since time immemorial. It is perfectly well known that they have been established from time to time—altered, improved, and refined from time to time. In many cases we know the names of the Chancellors who invented them. No doubt they were invented for the purpose of securing the better administration of justice, but still they were invented. Take such things as these: the separate use of a married woman, the restraint on alienation, the modern rule against perpetuities or the equitable rules of waste. We can name the Chancellors who first invented them and state the date when they were introduced into equity jurisprudence and therefore, in cases of this kind, the older precedents in equity are of very little value. The doctrines are progressive, refined and improved, and if we want to know what the rules of equity are, we must look of course rather to the more modern than the more ancient cases.

These observations emphasise at once the fact that equity is judgemade law and that it is of modern origin. From the examples which Jessel gives, it is a fair inference that he is thinking of the re-creation of equity from the time of Lord Nottingham onwards, and it is in that context that it merits discussion here. There was, indeed, an earlier equity, created by Chancellors who were mainly clerics. It is about this equity that the author of *Doctor and Student* writes in the reign of Henry VIII that it is founded on reason and conscience, and is a corrective of the Common Law in the hard case. In St Germain's phrase it tempers and mitigates the rigour of the Common Law. This was the philosophical basis of the jurisdiction of the Chancellors, as seen both by Wolsey and by his successor, Sir Thomas More. However whereas in the hands of Wolsey, equity seemed to threaten the basis of the Common Law itself, More invited the Common Law judges to introduce equitable considerations into their own administration of the law, and when they refused, he pointed out that they could have no case against the Chancellor for continuing to give equitable relief.

Whilst the Chancellors of this period have very notable achievements to their credit, it is in the following period, which begins with Lord Nottingham, that their function as law makers can be most clearly perceived. Appointed lord keeper in 1673, and created Lord Finch shortly afterwards, he was raised to the Chancellorship in 1675 and continued until 1682, having been created Earl of Nottingham the year before. From every point of view, his tenure of office was a notable one. With the fall of Cardinal Wolsey, the long line of great ecclesiastical Chancellors who were also statesmen came to an end. From this date, until the appointment of Nottingham, the Chancery's fortunes varied. Some Chancellors during this period were statesmen, others were courtiers, and there were one or two clerics, the last being Bishop Williams, Bacon's successor. Finally there were lawyers, such as Ellesmere, Nicholas Bacon and Francis Bacon. Even after the Restoration in 1660, the first Chancellor, Lord Clarendon, was a politician, not a lawyer. He was followed in 1667 by Sir Orlando Bridgeman (1667-1672), an eminent conveyancer, to whom the invention of the modern strict settlement is attributed. He again was briefly followed by another politician, Lord Shaftesbury, but when Shaftesbury was succeeded by Nottingham, the modern line of legal Chancellors begins; and from this date the development of equity as a distinct branch of English law is continuous.

Something must first be said in general terms of the Chancellors themselves, and of the nature of the system of equity which they developed. Although the Lord Chancellor is the head of the judiciary and until the Judicature Act of 1873 was the head of the Court of Chancery, the court in which equity was applied and developed, he was, and remained, an active politician. He was a member of the government, and a member of the cabinet, thus participating in the formulation of policy. Unlike the Lord Chief Justice, whose office is of indefinite duration, and who is not associated with any party, the Lord Chancellor takes office and leaves it with his party colleagues. From a theoretical point of view, the association of our highest judicial office with active party politics is quite indefensible, but it has also implied that some Chancellors, and particularly the ablest, have looked at equity with a statesman's eye, and have been fully conscious that in the development of equity, they had been law making in accordance with well-settled principles. This is particularly evident in the work of Nottingham, Hardwicke, Thurlow and Eldon. But whatever the political outlook of an individual Chancellor, he accepted the consequences of the Revolution of 1688, and the existence within the individual of certain natural rights which it was the business of the state to protect, as explained by Locke and other political philosophers. For Locke and those who thought like him, human beings were endowed with certain natural rights which formed the moral foundation for the rules of positive law. Although Locke does not pursue this line of thinking, it would be consistent with it to suggest that for the determination of these rights and for their translation into rules of positive law, the judiciary was a more sensitive instrument than the legislature.

In the eighteenth century, reason and the natural rights which flowed from its exercise, was dominant, and the concept of natural law was used as a theoretical basis for the changes which statesmen and judges wished to introduce. But since it was not open to question that the Revolution of 1688 had given birth to the most perfect and balanced of political systems, it followed that no fundamental changes of political structure were desirable. In this conclusion English political thinkers received striking support from Montesquieu whose conclusions, apparently based upon a reading of history, are echoed by Blackstone in his *Commentaries*, as well as by other later writers.

In the sphere of legal, as distinct from constitutional, change, the conception of natural rights proved a potent instrument for reform, and since in the eighteenth century, equity was a more flexible body of principles than the Common Law, it is not surprising that the most striking advances are to be found in equity, fashioned by the Chancellors, rather than in the Common Law courts, although it may be remembered that Lord Chief Justice Mansfield attempted similar changes in the Common Law. There was another reason why at this period equity served as a vehicle for law reform. The Court of Chancery was traditionally a court of conscience, applying principles which were regarded as having an ultimate origin in the law of nature—a fact to which Chancellors such as Lord Hardwicke frequently alluded. In giving wider scope to equitable principles, they were also applying principles of public utility or social policy, founded upon the protection of natural rights.

Since Chancellors have been chosen from the ranks of active and eminent political lawyers, it has occurred that relatively few of them had been Chancery practitioners at the time of their appointment. Before the Judicature Acts therefore, they not infrequently found it necessary to learn their equity on the bench afterwards. But this apparent anomaly has nevertheless had beneficial effects. The familiarity with judicial precedent shown by Chancellors with a Common Law background did something to strengthen the tendency which already existed in the Court of Chancery after Lord Nottingham's time to pay increasing attention to judicial precedents, which in turn stimulated the publication of equity law reports.

One other circumstance assisted this development. Until the nineteenth century the Court of Chancery was always understaffed. The Lord Chancellor himself was only a part-time judge, and the only other one was the Master of the Rolls. From 1660 onwards, therefore, there was an almost uninterrupted succession of leading Common Law judges, who sat in Chancery. Sometimes in cases of first importance, the Chancellor sat with at least three

Common Law colleagues, who naturally tended to give greater weight to judicial precedents than the Chancellor did. This divergence is plainly evident in the *Duke of Norfolk's Case* where the Common Law judges, and especially North, would have formulated the rule against perpetuities in narrower terms than Lord Nottingham did. Indeed in his judgement, Nottingham astutely dissected the artificialities with which the common lawyers had encumbered the topic, and in response to the hypothetical dangers which it was suggested might follow his judgement, he said:

> It has been urged at the bar, where will you stop. . . ? I answer I will stop everywhere when any inconvenience appears, nowhere before. It is not yet resolved what are the utmost bounds of limiting a contingent fee upon a fee, and it is not necessary to declare what are the utmost bounds to the springing trust of a term, for whensoever the bounds of reason or convenience are exceeded, the law will quickly be known.

Lord Nottingham's opportunity was an exceptional one, and he consciously took full advantage of it. At another point in the same case, he said (with a clear reference to reason and natural law as a source of legal principles):

> Pray let us so resolve cases here that they may stand with the reason of mankind when they are debated abroad. Shall that be reason here that is not reason in any part of the world besides? I would fain know the difference why I may not raise a new springing trust upon the same term, as well as a new springing term upon the same trusts; that is such a chicanery of law as will be laughed at all over the Christian world.

For Nottingham, a precedent was a useful servant, but a bad master. Even in Hardwicke's time, in the middle of the eighteenth century, the Chancellor would not hesitate to override a precedent if it seemed contrary to reason and nature. In his well-known letter to Lord Kames, Hardwicke wrote:

> Some general rules there ought to be, for otherwise the great

> inconvenience of *jus vagum et incertum* will follow, and yet the Praetor[2] must not be so absolutely and invariably bound by them, as the judges and by the rules of the Common Law, for if he were so bound, the consequence would follow that he must sometimes pronounce decrees which would be materially unjust.... This might lay a foundation for an equitable relief even against decrees in equity.[3]

It was only during the Chancellorship of Lord Eldon, at the beginning of the nineteenth century, that it became accepted doctrine that a precedent in equity was as substantially binding as a precedent at Common Law. For over a hundred and forty years after the Restoration in 1660, the Court of Chancery was deliberately establishing new principles of equity and extending them. Naturally the development varied in pace with almost every Chancellor, but as Jessel pointed out, almost every Chancellor contributed something.

If one were to attempt a compilation of how much Nottingham contributed to the development of the rules of equity, it would result in something like a text-book, covering almost every branch of equity practice. He took the decisions of his predecessors, often briefly and badly reported, often also conflicting, and out of them he attempted to extract a coherent principle, with a clear regard for the necessities of his age. There is a striking illustration of this in one of his best known decisions, *Cook v Fountain*,[4] where after analysing the facts he says: 'If after all this a man will still suppose that there was a secret lease or agreement between the parties to repurchase this rent, which no bill charges, no proof can make out, and the defendant denies upon oath, then it must be such a trust, security, or agreement as is only between a man and his confessor.'

> With such a conscience as is only *naturalis et interna* this court has nothing to do; the conscience by which I am to proceed is merely *civilis et politica* and tied to certain measures, and it is infinitely better for the public that a trust, security or agreement which is wholly secret should miscarry than that men

should lose their estates by the mere fancy and imagination of a Chancellor.

This care to confine the development of implied trusts within plain boundaries is evident throughout his judgement, for earlier he had stated that he was going to lay down some rules and distinctions upon trusts by which, he declared, he would govern himself, 'in all cases whatsoever'.

There followed a passage which is one of the best known in the whole of the Law of Trusts:

> All trusts are either, first, express trusts, which are raised and created, by act of the party, or implied trusts, which are raised or created by act or construction of law. Again, express trusts are declared either by word or writing; and these declarations appear either by direct and manifest proof, or violent and necessary presumptions. These are commonly called presumptive trusts[5] and that is when the Court upon consideration presumes there was a declaration, either by word or writing, though the plain and direct proof thereof be not exact. In the case in question there is no pretence of any proof that there was a trust declared either by word or in writing, so the trust, if there be any, must either be implemented by the law or presumed by the Court. There is one good, general and infallible rule that goes to both these kinds of trusts; 'tis such a general rule that never deceives, a general rule to which there is no exception, and that is this: the law never implies, the Court never presumes a trust, but in case of absolute necessity. The reason for this rule is sacred, for if the Chancery do once take a liberty to construe a trust by implication of law or to presume a trust unnecessarily, a way is opened to the Lord Chancellor to construe and presume any man in England out of his estate; and so at last every case in Court will become *casus pro amico.*

This is a very good illustration of Lord Nottingham's style. Once again, as in the *Duke of Norfolk's Case*, he was consciously formulating a general rule from a number of earlier decisions. He found equity in an extremely fluid state, with a scattering of decisions, often briefly and imperfectly reported. After his time the equity reports improve, and the judges in equity pay increased attention to precedents. They are conscious of what Nottingham has done, and references to his decisions are continuous for many years after his death. No other judge has exercised so profound an influence upon the development of a great branch of English law, and in what he did there is evidently a desire to make of equity a body of doctrines based upon clearly understood general principles, and at the same time to set plain limits to the extent of the Chancellor's jurisdiction. As in the *Duke of Norfolk's Case*, so in *Cook v Fountain*, he comes down firmly in favour of common sense. Pushed beyond the limits which Nottingham set, the doctrine of presumptive, or implied, trusts could have been employed to achieve many injustices, particularly in a disturbed society, following the Civil War, during which numerous undertakings concerning property could have been made. The establishment of an implied trust depends upon the operation of certain equitable presumptions. What these were Lord Nottingham makes clear in this and other cases.

It will be apparent that Nottingham's treatment of earlier decisions was that of an architect. They are not to be disregarded. Indeed he considers them with greater care than any of his predecessors; they are treated with respect, but he did not regard them as binding on him. They were evidence of what the law was thought to be. Similarly, whilst in equity he was prepared to follow a Common Law rule so long as it coincided with reason and conscience in the sense in which he understood these terms, he would not hesitate to depart from it (as in the *Duke of Norfolk's Case*) if it seemed to him to be out of date, and unduly formalistic. Nottingham's concern was to initiate what Pollock has described[6] as the process of transformation of equity from a system which 'varied with the length of the Chancellor's foot' to a settled but flexible system of principles. Thisc was a matter of delicate balance, for as Dr Yale has shown, the House of Lords, on appeal from the Chancery, continued to regard itself as free to administer a wider equity, not bounded by the pre-existing rules.

Once again, the *Duke of Norfolk's Case* is a good illustration of Nottingham's technique. He had called in the two chief justices and the chief baron to assist him, and although they were all against him, he nevertheless adhered to his formulation of the *Rule Against Perpetuities*. If their decisions are examined, it will be found that they were analysing what the Common Law learning upon this topic was, and this was greatly complicated by the rules relating to contingent remainders, and their relation to executory devises. Not unnaturally, they regarded this as limiting what they decided. One of the Common Law chief justices, Lord North, was, as his brother Roger North tells us, steeped in the learning of the Year Books, and in his own day was renowned for his Common Law learning. When, therefore, he succeeded Nottingham as Chancellor it was only to be expected that he would reverse Nottingham's decree, and this he did, remarking:

> A perpetuity is a thing odious in law, and destructive of the Commonwealth; it would put a stop to commerce and prevent the circulation of the riches of the Kingdom, and therefore is not to be countenanced in equity. If in equity you could come nearer to a perpetuity than the rules of Common Law would admit, all men being desirous to continue their estates in their families, would settle their estates by way of trust; which might indeed make well for the jurisdiction of the court, but would be destructive to the commonwealth.[8]

Thus spoke a pedantic lawyer whose transition to the Chancery had not broadened his outlook. Happily the House of Lords in 1685 restored Nottingham's decree. Parenthetically, it may be remembered that whenever a common lawyer disliked an equitable innovation, he was apt to regard it as destructive of the commonwealth. Hargrove, arguing against the trust for accumulation in the *Thellusson Case* over a century later, used exactly the same argument. Nottingham's outlook was broader.

North's succession to Nottingham was to the office of Lord

Keeper, not Lord Chancellor. This was a disappointment, although Nottingham himself had served initially as Lord Keeper, but for North there was no similar promotion. He served only for three years, until ill health caused his retirement in 1685. Although he had often been called upon to sit in cases of importance by Nottingham, he showed imperfect understanding of his predecessor's work, and a greater veneration for the rules of Common Law.

Even so, it is possible to trace some development of equity during North's three years as Lord Keeper. For example, he decided *Pusey v Pusey*,[9] decreeing specific restitution of the famous Pusey horn at the suit of the heir, and in the *Earl of Newbury v Wren*[10] he explained the relation of the equity jurisdiction of the Exchequer to the Court of Chancery. Even more interesting and important is *Earl of Arglasse v Muschamp*[11] in which North heard a suit relating to land in Ireland, thereby anticipating Lord Hardwicke's decision in *Penn v Lord Baltimore*[12] by nearly seventy years. In assuming jurisdiction, North commented: 'As to the objection that this court was deficient in power in this case to compel a performance of its decree, because it could not sequester the lands in question, he looked upon that as an objection of no weight, and it did not appear to him, but the defendant might have other lands in England, and then these would be subject to a sequestration.'

On the other hand, several cases show North acting very hesitantly where there were parol agreements for leases, which had been part performed.[13]

There is, in fact, in North's decisions in the Chancery, a clear recognition of the rules of equity as a developing system, and wherever it was possible, there is a reference to earlier decisions.

Nottingham's pioneer work required development, and a good deal of it is of major importance even today. For example, in *Re Diplock*[14] Wynn-Parry J at first instance had rejected a claim that, where executors under a will had transferred the estate to persons not entitled, the legatee (or, in the actual case, his next of kin or unpaid creditor) had a claim in personam against the persons wrongly paid for the return of the property. This decision was based upon an exhaustive survey of decisions from 1800 onwards. In the Court of Appeal, however, the inquiry was pressed back to the Restoration, and the court pointed out that it was in the period between 1660 and 1685 that the Court of Chancery was taking over from the ecclesiastical courts their jurisdiction over suits for legacies and suits for the distribution of the residue.

> The earliest cases cited to us [said the Court of Appeal] in which there is found any reference to the right of an unpaid creditor or legatee to go direct against a legatee already paid were three cases all reported in the first volume of Cases in Chancery, they are *Northrop v Hill*[15] before Lord Keeper Bridgeman, Windham J and Turner B, *Grove v Banson*[16] in the same year before Lord Keeper Bridgeman and Wyld J, and *Chamberlain v Chamberlain*[17] before Lord Keeper Finch. It is not necessary to refer further to these three cases. All were cited to Nottingham, LC, in the case *Noel v Robinson.*[18] The case may be regarded as having had the foundation for the later exercise of the equity jurisdiction for which the historical justification was the rivalry in regard to the administration of estates between the Court of Chancery and the spiritual courts.[19]

These early cases had been largely forgotten until the Court of Appeal restored them in their true place in equity jurisdiction.[20] In this instance North was willing to follow Nottingham, for the second decision in the series relied upon by the Court of Appeal was an *Anonymous*[21] one briefly reported, in which North came to the same conclusion as his predecessor. In fact, that he does so without doubt or comment would indicate that the jurisdiction was regarded as firmly established in his day. If the judgement of the Court of Appeal in *Re Diplock* is perused, it will be seen that it traces the entire course of the development of the jurisdiction during the eighteenth and nineteenth centuries.

Re Diplock (or in the House of Lords, *Minister of Health v Simpson*)[22] is the first of three equity cases of prime importance, which, in recent years, have involved a consideration of the foundations of equity jurisdiction which were laid in the second half of the seventeenth century. In 1953, three appeals reached the Court of Appeal, involving the power of the Court of Chancery (and the Chancery Division as its successor) to consent on behalf of infants or unborn persons to variations in a settlement of which they were beneficiaries. They were *Re Downshire Settled Estates*, *Re Chapman's Settlement Trusts*, and *Re Blackwell's Settlement.*[23]

The majority of the Court of Appeal took a restricted view of its powers, but Denning, LJ, dissented. He said:

> These three cases raise questions of great importance as to the jurisdiction of the Court of Chancery. It is said that the Court of Chancery has no jurisdiction to sanction acts which are not authorised by the trust instrument. That proposition is said to have been established by the decision of this court in *In Re New.*[24] In my opinion the jurisdiction of the court is not so limited. It was certainly not so limited in the days of Lord Hardwicke, LC. He proceeded on the broad principle that the court had power to deal with the property and interests of infants, or other persons under disability, in a manner not authorised by the trust whenever the court was satisfied that what was proposed was most advantageous for them, provided of course, that everyone of full age agreed to it. I hope to show that this is the true principle today; and for this purpose I will trace the history of the matter, for it is supported by the greatest names of English Equity.[25]

This he proceeded to do with very great learning, beginning with the *Earl of Winchester v Norcliffe*,[26] a decision of Sir John Trevor, MR. He added that his opinion on this point was accepted by Lord Jeffreys, LC, who, Lord Denning added, 'is said in equity matters to have been quite a good judge'. His account traces the jurisdiction through the eighteenth century, pointing out that Lord Hardwicke exercised it regularly. On this occasion the House of Lords agreed with the majority of the Court of Appeal[27] in taking a narrower view of the extent of its jurisdiction, and in doing so, they adopted the more hesitant views of a succession of nineteenth-century equity judges. Within a few years, nevertheless, the Variation of Trusts Act, 1958, had given statutory authority to a jurisdiction which the majority in two appellate courts had repudiated.

Lord Denning, moreover, certainly did not err in regarding Lord Jeffreys as a good equity judge, however unfamiliar he may appear to be in such a role. Although without any judicial experience in the Chancery before taking office (for, unlike North, he was never called in by his predecessor when Lord Chief Justice to assist him) his judgements, reported mainly in the first volume of Vernon's reports, show a grasp of equitable principle, and a desire to follow on the course which Nottingham had got. There was both political sympathy and personal friendship between Nottingham and Jeffreys. Nottingham's son, with Jeffreys, was the instigator of the restoration of Nottingham's decree in the *Duke of Norfolk's Case* by the House of Lords. The quality of Jeffreys's work may be assessed from the fact that although Jeffreys's decrees were challenged before the House of Lords after the flight of James II and the accession of William and Mary, practically every one of them was upheld. One further point should be mentioned. In the development of equity which occurred during the three years of Jeffreys's Chancellorship, one should mention the establishment of the doctrine of secret trusts in *Cook v Brooking*,[28] in this instance following and extending the decision of Lord North in *Thynne v Thynne*.[29]

There exists yet a third modern case in which the House of Lords has turned to the decisions of the late seventeenth century for inspiration. The main problem in *Re Baden's Deed Trusts*[30] was whether the objects of a trust power must be capable of being identified with the same certainty as the objects of a trust. A majority of the House of Lords led by Lord Wilberforce held that the test to be applied was that which was applicable to mere powers. In reaching this conclusion, Lord Wilberforce traced the practice of equity from the decisions in *Moseley v Moseley*[31] and *Clarke v Turner*.[32] These modern reconsiderations of the early decisions are not without importance. They exhibit modern equity judges seeking to escape from the fetters of a doctrine of judicial precedents which may confine equitable principles too narrowly.

The more one looks at successive Chancellorships, the more they illustrate Sir George Jessel's estimate of them. From 1660 until the Chancellorship of Lord Eldon, the doctrines of equity were in a state of continuous development which perhaps reached its peak during the long period of office of Lord Hardwicke, in the middle of the eighteenth century. Holdsworth has given us a concise account of the contributions of Hardwicke's eighteenth-century predecessors to the development of equitable principles[33] and of these one may perhaps notice that it was Lord Macclesfield who decided in *Cud v Rutter*[34] that the remedy of specific performance should be limited to cases in which damages was not an adequate remedy. Lord Macclesfield's successor Lord Keeper King decided the famous case of *Keech v Sandford*[35] which is regarded as the starting point of the law relating to constructive trusts, although there are decisions of Lord Nottingham and Lord Jeffreys which anticipate it. Here, as in the case of *Penn v Lord Baltimore*,[36] the eighteenth-century Chancellors were building on foundations laid in the reigns of Charles II and James II.

It is, nevertheless, the great figure of Hardwicke which dominates the eighteenth century, overshadowing those of all other Chancellors after Nottingham. He was preceded for four years by another Chancellor, Talbot, who in the view of many of his contemporaries, and also of Holdsworth,[37] would, if he had lived, have made the same mark upon the history of equity that Hardwicke subsequently did. Oddly, when King resigned in November 1733, both Yorke (subsequently Lord Hardwicke) and Talbot had strong claims to the Chancellorship, but as the Chief Justiceship of the King's Bench was also vacant, Hardwicke (who had just been created a peer) went temporarily to the King's Bench since Talbot was exclusively an equity lawyer—an unusual qualification for a law officer of the Crown.

Lord Hardwicke became Lord Chancellor in 1739, and he occupied that office for nearly two decades, until November 1756. In his day he enjoyed a great reputation not only as a lawyer of outstanding ability, but also as a statesman. In this, he compares only with Nottingham and Eldon. In learning he transcended both, for he had read widely in several systems of law,[38] and this is reflected in his judgements in the Court of Chancery. In addition his industry in the study of English law, whether as student, young practitioner, or judge, was inexhaustible and won tributes from the many distinguished lawyers who, at one time or another, had come before him. It was Hardwicke who settled the distinctive character and province of equity as it has existed down to the present time. Where no precedent existed Hardwicke did not hesitate to make one, and where a precedent conflicted with principle, he was prepared to overrule it. So it followed that equity was more fluid than the Common Law, and therefore more receptive to new ideas, until Lord Eldon, at the beginning of the nineteenth century, established the principle that precedents were substantially as binding in equity as at Common Law, clearly putting an end to a period of incessant development.

One illustration of Hardwicke's technique is his analysis of the various elements of fraud which can be redressed in equity in *The Earl of Chesterfield v Janssen.*[39] This has remained a guide to equity judges right down to the present day, and in *Lancashire Loans Co Ltd v Black*[40] Scrutton, LJ, pointed out that Lord Hardwicke's classic exposition goes beyond the Common Law formulation, and has at times been in conflict with it—for example in *Derry v Peek.*[41] As Lord Hardwicke pointed out in his famous letter to Lord Kames, a Scottish contemporary:

> fraud is infinite, and were a court of equity once to lay down rules how far they would go, and no further, in extending their relief against it, or to define strictly the species or evidences of it, the jurisdiction would be cramped, and perpetually eluded by new schemes which the fertility of man's invention would contrive.

These words have left an enduring mark upon the development of equity. They are implicit in the speech of Lord Haldane, LC, in *Nocton v Ashburton*[42] in which he analysed exhaustively the distinction between fraud at Common Law and fraud in equity. In doing so, he pointed out at Common Law, the action on the case for deceit was itself evolved by the judges in *Pasley v Freeman*[43] in 1789, ie forty years after Lord Hardwicke had defined the scope of fraud in equity. Lord Haldane's further observations explain the nature of the judicial law-making as clearly as anything which appear in the *Law Reports*. He says:

> Up to that date (1789) it was at least doubtful whether the action (ie for deceit) lay in the absence of a special duty. The doctrines of obligation to exercise care by persons in particular situations, who are doing acts which may injure the property or persons of others; of implied contract, as shown in the evolution of the action of *assumpsit* and its development from case; of the liability of the agent, who came at last to be treated as warranting the authority which he asserted; of the right to an injunction and an account in equity in cases of passing off goods, as explained and contrasted with claims based on deceit in Lord Westbury's judgment in *Edelsten v Edelsten*[44] and in such later authorities as the judgment of Mr Justice Farwell in *Bourne v Swan and Edgar; Bourne's Trade Mark, In re*;[45] these doctrines and the like illustrate the freedom which has been exercised by the judges in making new applications of recognised principles. Although liability for negligence in words has in material respects been developed in our law differently from liability for negligence in act, it is none the less true that a man may come under a special duty to exercise care in giving information or advice. I should accordingly be sorry to be thought to lend countenance to the idea that recent decisions have been intended to stereotype the cases in which people can be held to have assumed such a special duty.

Happily, the decision of the House of Lords in this case dispelled any such suspicion.

Unfortunately, it is not possible to give even the briefest account of Lord Hardwicke's massive contribution to equity—a contribution which decisively settled its nature and content for the future. Instead, one may perhaps refer briefly to some of the major advances made by equity during this period. Where today important reforms would be achieved by legislation, in the eighteenth century they were accomplished by the application of equitable principles, and this is therefore the Golden Age of equitable development.

It is during this period that the modern law of mortgages was developed. The principle 'once a mortgage, always a mortgage' and the allied principles that there can be no clog upon the equitable right to redeem dates from Lord Nottingham's decision in *Harris v Harris*[46] in 1681, and the doctrines of tacking and consideration were evolved at the same period.[47] It has already been noticed that Lord Nottingham established all the main features of the modern law of trusts, protecting the interest of the beneficiary against claims made against the trustee in his personal capacity. At the same time, it was established that the beneficiary's interest in a trust of land should, in general, be capable of being held for the same interests, and should devolve in the same way, as a legal estate. On the other hand, so far as their creation was concerned, the technical Common Law rules relating to contingent remainders were not introduced into equity.

One of the outstanding characteristics of the trust has always been its flexibility, permitting it to be applied to a very wide range of situations. It was this flexibility which caused it to be used to introduce a major social change by the creation of the married woman's separate estate in equity. Even before the Civil War, there were decisions which established that property could be given to a married woman through the intervention of trustees, thus making the first breach in the Common Law rule that on marriage, all the wife's personal property passed to the husband and, on the birth of issue capable of inheriting, all her real estate also. Coincidentally, the wife also lost the power to contract on her own account. She could only make contracts as the agent of her husband, who was therefore liable on them, as he was also liable in respect of her torts. Finally, she could not make a will of land at all, and she could only make a will of personal property with her husband's consent.

From the time of the Restoration onwards, the Court of Chancery consistently held that if property were given to a woman for her separate use, either before or after marriage, equity would protect her in her separate enjoyment of it, and when no trustees were appointed the husband himself was a trustee for her. By 1700 the practice of giving property in this way to a woman had become exceedingly common. During the first half of the eighteenth century, equity had gone a step further in the development of the doctrine of the wife's equity to a settlement. By virtue of this doctrine equity would not allow either the husband or his creditors to have recourse in equity against property which was to come to him in right of his wife, unless the husband made provision out of it for her.

One of the achievements of Lord Hardwicke was to settle the law relating to the married woman's capacity to dispose of her separate property by will. In *Peacock v Monk*[48] he decided that she possessed this power. At the same period, and a little later, courts were holding that a married woman had power to alienate during her lifetime, and further, that she was liable in respect of her contracts to the extent that she possessed separate property.[49]

The establishment of freedom of alienation, however, created a further problem. It might be a means of destroying the married woman's separate property altogether, if she used her power of alienation to surrender the property to her husband. In *Pybus v Smith*[50] Lord Thurlow was compelled to uphold a conveyance by a wife of the whole of her property as security for the payment of her husband's debts, and a footnote to the report of this case shows how greatly this freedom of alienation, in favour of a husband, was exercising the minds of Chancery judges at this period. It was to solve this problem that Lord Thurlow devised the clause providing that property might be given to a married woman with a restraint upon anticipation, it being inserted into the settlement of a Miss Watson, of which the Lord Chancellor was himself a trustee. Evidently, this development was in conformity with the wishes of his Chancery colleagues, for Lord Eldon says in *Brandon v Robinson*[51] that he had much conversation with Lord Thurlow upon it. As Lord Eldon points out, this restraint upon alienation was regarded as quite exceptional, and was due to the fact that the married woman's separate estate was itself the creature of equity.

> He did not [says Lord Eldon] attempt to take away any power the law gave her as an incident to property, which being a creature of equity she could not have at law: but, as under the words of the settlement it would have been hers absolutely, so that she could alien, Lord Thurlow endeavoured to prevent that by imposing upon the trustees the necessity of paying to her from time to time, and not by anticipation; reasoning thus; that equity, making her the owner of it, and enabling her, as a married woman, to alien, might limit her power over it, but the case of a disposition to a man, who, if he has property, has the power of aliening, is quite different.

In thus developing the separate estate of a married woman, and in the further conception of the restraint on alienation the Court of Chancery was consciously creating a new body of law, a task which today would be undertaken by Parliament. When from 1870 onwards, Parliament did legislate, creating the separate estate of the married woman *at law*, it incorporated also the equitable rules governing restraints on anticipation, which the Court of Chancery had evolved, nearly a century earlier. Since 1945, the relation of the parties to a marriage has changed to such a degree that the existence of this restraint became anomalous, and the incidence of modern taxation made it, in numerous instances, irksome. It has therefore been abolished.

Before leaving the creative work of the Chancellors between 1660 and Lord Eldon's Chancellorship, one may perhaps mention that most of them, and particularly Talbot and Hardwicke, were conscious of a philosophic basis for the rules which they were fashioning. The eighteenth century is the period in which theories of natural rights reached the peak of their development. If the leading decisions in equity are perused, it will be found there is frequent reference to natural rights, and to natural obligations, and in this infusion of these principles into equity the Chancellors recall, in some measure, the Roman praetors in their transformation of the civil laws of Rome by recourse to the law of nature, as they understood it. Much of the development of the law governing portions, hotchpot, satisfaction, election and marshalling can be traced to this source. Many are illustrations of the natural obligations of a father to provide for his children and to show equity between them. Others are illustrations of the maxim that 'Equity presumes an intent to fulfil an obligation'—obligation in this instance being extended beyond the area of legal to that of natural obligation. Many of Lord Mansfield's innovations in the Common Law have a similar origin. The eighteenth century was an age in which jurisprudence and philosophy were closer together than they have been since.

7

The Judges and the Constitution

The seventeenth century was the most critical century in the history of the English judiciary, and also in the history of the Common Law. It began with the Chief Justiceship of Sir Edward Coke and ended with that of Sir John Holt. Both of them were men of outstanding character, who did much to place the Common Law on a secure foundation. Between the dismissal of Coke in 1616 and the appointment of Holt in 1689 the essentials of the modern English constitution had been hammered out in the long struggle between King and Parliament, and during that struggle, the independence of the judiciary from executive control had become one of the principal matters of contention.

Coke's legal career divides into three phases. He achieved a commanding position as an advocate in the latter part of the reign of Elizabeth I. She appointed him Solicitor-General in 1594 at the age of 41, and in the following year the House of Commons appointed him Speaker, in recognition of his outstanding legal ability. His tenure of that office was very brief, for in April 1594, he was promoted to the office of Attorney-General and at this time the appointment was considered to be a disqualification for membership of the House of Commons.

As Attorney-General, Coke was remarkable for the vindictiveness with which he prosecuted those accused of high treason, in particular, the Earl of Essex in 1601, Sir Walter Raleigh in 1603, Guy Fawkes in 1606, and finally Father Garnett the Jesuit in the same year. At this stage of his career, there was little indication of the great achievements which lay ahead of him. His arrogance had made him an object of detestation to most of his professional colleagues, and in spite of his assertion in his *Institutes* that the use of torture in criminal trials was unknown to the Common Law, he did not hesitate to participate in the examination of persons accused of treason, in which torture was employed.

In 1606 James I appointed him Chief Justice of the Common Pleas and he remained in that office until 1613, when he was transferred to the Chief Justiceship of the King's Bench. Finding him too independent, James dismissed him in 1616. Four years later Coke, now almost seventy years of age, began a new career as a member of the House of Commons for Liskeard. Here he quickly became one of the leaders of a group of members who were opposed to the royal administration and who defended the privileges of the House against royal encroachments which increased after Charles I had succeeded his father. It therefore came about that Coke was the author and principal advocate of the Petition of Right which Parliament compelled a reluctant sovereign to accept in 1628. From the political point of view this was the crowning achievement of a great career, and it was virtually his last public act, although he lived in retirement until 1634.

This brief sketch can give no impression at all of the vastness of his contribution to the Common Law, nor of the importance of his surprisingly brief tenure of the office of Chief Justice. In the last years of Elizabeth's reign, the business of the Common Law courts had diminished and there was a danger that their jurisdiction would be replaced to a considerable extent by that of other courts, which had their origin in the council. Further, the great question of the relation of the judiciary to the royal administration was unsettled, and James I had no clear understanding of it. During his reign there was a sustained attempt to bring the administration of justice directly under royal control. Unlike some of his predecessors and the bulk of his successors until the Revolution in 1689, Coke had no intention of letting this question, so fundamental to the future development, both of the constitution and of the Common Law, go by default.

As a judge, Coke had a conception, medieval in origin, of the supremacy of the Common Law, which defined and limited the prerogative and might even invalidate legislation. Such a conception was already obsolescent in his day, and might in any case have produced conflicts between the judiciary and the executive. There are already hints of this in the latter part of the reign of Elizabeth I, when the Common Law courts showed restlessness at the increasing judicial activity of the council and of the numerous courts which exercised a jurisdiction outside the framework of the Common Law. These were of various kinds. The most famous for the part it played in enforcing the king's personal rule during the reign of Charles I was the Star Chamber, but it had been a major factor in the restoration and preservation of order in Tudor times. Looked at from the standpoint of the Common Law, even the Court of Chancery was a dangerous rival, and the fact that Wolsey had extended its jurisdiction was one of the charges in the proceedings for his impeachment. Again, while the Court of Admiralty's jurisdiction had been extended by statute in the reign of Henry VII, the Common Law courts regarded this extension of its activities into the sphere of mercantile law with suspicion. There was also the Court of High Commission, established to preserve the religious settlement achieved in Elizabeth's reign. This court, under the protection of the archbishops, resented the issue of writs of prohibition to it by the Common Law courts. Yet again, there were the Council of the North and the Council of the Welsh Marches, both with jurisdictions which were always capable of extension at the expense of the jurisdiction of the Common Law courts. To Coke the issue was a simple one. The supremacy of the Common Law courts must be asserted against all these threats.

This, in any event, would necessarily have involved a challenge to the royal prerogative; but the issue was made potentially more explosive by the willingness of James I to intervene directly in the struggle. Only a year after Coke's appointment to the Common Pleas, he was involved in a conflict which challenged at once the ecclesiastical courts and the claim of the king to administer justice in person. Already in 1605 Archbishop Bancroft had complained to the council that the ecclesiastical courts were being hampered by writs of prohibition. Coke immediately after his appointment declared that the writs of prohibition were issued in accordance with the Common Law. Two years later Nicholas Fuller, a barrister, applied to the King's Bench for a prohibition against the Court of High Commission. In the course of his argument he used words which the bishop interpreted as schismatic. For this he was fined and imprisoned in the Court of High Commission. The King's Bench, whilst not challenging the jurisdiction of the High Commission in matters of doctrine, asserted that a barrister could not be punished for words said in court, and also unequivocally asserted its right to determine the extent of the jurisdiction possessed by the ecclesiastical courts. Bancroft appealed to the king, asserting that the limits of ecclesiastical jurisdiction or any other doubtful question of law could only be determined by the king, since the judges were only his delegates. James incautiously adopted this argument in full, whereupon Coke, with the support of all the Common Law judges, declared such a claim to be contrary to law. When James angrily asserted that he had often heard the boast that English law was founded on reason, and that he had reason as well as the judges, Coke made the classic reply:

> True it is, please your Majesty, that God has endowed your Majesty with excellent science as well as with great gifts of nature; but your Majesty will allow me to say, with all reverence, that you are not learned in the laws of your realm of England, and I crave leave to remind your Majesty that causes which concern the life or inheritance, or goods or fortunes of your subjects are not to be decided by natural reason, but by the artificial reason and judgement of law, which law is an art which requires long study and experience before that a man can attain to the cognizance of it. This is the golden met-wand and measure to try the causes of your Majesty's subjects, and it is by the law that your Majesty is protected in safety and peace.

To this an infuriated sovereign replied:

> Then I am to be *under* the law—which it is treason to affirm

and Coke replied:

Thus wrote Bracton, *Rex non debet esse sub homine, sed sub Deo et lege.*

From this moment the conflict between the king and his chief justice was continuous, but there was a point of some significance about this episode which did not escape the king's attention. Coke had had the support of all the judges in this confrontation. Many of them had been appointed in Elizabeth's reign, and Coke himself had succeeded Popham, whose independence and assertion of the primacy of the Common Law was comparable with Coke's. Such independence, from the point of view of the royal administration, was inadmissible. The judges were the king's servants in fact, as well as in name, and henceforth care would be taken in selecting them, to ensure that they were more amenable to royal direction. Even so, the judges did not relinquish their independence without a struggle. In the most celebrated case of all, during the troubled period between the accession of James I and the outbreak of the Civil War, the case of ship money (*R v Hampden*) in 1637[1] which was heard in the Exchequer Chamber before twelve Common Law judges, seven of the twelve judges found in favour of the king, and five for Hampden. It is true that some of the five decided on technical grounds, but this was no more than an illustration of judicial caution at a time when the king's direct rule, without a Parliament, was at its height.

There is also another side to this great case. The seven judges who decided in favour of the king must have known that when a Parliament did meet—as it did in 1640—their decision, and possibly their persons, would be the object of bitter attack; and, in fact, a number of them were impeached. Accordingly, although it has been the fashion to attack them as time servers, lacking in principle, it should be appreciated that the desire for judicial office was not their only motive, and it may not have been the dominating one. At this difficult time in our history, at least three theories of the constitution were sincerely held, and the attitudes of those who held them tended to harden and their views became more extreme as the conflict deepened. At one extreme were those who accepted the view that the king was sovereign in fact as well as in name. He governed by virtue of the royal prerogative with the advice of Parliament, when Parliament was in existence, but at other times, by the authority which he enjoyed by virtue of his kingly office. It was only by degrees that there evolved the opposite theory that Parliament was sovereign, by which it was understood that Parliament consisted of King, Lords and Commons. At the outset of the struggle the majority of Englishmen would have maintained that neither King nor Parliament was sovereign. Both exercised their authority in accordance with the Common Law, and the constitution was 'balanced' by the relation of one to the other. This was the ideal of Edward Hyde, later Lord Clarendon, and it was an idea that persisted until 1689, when the sovereignty of Parliament became the bedrock of the English constitution. All this would have seemed very strange at the beginning of James I's reign, when Dr Cowell, Regius Professor of Civil Law at Cambridge, published, under the patronage of Archbishop Bancroft, a volume, *The Interpreter*, a species of law lexicon, in which there appeared an exposition of the king's absolute power in extreme terms. Under the heading *King* he had written:

> He is above the law by his absolute power, and though for the better and equal course in making laws he do admit the three estates unto council, yet this in divine learned men's opinion is not of constraint, but of his own benignity or by reason of his promise made upon oath at the time of his coronation. And though at his coronation he take an oath not to alter the laws of the land, yet, this oath notwithstanding, he may alter or suspend any particular law that seemeth hurtful to the public estate. Thus much in short, because I have heard some to be of opinion that the laws are above the King.

The publication of this book provoked such a commotion that James found it prudent to disown it. Nevertheless, as late as the case of ship money, in 1637 Chief Justice Finch was saying:

> The defence of the kingdom must be at the charge of the whole

> kingdom. The sole interest and property of the sea, by our laws and policy is in the king and sea and land make but one kingdom, and therefore the subject is bound to the defence of both. Parliament is not the only means of defending the kingdom. The king is not bound to call it but when he pleases, and there was a king before a Parliament. The law which has given the interest and sovereignty of defending and governing the kingdom to the king, also gives him power to charge his subjects for its defence, and they are bound to obey.

Pursued to its logical extreme, this meant that the king could dispense with Parliament altogether, and that he could legislate without its intervention. This is what Lord Ellesmere, as Lord Chancellor (and by no means the most extreme advocate of the prerogative), meant when, in the *Case of Proclamations* in 1611,[2] he advised the judges

> to maintain the power and prerogative of the king; and in cases in which there is no authority and precedent, to leave it to the king to order in it according to his wisdom,

but the judges, at Coke's direction, ignored this advice and held

> that the king by his proclamation cannot create any offence which was not an offence before, for then he may alter the law of the land by his proclamation in a high point; for if he may create an offence where none is, upon that ensues fine and imprisonment. Also the law of England is divided into three parts, common law, statute law, and custom, but the king's proclamation is none of them.

This pronouncement negatived the king's assertion of a law-making power independent of Parliament, but so long as the Star Chamber was there to enforce proclamations, the threat was always there, and both the Civil War and the Revolution of 1689 were to intervene before it was finally dissipated.

Throughout his judicial career Coke was involved in a two-fold struggle to resist further encroachments upon the Common Law by other jurisdictions. His Reports relate the way in which he curbed the judicial and administrative activities of the Councils of Wales and the Council of the North, although the jurisdiction of the latter was extended again in the next reign during the presidency of Strafford. In his conflict with the Court of Chancery he was unsuccessful, and it was well for the future development of English law that he was. In the struggle between the King's Bench of which Coke was the Chief Justice, and the Chancery of which Lord Ellesmere was Chancellor, only the King in Council could decide, and in the *Earl of Oxford's Case*[3] and its aftermath, James, following the advice of Bacon, then Attorney-General, decided that where Common Law and equity conflicted, the rules of equity were to prevail.

In his conflict with the Court of Admiralty in respect of jurisdiction in mercantile matters, which Coke sought to restrain by writs of Prohibition, a working compromise was reached, whereby the two systems had concurrent jurisdiction. In this dispute, and that with the Court of Chancery, the royal prerogative was only indirectly involved. They were lawyers' struggles, ultimately about the application of differing systems of law—Common Law, equity and admiralty law. A far more serious conflict, and the culminating point in Coke's resistance to the excessive claims of the king in respect of the prerogative, arose upon the question of whether the king had the right to stop or delay proceedings in the Common Law courts by the issue of the writ *de non procedendo rege inconsulto*. After simmering for some time, the question came to a head in the *Case of Commendams* in 1616.[4] The king had given to the Bishop of Coventry an ecclesiastical living to be held *in commendam* with his bishopric. When a dispute arose with regard to the right to present (which, being a right of advowson, was triable in a Common Law court) the Attorney-General on the king's instruction issued the writ to stay the proceedings, whereupon the judges, on the advice of Coke, wrote the king a letter, in the course of which they said:

We hold it our duties to inform your Majesty that our oath is in these express words: that in case any letters come unto us contrary to law, we do nothing by such letters, but certify your Majesty thereof, and go forth to do the law notwithstanding the same letters. We have adversely considered of the said letters of Mr Attorney and with our consent do hold the same contrary to law.

They added that they had therefore not proceeded upon the case.

The result was that all the judges were summoned before the council, where they were admonished by the king himself. Only Coke maintained the position which they had adopted in their letter. The rest asked for pardon, and promised that they would uphold the king's prerogatives both in the actual case, and in the future.

All this occurred whilst the conflict between Coke and the Chancery was still fresh in everyone's mind, and accordingly, his dismissal followed in November of the same year. His successor, Montague, was a man of much more pliant temperament, and Ellesmere in his speech to him upon his appointment made it quite clear that the judges were subordinate to the king. Coke's dismissal, said Ellesmere, was 'a lesson to be learned of all and to be remembered and feared of all that sit in judicial places'. And in a speech in the Star Chamber in the same year, James admonished the judges not to encroach upon the royal prerogative: 'If there fall out a question that concerns my prerogative or mystery of state, deal not with it till you consult with the king or his Council or both.'

In such a political climate, the maintenance of judicial integrity became impossible and only prerogative lawyers could hope to receive judicial appointments. One result of this was that judicial decisions—of which the *Case of Ship Money* was only one—became a matter of public controversy and parliamentary debate. The judiciary had been thrown into the political arena and the denunciation of many of them by the Long Parliament was a logical step by the parliamentary opposition, which gradually came to believe that the solution was to be found in the supremacy of Parliament over the judiciary. To this Coke in the parliamentary phase of his colourful career offered an alternative in the supremacy of the Common Law and the independence of the judiciary.

It has often been said that the restoration of Charles II in 1660 settled nothing beyond the fact that England preferred a constitutional monarchy to republican government or rule by the army. The main constitutional problems—and especially the problem of the position of the prerogative in the constitutional framework—was still unresolved, and there were widely differing views upon it. The context had, however, changed. It was no longer possible for a king to claim the power to rule without Parliament. The strength of that institution had been established by the Long Parliament before the opening of the Civil War. What had been accomplished in these years remained after 1660, and in particular, there was no longer a Star Chamber in which royal policy could be enforced by fine, imprisonment and mutilation. Further, the position of the Common Law was now secure. What did remain of the earlier royal pretensions was the claim of Charles II and James II to dispensing and suspending powers, ie the claim to dispense with the operation of legislation in favour of a particular individual or generally. This claim was finally ended by the Bill of Rights in 1689.

What had not been solved was the status of the judiciary. Judges were still appointed by the king, in fact as well as in form, and they still held office during the royal pleasure. Both Charles II and James II controlled judicial appointments, and dismissed judges repeatedly, when they no longer acted as instruments of royal policy. Control of the judiciary after the Restoration was even more important to the Crown than it had been before 1640, because the abolition of the Star Chamber and other prerogative courts made it necessary for the royal policy to be enforced in the ordinary courts. At times this might lead to stalemate, for while the Crown controlled the judiciary, juries were selected, especially in London, by officers who were responsible to magistrates who were members, and sometimes leaders, of the opposition. In such circumstances, they could be relied on not to convict. It was reliance upon the verdicts of packed Whig juries which gave Shaftesbury his immunity, and when the Whigs of the City lost control of the selection of juries, it was immediately necessary for him to take refuge in Holland. Had the Star Chamber still existed, it is doubtful whether opposition to the Crown on the scale which Shaftesbury organised it would have been possible at all. It is equally open to question whether the scandals of the Popish Plot trials, where verdicts were given in accordance with the prejudices of the London mob, whipped up by Titus Oates, Dangerfield and others, could have taken place.

The consequences of bringing the judges into the political arena were quite disastrous, and at no other period of English history had the judiciary shown to greater disadvantage. The early appointments of the reign of Charles II were sound, even distinguished. Sir Matthew Hale and Sir Robert Vaughan were among the early appointments as Chief Justices, and Orlando Bridgeman was the first post-Restoration Chief Justice of the Common Pleas. These are distinguished names by any test, and Sir Matthew Hale is one of the leading judicial writers upon English law and its history. Lord Nottingham is one of the three outstanding architects of equity. Even the erudition of Lord North, Chief Justice of the Common Pleas and later Lord Keeper, at the end of the reign, is not open to question. In between there were many lesser men, and one or two whose personal integrity was doubtful, and who were at best pliant instruments of royal policy. When they were dismissed, they provided the spectacle of judges returning to private practice, which again is a characteristic of this age alone.

As the struggle between the Crown and the Whigs intensified in the latter part of Charles II's reign, even unscrupulous time servers proved inadequate as instruments of royal policy, and they were replaced by ruthless adherents of the court, such as Jeffreys, Sir Thomas Jones, Herbert and Wright. In the brief reign of James II, royal control of the judiciary was pushed to the furthest limit, and it is related that when James II dismissed Sir Thomas Jones, James told him that he was determined to have twelve judges of his opinion, to which Jones is reported to have replied that he might find twelve judges, but not twelve lawyers. James's last intervention was designed to bring about the replacement of Anglican judges by Roman Catholics, an enterprise which was already well advanced at the Revolution.

With a bench which either sincerely believed in the royal prerogative, or was overawed by the monarch, even the Common Law could be distorted and used as an instrument of oppression. For this situation the two contending factions must share the blame, although perhaps not in equal measure. The opposition has jury-packing and the miscarriages of justice in the Popish Plot trials to its discredit. On the other side must be placed the straining of the law of treason in the Rye House Plot Trials, and decisions such as *Godden v Hales* in 1686,[5] temporarily legalising the Crown's dispensing power in respect of the penal laws debarring Roman Catholics from holding public office. Before giving judgement, Chief Justice Herbert fortified his opinion by consulting all the Common Law judges, and eleven out of the twelve concurred in upholding the dispensing power in extravagant terms. They held:

1 That the Kings of England are sovereign princes.
2 That the laws of England are the King's laws.
3 That therefore 'tis an inseparable prerogative in the Kings of England to dispense with penal laws in particular cases, and upon particular necessary reasons.
4 That of these reasons and those necessities the King himself is sole judge; and then which is consequent upon all.
5 That this is not a trust invested in or granted to the King by the people, but an ancient remains of the sovereign power and prerogative of the Kings of England; which never yet was taken from them, nor can be. And therefore such a dispensation appearing upon record to come time enough to save him from the forfeiture, judgment ought to be given for the defendant.

The solitary judge who dissented from these extravagant pretensions was Mr Justice Street who, as Narcissus Luttrell remarked, 'hath lately married a wife with a good fortune, since his opinion against the King's power of dispensing'. This was prudent, as he was dismissed almost immediately afterwards.

During the reign of James II the overriding problem for a judge was the degree of his subservience. There occurred immediately before the Revolution the historic trial of the seven bishops. Several major constitutional questions were argued before the Chief Justice, and the other three King's Bench judges who heard the case. James had ordered a 'Declaration of Indulgence' to be read by the bishops and clergy in all churches. This document purported to be a pronouncement in favour of religious toleration, but its true object was to remove all the disabilities upon Roman Catholics, imposed by the Test Act and other statutes. In reality, therefore, it was an exercise of the suspending power, although it was argued on behalf of the Crown that it was simply an extension of the dispensing power. The seven bishops refused to authorise the publication of the declaration in their dioceses, and they drew up a petition to the king, asking that they should not be compelled to read and distribute the declaration, since the alleged prerogative power (whether suspending or dispensing) had frequently been declared to be illegal by Parliament. For this they were prosecuted for seditious libel. This time the king had pressed even a compliant judiciary too far. Chief Justice Wright and Mr Justice Alibone (a Roman Catholic, in respect of whose appointment James had already exercised the dispensing power) held that the bishops' petition was a seditious libel, but the other two—Holloway and Powell—held that it was not. The jury found the bishops 'not guilty'. Dismissal of Holloway and Powell quickly followed. This was at the end of June 1688. Before the end of the year, the Revolution had occurred, and when Parliament met in the new reign, not only did the Bill of Rights declare illegal the suspending power and also the dispensing power 'as it hath been exercised of late', but also *Godden v Hales* and numerous other decisions in the two decades preceding the Revolutions were declared unlawful.

The signs of judicial venality were plain before the end of the reign of Charles II. In a pamphlet written in 1684 or 1685, the

Marquis of Halifax had written:

> To see the laws mangled, disguised, made to speak quite another language than their own; to see them thrown from the dignity of protecting mankind to the disgraceful office of destroying them, and, notwithstanding their innocence in themselves to be made the worst instruments that the most refined malice and villainy can make use of, will raise men's anger above the power of laying it down again, and tempt them to follow the ill example given them of judging without hearing when so provoked by their desire for revenge.

Holdsworth summarised the results of this policy in two striking paragraphs.[6] The list of dismissed judges was a long one. It included some who had exalted the royal prerogative, but who could not stomach the wholesale use of the dispensing power under James II. It included Chief Justice Herbert, who, in spite of his judgement in *Godden v Hales*, nevertheless refused to order a soldier, who had been condemned and sentenced at Reading, to be executed at Plymouth; and also Jones, who had sat with Scroggs in the worst of the Popish Plot trials, and had then been impeached by the House of Commons, again with Scroggs, for acquitting the queen's physician. Jones had also shared in the decision forfeiting the Charter of the City of London, and had behaved brutally in the trials of Elizabeth Gaunt and Cornish. He, too, went in 1686 for refusing to uphold the dispensing power. As a result of these dismissals many of the judges had returned to practise by the end of the reign, and the counsel for the seven bishops included Pemberton (who had been dismissed more than once from his office of Chief Justice); Levinz, also dismissed from the Bench for his opposition to the dispensing power; Sawyer, dismissed from the office of Attorney-General; Heneage Finch, son of Lord Nottingham, dismissed from the office of Solicitor-General; Pollexfen, who was to be the first Chief Justice of the Common Pleas under William III; his successor in that office, Sir George Treby; and finally, Somers, William's first Lord Chancellor who, with Holt as Chief Justice of the King's

Bench, was to play a leading part in the rehabilitation of the judiciary. Holt himself had been dismissed from the Recordership of London, and was missing from the list of defence counsel for the seven bishops only because, as king's serjeant, he was not able to be included, and he refused to appear for the prosecution. One other name was missing for the same reason—that of Serjeant Maynard, whose long life covers almost the whole of the seventeenth century. He had been one of the managers of the impeachments of Strafford and Laud, and had served in Parliament during the Commonwealth. He had only escaped high judicial office because of his unwavering Whig principles, and when William III remarked that he seemed to have outlived all the eminent lawyers of his time, made the famous remark that 'he had like to have outlived the law itself if his highness had not come over'. Few would wish to quarrel with that verdict.

From the Revolution onwards, judges enjoyed security of tenure, and this was given statutory protection by the Act of Settlement, which provided that they were removable only upon the address of both Houses of Parliament. This far seeing change not only made it impossible for the Crown at any future date to put pressure upon them, but also removed a possible threat from the House of Commons which, in the reigns of Charles I and Charles II, had sought to impeach some members of the judiciary for decisions of which they disapproved. At long last, therefore, the judges were removed from the sphere of political action, and since 1688, not only has no judge been removed by the procedure prescribed in the Act of Settlement, but no judge has been threatened by its invocation. Moreover, it was established in the seventeenth and eighteenth centuries that no judge of a superior court can be made responsible in law for acts done by them in his judicial capacity. In the words of Chief Baron Kelly, in *Scott v Stansfield*:[7]

> ... it has been uniformly held, from the time of Lord Coke to the present day, that no action will lie against a Judge for any act done or any word spoken in his judicial capacity in a court of justice; and the whole current of decisions from that time to

this is uniformly to the same effect. . . And this provision in the law which is as ancient as the law itself, is not for the protection or in any wise for the benefit of a malicious, corrupt, or offending judge, but for the benefit of the public who are entitled to require that the judges should be independent, and should be protected by the law in exercising their functions without fear.

So far as the constitution was concerned the changes brought about in the position of the judiciary have proved to be of first importance in subsequent developments. Successive generations of lawyers have accepted the doctrine that the Common Law, as expounded by the judges, is the surest guarantee of personal liberty, and a succession of decisions from the time of Lord Chief Justice Holt onwards have confirmed this. Freedom of the person, freedom of speech, and the right of public meeting rest, not upon any legislative pronouncement—not even upon the Bill of Rights—but upon decisions defining the extent of the right in particular cases. The constitutional doctrines built upon these decisions are elaborated systematically in Dicey's *Law of the Constitution* and many similar volumes. It is in the fullest sense, judge-made law.

The removal of the judiciary from the political arena was necessarily accompanied by a limitation of function. Since Parliament was now supreme, its legislative pronouncements could not be questioned in any court. It would have been otherwise if the English Revolution, like the American a century later, had given birth to a written constitution. Under that constitution the American Supreme Court has exercised the power to invalidate legislation of Congress which it deems to be in conflict with the provisions of the constitution, which is the fundamental law. Often such constitutional decisions have involved the protection of personal rights, guaranteed to American citizens by the constitution. But while English judges have ordinarily exercised their functions in an atmosphere remarkably free from conflict, it has been otherwise in the United States. At times the federal judiciary has been in the centre of violent controversy, its decisions have been attacked, there have been threats of impeachment of one or more members, and there have been prolonged disputes over Presidential nominations to the Supreme Court. In so far as these things focus attention upon the work which judges do, and the way in which they perform it, this is not necessarily a bad thing. The statement that justice must not only be done, but must be seen to be done, has a wider application than to the determination of a particular case.

American writers have gone further, however. They have examined the family background, education, interests and prejudices of judges in the hope of discovering their ultimate motivation, although in recent years they appear to have wearied a little in the performance of this task. Their inquiry was in no sense novel. Anyone who has read the history of the seventeenth century in England knows that political writers of that age did not scruple to expose the prejudices of contemporary judges, as indeed they did a century later, in attacking Lord Mansfield. In our own day, more general attacks have been mounted upon the judiciary by trade unionists and others for alleged political and social bias. It was Jerome Frank, in a searching analysis of the judicial function in *Courts in Trial*, who revealed the great truth that, after all, judges were human, but not sub-human. In a dispatch to the Foreign Secretary by Sir Robert Hart, a famous British diplomat in China a century ago, Sir Robert wrote: 'My lord I beseech you to believe that Her Majesty's representatives in China are not naturally more prejudiced than other men.' Much the same could be said of judges, with the addition that, by training, a judge may consciously isolate his prejudices, and discount them.

The late Justice Robert H. Jackson in an essay written not long before his death[8] said:

> The Supreme Court of the United States was created in a different manner from most high courts. In Europe most judiciaries evolved as subordinates to the king, who delegated to them some of his functions. For example, while the English judges have developed a remarkably independent status, they still retain the formal status of Crown servants. But here the Supreme Court and the other branches of the Federal Govern-

ment came into existence at the same time and by the same act of creation.

Later he adds:

> From what I have said it might almost be assumed that the Supreme Court could be ignored in the power equation of the American Government. But in living history this institution has profoundly influenced, for better or for worse, the course of the nation. Not only has it been the centre of bitter debate itself, but its decisions have played some part in nearly every great political issue that has vexed our people.

And finally:

> Our history has not been free of sanguinary internal conflicts. It would not be realistic to contend that judicial power always has been used wisely. The Court has been sharply attacked by Presidents Jefferson, Jackson, Lincoln and both Roosevelts. Yet no substantial sentiment exists for any curtailment of the Court's powers. Even President Roosevelt in the bitterest conflict with judicial power in our history suggested only change in the Court's composition not in its constitutional prerogatives. The real strength of the position of the Court is probably with its indispensability to government under a written Constitution. It is difficult to see how the provisions of a 150-year-old written document can have much vitality if there is not some permanent institution to translate them into current commands and to see to their contemporary application. Courts will differ from time to time in the emphasis they will place on one or another of the Constitution's provisions, in part no doubt responsive to the atmosphere of the changes in public opinion. Interpretations will change from one generation to another, precedents will sometimes be overruled, innovations will be made that will not always be predictable. That has always been the history of the Court.

The legal profession in all countries knows that there are only two real choices of government open to a people. It may be governed by the will of one or of a group of men. Law, as the expression of the ultimate will and wisdom of a people, has so far proven the safest guardian of liberty yet devised. I think our constitutional and judicial system has made a valuable and enduring contribution to the science of government under law.

Although the United States Supreme Court and the House of Lords are often compared, they differ fundamentally in origin and function. The Supreme Court was created in the original compact between the states from which the constitution emerged, and as a result of a rather literal application of the doctrine of the separation of powers it was regarded as distinct from, and in no way subordinate to, the executive or Congress. Further there was implicit in its terms of creation the power to interpret the articles of the American constitution—a power which Chief Justice Marshall freely availed himself, and following him, the Supreme Court has done so ever since. The result has been that in the interpretation of the Articles of the Constitution, there exists a great body of constitutional law, which is judge-made by the Supreme Court, and one important section of which defines the limits of power of the other branches of government, whose activities it not infrequently invalidates. Indeed, the invalidation of much of President Franklin Roosevelt's New Deal legislation in the thirties not only brought the Supreme Court into the middle of the political arena, but for a time threatened to provoke a major constitutional crisis.

There is nothing of this in the history of the House of Lords as a final court of appeal. In England, the Crown is still in theory 'the fount of justice' and the supremacy of its courts can ultimately be traced back to the royal prerogative. When at the end of the seventeenth century the judges ceased to be the king's servants and established their *de facto* independence, they remained subordinate to Parliament in the sense that they had no power to challenge the validity, constitutional or otherwise, of any statute passed by Parliament. This has preserved the judiciary from the fires of controversy which have swept over its American counterpart, and it has compelled it to exercise its influence and its law-making functions in a subtler way. Unlike the Supreme Court it would disclaim any desire consciously to frame social policy.

8

Judicial Failure in the Law of Charities

After considering some aspects of the massive achievement of the Chancery judges in the general field of equity, it will serve as a corrective to study their failure in a related, but distinct branch of the law. The law of charities substantially overlaps the law of trusts but it is not coterminous with it. There are charitable institutions of many kinds, including charitable corporations, and problems frequently arise in relation to gifts to them. Moreover, there exist the Charity Commissioners, who have a concurrent jurisdiction with the courts in charity matters, whilst the Commissioners of Inland Revenue are frequently called upon to determine whether a gift or trust is charitable or not, in order to establish its status in respect of taxation. In both cases, there is an appeal from the decisions of the Commissioners to the Courts. Appeals from the Charity Commissioners are heard by the Court of Appeal; appeals from the Commissioners of Inland Revenue come before a judge of first instance, with the possibility of further appeals. A high proportion of these ultimately reach the House of Lords which, therefore, in modern times, has been called upon to decide questions affecting charities much more frequently than it would otherwise have done.

Charity was a matter of direct concern to the church courts, for prior to the Reformation in England the Church was the most frequent beneficiary. The christian was exhorted to remember the poor and sick as part of his religious duty, and to make provision for them either during life or by his will. This finds clear expression in *The Vision of Piers Plowman*, a fourteenth-century poem in which merchants are urged to obtain remission of sins and a happy death by using their fortunes to benefit charitable purposes, which are described in the following way:

> And therewith repair hospitals, help sick people,
> Mend bad roads,
> Build up bridges that had been broken down, help maidens to marry or make them nuns, find food for prisoners, and poor people, put scholars to school, or to some other craft, help religious orders, and ameliorate rents or taxes.

In the Statute of Charitable Uses of 1601, the preamble describes charitable purposes in strikingly similar language and these objects were evidently traditional. What is particularly interesting is that the intervention of the Reformation had not changed them. What had changed was the place and mode of administration of the law of charities, for after the Reformation the church courts declined rapidly, and although they were called upon from time to time to determine whether a gift in a will was charitable the great bulk of work in charity matters had passed to the Court of Chancery, which administered the law as a body of secular rules. The church court had always administered the law of charity in the context of 'pious uses', to which, in the long run, all charitable gifts could be related. The Court of Chancery has no such overriding test, and its decisions therefore have not been related to any general principle. They therefore lack coherence, and many of them are, from the standpoint of social utility, lacking any kind of unity. The unsatisfactory state of this branch of the law has frequently provoked judicial criticism. To give only one example, Lord Sterndale, MR, said in the Court of Appeal in *Re Tetley*:[1]

> I . . . , am unable to find any principle which will guide one easily, and safely, through the tangle of the cases as to what is and what is not a charitable gift. If it is possible I hope sincerely that at some future time or other a principle will be laid down. The whole subject is in an artificial atmosphere altogether. A large number of gifts are held charitable which would not be

called charitable in the ordinary acceptation of the term, and when one takes gifts which have been held to be charitable, and compares them with gifts which have been held not to be charitable, it is very difficult to see what the principle is on which the distinction rests. I confess I find considerable difficulty in understanding the exact reason why a gift for the benefit of animals and for the prevention of cruelty to animals generally should be a good charitable gift, whilst a gift for philanthropic purposes which, I take it, is for the benefit of mankind generally, should be bad as a charitable gift. The gift for the benefit of animals apparently is held to be valid because it is education of mankind, it being good for mankind that they should be taught not to be cruel, but kind to animals, and one could quite agree with that. But if the benefit of mankind on that particular side makes that a good charitable gift, it is a little difficult to see why any philanthropic purpose to benefit mankind on all sides is a bad one. But it is so; it has been so decided, and therefore the present case is made very difficult, as every case is when there is no governing principle which can be applied.

Lord Sterndale was speaking with feeling, for in the absence of a general principle, the courts, with totally misplaced ingenuity, have resorted to technicalities and over-subtle distinctions, blandly attributing the fault to donors and testators, and their legal advisers, for failing to be sufficiently precise.

Although the Court of Chancery, and now the Supreme Court, has been applying the law of charities for centuries it has not yet evolved a definition of a charitable purpose, and so long as its present attitude continues, it never will. It has already been mentioned that the Statute of Charitable Uses, 1601, took over from the Church its traditional idea of charitable purposes, but without the overriding concept of 'pious uses'. Even in 1601, it was recognised that the list contained in the preamble was not an exhaustive enumeration of charitable purposes. If it had been, the courts' jurisdiction would have been seriously circumscribed. There were at that date some charities of first importance, such as the Church and the colleges of Oxford and Cambridge, which were entirely outside the operation of the statute, the main purpose of which was to introduce new machinery to ensure that funds devoted to charity were properly used. For the Church and the Oxford and Cambridge colleges, there were other means of supervision and control. Since the statute was not all-inclusive, it was possible for the court to regard the list in the preamble as illustrations of charitable purposes, to which they were free to add others. This they did, as they frequently explained, within 'the spirit and intendment' of the statute of 1601.[2] This, however, is nothing more or less than a legal fiction, for many objects which are now regarded as charitable, cannot possibly be regarded as having any connection at all with the objects then set out. Moreover, at the present time, the absurdity has been taken one stage further. The preamble to the Statute of Charitable Uses was re-enacted in the Mortmain and Charitable Uses Act, 1888. This Act was totally repealed by the Charities Act, 1960; so that today the courts are interpreting charitable purposes in accordance with the spirit and intendment of a non-existent statutory provision—a highly interesting jurisprudential enterprise.

Had the courts accepted the opportunity, the absence of a statutory definition could have assisted in the development of the law. Charitable purposes change with changing social conditions. Further, purposes which were once primary objects of charitable bounty, such as hospitals and schools, have become branches of state activity. Presumably no one today would wish to give sums of money by way of charity for the repair of bridges, roads and havens, when he has already contributed heavily by way of taxation. It is, as the Nathan Report on Charities pointed out, one of the characteristics of a healthy society that as often as the state assumes responsibility for an activity which was previously charitable, its public-spirited members seek out new purposes which they can support by charitable bounty. But the readiness of donors to give implies also a readiness on the part of the courts to accept purposes as charitable, provided they are socially beneficial.

While it is quite plain that the list of charitable purposes is progressively expanding, it is quite impossible, as Lord Sterndale pointed out, to discover any principle governing that expansion, and it is at once apparent that a major opportunity for the elaboration of one has been missed. Even at the present time, there is no indication that the search for such a principle is in progress. Instead, there are frequent references to the famous fourfold classification of charitable purposes which is contained in Lord Macnaghten's speech in *Commissioners of Income Tax v Pemsel.*[3] This in turn is founded upon Sir Samuel Romilly's learned argument before Lord Eldon in *Morice v Bishop of Durham*[4] in which he distinguishes 'charity' in the legal sense from liberality or benevolence. Liberality, he says, is a word whose meaning is so extensive that it is impossible to define it, and he follows this by a number of examples, some of which, interestingly, have since been held to be instances of charity in the legal sense. He continues:[5]

> There are four objects, within one of which all charities, to be administered in this Court must fall: First, relief of the indigent in various ways: Money, Provisions, Education, Medical Assistance etc, Secondly, The Advancement of Learning, Thirdly, The Advancement of Religion, and Fourthly, which is the most difficult, the advancement of objects of general public utility.

Eighty-six years later, Lord Macnaghten adopted this classification in *Pemsel's Case.*[6] He says:

> No doubt the popular meaning of the words 'charity' and 'charitable' does not coincide with their legal meaning and no doubt it is easy enough to collect from the books a few decisions which seems to push the doctrine of the Court to the extreme, and to present a conflict between the two meanings in an aspect almost ludicrous. But still it is difficult to find the point of divergence, and no-one as yet, has succeeded in defining the popular meaning of the word 'charity'. . . How far then, it may be asked, does the popular meaning of the word 'charity' correspond with its legal meaning? 'Charity' in its legal sense comprises four principal divisions: trusts for the relief of

poverty; trusts for the advancement of education; trusts for the advancement of religion; and trusts for other purposes beneficial to the community not falling under any of the preceding heads. The trusts last referred to are not the less charitable in the eyes of the law, because incidentally they benefit the rich as well as the poor, as indeed every charity that deserves the name must do either directly or indirectly.

This, it will be seen, is not so much a definition, as a fourfold classification, in which the fourth class is of variable and uncertain content. It would not have been, had it been acceptable that all purposes beneficial to the community were charitable, but this is not the case. Although all the objects within the fourth class must contain the element of public benefit, not all purposes for the public benefit are charitable, and judges have differed widely in their views upon where the line should be drawn.

The decision of the House of Lords in *Pemsel's Case* settled two points: (1) that in English law, 'charitable purposes', as interpreted by courts of equity, means exactly the same when it is being interpreted in revenue cases; and (2) that although in Scottish law, 'charity' has a rather different and broader meaning than it has in English law, when applied to the validity of gifts and trusts, so far as revenue law is concerned, the test to be applied is the English not the Scottish test. So the Scottish judge is under the necessity of discovering the meaning of 'charity' in English law when, for over three centuries, English judges have failed to agree upon it. Cases involving the determination of the question whether the purpose of a gift is charitable or not are among the most difficult in the whole of English law, upon which to make a prediction. Each one of Lord Macnaghten's four heads contains decisions which between themselves, are difficult, if not impossible to reconcile, and in which many judges have adopted a hit or miss attitude with regard to earlier decisions. In *Re Ward*[7] MacKinnon, LJ, who was rarely called upon to sit in charity cases, said:

Thanks to the industry of counsel I have made my first acquaintance with a number of authorities in most of which the manifest intentions of various testators seem to me to have been defeated by their artless use of language. Of the authorities so cited only one seems to me to be of any value, because it is the only one which laid down a principle which I can follow.

As a direct consequence of the absence of principle, too much emphasis in charity decisions is laid upon fine grammatical distinctions, and also upon the meaning of particular words or phrases. Very great learning has been expended, sometimes with disastrous results, upon the meaning of 'and' and 'or'. 'Charity' is used in law in a technical sense, and because words like 'benevolent', 'philanthropic' or 'patriotic' have been held to be vague, and of wider import than 'charitable', they have brought about a failure of the gift when 'charitable' has been linked with one or other of them. It is sometimes said that the word 'and' is conjunctive whilst 'or' is disjunctive, but this is not always true. Where a testator leaves money for 'such charitable and philanthropic purposes as my trustees may select' the courts have held that he intends to benefit purposes which are both charitable and philanthropic. The gift must satisfy two tests, and logic therefore insists that the gift is necessarily charitable. This is because both adjectives are used to qualify the noun 'purposes'. If, however, the testator leaves property to 'such philanthropic purposes and charitable institutions' as his trustees select, two different conceptions are linked by the word 'and', with the result that the object of the testator's bounty goes outside the range of legal charity, and the courts have held that in such cases, the whole gift fails, since neither the trustee nor the court can apportion between charitable and non-charitable objects. This appears to be a little arbitrary. It could have been equally possible to hold that in such a case, the maxim 'Equality is Equity' applies, so that, one half of the gift is applied effectively to charitable purposes, and as to the other half, the gift fails for vagueness.

There are similar difficulties in the construction of the word 'or'. It is used to indicate alternatives, but it can also be used to indicate that the second term is in fact a synonym for the first. In

Chichester Diocesan Trust and Board of Finance v Simpson[8] Lord Simonds commenting on a gift 'for charitable or benevolent purposes' said:

> Since the test of validity depends on the area of choice not being extended beyond the bounds of legal charity a meaning must be given to the words 'or benevolent' which retains them within these bounds. This result, it has been contended, may be reached by giving the word 'or' not its primary disjunctive meaning but a secondary meaning which may perhaps be called exegetical or explanatory. Undoubtedly 'or' is capable of this meaning; so used, it is equivalent to 'alias' or 'otherwise called'. The dictionary examples of this use will generally be found to be topographical as 'Papua or New Guinea' but, my Lords, this use of the word 'or' is only possible if the words or phrases which it joins connote the same thing and are interchangeable the one with the other.

The employment of this grammatical exercise by the House of Lords in *Chichester Diocesan Trust and Board of Finance v Simpson*[9] brought about the greatest miscarriage of justice to be found in the modern Law Reports, the decision exactly corresponding with MacKinnon, LJ's, description in *Re Ward* of many of the charity decisions to which his attention had been directed. Caleb Diplock, who died on 23 March 1938, left a will, dated 5 November 1936, in which he left the whole of his residuary estate to his executors in trust to apply it 'for such charitable institution or institutions or other charitable or benevolent object or objects in England' as they should select. As will be seen, the disposition would have been a perfectly good charitable bequest except for the inclusion of the two words 'or benevolent'. The residuary estate was large and the testator had no near relation. In addition (although this could not be led in evidence) he had already benefited a number of charities, primarily hospitals, in his lifetime. The executors themselves had no doubt of the testator's intentions, and they distributed the estate amongst a large number of charities, many of them hospitals, before the next-of-kin put in a claim.

One may contrast the over-indulgence of the House of Lords in grammatical exercises with the broader outlook of Farwell, J, at first instance.[10] His judgement is not only full of common sense, but it is a model of the way in which the question of construction should be approached in cases such as this. He says:

> Where the Court is being asked to construe a will there are, no doubt, certain rules of construction which it must observe, but when it is a question of determining the meaning of certain words read in conjunction with other words, and of reading the whole will, so as to ascertain the true intention of the testator from the language used, then it is, I think, a fallacy to say that the court is necessarily bound to approach the question of intention blindfolded because of the decision, even a decision of the House of Lords, in some other case of construction where the same words were used in a different connexion; and that such a decision is necessarily binding in every other case where these words appear, although the connecting language as a whole may not be the same. The fact that other courts have come to a particular conclusion as to the meaning of such words as 'benevolent' is, of course, a matter which this court must take into the most careful consideration and if there is a definite authority binding on it that in every case 'charitable or benevolent' must be construed so as to render a gift of this kind invalid, no doubt effect must be given to it. But there is, in my judgment, nothing in any binding authority cited to me which creates that position, the truth of the matter being that the court in each case has to consider the actual language of the testator.

Farwell, J, then pointed out, from the text of the will, that there was very significant evidence (which was entirely disregarded in the House of Lords) that the testator had been thinking only of charitable institutions as the beneficiary of his residue, and he concluded:

> In these circumstances am I constrained by authority to read

the words 'or benevolent' so as to defeat what I am quite clear in my own mind was his intention? I do not think I am. In this case I am construing this particular will and the particular language which the testator has used. He has shown quite clearly a definite intention to benefit charities in the proper sense of the word. His decision was that his very large residue should be distributed by his executors among institutions and hospitals and such like establishments, for their benefit. The reference to these particular institutions shows a good charitable intention, and though it may be by a slip the word 'or' was inserted between 'charitable' and 'benevolent' he did not in my judgment, intend in this particular case so to extend the scope of his bounds as to bring ambit of the power of the executors objects which are not charitable, because the overriding intention of this will is that only these objects are to benefit which are charitable in the strict legal sense.

In the House of Lords, Lord Wright, who delivered the only dissenting judgement, observed: 'I confess I am convinced that the time has come when modern minds imbued with modern ideas should attempt to achieve a clear, workable and comprehensive definition of what is meant to be charitable and its cognate terms, such as benevolent, philanthropic and the like. That is a task for the legislature.' Later, after pointing out the bewildering range and variety of the decisions, and the difficulty or even impossibility of reconciling them, he stresses that they have produced the greatest uncertainty which is reflected in the great mass of litigation. He also points out the striking omission by the courts to apply the 'blue pencil' test to gifts in which the term 'charitable' is used disjunctively with some other form.

Unfortunately, English law now provides no means—apart from legislation—for redressing the disastrous effects of decisions such as that of the House of Lords in this case, and it has recently rejected an opportunity of providing one. The Australian states of Victoria, New South Wales, Western Australia, and also New Zealand, have enactments which provide that where non-charitable purposes are included with charitable purposes a trust which is thereby rendered invalid, the court has power to construe it as if no application of any part of the funds for non-charitable purposes had been directed. In effect, therefore, the words creating the invalidity are omitted, and had there been such a statutory provision in English law the court in *Re Diplock* would have been able to omit the words 'or benevolent', and uphold the disposition as being for charitable purposes only. English appellate judges are familiar with the operation of these Australian and New Zealand statutes through appeals to the Privy Council, a recent example being *Leahy v Attorney General* decided by the Privy Council in 1959.[11] Nevertheless, no similar provision appears in the draft of the Charities Act, 1960, and an amendment to include such a provision during the debate on the bill in the House of Lords was rejected. Instead, a badly drafted act, The Charitable Trusts (Validation) Act, 1954, was passed as a consequence of the report of the Nathan Committee on Charities, validating imperfectly drafted trust provisions in instruments taking effect before 16 December 1952. The Nathan Committee did not recommend a provision unlimited in time, on the grounds that testators, or their legal advisers, ought to know what the law is. Unfortunately the reports contain a large number of decisions showing that testators often do not know, and that (which is still more unfortunate) the fault is by no means always theirs.

Very many examples could be adduced in support of this last observation. It will be sufficient to mention a few cases concerned with the meaning of charity in its application to the advancement of religion. Ever since the spread of toleration in religious matters put an end to the invalidity of bequests for the advancement of the christian religion, or for the advancement of variations to the christian faith, other than that of the Anglican Church, the courts have adopted a remarkably liberal attitude towards gifts under the head of charity. As Sir John Romilly, MR, said in *Thornton v Howe*,[12] the court now makes no distinction between one sort of religion and another or between one sect and another. He pointed out that a trust for a sect whose doctrines were subversive of all morality would still be void, and this limitation might possibly have some relevance today, when a number of strange beliefs and practices might seek to masquerade as religions. Formerly, too, the English law of charities contained the strange doctrine of superstitious uses, of extremely dubious origin[13] and fashioned for the purpose of obstructing the spread of the Roman Catholic faith in England. For practical purposes it ceased to have relevance after the passing of the Roman Catholic Relief Act, 1829, and the Roman Catholic Charities Act, 1832. Its last vestiges, so far as the Roman Catholic religion are concerned, disappeared with the decision of the House of Lords in 1919 in the case of *Bourne v Keane*[14] but in *Gilmour v Coats*[15] the House of Lords held, in 1949, that a gift to a closed order of purely contemplative nuns was not a charitable gift, since it lacked the necessary element of public benefit. This is obviously a decision of considerable social significance. In *Gilmour v Coats*[16] it adversely affected the work of the Roman Catholic Church in England. Ironically, four years later Harman, J, in *Re Warre's Will Trusts*[17] also held invalid a bequest for the establishment of a retreat house for members of the Church of England.

Whatever criticisms may be made in respect of these two decisions they are criticisms of judicial policy, and not of judicial technique. The cases considered next are unsatisfactory on the latter ground.

It was held, as long ago as 1669 in *West v Knight*,[18] that a gift to the parish was good as a charity. This was in line with other decisions upon gifts to localities, such as towns, countries, and other territorial units. When such gifts were made, it was ruled, they must necessarily be applied for charitable purposes within the area. Similar reasoning was applicable in *Re Norton*[19] where the gift was for 'the benefit of the church or parish'. Here it was apparent that the parish to which the gift was applicable was a religious parish. In *Re Garrard*[20] a gift to the vicar and churchwardens of a parish to be applied as they in their discretion should think fit was held good, and Joyce, J, observed:

> It is quite clear, having regard to the authorities, that a gift to the vicar for the time being of a parish is a charitable gift for the benefit of the parish for ecclesiastical purposes. The

churchwardens are the officers of the parish in ecclesiastical matters, so that a mere gift or legacy to the vicar and churchwardens for the time being of a certain parish, without more, is, I do not hesitate to hold, a gift or charitable legacy to them for ecclesiastical purposes in the parish.

On the other hand in *Dunne v Byrne*[21] the words were:

I will and bequeath that the residue of my estate should be handed to the Roman Catholic Archbishop of Brisbane and his successors to be used and expended wholly or in part as such Archbishop may judge most conducive to the good of religion in the diocese.

Lord Macnaghten in delivering the opinion of the Privy Council held that the clause was not identical with 'for religious purposes'. That is to say, the archbishop in expending the fund in ways 'most conducive to the good of religion in the diocese' might possibly include purposes which were not religious. The reasoning is distinctly hard to follow, when one remembers that if the gift had been to the archbishop without more, the court would have held that it must necessarily be used for religious purposes in the diocese.

The consequences of this narrow and illiberal construction have been wholly unfortunate. In the first place it has been frequently followed and its authority was formally imposed upon English law, (1) in *Re Stratton*[22] where the gift was to the vicar and churchwardens of the parish 'for parochial institutions or purposes'. This phrase, said the Court of Appeal, could include purposes which though excellent in themselves were not charitable; and (2) in *Farley v Westminster Bank*[23] by the House of Lords. In this case there was a gift to the vicars and churchwardens of two named churches 'for parish work', and it was held that the phrase might also include non-charitable activities. Lord Atkin, with some lack of humour, observed:

I think that this case is a warning to those persons who desire

> to make wills with a benevolent intention, giving legacies for charitable purposes in the broad sense of the word, that they should make it clear that their objects are within the legal definition of charity, and are certain.

An admonition to the judges in similar terms would not be misplaced, for in addition to this line of decisions *Re Garrard*[24] has also had its supporters, and the law on this topic is at present in a state of confusion. No one seems to have noticed that in every one of the cases in which the clause was held to be too wide, there could be no doubt that even on the widest possible construction the objects were for the benefit of the public or for a section of them—thereby again demonstrating that by no means all gifts for the benefit of the public are charitable in the legal sense.

Even in the terms of logic, the present state of the authorities is uncomprehensible. A gift to the vicar and churchwardens alone is necessarily charitable. So is a gift to the parish, from which it follows that a gift to the vicar and churchwardens of a parish 'for the parish' is good; but if it is to the vicar and churchwardens of a parish 'for parish work', then following *Re Ashton's Estate* it is too wide and invalid. Such distinctions tend to bring the law into discredit and consciousness of this led Jenkins, J, in *Re Eastes*[25] to attempt to sort out the mess. In this case, the gift was again to the vicar and churchwardens of the parish 'for purposes in connection with the said church', and Jenkins, J, preferring *Re Garrard* to *Re Ashton's Estate* held the gift good. In analysing the distinctions which these cases have established Jenkins, J, said: 'It seems to me that there is a limit to the fineness of distinctions which can reasonably be drawn between gifts of this type.' There is, indeed, and the present situation is extremely unsatisfactory. One looks in vain in these verbal exercises by counsel and judiciary for any recognition that every one of these gifts had been intended by the donor to improve the welfare, material or spiritual, of the inhabitants of the parishes or dioceses to which they were given; that in the fullest sense, they are for the benefit of the public, or a section of it.

It is not without interest to notice that although the courts have generally condemned certain words (such as 'benevolent' or 'philanthropic') and phrases (such as 'parish work' or 'for parochial institutions or purposes') as expressions which are either too vague, or as capable of including non-charitable purposes, they apparently regard 'public benefit' as a term to which a precise meaning can be attached, although they studiously avoid saying what it is. Similarly there is apparently some judicial consciousness of a distinction between a member of a public class of the community and a member of a private class, though it seems to be one of those distinctions which are felt rather than one which is capable of definition. A railway porter (an employee of British Rail) is a member of a private class, while a barrister or a solicitor is a member of a public class, so that gifts for the education of railway porters are not charitable, whilst gifts for the education of solicitors or barristers are. One may justifiably ask why this should be so. The 'private' character of a class, we are told, is determined by the fact that the tie between the member is either kinship or contact of employment, and that this concept continues to prevail even when the enterprise in respect of which the employment exists is a national monopoly. It is, at best, a slippery test, and Lord Greene, MR, said in *Re Compton*:[26]

> No definition of what is meant by a section of the public has, so far as I am aware, been laid down, and I certainly do not propose to be the first to make the attempt to define it. In the case of many charitable gifts it is possible to identify the individuals who are to benefit, or who at any given moment constitute the class from which the beneficiaries are to be selected. The circumstance does not, however, deprive the gift of its public character. Thus, if there is a gift to relieve the poor inhabitants of a parish, the class to benefit is readily ascertainable. But they do not enjoy the benefit when they receive it by virtue of their character as individuals, but by virtue of their membership of the specific class. In such a case the common quality which unites the potential beneficiaries into a class is essentially an impersonal one. It is definable by reference to what each has in common with the other, and that is something

into which their state as individuals does not enter.

What this means in practical terms is explained, at least in part, in the speech of Lord Simonds in *Inland Revenue Commissioners v Baddeley*.[27] In discussing whether a trust, otherwise charitable under the fourth head (in Pemsel's Case) is valid if the beneficiaries are limited to the members or potential members of a particular church within a particular area, he says:

> It is, however, in my opinion, particularly important in cases falling within the fourth category to keep firmly in mind the necessity of the element of general public utility and I would not relax this rule. For here is a slippery slope. In the case under appeal the intended beneficiaries are a class within a class, they are those of the inhabitants of a particular area who are members of a particular church: the area is comparatively large and populous and the members may be numerous. But, if this trust is charitable for them, does it cease to be charitable as the area narrows down and the numbers diminish? Suppose the area is confined to a single street and the beneficiaries to those whose creed commands few adherents, or suppose the class is one that is determined not by religious belief but by membership of a particular profession or by pursuit of a particular trade. These were considerations which influenced the House in the recent case of *Oppenheim*.[28] This was a case of an educational trust but I think that they have even greater weight in the case of trusts which by their nominal classification depend for their validity upon general public utility.

Even so there seems to be something distinctly artificial in regarding members of a particular church as a *private* class (presumably linked by contract).

It is not only in the determination of what constitutes a valid charitable trust that decisions in English courts have proved to be inconsistent and unsatisfactory for want of any general principle. They inherited from the ecclesiastical courts the *cy-près* jurisdiction which extended both to original gifts and *cy-près* modification of schemes. Although knowledge of the way in which this was exercised before the Reformation is scanty, it can at least be said that, since the church courts regarded gifts to charity as gifts to 'pious use', made for the benefit of the soul of the donor, and the assurance of felicity in the after-life, there was always the general 'pious' character of the gift to which an appeal could be made in charity cases. In the hands of secular courts, it became established doctrine that there could, in general, be a *cy-près* application of charitable funds only if a general charitable intent had been shown, and the duty of the court in such a case became limited to discovering the next nearest object to that indicated by the donor. Once again, the law on this branch of the law of charities became exceedingly technical, and the jurisdiction became confined within extremely narrow limits. Chapter 9 of the Report of the Nathan Committee[29] discusses the problem in detail, and emphasises that for a century—from 1853 onwards—the Charity Commissioners had unsuccessfully advocated a wider jurisdiction. As the law stood *cy-près* could only be invoked when it was clearly established that the mode specified by the donor could not be carried into effect, and even then, only when a general charitable intent was shown. Impossibility of execution was narrowly construed, and general charitable intent has not always been easy to determine.

Impossibility of execution may be illustrated by the *Weir Hospital Case* in 1910.[30] The testator devised two freehold houses—one in Balham and the other 'The Hawthorns' Clapham—to trustees to be employed as a dispensary or cottage hospital for the inhabitants of Streatham, together with substantial personal property, the income of which (approximately £3,000) should be applied towards the maintenance of these activities. There was a restrictive covenant on 'The Hawthorns' which came to an end in 1907 at which date it was found impracticable (though not impossible) to use the house as it had been intended, that is as a cottage hospital. The trustees consulted the Charity Commissioners, who pointed out that there already existed a general hospital in Battersea, about half a mile from the Streatham boundary. They suggested that the Weir Charity should be administered with this hospital under a joint scheme in which the dispensary was to be continued, and 'The Hawthorns' would be used as a nurses' home for the staff of the hospital, a certain number of beds in which were to be reserved for the benefit of the inhabitants of Streatham. The Court of Appeal set aside this scheme, sharply reminding the Charity Commissioners that their *cy-près* jurisdiction was no wider than that of the court, Cozens-Hardy, MR, remarking rather bleakly that 'there can be no question of *cy-près* until it is clearly established that the directions of the testator cannot be carried into effect'. All three members of the Court of Appeal endorsed the observations of Lord Romilly in *Philpott v St George's Hospital*[31] when he said:

> If the testator has, by his will, pointed out clearly what he intends to be done, and his directions are not contrary to the law, this Court is bound to carry that intention into effect, and has no right and is not at liberty to speculate upon whether it would have been more expedient or beneficial for the community that a different mode of application of the funds in charity should have occurred to the mind of the testator, or that he should have directed some different scheme for carrying his charitable intentions into effect. Accordingly, instances of charities of the most useless description have come before the court, but which it has considered itself bound to carry into effect. But there are other cases where the testator has devoted funds to charity generally, and has not specified any particular charity or application of the funds. In these cases the queen, by her sign-manual, directs the charity to be carried into effect by the Attorney-General, or by the Court, which then has the full power to adopt any scheme which the Attorney-General, after considering the matter fully, should deem expedient. So, also, where there are accretions to a charity, which are not specifically disposed of, the Court, in that case, may, to some extent, act in a similar way. So, also, where a fund is given for a particular object which entirely fails.

An instance of the latter is *Attorney-General v Gibson*[32] where a large property was given for the redemption of christian slaves in Barbary. After the suppression of piracy along the Barbary Coast, there were no longer christian slaves to be redeemed.

The courts have also failed to devise any satisfactory general test for discerning whether a genuine charitable intent has been shown, and the decisions are by no means easy to reconcile.[33] This problem arose in acute form in respect of a number of public appeals, either for funds to build hospitals, in the days when many of these were still voluntary, or in respect of other public objects, for which there were surplus funds after the object had been achieved. Widely differing views were expressed by judges of first instance and also by appellate judges upon the presumed intent of donors at the time when they contributed. A majority of judges, in a majority of cases, inclined to the view that donors intended to benefit a particular charity only, so that when the object failed, wholly or partially, the trustees were placed in the impossible position of being under an obligation to return the contributions, either wholly or in part, to donors who were, in a number of cases, undiscoverable. This particular oddity has now been redressed by section 14 of the Charities Act, 1960, and the *cy-près* doctrine itself has received a broadened application by section 13, although it is not yet clear how the courts will interpret their extended powers.

Whatever may be thought of the administration of the general law of charities by the courts, there has long been a feeling that the courts are inappropriate for the exercise of *cy-près* jurisdiction. The Reports of the Schools Inquiry Commission 1867–8, on which the Endowed Schools Acts were based, stated that all the witnesses who had appeared before them (and they included Vice-Chancellor Wood, Lord Romilly and Lord Selborne) had recommended that the *cy-près* modification of schemes should be taken away from the courts, and should be given to an administrative board or committee. There seems, indeed, no convincing reason why the Charity Commissioners should not exercise it, free from the cramping appellate jurisdiction of the courts. The need for periodic revision of the activities of charities in a rapidly changing social context requires no emphasis, and the courts have shown neither aptitude nor liking for the task of applying the *cy-près* doctrine. The Report of the Schools Inquiry Commission of 1867–8, which has been mentioned above, concluded:[34]

> A court of law is in many respects not the best tribunal for deciding questions of this kind, which are much more often administrative than judicial, rather matters of policy and commonsense than of law. To decide such questions it is absolutely necessary to have large discretionary powers, and, as Lord Westbury remarks, 'the habits of a court of justice unfit them for the large views which should regulate the exercise of such powers'. And, if this is the case in dealing with schemes as they have been hitherto dealt with, *a fortiori* it applies to any reorganisation of trusts over a whole district, which is to treat them in their mutual relations, instead of dealing with them one by one. It would be quite out of the usual course of a court of equity and a matter for which its machinery is unfitted, to consider not only the trust before it, but its relation to all the other trusts over a considerable district. Both the reason of the thing and the weight of evidence applied to concur in pointing to the expediency of removing these questions from the Court of Chancery, and this opinion is confirmed by the adhesion of several of the highest legal authorities.

This opinion was echoed by Lord Davey, when giving evidence before a select committee of the House of Commons in 1894,[35] and it was in conformity with these expressions of opinion from the highest legal authorities that it was decided by Parliament to remove the administration of educational trusts, and particularly the *cy-près* jurisdiction, from the Courts to the Board (now the Department) of Education. It is for this reason surprising that the Charities Act, 1960, preserved to the courts their *cy-près* jurisdiction in charitable trusts generally, and continued the restriction of the activities of the Charity Commissioners in this field. If there is, in the tangled story of the law of charities, one prediction which can be made with confidence, it is that eventually the general *cy-près* jurisdiction must be transferred to the Charity

Commissioners, to the exclusion of the courts, and that there is much to be said for a general transfer of the law of charities to the same administrative body.

9

The Law Merchant and the Common Law

Today, mercantile law is one of the most orderly parts of English law, containing some well-drafted statutes codifying particular branches of it. Outstanding amongst these are the Bills of Exchange Act, 1882 and the Partnership Act, 1890. These acts have worn very well indeed, and they have needed little amendment since they were first passed. Both for the most part codified pre-existing practice, embedded in judicial decisions, and in consequence, the judicial task of construing the statutes has not been difficult. There had been a continuous stream of development, into which the statute has been smoothly fitted—so smoothly, that it is only rarely necessary to refer to an earlier state of things.

Mercantile law is an area in which Common Law judges, with occasional assistance from their colleagues in equity, created a comprehensive body of law, in a manner which the modern judiciary could not imitate, not so much because of judicial timidity, but because it is now settled practice that when a matter of this magnitude is to be considered it is the concern of Parliament acting on the initiative of the executive. In the eighteenth century the opposite view prevailed. Although Parliament was the arena for political combat it was not a suitable place for the consideration of changes in the sphere of private law. This was the province of the courts. Judges such as Hardwicke in the Chancery, and Mansfield in the Common Law courts, were conscious of their role as law makers, and willingly accepted it. So far as mercantile law was concerned, Mansfield brilliantly carried to its logical conclusion a process which had been initiated by Coke, and which had been continued by Lord Chief Justice

Holt at the beginning of the eighteenth century.

Half a century ago, an English practitioner, Mr W. A. Bewes, wrote a little work entitled *The Romance of the Law Merchant*. It was little more than a sketch of a vast process, extending over several thousands years—the transmission of a body of mercantile customs, relating to sale, banking, negotiable instruments, agency, general average, and many other incidents of mercantile law from their birthplace by the banks of the Euphrates and Tigris, not later than 3000 BC to the modern world. Even today, the wealth of contract tablets from Sumeria, Babylonia and other centres of ancient civilisation in Western Asia has attracted the attention of disappointingly few lawyers, and much of the work of translation and criticism has been done by Assyriologists. Yet it is in these tablets that the origin of a large number of the institutions of modern mercantile law are to be found. Mr Bewes, in his sketch, shows how these institutions were transmitted in turn, to the Phoenicians, the Greeks, the Romans, the Arabs, and then to the Italian merchants, through whom they became known to Western Europe. As an illustration of this continuing process, Sir Alexander Cockburn says in *Goodwin v Robarts*:[1]

> Bills of Exchange are known to be of comparatively modern origin, having been first brought into use, so far as is at present known, by the Florentines in the twelfth, and by the Venetians about the thirteenth century. The use of them gradually found its way into France, and still later and but slowly, into England.

Cockburn then points out the significant fact that Richard Malynes, a London merchant, who published his *Lex Mercatoria* in 1622, gives an account of Bills of Exchange as used by the merchants of Amsterdam, Hamburg and other places, and he expressly states that such bills were not used in England. Cockburn points out, however, that promissory notes payable to bearer were certainly known in the reign of Edward IV, and that a statute of Richard II's reign referred to bills of exchange as a means of carrying money out of the realm. The explanation of this apparent contradiction is that when Malynes wrote, the Common Law had not yet taken cognizance of bills of exchange or, indeed, of most other institutions of mercantile law. Cockburn points out that the practice of making bills payable to order, and transferable by endorsement, was taking shape among the merchants of western Europe at the beginning of the seventeenth century. In *Bromwich v Lloyd*[2] Treby, CJ, summarised a lengthy chapter of legal history when he observed:

> Bills of Exchange were originally between foreigners and merchants trading with the English; afterwards, when such bills came to be more frequent, then they were allowed between merchants trading in England, and afterwards between any traders whatsoever, and now between any persons, whether traders or not.

The dominant position held by the merchants of the Italian cities in European trade, until the fall of Constantinople and the discovery of America, made their mercantile practice the models upon which the trade of western Europe was fashioned. At an early date, it became their custom to demand specific privileges in the cities and countries with which they traded. First among these was the right to have commercial disputes decided by a consult in accordance with mercantile custom. Although there were some local variations in these, it would not be inappropriate to regard them as a body of custom which merchants in general recognised as binding. Although from the beginning of the seventeenth century, the system was ceasing to be a feature of European commerce, it was recreated in Asia when the European traders began to establish themselves there.

In describing the courts which, in the Middle Ages, administered the Law Merchant, Holdsworth[3] points out that this law included both the maritime and commercial law of modern codes:

> Both [he says] applied peculiarly to the merchants, who, whether alien or subject, formed in the Middle Ages a class

very distinct from the rest of the community. Both laws grew up in a similar manner from the customary observances of a distinct class. Both laws were administered in either the same or in similar courts, which were distinct from the ordinary courts. Both laws differed from the Common Law, both had in the Middle Ages an international character; and both continued to possess this international character down to modern times.

At a late period, when the customs of the merchants were being incorporated by judicial decisions into the Common Law, they were often described as a *jus gentium.* In 1759, Lord Mansfield (whose knowledge of the origin and development of the Law Merchant was more extensive than that of any other English judge), said: 'The maritime law is not the law of a particular country, but the general law of nations.'[4] He held exactly the same view of the mercantile customs which were applicable in cases where there was no maritime element.

It is one of the major achievements of the Common Law judges that this great body of law became part of the law of England, not by the enactment of a commercial code as was often the case abroad, but by judicial decision. It was only when this had occurred that, in the nineteenth century, important parts of it were codified in statutes such as the Bills of Exchange Act and the Partnership Act. Long before that date, mercantile customs had been made applicable to all transactions irrespective of the status of those who entered into them.

In the Middle Ages, however, the right to have mercantile transactions between merchants whether native or foreign decided by mercantile customs was a highly prized privilege, obtained by royal franchise. So far as the internal trade of the kingdom was concerned, it was an incident of the right to hold a fair with its attendant court, and such a right might be enjoyed by a judicial body or by a corporation and attendant court. In the development of such market courts, applying a law distinct from the local law, England was simply following the common pattern in western Europe from the tenth century onwards, and already by the reign of Henry I a court was an ordinary appurtenance to a fair.[5] Very soon, such courts became commonly known as courts of piepowder, apparently from the dusty feet of the chapmen who frequented the markets, and by the second half of the fifteenth century it was established Common Law doctrine, that in every market or fair there was a court of piepowder, and there are frequent references to their activities in the literature of the seventeenth century, and even later.[6] Nevertheless, their activities had declined greatly by Blackstone's time. At this date, the fairs in respect of which they existed were no longer the great concourses of merchants that they had been in earlier times, and further the Common Law had extended its frontiers to incorporate much of the Law Merchant.

Besides the courts of fairs and boroughs, there were also the courts of the staple. In the Middle Ages, foreign trade was concentrated in certain designated areas, which were termed staple towns, and accordingly the courts of the staple were largely concerned with disputes arising out of the foreign trade. The foreign merchants themselves enjoyed a special status as a result of the grant of privileges by the Crown, and these privileges were jealously watched by their English competitors. The *Carta Mercatoria* of 1303 gave to certain specified alien merchants, in return for customs dues paid to the Crown, exemption from a number of municipal imports, freedom to trade and to live in the cities where they traded. Above all, it gave the right to speedy justice according to the Law Merchant from specially appointed mercantile justices. In the Eyre of London in 1321, for example, the German merchants tenaciously affirmed their privileges, which they had secured by grant from Henry III, and which had been confirmed in 1317 by Edward II. For the elucidation of those liberties they say that they claimed the right to elect for themselves from their own society an Alderman,

> and to present him thus elected to the Mayor and Aldermen of London, and that he shall take an oath before the said Mayor and Aldermen of London to do right and justice to all and each of the Hansa of the Society of the said German merchant, and this same Alderman of the said Society shall hold his

Court in the house which is called the German's Guildhall in the said city for all pleas of covenants, debts and contracts which may chance to be moved between the merchants of the said Hansa and if any one of the said Hansa be impleaded before the Mayor or sheriffs of London in any plea of covenant, debt or personal contract the same Alderman of the Society aforesaid shall claim his court of it and shall obtain it and do justice in it in the aforesaid Hall of the Germans.[7]

Holdsworth points out[8] that the courts of the staple had a very wide jurisdiction in all matters (except matters of freehold or felony) touching the merchants, that the law they applied was the Law Merchant, and that the courts comprised the Mayor and Constables of the town, plus two alien merchants, one of whom came from the northern foreign merchants (ie the merchants of the Hansa) and the other from the merchants of the south (who would normally be Italians). In jury trials affecting alien merchants, there were to be mixed juries, one half English and the other half foreign; finally in cases of difficulty, there could be an appeal to the Chancellor and the Council.

In seaport towns, there were local courts with jurisdiction in maritime cases. Some of these may have existed before the Norman Conquest, and it is certain that many more came into existence shortly afterwards.[9] Later when in the reigns of Edward I and his successors, jurisdiction was conferred on the Lord High Admiral to control maritime conduct in the seas round Britain, and to decide matters both civil and otherwise which arose there, a number of these ancient local maritime courts successfully claimed exemption from his jurisdiction. One extremely important illustration of this was the Cinque Ports, where privileges were unusually extensive and included regular admiralty jurisdiction. At first there were several admirals, and several courts, but by Tudor times there was only a single Court of Admiralty, from which there was an appeal to the Council, which in Tudor times appointed delegates, who were doctors of civil law, to hear appeals. This was appropriate, for there was an important Roman Law element in the maritime law applied by the admiralty. This extended over a very wide field, including all contracts made abroad, bills of exchange (which until Tudor times were mainly drawn abroad), foreign commercial agencies, charter, pirates, insurance, average freight, non-delivery and damage to cargo, and general shipping business.

From very ancient times all these matters had been regulated by codes of maritime practice, which, though probably unofficial in origin, were accepted as binding by the courts of the countries in which they were applied. Of these codes, the oldest was the Rhodian Sea Law, parts of which were incorporated into Justinian's *Digest*.[10] Other codes regulated the conduct of maritime matters in other parts of the western world. For example, the so-called *Laws of Oleron* were incorporated into *The Black Book of the Admiralty* in the reign of Edward II. Oleron at that time was an important port and commercial centre in Bordeaux, with which the connections of English merchants were very close. Later, English maritime practice was influenced by the *Laws of Wisby*. This town was for a time the commercial centre of the trade to the Baltic. The laws, written in Saxon, in part incorporate rules from the *Laws of Oleron* and their influence in the development of English maritime law reflected the growing importance of the Hansa in the history of English commerce.

All these courts, whether mercantile or maritime, were administering bodies of law derived from the international usages of merchants and seamen, and which therefore had an origin and development quite distinct from that of the Common Law. They were, in consequence, regarded with suspicion by the Common Law courts, which attempted to limit their activities, especially those of the Court of Admiralty, against which the Common Law courts issued writs of prohibition from time to time. These were pressed with great persistence during the chief justiceship of Sir Edward Coke, who was anxious to avert any decline in the status of the Common Law courts, and who, at the same time, sought to attract into them the increasingly important commercial business of the country. In so doing, he followed earlier examples, in which the Common Law courts had hampered the local mercantile courts. These, in any event, were already in decline, as the medieval fairs themselves lost their importance.

The Common Law courts assumed jurisdiction over mercantile matters, even over transactions which occurred abroad, by the bold expedient of describing the places at which they occurred as being situated near the parish of St Mary-le-Bow in the ward of Cheap, and by making this impudent fiction untraversable. They accepted the fact that the Common Law, as it then existed, could not be applied to mercantile transactions, and they therefore permitted the relevant mercantile customs to be proved in each case by a jury of merchants. Thus, an entire process of incorporating the great body of mercantile customs into the Common Law, with all the consequential adjustments, was accomplished by way of judicial recognition of mercantile customs, proved in the Common Law courts in actual cases brought before them. It was a continuing process which extended from the sixteenth to the nineteenth century, and which is still in progress. For example, in *Goodwin v Robarts*, a case brought on appeal before the Court of Exchequer Chamber in 1875,[11] the question was whether bearer bonds of a foreign government were negotiable instruments, and a custom that they were was proved before the court of first instance. That great authority on commercial law, Benjamin, argued against their negotiability on the ground that such bonds did not correspond with any of the forms of securities which had previously been held to be negotiable. Cockburn, CJ, in delivering the judgement of the court, examined with great learning the history of negotiable instruments, both before and after their recognition by English Common Law courts, and in reply to Benjamin's argument, he said:

> Having given the fullest consideration to this argument, we are of the opinion that it cannot prevail. It is founded on the view that the law merchant thus referred to is fixed and stereotyped, and incapable of being expanded and enlarged so as to meet the wants and requirements of trade in the varying circumstances of commerce. It is true that the law merchant is sometimes spoken of as a fixed body of law, forming part of the common law, and, as it were, coeval with it. But as a matter of legal

history, this view is altogether incorrect.

The law merchant, thus spoken of with reference to bills of exchange and other negotiable securities, though forming part of the general body of the *lex mercatoria*, is of comparatively recent origin. It is neither more nor less than the usages of merchants and traders, in the different departments of trade, ratified by the decisions of courts of law, which, upon such usages being proved before then, have adopted them as settled law, with a view to the interests of trade and the public convenience, the courts proceeding herein on the well-known principle of law with reference to the different departments of trade. Courts of law in giving effect to the contracts and dealings of the parties, will assume that the latter have dealt with one another on the footing of any custom or usage prevailing generally in the particular department. By this process, what was before usage only, unsanctioned by legal decision, has become engrafted upon, or incorporated into, the Common Law, and may thus be said to form part of it. 'When a general usage has been judicially ascertained and established' says Lord Campbell in *Brandao v Barnett*,[12] 'it becomes a part of the law merchant, which courts of justice are bound to know and recognise.'

By proceeding in this way, the Common Law courts gave the maximum flexibility to the development of this part of English law. They also made this body of law applicable to mercantile transactions, as distinct from the transactions of merchants as a class. The Common Law courts in the seventeenth and eighteenth centuries carried out, unfettered by legislation, a process of development of this branch of the law which was as fundamental for the future of English law as a whole, as the development of equity by the Court of Chancery at the same period. That development is continuing. For example, in *Bechuanaland Exploration Co v London Trading Bank*,[13] a mercantile usage was proved attaching negotiability to the debentures of an English company, the usage being of recent origin. Kennedy, J, in a closely reasoned judgement, surveyed the authorities exhaustively, and decided that it was in many cases necessary to set out the custom as the basis of the right claimed, in respect of which *assumpsit* would then be given.

By the end of the seventeenth century, the allegation in the pleadings that the parties were merchants was dropped, and henceforth mercantile law, though a distinct part of the Common Law, was applied to all mercantile transactions, irrespective of the status of the parties. Until part of it, such as the law of negotiable instruments, was embodied in statutes, it remained a product of judicial reasoning, founded on mercantile customs, and it was for the judges to define the orbit and incidents of the custom which they were incorporating. In Holdsworth's words,

> it was a familiar task upon which the common law judges were engaged when they thus set themselves to construct from a basis of commercial custom new branches of the Common Law. These same judges were in a similar manner constructing our modern law as to copyhold tenure; and their forefathers in the thirteenth century had thus laid the foundations of the common law itself.[14]

In any consideration of the nature and magnitude of the judicial achievement in the sphere of mercantile law, recognition should be given to the enormous importance of the flexibility of the action of *assumpsit*, which was the principal instrument by which the law merchant was incorporated into the Common Law. Thus, Spence says, in his *History of Equity Jurisdiction*:[15]

> It is under the action of *assumpsit* that the modern law merchant has been incorporated into the common law. In the time of Edward III we discover that in the ordinary transactions among merchants, a distinct law prevailed... This was called the *Lex mercatoria*...
>
> As regards the modern law merchant. In the reign of James I, it was held that if a merchant direct a bill of exchange to another merchant, payable to A, or to order, and the other accept it, by the law merchant a promise was to be implied in

the acceptor to pay; afterwards an action of *assumpsit* was given to every endorsee to whom the bill was assigned.

So every endorser who assigned such a bill, was held liable to an *assumpsit* by every subsequent indorsee; and if the merchant to whom it was directed refused it, the director (or drawer) was liable to every indorsee. . .

A comprehensive and rational system of law on the subject of bills of exchange and promissory notes has, with some help from the legislature, been established by the judicial decisions of Lord Mansfield and his colleagues, and their distinguished successors.

Through the medium of the action of *assumpsit*, also under the auspices of Lord Mansfield, the law of Insurance was formed into a system, which has been found to be adaptive to all the exigencies of society; indeed, the whole of the modern system of commercial law may be said to have almost originated with some eminent judge.

Holdsworth, it may be added, regarded the creation of the law of marine insurance as the greatest of all Lord Mansfield's achievements.

Looking back on this expansion of the Common Law by the judges over a period of nearly four centuries, we are conscious of the inevitability of the process. Through the abilities and insight of the judges who participated in it, it produced a body of English commercial law which, though bearing clear traces of its origins in commercial customs which were international in character, developed in a characteristically English fashion. One aspect of this has already been mentioned—viz, the discretion which the judges exercised to limit the orbit of a custom, or even to recognise one, if it appeared to be unreasonable. A second was the remarkably small body of text book literature—especially foreign text book literature—upon which practitioners and judges relied for their knowledge of mercantile customs. The literature was abundant, but it remained largely unread. Once a custom had been recognised, it generated its own body of case-law. In *Goodwin v Robarts*,[16] for example, the history of negotiable instruments is traced through the English decisions. Except for references to their first introduction into England, references to foreign practice are rare. Similarly, Kennedy J's judgement in *Bechuanaland Exploration Co v London Trading Bank*[17] is to some extent complementary, in that it reviews the nineteenth-century decisions, without making a single reference either to text books or to what is happening abroad. Obviously, this is at once a strength and a weakness. Only in the eighteenth century, during the Chief Justiceship of Lord Mansfield, did English law for a short period look outside itself in this area of law.

The distrust of the foreign source is traditional in the practice of English law. In the introduction to his *Mercantile Law*[18] written in 1834, John William Smith wrote:

> It should be observed that the foreign laws and foreign lawyers who have been first mentioned as having influenced the formation of the mercantile law of this country, were never, at any period, recognised by the judges of our courts as being, *per se*, of any authority whatever. Respect for the rules which they lay down may be for the learning and sagacity which they evince, but, when they are obeyed, it is as part of the law and custom of England, declared to be such, either by being usage and tradition or by the decisions of our own courts of justice containing an enlightened adaptation of ancient principle to modern convenience.

The foreign lawyers to whom Smith referred laboured under a double disability. They were foreigners *and* they were text-book writers!

There would have been a very different course of development, had mercantile law in England been developed by courts outside the Common Law. It would have lacked some of the clarity and precision which came from the successive extensions of the action of *assumpsit* to mercantile matters. It might not have been achieved by the end of the seventeenth century. It might not have been regulated in its development by the doctrine of judicial precedent. Looking back we can consider that the possibility of a rival development was remote, but during the sixteenth century it seemed quite feasible, which to some degree explains the vigour of Coke's attacks upon the prerogative courts, and particularly upon the Court of Admiralty in which civilians, rather than common lawyers, practised. The civilians in developing maritime law were in closer contact with their counterparts on the continent than the common lawyers were. Admiralty law has always preserved a certain Roman law element. There were, however, other potential rivals. The charter of a number of trading companies formed at the end of Elizabeth I's reign, and during that of her successor, frequently contained clauses giving the companies power to settle disputes in which a member was involved, and to establish a court in which merchants should be members. For example, the charter of the Company of Merchants Trading to France, dated 12 July 1611, provides:

> And whereas by the said Articles of Treaty concluded at Paris as is aforesaid for this more commodious intercourse of traffic between the subjects of Us and the subjects of the said Most Christian French King it is among other articles comprehended and agreed that for the better provision and remedy of any grievences or difficulties which may arise in commerce or traffic between the subjects of either Kingdom there should be in the City of Roane [ie Rouen] named and appointed by the said Christian King or his successor two merchants of good credit and reputation, which with two English merchants of good credit and reputation, which Us our heirs and successors residing for the time in France shall jointly receive and hear the complaints and controversies of the merchants of Us our heirs and successors that may arise by commerce of traffic either at Roane or any of the ports of that province, and the same forthwith according to equity and right having respect to the said Treaty shall speedily finish and compose, as also that ourself our heirs and successors shall name two English merchants which, likewise taking unto them two French merchants of like quality to be names by the Ambassador of the said French King or his successors residing in England for the time,

shall do the like, which four if they could not agree then by mutual assent between themselves they should choose and take unto them a fifth, the same being in Roane a Frenchman and in London an Englishman, and so by the greater number of these the judgement pass, the like order to be observed in all places of mart and market and cities of France and likewise in the cities of Great Brittayne and Ireland, for the better execution whereof commission with authority to perform the same or either part should be given which Merchants as well English as French so to be chosen on either part should be called *Conservators of Commerce* and *Traffic* and be appointed from year to year and should take oath faithfully to perform the office and authority given and committed into them.[19]

Many other examples of concessions of jurisdiction appear in other charters, the outstanding example being perhaps that which is contained in the Charter of the East India Company granted in 1600.

The community of merchants as a whole were reluctant to relinquish their functions in the administration of mercantile law, even within the realm. Thus, the Commissioners in Bankruptcy, established by Statute in 1571, were a mixed tribunal of lawyers and merchants, and an Act of 1601 established a special court of mixed merchants and lawyers (both common lawyers and civilians) to decide disputes arising out of insurances. The struggle for the supremacy of the Common Law courts in mercantile matters was a prolonged one, and its successful issue owes much to the energetic actions of Coke as Chief Justice. It is in this rather than in his actual contributions to the substantive law, that his primary importance in the history of mercantile law is to be found, for as Marsden, Holdsworth and others have pointed out, the Common Law courts were initially quite unfamiliar with the usages of the mercantile community. Marsden, in his learned analysis of the work of the Court of Admiralty, says of the development of English maritime and commercial law:

It seems to be clear that its earliest growth was in the Admiralty, and not in the common law courts. Before the latter had finally established their supremacy, many points of maritime law that were afterwards painfully elaborated by the common lawyers had for at least a century been familiar to civilians. The liability of the shipowner as carrier for loss by thieves, which was discussed at Westminster in 1671[20] was treated as clear law in the Admiralty as early as 1640, and probably earlier. Similarly general average, insurance, and the negotiability of bills of exchange and bills of lading, all matters of rare occurrence in the Westminster Courts during the Elizabethan and Stuart period, were very frequent in the Admiralty. These were probably treated as decisions of an inferior court that had no jurisdiction. Nevertheless the Common Law, with tardy steps, followed the Admiralty in many of its decisions, perhaps unconsciously, and certainly without acknowledgement. Sir Matthew Hale is careful to point out that the common law courts, as well as the Admiralty, administered the civil law, so far as, by the law of England, the civil law was applicable to maritime cases; and the supremacy of the former being established, the decision as to what was the law of England was necessarily in their hands.[21]

In an article entitled *Bills of Exchange during the Seventeenth Century*,[22] Dr Holden has drawn attention to the major advances made in this branch of mercantile law whilst Holt was Chief Justice of the King's Bench. Holt was a Whig, and a strong supporter of the Whig Revolution of 1688, and he held office from the accession of William and Mary until shortly before his death in 1710. It was, therefore, not surprising that he was conscious of, and responsive to, the needs of a rapidly expanding commerce. The trade with India was already extensive, and in the very year of William's accession, the East Company's ship *Defence* reached Canton. Thereafter the China trade was continuous, and it rapidly rose in importance.

Holt's influence, during over twenty years as Chief Justice, at an unusually important time, is written large in many branches of the law. In *Smith v Brown*[23] he anticipated Lord Mansfield's decision in *Somersett's Case*[24] by holding that 'as soon as a negro slave comes into England he is free', Holt's beneficial influence upon the conduct of political trials and the law of evidence is part of constitutional history, and every lawyer is familiar with his judgement in *Coggs v Bernard*[25] in which he elaborately set out the law of bailments in terms derived from Roman law, attempting to introduce in this way the Roman law conceptions of the standards of care—an attempt which, in this instance, was unsuccessful. But in the wider sphere of mercantile transactions, his influence has been more enduring. It is not necessary to speak of his work in the extravagant terms used by Campbell[26] but his general conclusion upon the permanent importance of Holt's work, especially in the field of negotiable instruments, is sound. It is echoed by Holdsworth, and has been exemplified by Dr Holden in his *History of Negotiable Instruments in English Law.* Holdsworth emphasises that, although Holt cited, not only Justinian's *Institutes* but also the commentaries of Vinnius, he had no deep learning in Roman law. He was essentially a common lawyer, who knew both his Bracton and the Year Books. Above all, he was aware of the need for the Common Law to take account of the needs of contemporary commerce. His links with the City were close, and it was therefore natural for him to depend upon the evidence of the merchants in the elaboration of principles to mould their usages into a coherent body of law. In *Mutford v Walcot*[27] he said that in an earlier case he had had all the eminent merchants in London with him at his chambers at Serjeant's Inn in the long vacation about two years before. This was not an isolated instance of the close connection between the Chief Justice and the mercantile community. It perpetuated, in a new and less formal way, the participation of the merchants in the expansion of the Common Law.

One of Holt's decisions, which might seem in some respects to be at variance with their general tendency, was that of *Clerke v Martin*[28] in which he held that promissory notes were not negotiable. A number of subsequent judges, and many legal writers, have condemned this decision as an obstruction to commerce. Dr Holden, however, has considered it in detail, and has reached the conclusion that earlier decisions bound (or at any rate, very strongly influenced) Holt against a contrary decision, and that, if the writing on bills of exchange and promissory notes is adequately considered, there were good reasons why promissory notes should at this date be treated in this way. The decision was quickly followed by the Promissory Notes Act, 1704, which made such notes both transferable and negotiable. It was high time for such a step to be taken, as the importance of negotiable instruments grew year by year, side by side with growth of commerce, and new forms of them (for example, bankers' notes and Exchequer bills) were already in common use.

The judges of the first half of the eighteenth century continued the work which Holt had initiated, combining caution and an increasing familiarity with mercantile practice. Holt had given this body of law a characteristically English shape. He was a common lawyer to his finger-tips, and his receptiveness to commercial practice did not lead him to a comparative study of the law which he was shaping. This task was reserved for Lord Mansfield, who was Chief Justice from 1756 until 1788, a period during which the commercial predominance of England was established from China to the Caribbean and the North American continent. Each judge was admirably fitted to respond to the needs of the age in which he lived, and Holdsworth has acutely expressed the difference between them.[29] He points out that Holt's legal conservatism, or the strength of his Common Law background, caused him to proceed cautiously, and set limits for the changes which he introduced; but, from another point of view, this had important and valuable consequences. If, says Holdsworth, Holt had been more familiar with other systems of law, he might have been tempted to borrow largely from them with the result that commercial law would have become a separate body of law. As it was, the developments for which he was responsible were made an integral part of the Common Law. Holt made good progress in the settlement of the domain on Common Law principles. No doubt to complete its settlement the cosmopolitan learning of a jurist like Mansfield was essential. But the fact that a common lawyer like Holt had begun that settlement, made it easier for the Common Law at a later date to assimilate intelligently the foreign ideas which were necessary for its completion.

It is not an easy task to attempt to assess the contribution of John Murray, Lord Mansfield, to English law. The names of Hardwicke and Mansfield span five decades of the eighteenth century. Hardwicke was appointed Chancellor in 1737 and Mansfield retired in 1788. The work of each was of the very first importance, and has proved enduring. What Hardwicke did for equity, Mansfield did for the Common Law. Mansfield had been Solicitor-General for eleven years during Hardwicke's Chancellorship—one of the longest tenures of that unspectacular office, although for much of it, he had almost completely replaced the Attorney-General in the councils of the government. The younger man had therefore full opportunity to observe the great Lord Chancellor's work at close quarters, and, in his appointment as Chief Justice, in taking leave of Lincoln's Inn, preparatory to entering Serjeant's Inn, he paid an eloquent tribute to Lord Hardwicke in these words:

> If I have had, in any measure, success in my profession it is owing to the great man who has presided in our highest courts of judicature the whole time I attended the bar. It was impossible to attend him, to sit under him every day, without catching some beams from his light. The disciples of Socrates, whom I will take the liberty to call the great lawyer of antiquity, since the first principles of all law are derived from his philosophy, owe their reputation to them having been the reporters of the sayings of their master. If we can arrogate nothing to ourselves, we can boast the school we were brought up in, the scholar may glory in his master, and we may challenge past ages to show us his equal.
>
> My Lord Bacon had the same extent of thought, and the same strength of language and expression; but his life had a stain.
>
> My Lord Clarendon had the same ability and the same zest for the constitution of his country: but the civil war prevented his laying deep the foundations of law, and the avocation of

politics interrupted the business of the Chancellor.

My Lord Somers came the nearer to his character; but his time was short, and envy and faction sullied the lustre of his glory.

It is the peculiar felicity of the great man I am speaking of, to have prevailed very near twenty years, and to have shone with a splendour that has risen superior to faction and that has subdued envy.

Even before his appointment to the bench, Mansfield had given clear intimation, not only of the greatness of his intellect, but of his attention to commerce. In 1744, in *Omichnund v Baker*[30] he had argued that a Hindu should be sworn as a witness according to the forms of the Hindu religion. On this, the philosopher Burke wrote:

The sentiments of Murray, the Solicitor-General, are of no small weight in themselves, and they are authority by being judicially adopted. His ideas go to the growing amelioration of the law by making its liberality keep pace with the demands of justice and the actual concerns of the world—not restricting the infinitely diversified occasions of men, and the rule of natural justice, within artificial circumscriptions, but conforming our jurisprudence to the growth of our commerce and of our empire. This enlargement of our concerns he appears in the year 1744, almost to have foreseen; and he lived to behold it.

For thirty years Mansfield dominated the Common Law courts as no other Chief Justice has done, and his aim was to re-interpret the Common Law in the light of natural law principles and his knowledge of other legal systems. In this enterprise, he necessarily encountered opposition, he provoked much hostile criticism, and his judicial colleagues and successors did not invariably share his outlook. In 1770 Junius launched a frontal attack upon Mansfield's administration of justice:

In contempt or ignorance of the common law of England [he

said] you have made it your study to introduce into the court where you preside measures of jurisprudence unknown to Englishmen. The Roman Code, the law of nations, and the opinion of foreign civilians, are your perpetual theme; but who-ever heard you mention *Magna Carta* or the *Bill of Rights* with approbation or respect? By such treacherous arts the noble simplicity and free spirit of our Saxon laws were first corrupted. The Norman Conquest was not complete until Norman lawyers had introduced their laws and reduced slavery to a system. Instead of these certain positive rules by which the judgements of a court of law should invariably be determined, you have fondly introduced your own unsettled notions of equity and substantial justice. Decisions given upon such principles do not alarm the public so much as they ought, because the consequences and tendency of each particular instance is not observed or regarded. In the meantime the practice gains ground; the Court of King's Bench becomes a court of equity; and the judge, instead of consulting the law of the land, refers only to the wisdom of the court and the purity of his own conscience.

It is a little unexpected to find Junius among the Common Law diehards, but there is no doubt that he was expressing an alarm shared by many common lawyers, intensified by recollections that Mansfield was, after all, a Scot. This point was expressly made against him by Lord Redesdale, when Lord Chancellor of Ireland, in *French v Woolston.*[31] Such criticisms were examples of judicial pettiness which reflected little credit upon those who uttered them, for it is not possible to put into short compass a final assessment of the extent to which English law benefited from Lord Mansfield's long tenure of the Chief Justiceship, and his actual achievements were based upon a consistent philosophy, allied with remarkable insight. For example, in *Mostyn v Fabrigas*[32] he established the great principle that the subject of a British colony has a right of redress in a British court against the government for a wrong. Fabrigas was an inhabitant of Minorca, which was a British colony from 1714 to 1759. Lord Mansfield's judgement opens with words which go to the root of the matter. He says:

> It is impossible there ever should exist a doubt but that a subject born in Minorca has as good a right to appeal to the King's courts of justice at Westminster as one who was born within the sound of Bow-Bells; and the objection made in this case, of its not being stated on the record that the plaintiff was born since the Peace of Utrecht, by which Minorca was ceded to this country, is untriable for from the moment of the cession all the inhabitants of the island were under the allegiance, and were entitled to the protection of the British Crown.

Mansfield's lively appreciation of the great international changes which were in progress was derived, partly from his close association with the leading English statesman of his day, but more from his close associations with the mercantile community. Campbell records:

> He likewise did much for the improvement of commercial law in this country by rearing a body of special jurymen at Guildhall, who were generally returned on all commercial cases to be tried there. He was on terms of the most familiar intercourse with them; not only conversing freely with them in court, but inviting them to dine with him. From these he learned the usages of trade, and in return he took great pains in explaining to them the principles of jurisprudence by which they were to be guided. Several of these gentlemen survived when I began to attend Guildhall as a student, and were designated and honoured as 'Lord Mansfield's jurymen'. One always wore a cocked hat, and had almost as much authority as the Lord Chief Justice himself.[33]

One may regret that this character never attracted the attention of Charles Lamb, for Mr Vaux would have made a perfect subject for one of his essays.

One very specialised field of mercantile and maritime law, that of marine insurance, merits special mention, for the attention which Lord Mansfield paid to it. In the introduction to his work on *Marine Insurance*, Park mentions that from the reign of Elizabeth I until 1756 there were only sixty reported decisions on marine insurance, and most of these were so briefly reported as to be almost valueless. Lord Mansfield set himself the task of establishing this branch of law on sound principles, and in doing so, he made extensive use of foreign mercantile usage and commercial codes, and he trained a body of special jurors to try marine insurance cases. His decisions were supported by an exposition of the principles underlying this branch of commercial law, which long remained of first importance in its development.

The contact between the mercantile community and the courts, initiated by Lord Mansfield, has always remained close. In 1810 Lord Ellenborough, in *Livie v Janson*,[34] decided, in accordance with maritime practice that if a ship was damaged in consequence of an insured risk, and subsequently became a total loss through circumstances in respect of which no marine insurance had been taken out, the owners could not recover on the policy in respect of deterioration. The rule at first sight appears a hard one, but as Lord Ellenborough put it: 'If the property, whether damaged or undamaged, would have been equally taken away from him, and the whole loss would have fallen upon him had the property been ever so entire, how can he be said to have been injured by its having been antecedently damaged?'

The rule was discussed and applied by a succession of nineteenth-century cases, and was finally confirmed by the House of Lords in *British & Foreign Insurance Co Ltd v Wilson Shipping Co Ltd* in 1920.[35] After reviewing the development of the rule (which was unaffected by the Marine Insurance Act, 1906) Lord Birkenhead, LC, said:

> The true rule is capable of statement in the following proposition. When a vessel, insured against perils of the sea, is damaged by one of the risks covered by the policy and before the damage is repaired, she is lost, during the currency of the policy, by a risk which is not covered by the policy, then the insurer is not liable for such un-repaired damage. The rule so

stated embodies the principle upon which underwriters and merchants have based their practice in such matters for upwards of a century, and, even if this House were of opinion that the rule did not state the law correctly, it would be a matter of grave consideration whether such a rule which has been observed for so long, which has been expressly or impliedly incorporated in so many contracts and has profoundly influenced the course of dealing between merchants, should be reversed at this period of its history. In my opinion the question does not arise.

Of Mansfield's work, the ablest of his judicial contemporaries, Mr Justice Buller, said in *Lickbarrow v Mason*:[36]

Before that period we find that, in courts of law, all evidences in mercantile cases were thrown together; they were left generally to a jury, and they produced no established principle. From that time, we all know the great study has been to find out some certain general principles, which shall be known to all mankind, not only to rule the particular case then under consideration, but to serve as a guide for the future. Most of us have heard those principles stated, reasoned upon, enlarged and explained, till we have been lost in admiration at the strength and stretch of the human understanding. And I should be very sorry to find myself under the necessity of differing from any case which has been decided by Lord Mansfield, who may be truly said to be the founder of the commercial law of this country.

Mansfield's outlook on law was more comprehensive than that of any other English judge. Whilst his Year Book learning was not as profound as that of Coke or Holt, it was extensive, as was his knowledge of the reports as they existed in his day. Not infrequently his judgements contain adverse comments upon the quality of some of them, but as Holdsworth suggests,[37] these criticisms may in part be due to the fact that they may contain matter which he was not prepared to accept. If this is the case, it emphasises Lord Mansfield's function as a conscious law-maker. No judge today, however valorous, could act in so downright a fashion. Mansfield's outlook on law was always influenced by his consciousness of the historical development of legal rules, and his reading was exceptionally wide. It included French and Dutch writings on commercial and maritime law, and also upon international law, whilst there is abundant evidence in his decisions of his familiarity with both Roman and canon law. As a Scotsman, though educated in England, he was naturally familiar with Scottish law. In all he did as chief justice, he showed himself a jurist of the first rank. In the field of international law, when Attorney-General, he prepared a reply to the seizure by Frederick the Great of Prussia, of the money due to private British subjects, as a reply to the exercise by British ships in time of war of their right to arrest Prussian ships suspected of carrying contraband. This has always been regarded as a masterpiece, and it is evidence of his extensive learning and eminence in a field remote from the Common Law. It is also evidence of one of Mansfield's outstanding characteristics, to which he referred in the trial of John Wilkes,[38] where he says:

> I never give a judicial opinion upon any point, until I think I am master of every material argument and authority related to it.

Mansfield was probably the most important, as well as the ablest, judicial law-maker to sit in an English court. There is this much to be said in support of the criticism of Junius—Mansfield wished to broaden the Common Law, by infusing new rules into it. This naturally produced opposition, both from contemporaries and from successors—particularly from Kenyon and Eldon, and Holdsworth has summed up his work in the following way:

> He exercised a profound influence upon many makers of the Common Law by his judgement in a large number of cases in which his views were accepted; . . . in some of the cases in which his views were rejected, they have had an indirect in-

fluence upon the development of the law; . . . and in other cases in which they were rejected, they show an astonishing foresight of the course taken by the legislative reforms of the succeeding centuries.

Even amongst so much achievement, his development of commercial and maritime law stands pre-eminent. He was always conscious that both of these branches of law were applicable, not in Great Britain alone but universally, and that the principles underlying it should be clear, coherent, and acceptable to the merchants who were primarily concerned with it. It was here, therefore, that Mansfield's erudition in continental legal literature and his philosophic outlook on law as a rational system was of first importance. Equally important was his consciousness that in a world of rapidly developing commerce, although the general principles might be clear and settled, the actual usages of the merchants were constantly expanding, and that the function of the judge was to establish a balance between certainty and change. It was in this that Mansfield excelled, and it was the special good fortune of English law that it should have attracted an intellect so dominating as that of Mansfield's at one of the greatest periods in England's mercantile history.

10

Public and Private International Law

A perusal of Lord Mansfield's judgements will show that he was at all times aware that mercantile and maritime law were applicable in an international context, and in incorporating their usages so extensively, he was extending the frontiers of the Common Law. At the same time, he was impressing these usages with an English quality by confining them within the doctrine of judicial precedent. In both these areas, however, what was fashioned by Mansfield and his successor was a complete system. The treatment of public international law by the common lawyers has been rather different. They have been troubled by the nature of international law (and also by the evidence from which its existence can be presumed). So far as the first question is concerned, international law is a law which exists between states, and therefore, it is often not a matter for determination by the courts at all. But the acts between states often have a direct impact upon individual citizens, and when they do, it is necessary for courts to take cognizance of them. In such circumstances, it is now the invariable practice of English courts to accept the ruling of the executive on the policy decisions of the state. This principle was emphatically affirmed by Lord Atkin in the House of Lords in *Republic of Spain v Arantzazu Mendi*,[1] one of the many cases arising out of the Spanish Civil War, which came before the English courts. The ship was in an English port, and was claimed by both the Republican Government of Spain and the Nationalist Government. The main question arising for decision was whether the National Government enjoyed the status of a foreign sovereign state, and on this point Lord Atkin said:

Bucknill, J, took the correct course of directing a letter dated May 25, 1938, to be written by the Admiralty Registrar to the Secretary of State for Foreign Affairs, asking whether the Nationalist Government of Spain is recognised by His Majesty's Government as a foreign Sovereign State. I pause here to say that not only is it the correct procedure but that it is the only procedure by which the Court can inform itself of the material fact whether the party sought to be impleaded, or whose property is going to be affected, is a foreign Sovereign State. This I think is made clear by the judgment in this House in *Duff Development Co v Kelantan (Government) and Attorney-General.*[2] With great respect I do not accept the opinion implied in the speech of Lord Sumner in that case that recourse to His Majesty's Government is only one way in which the Judge can ascertain the relevant fact. The reason is, I think, obvious. Our Sovereign has to decide whom he will recognise as a fellow Sovereign in the family of States, and the relations of the foreign state with ours in the matter of State immunity must flow from that decision alone.

In the case with which Lord Atkin was dealing, the question to be settled determined the immunity or otherwise of one of the parties to it. The rule that the courts accept the pronouncement of the executive on such matters as final, can, however, press very heavily upon the private citizen, as was shown in striking fashion by the decision of Sir Jocelyn Simon, President of the Probate, Divorce and Admiralty Division, in *Adams v Adams.*[3] An Englishwoman obtained a final decree of divorce from her Rhodesian husband in Rhodesia, but was declared by the president unable to marry in England, because English courts do not recognise such a decree, which was pronounced by a judge appointed in November 1968. Apparently there does not exist for judges any convenient doctrine similar to that of apostolic succession, which bolstered the position of English bishops, and regularised their activities, after the separation from Rome in the sixteenth century. Once again the English court accepted in full the certification by the foreign secretary that Southern Rhodesia was not recognised as a separate state, so that a judge appointed since the Unilateral Declaration of Independence was acting without authority which an English court would recognise. This anomalous state of affairs was ended by the Southern Rhodesia (Marriages, Matrimonial Causes and Adoptions) Order, 1972. There are, of course, other possibilities, discussions of which produced a clear division of opinion, a voluminous citation of authority and some dissent in the House of Lords in *Madzimbamuto v Lardner-Burke* in the previous year.[4] Lord Pearce's speech in that case, setting out the views of the dissenting minority, is notable for its able discussion, not only of text-book literature, but also of the decisions of American courts following the Civil War, on acts done by Confederate courts and other public authorities during the period of secession. A wide class of these was given retrospective validity after the war ended, on the ground of necessity. Thus, in *Texas v White*,[5] the American supreme court said, of acts done by the State of Texas during the period of secession:

> It is not necessary to attempt any exact definitions, within which the acts of such a State government must be treated as valid, or invalid. It may be said, perhaps with sufficient accuracy, that acts necessary to peace and good order among citizens, such for example, as acts sanctioning and protecting marriage and the domestic relations, governing the course of descents, regulating the conveyance and transfer of property, real and personal, and providing remedies for injuries to person and estate, and other similar acts, which would be valid if emanating from a lawful government, must be regarded in general as valid, when proceeding from an actual, though unlawful government; and that acts in furtherance or support of rebellion against the United States, or intended to defeat the just rights of citizens, and the acts of like nature, are in general to be regarded as invalid and void.

Lord Pearce also pointed out that Lord Mansfield had recognised this doctrine of necessity in *R v Stratton*[6] in 1779, a case in which the Governor of Madras ordered the arrest of certain persons under the plea of necessity. Lord Mansfield expressly recognised the plea of necessity, and having defined it, left it to the jury to decide whether the case before him came within it. In *Adams v Adams*, however, the president preferred to leave the question how far recognition should be accorded to executive, judicial or legislative acts in Rhodesia to Parliament—a clear abdication by the judiciary, and an implied denial of the existence of any doctrine of necessity.

If one turns to the evidence of the existence of a rule of international law before English courts, the fullest discussion of this is probably to be found in judgements of Cockburn, LCJ, and Lord Coleridge, CJ, in *R v Keyn*.[7] In that case, Keyn had been indicted at the Central Criminal Court for the manslaughter of Young, a passenger in the British steamship *Strathclyde*, en route from London to Bombay. When off Dover, the *Strathclyde* was run into by the *Franconia*, a German vessel, and sunk with some loss of life among the passengers and crew of the *Strathclyde*, amongst whom was Young. The collision occurred approximately two miles from Dover, and when the *Franconia* reached an English port, her captain, Keyn, was arrested, tried and found guilty of manslaughter. The Central Criminal Court reserved for the consideration of the Court for Crown Cases Reserved the question whether an English court had jurisdiction, there being at this date no statute conferring such jurisdiction in territorial waters. The court decided, by a majority of seven to six, that English law did not confer such jurisdiction, and when it was urged that international law conferred such a right on every state, the majority view was that there was no certainty in the writings of international lawyers upon its extent or nature. Cockburn, CJ, who delivered the leading judgement for the majority, pointed out that some writers contended for a three-mile limit, others for the range of cannon-shot. Some claimed an absolute dominion over territorial waters, others a dominion subject to a right of passage by the ships of other nations. Others again claimed dominion but asserted a jurisdiction for a number of specific purposes, eg police, revenue, or fishery protection. Cockburn added that even if the opinion of text-book writers (of many nations) had been unanimous instead of divergent, their opinions could not make law apart from the assent of civilised nations within the orbit of international law. Further, even if such an assent could have been proved, it was very doubtful whether the principle, embodying new law, could be applied by English courts without an Act of Parliament. Cockburn pointed out, in addition, that the right of jurisdiction could have been conferred by treaty or usage, but no treaty embodied it in respect of passing vessels, although some had dealt with the enforcement of neutrality in time of war, and others with the regulation of fishing, and there was certainly no usage which covered general jurisdiction in territorial waters.

Lord Coleridge's judgement, which expressed the substance of the minority view, stands in sharp contrast with this restrictive opinion. He pointed out that all the writers on international law declared that some portion of waters adjacent to the coasts of a country were regarded as territorial waters, over which the courts of that country exercised jurisdiction. Although in the realm of international law there was no law-giver, and no tribunal with a general compulsory jurisdiction, there existed nevertheless a body of usages which civilised states had agreed to observe in their dealings with one another. Whether a particular usage had been accepted was really a matter of evidence. Treaties and acts of states were among such evidence, and so was the general opinion of international jurists; and on points which arise in English courts, and to which such usages might be applicable, the English courts consider the usages, and where they were proved to exist, applied them as part of English law. This, one ventures to suggest, is a judgement in the tradition of Lord Mansfield.

It will be noticed that in discussing the materials from which English courts derive rules of international law applicable in English courts, the English judges consistently minimise the authority of text-writers, and stress the importance of usage. This is not only in line with the general development of English law, it also forms the basis for the positivist as contrasted with the naturalist approach to international law, which the same judges have universally adopted. Incidentally, the positivist approach, by emphasising consent of states and usage as the determining factors, leave free scope to the executive in policy making, and the same attitude thus avoids the possibility of conflicts between executive and judiciary, such as Lord Atkin feared. It is not accidental that the American Supreme Court, in the cases which followed the Civil War, which have already been mentioned, adopted a rather bolder attitude; for the position of the American Supreme Court is guaranteed by the Constitution. Possibly the clearest statement of the position of the English judiciary is to be found in Lord Alverstone's judgement (with which his two colleagues concurred) in *West Rand Gold Mining Co v The King.*[8] The question in that case was the extent of the liability for pre-existing obligations incurred by Great Britain on the annexation of the Boer Republics at the end of the Boer War. For the suppliants it was argued by Lord Robert Cecil that although a conquering state, in annexing, could make any terms it liked as to taking over the obligations of the state annexed, if nothing was said about a particular obligation, the conquering state was liable on it, and its courts must enforce it. Lord Alverstone in his judgement pointed out that Lord Robert Cecil's argument involved three propositions:

1 That in international law, the sovereign of a conquering state was liable for the obligations of the conquered state.
2 That international law was part of the law of England.
3 That rights and obligations which were binding on the conquered state must be protected and enforced by the courts of the conquering state.

In support of the first proposition, Lord Robert cited passages from numerous writers on international law, both English and foreign, but Lord Alverstone did not hesitate to circumscribe their authority narrowly. He said:

> In regard to this class of authority it is important to remember certain necessary limitations on its value. There is an essential difference, as to certainty and definitions, between municipal law and a system or body of rules in regard to international

conduct, which, so far as it exists at all (and its existence is assumed by the phrase 'International law'), rests upon a consensus of civilised states, not expressed in any code or pact, not possessing, in case of dispute any authorised or authoritative interpreter, and capable, indeed, of proof, in the absence of some express international agreement, only by evidence of usage to be obtained from the action of nations in similar cases in the course of their history. It is obvious that in respect of many questions that may arise, there will be room for difference of opinion as to whether such a consensus could be shown to exist. Perhaps it is in regard to the extraterritorial privileges of ambassadors, and in regard to the existence of limits as to territorial waters, that it is least open to doubt or question.

The views expressed by learned writers on international law have done in the past, and will do in the future, valuable service in helping to create the opinion by which the range of the consensus of civilised nations is enlarged. But in many instances their pronouncements must be regarded rather as the embodiments of their views as to what ought to be, from an ethical standpoint, the conduct of nations *inter se*, than the enumeration of a rule or practice so universally approved or assented to as to be fairly termed, even in the qualified sense in which that word can be understood in reference to the relations between independent political communities, 'law'. The reference which these writers not infrequently make to stipulations in particular treaties as acceptable evidence of international law is as little convincing as the attempt, not unknown to our courts, to establish a trade custom which is binding without being stated, by adducing evidence of express stipulations to be found in a number of particular contracts.

In spite of this low assessment of the work of text-book writers, it may be mentioned that only five years before the *West Rand Mining Company* case, Mathew, J, had decided a case exclusively on the statements of international law to be found in text books. In *Macartney v Garbutt and Others*,[9] the plaintiff was a British subject employed as English secretary at the Chinese Embassy in London, and the question was whether he was immune from the jurisdiction of the English courts in virtue of his diplomatic status, Mathew, J, considered the treatment of this problem by Bynkershoek, Wharton, Calvo, and Phillimore, and decided that Macartney was entitled to the exemption which he claimed.

In conformity with Lord Alverstone's opinion of the text-writers it was possible for him, in discussing international law, to state without equivocation the proposition that English courts would only accept as binding rules to which Great Britain, along with other states, had assented, and which could be clearly proved —thus leaving a very considerable latitude to accept or reject. He says:

> Any doctrine so invoked must be one really accepted as binding between nations, and the international law sought to be applied must, like anything else, be proved by satisfactory evidence, which must show either that the particular proposition put forward has been recognised and acted upon by our own country, or that it is of such a nature, and has been so widely and generally accepted, that it can hardly be supposed that any civilised state would repudiate it. The mere opinions of jurists, however eminent or learned, that it ought to be so recognised are not in themselves sufficient. They must have received the express sanction of international law by their frequent practical recognition in dealings between various nations. We adopt the language used by Lord Russell of Killowen in his address at Saratoga in 1896, on the subject of international law and arbitration: 'What then is international law? I know no better definition of it than that it is the sum of the rules or usages which civilised states have agreed shall be binding upon them in their dealings with one another.' In our judgment, the second proposition for which Lord Robert Cecil contended in his argument before us ought to be treated as correct only if the term 'International Law' is understood in the sense, and subject to the limitations of application, which we have explained. The authorities which he cited in support of the proposition are entirely in accord with and, indeed, will illustrate

our judgment upon this branch of the arguments advanced on behalf of the suppliants.

The authorities which Lord Robert Cecil cited, and which Lord Alverstone mentioned, are *Barbuit's Case*, decided in 1737;[10] *Triquet v Bath*,[11] in 1764, and *Heathfield v Chillon*,[12] decided in 1767. Significantly, all three are connected with Lord Mansfield. He was counsel in the first, and he decided the other two. In all of them, it is asserted that international law is part of the law of England—a broad proposition, characteristic of Lord Mansfield, but in the *West Rand* case, Lord Alverstone greatly restricts the application of principle, by saying:

> The expressions used by Lord Mansfield when dealing with the particular and recognised rule of international law on this subject [ie the privileges of ambassadors], that the law of nations forms part of the law of England, ought not to be construed so as to include as part of the law of England opinions of text-writers upon a question as to which there is no evidence that Great Britain has ever assented, and *a fortiori* if they are contrary to the principles of her laws as declared by her courts.

There is no evidence that Lord Mansfield would have accepted the first part of this dogmatic assertion; and those who investigate this problem in the English decisions will notice the curious fact that, although the English judges occasionally refer to American decisions, they seem to be oblivious of the decisions of municipal courts of other states, as possible evidence of what international law might be.

There exists, nevertheless, one area of international law in which English judges have adopted a broader outlook. This is in the law of prize, which has been continuously administered by Admiralty judges, and which was a monopoly of the civilians until the middle of the nineteenth century. The list of English judges who have sat in matters of prize is a long and distinguished one, but the name of Lord Stowell is nevertheless pre-eminent.

Holdsworth says: 'It was under his guidance that the civilians made, in the creation of the system of prize law, one of their largest contributions to English law, and a very considerable contribution to the jurisprudence of the world.'[13]

William Scott, the elder brother of Lord Eldon, was born on 8 October 1745, and the careers of these gifted brothers showed remarkable parallels. When William was Advocate-General, John Scott was Solicitor-General. William became Judge of Admiralty in 1798, less than a year before John became Chief Justice of the Common Pleas; and William resigned the Judge of the Court of Admiralty the year after John's resignation of the Chancellorship. William Scott, Lord Stowell, was therefore Judge of the Court of Admiralty throughout the long years of the struggle with Napoleon, when the Court of Admiralty was busier in prize matters than it had ever been before. Oddly, through much of the period, he was a member of the House of Commons—from 1790 until 1821, when he was raised to the peerage. He resigned his judgeship in Admiralty in 1827, and died, at the great age of ninety-one, in 1836.

Lord Stowell was in the highest tradition of English legal statesmanship. He combined the widest knowledge of classical and modern learning, he was a master of both Common Law and civil law, but he also had an acute appreciation of legal rules as a developing system. In addition, his judgements were couched in elegant language which still makes them a pleasure to read; and they contain expositions of the policy of the law in terms reminiscent of some of Lord Mansfield's classic judgements. So high an authority as Lord Sumner has written: 'For a generation he was rather a law giver than a judge in the ordinary sense of the term. Upon many maritime points his judgements are still the only law.'[14] And his great American contemporary, Judge Story, wrote of him, saying that he had taken care that Lord Stowell's judgements should form the basis of the United States' maritime law.

The greatness of Lord Stowell's work in the law of prize can be attributed primarily to two factors. In the first place, he created a coherent body of law, based upon principles which he defined with precision. The second was that, throughout his judicial career, he emphasised that a prize court administers international law. In the *Maria*[15] he declared that it was the duty of such a court 'to administer with indifference that justice which the law of nations holds out without distinction to independent states, some happening to be neutral and some belligerent. The seat of judicial authority is indeed, locally here in the belligerent country, according to the known law and practice of nations; but the law itself has no locality.' In conformity with this principle, Stowell repeatedly and exhaustively examined the writings of continental writers upon international law, as well as the relevant decisions of courts of other countries.[16]

The principle so firmly established by Lord Stowell in the *Maria* and other cases, that a prize court is an international, and not a municipal court, was strongly reaffirmed by the Privy Council during World War I, in its famous judgement in the *Zamora*,[17] in which it was held that an Order in Council violating the rules of international law was not binding upon a prize court sitting in England. Only an Act of Parliament could modify the law which it applied. In the words of Lord Parker:

> The law which the Prize Court is to administer is not the national or, as it is sometimes called, the municipal law, but the law of nations—in other words, international law. It is worth while dwelling for a moment on this distinction. Of course the Prize Court is a municipal court, and its decrees and orders owe their validity to municipal law. The law which it enforces may therefore in one sense be considered a branch of municipal law. Nevertheless, the distinction between municipal and international law is well defined. A court which administers municipal law is bound by and gives effect to the law as laid down by the sovereign state which calls it into being; it need enquire only what that law is; but a court which administers international law must ascertain and give effect to a law which is not laid down by any particular state, but originates in the practice and usage long observed by civilised nations in their relations towards each other, or in express international agreement. It is obvious that, if and so far as a Court of Prize in

this country is bound by and gives effect to Orders of the King in Council purporting to prescribe or alter the International Law, it is administering not international, but municipal law, for an exercise of the prerogative cannot impose legal obligations on anyone outside the King's dominions who is not the King's subject. If an Order in Council were binding on the Prize Courts, such Court might be compelled to act contrary to the express terms of the commission from which it derives its jurisdiction.

If the struggle with Napoleon had not been so lengthy, it is probable that the full range of Stowell's genius would not have been so apparent, although his contributions to ecclesiastical and maritime law would still have been of great worth. Holdsworth penetratingly sums up:

> It is, I think, true to say that what Hardwicke and Eldon did for equity and what Mansfield did for the Common Law, Stowell did for all these branches of law which fell within the sphere of the civilian's practice. Their achievement was possible not only because they were all very great lawyers, but also because they held their offices for sufficiently long periods to make their influence felt, and because they all came at periods when English law especially needed this kind of guidance. Consequently they all succeeded in creating large parts of the law which govern us today.[18]

To this, a further comment may be added. Of these four outstanding judges, three—Hardwicke, Mansfield and Stowell—had a universal view of the nature of law, and a philosophic approach to the solution of legal problems. For this reason, all three were conscious law-makers, whose contributions to modern English law have been of enduring value.

The nineteenth century saw only one contribution to English law comparable with those of the three judges just mentioned, and this was a collective, rather than an individual achievement. Already in Lord Stowell's time, some of the problems in what came to be termed the 'conflict of laws' were demanding the elaboration of general principles, and a few of them were framed by Lord Stowell himself. A number of them were concerned with the validity of marriages and with questions of personal status. One of considerable interest was *The Slave Grace*,[19] in which he held that a slave, who had accompanied her master to England from Antigua, where slavery then existed, though free in England, reverted to her former status when she returned to Antigua. Not unnaturally this decision was much discussed, though its soundness in law is now recognised.

There is, however, a more famous decision of Lord Stowell—that which he gave in *Dalrymple v Dalrymple*,[20] which is rightly regarded as a landmark in the development of this branch of the law. However, before discussing this case we should first consider why its development in England was so late. For example, it is not mentioned by Blackstone at all.

Blackstone's silence is the more noteworthy, because on the continent, the problems arising in the conflict of laws had long been familiar to writers and courts. The great Italian jurists, commenting upon the *Corpus Juris*, had discussed some of the basic principles as early as the twelfth century. Round about the middle of the thirteenth century, Accursius, in his gloss on the Code, included a discussion of some of the main problems, and in the fourteenth century the number of writers increased considerably. They included the distinguished names of Bartolus and Saxo Grammaticus. In England, however, these problems were almost unknown until the time of Hardwicke and Mansfield, as Kent pointed out in his *Commentaries on American Law*, published in 1827. Significantly, the United States was ahead of England in the development of this branch of the Common Law, and all English writers have been influenced, directly or indirectly, by Story's commentaries upon the conflict of laws published in 1834. Even Story's work had been preceded by a *Dissertation on questions which arise from the contrarety of the Positive Laws of Different States and Nations*, published by Samuel Livermore in 1828. The first English work, that of Westlake on *Private International Law*, only appeared in 1858. The reason for this

American leadership is clear enough. Under the American federal constitution these problems were arising between state and state almost from the foundation of the republic.

It is necessary to say something by way of explanation of the late emergence of the conflict of laws as a branch of English law, more especially in contrast with its early development on the continent. It can be traced to several factors. In the first place, the development of the conflict of laws by the jurists which had occurred in Italy and France during the Middle Ages was a by-product of their study of Justinian's *Corpus Juris*. It was not purely a theoretical study, since the *Corpus Juris* was the basis of the law of both countries. There was not, nor could there be, any comparable development in England.

Secondly, these jurists had been led to explore the subject because the laws of the Italian city states differed, as did the laws of the different French provinces, so that the problem of the application of another system of law to the solution of a legal problem was of common occurrence. In England, the centralisation of justice which occurred after the Norman Conquest gradually established a law common to the whole country. There was consequently little scope for conflicts of laws to arise within the realm, although there exists in the reports a number of decisions, especially in the latter part of the seventeenth century, upon the extent of the applicability of local customs, and possible conflicts between two bodies of custom. These indicate that, had not the supremacy of the central courts been so firmly established, it might have been necessary for English law to take cognisance of the conflict of laws centuries before it actually had to. To take only one example: in *Chambry v Chambry*,[21] Chambry, a freeman of the city of London, died intestate in the province of York, leaving a house in York, and a personal estate of twenty thousand pounds. There were two sons and a daughter; and by the custom of York his elder son, who had already received lands from his father, would have been excluded from any share of the personalty. It was held that the custom of York is local, but that of London follows the person, and therefore prevails over it so far as a freeman of London is concerned. These cases were mainly decided at the period when these local customs were beginning to be circumscribed by statute. Thus, statutes of 1696, 1703 and 1724 abolished for Wales, York and London respectively the restrictions on testation which had formerly existed there by local custom. With the passing of these statutes, questions of the applicability of local customs to the distribution of the estates of intestates no longer arose.

So far as problems of foreign law were concerned, the principle of the Common Law was that matters arising in England were decided by English law. If they arose abroad, they should be left for the appropriate foreign court to decide. This applied to transactions of English merchants abroad, as much as to aliens. It was to surmount this principle that the Common Law courts, in mercantile cases in respect of transactions entered into abroad in the latter part of the sixteenth century, invented the procedural fiction (which was untraversable) that a contract made in a foreign city was alleged to be made in the parish of St Mary-le-Bow in the city of London. When such cases became common, the problem of the law applicable was solved by the application of the law merchant which, as applied by the Common Law court, was progressively treated (as we have seen) as a part of English law.

In making this development the Common Law courts were deliberately entering into rivalry with the Admiralty Court, which had been given statutory jurisdiction to try cases arising outside the realm, and the Admiralty had always applied the law merchant and maritime law, both of which were regarded as international in character. Although at the period when Coke was Lord Chief Justice there was a memorable attack by the Common Law courts upon the jurisdiction of the Admiralty by means of writs of prohibition, the conflict was over jurisdiction, and only incidentally over the law applicable. Even that conflict was concerned with cases arising in England, over which the Admiralty had been claiming jurisdiction on account of their commercial character. Over others the Common Law courts at this period had no wish to exercise any jurisdiction, with one important qualification. Even before the end of the fourteenth century, it had been established that if a contract were made in England, then even if it were performed abroad, it was triable in the Common Law courts. In these cases, however, no question of foreign law arose. The cases were decided in accordance with the Common Law. One such case, of very special interest since it was one of the earliest decisions on marine insurance, was decided in 1589, and is mentioned in *Dowdale's Case*,[22] decided in Coke's time. In the earlier case, an *assumpsit* was brought on a policy of insurance issued in London, on a ship arrested in France. The court found for the plaintiff, the insurer, but it was moved in arrest of judgement that as the act had occurred outside the realm, the case was not triable in a Common Law court. But it was held that the action was properly brought, because the substance of the action was the contract of assurance made in London, which was the foundation of the *assumpsit*.

It has already been noticed that the Common Law judges avoided problems of conflicts between domestic law and the law merchant by treating the rules of the law merchant as mercantile customs, suitable for progressive incorporation in to the Common Law, and when this had taken place, the rules were applied, wherever appropriate, to all cases, whether domestic or foreign, and to all persons whether technically merchants or not, and whether English or foreign. This was because, until the close of the eighteenth century, the law merchant was regarded as part of the *jus gentium* and as Lord Mansfield said, in *Pillans v Van Mierop*:[23] 'All nations ought to have their laws conformable to each other on such commercial cases.'

Unfortunately, foreign laws could not be treated in a similar fashion, and by the second half of the eighteenth century, it was already evident that the traditional outlook of English law—that each nation administered its own system, and only its own system —would have to be modified. Already for a century and a half, the English courts had been compelled to consider, from time to time, the effect of foreign judgements. Throughout the seventeenth century, the attitude which they invariably adopted was that the foreign judgement was necessarily executed in England, since, as one judge put it, 'the justice of our nation should be aiding the justice of another nation', and further, the English court could not examine the justice of the foreign decree.

Later, it became established that a foreign judgement creates a new cause of action in the nature of a simple contract, in an English court. The English court will not review the foreign judgement, nor will it consider whether the foreign court has correctly applied the law. But the English court will investigate whether the foreign court had jurisdiction, and it will also investigate any case in which it is alleged the judgement has been obtained by fraud.[24]

Hardwicke, Mansfield and Stowell were all conscious of the difficulties of maintaining the attitude that an English court could not have recourse to foreign law, nor take cognisance of acts done abroad. In *Robinson v Bland*[25] Lord Mansfield decided a case in which money was lent between two English subjects in France, to be repaid in England, and he observed: 'The general rule established *ex comitate et juri gentium* is that the place where the contract is made, and not where the action is brought, is to be considered in expounding and enforcing the contract. But this rule admits of an exception where the parties had a view to a different Kingdom.' In *Mostyn v Fabrigas*[26] he heard an action for trespass and false imprisonment against the Governor of Minorca, in respect of acts done by him against a Minorcan in Minorca. In the following year, in *Holman v Johnson*,[27] he laid down the basic principle: 'Every action tried here must be tried by the law of England, but the law of England says that in a variety of circumstances with regard to contracts legally made abroad, the laws of the country where the cause of action arose shall govern.'

The ecclesiastical courts not infrequently were called upon to consider the validity of marriages celebrated abroad. In *Scrimshire v Scrimshire*, in 1752,[28] the ecclesiastical court was asked to decide upon the validity of a marriage of British subjects in France. The marriage was clandestine, and was forbidden by both English and French law. In France, the marriage was completely void, while in England the marriage could be voided by the court under certain conditions. When the suit was brought by the wife for restitution of conjugal rights, the Parliament of Paris had already declared the marriage void, and the English ecclesiastical court decided that the validity of the marriage was to be determined by French law, as the *lex loci actus*. The report states that the opinion of Lord Hardwicke had been sought upon the problem, and the reasoning for the decision seems to reflect his own outlook.

> The *Jus Gentium* [it was stated] is the law of every country and is obligatory on the subjects of every country. Every country takes notice of it; and this court observing that law in determining upon this case, cannot be said to determine English rights by the laws of France, but by the law of England, of which the *Jus Gentium* is part . . . as the law of England takes notice of the law of nations in commercial and maritime affairs; because all countries are interested in these questions; and as all countries are equally interested to have matrimonial questions determined by the laws of the country where they are heard, and the mischief would be infinite to the subjects of all nations if it was not so I am of opinion that this is the *Jus Gentium* of which this and all courts are to take notice.

So these rules governing the conflict of laws were regarded as part of the *jus gentium*, which like the law merchant and public international law, were to be incorporated into the Common Law by way of judicial decision. In *Dalrymple v Dalrymple*,[29] Lord Stowell defined the position in English law in terms which have become classical, and which have proved the starting point of a century and a half of continuous development by the courts. The problem was of a marriage in Scotland. Lord Stowell said:

> Being entertained in an English Court, this case must be adjudicated according to the principles of English law applicable to such a case. But the only principle applicable to such a case by the law of England, is that the validity of Miss Gordon's marriage rights must be tried by reference to the law of the country, where, if they exist at all, they had their origin. Having furnished this principle the law of England withdraws altogether and leaves the legal question to the exclusive judgment of the law of Scotland.

In conformity with this view, it has been maintained by many writers in England and the United States, and more particularly by Dicey and Beale, that the English court enforces, not a foreign law, but a right acquired under the law of a foreign country. This theory has been energetically attacked, and in England, especially by Cheshire, although he concedes that it performed a useful role in the development of the conflict of laws in the nineteenth century.

From Cheshire's analysis of this development, several conclusions emerge. The first is that, so long as the conflict of laws was regarded, as it was by Hardwicke, Mansfield and Stowell, as a derivative from the *jus gentium*, emphasis was necessarily placed upon the writings of philosophers and jurists, both English and continental. Today, this approach has been abandoned by the courts for one which is more pragmatic. Cheshire decisively rejects the suggestion that there is a body of principles from which the rules are deducible.

> So far as the Common Lawyer is concerned [he writes] his instinct is to test a proposed rule by its practical bearing upon normal human activities and expectations. It is by this method that in his opinion the purpose of law, which at bottom is to promote justice and convenience, can best be furthered. He is nothing if not an empiricist and a pragmatist. That is the spirit in which the rules for the choice of law are conceived. There is no sacred principle that prevails in all decisions, but when the circumstances indicate that the internal law of a foreign country will provide a solution more just, more convenient and more in accord with the expectations of the parties than the internal law of England, the English judge does not hesitate to give effect to the foreign rules. What particular foreign law shall be chosen depends upon different considerations in each legal category. Neither justice nor convenience is promoted by rigid adherence to any one principle. It is preferable that the various principles should fit the needs of the different legal relations, and should harmonize with the social, legal and economic traditions of England.

In conformity with this view, Cheshire, whilst paying a full tribute to the pioneer work of Mr Justice Story in reducing the decisions and juristic literature to an orderly system, at the same time criticises his lack of discrimination, which, he says, caused him to pay excessive respect to continental writers. It is plain that Cheshire regards the conception of a comity of nations and a *jus gentium* from which the development of the conflict of laws can proceed as altogether replaced by a concept of social engineering which, on analysis, proves to be no more than empiricism.

It cannot be disputed that the weight of modern decisions in this branch of law supports Cheshire's view, with the necessary consequence that we today speak of an English conflict of laws, in contrast to a French or German conflict. Whilst they share a common stock of ideas, they show marked differences in application which, year by year, renders the task of unification more complex, more especially because even the English conflict of laws is still in a fluid state. For this reason, as Cheshire points out, the early decisions are unsafe guides to the modern: 'The early judges [he says] worked on virgin soil, and their decisions were necessarily hesitating and tentative. Circumstances have necessitated a process of trial and error, and unless it is realised that the early decisions frequently represent the halting steps of pioneers it will be long before this branch of law attains a state of elegant cohesion.'

That elegant cohesion, one may perhaps add, will be one which bears the hall mark of the Common Law technique. Once again, the English judiciary, in applying themselves to problems in the conflict of laws, have preferred to base themselves upon the logic of the English decisions, rather than upon the philosophical speculations of the jurists. In reaching such a conclusion, one may perhaps regret that the initial impulse given by Hardwicke, Mansfield and Stowell is now apparently spent, more particularly because this represents a retreat from the conception of a community of civilised nations amongst whom certain principles of conduct were universally accepted.

II

Trade Unions and the Courts: An Unsolved Problem

In *United Engineering Union v Devanayagam*,[1] Lords Guest and Devlin said, in a joint dissenting judgement:

> It is a commonplace that with respect to industrial relations the Common Law of master and servant has fallen into disuse. Disputes about conditions of employment are not usually settled by the courts, in accordance with the terms, express or implied, of the contract of service. Trade unionism could no doubt have used its increased bargaining power to obtain more realistic and elaborate contracts of service within the framework of the old Common Law, but it preferred to use it to seek advantages irrespective of contract and enforceable not by legal machinery but by threat of the strike. The law has therefore had to make a new entry into the field of industrial relations. It has had to start again from the beginning, and, as in the field of international relations, has had to make its way in by formulating methods of securing the peaceful settlement of disputes.

These observations make a useful starting point for the consideration of the growth of the law relating to trade unions. There exists a deep-rooted conviction among trade unionists that the law, and particularly the judges, are hostile to them. It will be the purpose of this chapter to discover, from the development of the law relating to trade unions by the courts, whether this conviction can be supported, but first, one should observe one curious feature about this branch of the law. A great and comprehensive trade union structure has grown up, so that today, it would not be inaccurate to say that trade union policy is a major factor in the formation of national policy. This structure has evolved out of agreements between members to form or to join a union, and between unions to establish the Trade Union Congress, but until the Industrial Relations Act 1971 there was no comprehensive statute defining what a trade union is, or attributing to it rights and duties, either between members or in respect of third parties. It is as if modern commercial companies had grown up, without the regulatory Companies Acts. Possibly in those circumstances business men acting corporately would have had reason to complain of the attitude of the courts, since many of the decisions would necessarily have spelled out the limitations of their activities. Further, the legislation which exists in the sphere of trade unionism is too often little more than the formal recognition of a political victory or a political defeat. It has often been piecemeal, and sometimes ambiguous.

First, it is necessary to say what a trade union is. The Trade Union Act 1876 says:

> 'Trade Union' means any combination whether temporary or permanent for regulating the relations between workmen and masters, or between workmen and workmen, or between masters and masters, or for imposing restrictive conditions on the conduct of any trade or business, whether such combination would or would not, if the principal Act [ie the Trade Union Act 1871] had not been passed, have been deemed to have been an unlawful combination by reason of some one or more of its purposes being in restraint of trade.

Recently, Lord Denning, MR, said of a trade union of workers in the Court of Appeal: 'A trade union exists to protect the right of each one of its members to earn his living and to take advantage of all that goes with it. It is the very purpose of its being.'[2]

Trade unions, therefore, exist for what may comprehensively

be described as industrial purposes, though today they do many other things. They may be friendly societies, providing benefits for members. They may pay contributions to support members of Parliament. But what is fundamental to the definition is that it describes a union as a combination, whether of workers or employers, and that such a combination is not, because of contemplated activities, eg strikes aiming to modify the conditions of employment, to be regarded as being in restraint of trade. Parenthetically it may be noted that at the date when this Act was passed, the possible impact of agreements of various kinds upon *laisser-faire* principles was giving the courts a good deal of trouble and was to give rise to much conflict of judicial opinion before the boundaries of the modern tort of conspiracy were traced.

This will be discussed later, but at this point it is necessary to stress that in the early history of trade unionism, hostility was to be traced, not primarily to the courts, but to the legislature. The legend of judicial hostility was energetically challenged by Fletcher Moulton, LJ, in *Gosney v Bristol etc Trade and Provident Society*[3] in characteristically plain language:

> The real fallacy of the argument on the part of the defendant lies deeper. It proceeds on the proposition that strikes are *per se* illegal or unlawful by the law of England. In my opinion there is no foundation for such a proposition. It is true that occasional *dicta* are to be found to the effect that combinations to better the conditions of labour are unlawful at Common Law; but the Courts have never accepted the law thus laid down, and very eminent Judges have expressed views to the contrary.
>
> But the point is, in my opinion, best decided by an examination of the actual decisions of the Courts. There is no trace of any such doctrine during the centuries when the Common Law of England was formed, nor in fact until the end of the eighteenth century. This was not due to any friendliness towards freedom of action on the part of workmen in this respect. On the contrary, during the seventeenth and eighteenth centuries a long succession of legislative enactments were passed restrict-

ing, with a severity which shocks our modern ideas, all attempts on the part of workmen to better their conditions of labour. Yet during the whole of this period no Court treated combinations to better the conditions of labour as being contrary to Common Law, and none of these statutes purported to declare or rest upon the Common Law. If we except an *obiter dictum* by Mr. Justice Grose in *Rex v Mawberry*[4] in 1796—which to my mind was not intended to refer to Common Law but to the effect of statutes then in force—I cannot find that there were any judicial *dicta* in support of the suggested proposition until after this legislation swept away all these statutes by the Act of 1825. It does not surprise me that after the Courts had for such a long series of years been occupied in enforcing statutory prohibitions of very varied kinds against combinations among workmen, there should come to be an idea in some minds that the Common Law itself must have disapproved of that which legislation so persistently persecuted. But conclusions as to the Common Law which first appear in recent times and are based on no accepted principle of earlier date are to be looked upon with great suspicion. Ever since 1824 the weight of authority is against this doctrine. Strikes *per se* are combinations neither for accomplishing an unlawful end nor for accomplishing a lawful end by unlawful means, and I therefore come unhesitatingly to the conclusion that the fact that the arrangements for giving strike pay do in a sense facilitate strikes is quite immaterial for the purposes of our decision, and that the defendant society does not become illegal by reason of its having this as one of its 'objects'.

This passage from Fletcher Moulton's judgement very clearly attributes responsibility where it properly belongs—not to the courts but to the legislature. Nevertheless, the legend persists, and has been repeated many times since this decision. A second point should also be mentioned. Trade union spokesmen have frequently suggested that they will not accept control of their activities by the law. This is a misleading expression. In a political community no one, and no association, can act outside the law.

If, by their expressions and attitude, union leaders express their determination not to accept the principle that agreements between unions and employers should be legally binding, they cannot complain if the courts re-examine with care the union machinery by means of which such a principle is carried into effect. Much of trade-union activity is already regulated by law; for example, the investment of its funds and the payment of benefits are controlled by statutes and by the law of trusts and contracts. So too is the relation between a union and its members —a matter which has been frequently before the courts in recent times. The objects of a union, as of every other voluntary association, must be lawful. Thus, at Common Law, certain acts in furtherance of a trade dispute do not involve the union in liability. This has been established by the Trade Disputes Act, 1906. A member has certain legally enforceable rights against the members, as a normal consequence of the contractual relationship between them; and the manner in which these are exercised may involve questions of public policy of which the courts are the interpreters.

In 1926 the General Strike collapsed because Astbury, J, a judge of first instance, held that those who participated in it were outside the protection conferred by the Trade Disputes Act, 1906. Trade union activity is therefore not a political jungle, but an area of social activity in which the vast majority of activities are conducted within a legal framework. The problem whether the state should intervene further into trade-union activities is therefore not whether trade unions should be regulated by law, but how far it is desirable or politic to extend a regulation which already exists.

A second point to be noted is that, although freedom to associate is fundamental to the Common Law, the law has always exercised the right to regulate the constitution and activities of certain kinds of association. For example, at the very time when the legislature was regulating industrial combinations, by the Acts of 1824 and 1825, an Act of 1826 had regulated the formation of joint stock banking companies. This was the precursor of a succession of Acts during the following hundred and forty years, regulating the formation, activities, and winding up of commercial companies of every kind.

For many centuries, Parliament had exercised the right to regulate the conditions of employment, and it had conferred on the magistrates the power to fix wages, but the regulating system which statutes had established became obsolescent in face of the development of large-scale industry in the eighteenth century. Where large bodies of men acted in concert, it was impossible to imprison them all, and in a quite short time, their associations became permanent and powerful enough to organise strikes for higher wages and better conditions of employment and all attempts by way of petition or legislation against combinations in particular industries, proved ineffective to check them. Finally, at the height of the war with France, following the French Revolution, a comprehensive Act was passed, forbidding combinations of workmen generally, expressed in the broadest terms, and forbidding union activity of any kind. The Combination Act of 1799 provoked so much opposition that it was modified in the following year, but it remained the law until 1824.

These repressive statutes followed directly upon the abandonment by Parliament of any attempt to regulate the relation of masters and men. Indeed, under prevailing theories of *laisser-faire*, any such attempt was regarded as completely futile. The results of this abdication have been enduring. It left employers and men face to face, so that the strike became the normal weapon of the workers. It also bred among workers the conviction that appeals to Parliament and also to the courts were useless, since they were controlled by men antagonistic to them. That attitude is today as deep rooted as ever it was. Holdsworth has remarked:

> The fact that it was possible in 1906 to pass a statute which perpetrates the enormous injustice of freeing trade unions of masters and men from liability for torts is, I think, due primarily to the prevalent *laisser-faire* doctrines which induced Parliament at the end of the eighteenth century and the beginning of the nineteenth to refuse to set up any legal machinery for the equitable adjustment of industrial disputes.[5]

In 1824, under the influence of Benthamite ideas, and the propagandist zeal of Francis Place, Parliament repealed all the combination laws (in all, thirty-five statutes, stretching from the reign of Edward I to that of George III), and provided that any association, whether of masters or men, for purposes relating to the conditions of, or rates of payment for, employment should not be liable to any prosecution or other criminal proceedings for conspiracy. Previously any such combination, being for a purpose declared illegal in one or several statutes, was *ipso facto*, a criminal conspiracy. Unfortunately, the high hopes generated by this Act were not realised. It was followed by a wave of strikes, some of them accompanied by violence (which had continued to be illegal under the Act) with the consequence that in 1825, Parliament replaced the 1824 Act with another, which spelled out in greater detail than before the penalties for violence, threats or other pressure designed to interfere with the course of employment. The Act contained a proviso that its penal provisions did not extend to any persons who met together for the sole purpose of consulting on and determining wages or prices which those meeting together should demand in respect of their work, and for certain allied objects, eg hours of work.

It will be seen that the right to combine as contained in the Act of 1825 was a very restricted right, and unless the trade union and its activities fell within the words of the proviso, the union was outside the protection given by the Act. Accordingly, a series of judicial decisions during the forty years after 1825 made it in the highest degree hazardous for a trade union or its officials to take any part at all in the organisation or incitement of a strike. Further, although by the Act of 1825, even if the trade union confined its activities within the limits there established, it did not thereby become an association protected by the law. This emerged in the highly interesting case of *Hilton v Eckersley*,[6] in which a combination of employers had entered into a mutual bond to thwart the activities of trade unions which sought to alter the hours of work or scales of payment of their employees by agreeing to organise a lock-out in reply. The case was heard by three judges —Lord Chief Justice Campbell, Crompton, J, and Erle, J (who later was to preside over an extremely important Royal Commission, on whose findings the Trade Union Act of 1871 was based). Lord Campbell and Crompton, J, held that the bond was illegal at Common Law as being contrary to public policy, and in restraint of trade and of the free action of individuals. It was therefore void at law, although neither by Common Law nor statute illegal. Erle, J, who dissented, thought that the bond was legal both at Common Law and under the Act of 1825, the restraint of trade, if any, not being greater than was required to protect a lawful interest.

Both Campbell and Crompton considered the decision of Grose, J, in *R v Mawbey*,[7] in which he had stated that combinations of workmen to raise the rate of wages were illegal, and that those participating could be indicted for conspiracy at Common Law. Crompton, J, apparently accepted this, but Lord Campbell was doubtful whether this truly represented the law, and, as has already been noticed, Lord Moulton had no doubts on this point.

As the nineteenth century progressed, and the convictions for unlawful practices in relation to strikes multiplied, judges, as well as the general public, became increasingly puzzled concerning the role of trade unions in industrial life, and of the extent of the tolerance which the Act of 1825 had conceded. In 1867 and 1869 there were decided two cases at the very time when the Royal Commission, presided over by Sir William Erle, was sitting—*Hornby v Close*[8] and *Farrer v Close*,[9] which illustrated both the varying views of the judges, and also the curious twilight in which trade unions then existed. In *Hornby v Close* an addition of rules to the general rules of a society, clearly designed to protect members in the course of trade disputes, was held to place the society outside the benefits conferred by the Friendly Societies Act, and more particularly, outside the powers conferred for the punishment of members misappropriating money. Such powers were an exception to the Common Law rule that a co-owner cannot commit theft of jointly owned property. In the second case, the offending rules did not appear, but evidence was given that the society gave strike pay at discretion to men in any trade dispute. In a court of four, two judges thought that this society was to be treated as a trade union, and therefore the case was within the earlier decision of *Hornby v Close*. The other two judges, however, thought there was nothing to show there was any illegal purpose, and therefore the society was entitled to the protection of the Friendly Societies Acts. The court being equally divided (on an appeal from the magistrates) the decision of the justices stood. This was particularly unfortunate, for Close, the secretary of the society, was clearly proved to have embezzled the funds of the society, but because it could not take advantage of the Friendly Societies Acts, it was unable to take action against him. An Act of 1868 enabled a trade union to prosecute its members in such cases.

The position of the union, *vis-à-vis* its officers, was very little better in the law of trusts. If the objects of the union included illegal purposes, and they included objects which could be comprehensively described as in restraint of trade, then a trust of union property was void.

A further disability arose from the illegal character of a trade union. Members who left a union could not be proceeded against for failure to observe the rules, including those relating to arrears of dues and fines.

It is not possible here to make a study of the social and political background of the judges who decided the cases concerning trade unions between 1830 and 1914, but the results of it might prove illuminating. What is clear is that the majority regarded the steady rise in importance of trade unions as the century progressed with trepidation, and that their decisions, in consequence, were restrictive of union activities. There were others (a minority) who took a more liberal view, and the outlook of these probably was most fully reflected in the report of the Royal Commission. By this time, unfortunately, strikes and lock-outs had come to be regarded as the normal instruments of industrial pressure, each side only appealing to the courts where some illegality by the other was alleged. In such a conflict it was only to be expected that employers should have more occasions for complaint than workmen, or that outbreaks of violence were recurrent, frequently destructive of property, and sometimes endangered life. In 1893, for example, there were widespread strikes in the cotton industry in Lancashire, among the dockers at Hull, and finally among the coalminers of Yorkshire, Lancashire and the Midlands. All except the cotton strike were accompanied by intimidation, and destruction of property. At Featherstone Colliery in Yorkshire, a mob burned and pulled down part of the colliery works and threatened the destruction of the entire colliery. The militia having been summoned, and the Riot Act having been invoked, soldiers fired on the mob, inflicting fatal casualties. Mr Gladstone's last Liberal Government, then in office, set up a commission of inquiry comprising Lord Bowen (a lord of appeal of very high reputation and liberal outlook), Sir A. Rowlatt, and Mr Haldane, a leading practitioner and Liberal Member of Parliament, who subsequently became a Labour Lord Chancellor. The commission was unanimously of the opinion that the disorders were so extreme, that the action of the military in firing on the mob was completely justified.

It is well to remember these things in considering the long and painful struggle of the trade unions to establish their place, and to define their functions, in a free industrial society. Unfortunately the struggle itself most frequently placed the judges in the position of passing sentence upon the perpetrators of violence, and of holding invalid acts by unions or their agents which passed beyond the limits of their functions as defined by piecemeal and sometimes inconsistent legislation. Over the prolonged struggle, there hung the long shadow of *laisser-faire* and restraint of trade. Finally, the extension of the factory system and large-scale industry in time led to the replacement of those historic terms 'masters and men' by the impersonal 'employer and employee'.

In a brilliant sketch in the latter part of Chapter XVII of his now almost forgotten *Short History of English Law*, the late Professor Jenks described the interplay of these various factors in the developing conflict between what we now, equally impersonally, describe as Capital and Labour. He describes the unhappy genesis of the doctrine of common employment (now at long last finally laid to rest by statute) in the decision of Lord Abinger in *Priestley v Fowler*.[10] Professor Jenks criticises the reasoning of the Court of Exchequer chamber. To this one might add that the language of the judgement appears quaint, even for the year 1837. The plaintiff was a butcher's delivery man. The butcher directed him to take and deliver goods in a van, owned by the defendant butcher, and driven by another of his servants. The van was overloaded and broke down, and the plaintiff was injured. As every Common lawyer knows, the plaintiff was unable to recover, because he and the van driver were in the common employment of the butcher. Lord Abinger gave no prior judicial authority for the introduction of the principle, and he explained that the court was therefore at liberty to look to general principles and to the consequences of the decision. He then proceeded:

> If the master be liable to the servant in this action, the principle of this liability will be found to carry us to an alarming extent. He who is responsible by his general duty, or by the terms of his contract, for all the consequences of negligence in a matter to which he is principal, is responsible for the negligence of all his inferior agents. If the owner of the carriage is therefore responsible for the inefficiency of his carriage to his servant, he is responsible for the negligence of his coach-maker or his harness-maker or his coachman. The footman, therefore, who rides behind the carriage, may have an action against his master for a defect in the carriage owing to the negligence of the coachman, or for a defect in the harness arising from the negligence of the harness-maker, or for drunkenness, neglect or want of skill in the coachman, nor is there any reason why this principle should not, if applicable in this class of case, extend to many others. The master, for example, would be liable to the servant for the negligence of the chambermaid for putting him in a damp bed; for that of the upholsterer for sending in a crazy bedstead, whereby he was made to fall down while asleep and injure himself; for the negligence of the cook, in not properly cleaning the copper vessels used in the kitchen; of the butcher in supplying the family with meat of a quality injurious to the health; of the builder, for a defect in the foundations of the house, whereby it fell, and injured both the master and the

servant by the ruins.

There is more in this vein, but apart from the faulty reasoning to which Professor Jenks draws attention, who would conclude from this that in 1837 England was leading the Industrial Revolution, that large areas of Lancashire were covered with cotton mills, that large areas of Yorkshire, Nottinghamshire and Lancashire were disfigured by coalmines, that the Midlands was alive with furnaces, and that ships were being built around the coasts? Surely these activities merited at least a word, in considering the consequences of the decision, even if only to attempt to define, in relation to these larger scale enterprises, how far the doctrine of common employment could be expected to extend. Lord Abinger, however, was no Lord Mansfield, and the Common Law had passed into a different phase of expansion.

It was, nevertheless, in the sphere of the criminal law that the unions felt themselves to be most oppressively treated, and they can be scarcely blamed for failing to appreciate the subtleties of the law of conspiracy, developed by the nineteenth-century judges. It was the more unexpected, because the Act of 1825 had appeared to establish that so long as unions confined their activities within the terms of that Act, their activities were not illegal. This is, in fact, what Rolfe, B, had expressly stated in *R v Selsby* in 1847.[11] It is true that his exposition of the law relating to trade union activities suggested that union discussions of strikes and wages might be carried on in an atmosphere of lofty, academic abstraction, and the facts were often far different. Still *R v Selsby* seemed to indicate that the threat of conspiracy had gone for lawful union activities. Such an attitude, however, failed to take into account the alarm felt by employers and by wide sections of the public at the rapid growth in size, resources and power of many unions, and also the alarm felt at the persistence of violence and intimidation in many strikes. Accordingly, when the courts refurbished the ancient weapon of criminal conspiracy, they were regarded as the defenders, not only of public order, but also of society itself. Only in this way can some of the decisions of the forty years following the Act of 1825 be explained.

It was only too apparent that section 3 of the 1825 Act offered a ready means of stifling union activity. This section forbade, under penalty of three months' hard labour, any attempt to force, by violence, threats or intimidation, any workman to leave his employment, return his work unfinished, or refuse to enter any employment, or to join or remain a member of any society, or to seek to coerce any employer to alter his method of carrying on his business. There followed a series of decisions in which judges came to regard almost every act done in furtherance of a trade dispute as a breach of the section. Moreover the courts held that an agreement or combination to procure the commission of a statutory offence, ie an infringement of section 3, was a criminal conspiracy. This made all proceedings at union meetings which resulted in a breach of the section criminal conspiracies. In *R v Rowlands*,[12] Erle, J, ruled that quite apart from conspiracies to commit acts forbidden by the Act of 1825 a combination of workmen for the purposes of obstructing an employer in his business, thereby constraining him to a certain schedule of prices, by 'persuading' persons to leave the employer's service, was a crime. This was the starting point of the doctrine of 'conspiracy at Common Law', for which it was in *R v Rowlands* impossible to find any decided case earlier than 1825.

Behind this (at first sight) startling development there existed a philosophy derived, once again, from *laisser-faire*. It was based upon the principle of the free and untramelled worker making an agreement to employ his industry and to be taken in the service of a free and untramelled employer. The freedom of both to decide judiciously was to be protected from outside pressure. It was expressed in clear terms by Bramwell, B, in *R v Druitt*;[13] it was affirmed by the Royal Commission on trade unions in 1869; and it was approved by the House of Lords as recently as 1915 in *Larkin v Long*.[14] But its existence necessarily implied that almost any actions done by or on behalf of a union in the prosecution of a strike would be regarded as unlawful pressure on the employer. The minority report on trade unions in 1869 gave a number of instances. Holdsworth regards them as normal applications of the Common Law,[15] but it is not open to question that each decision extended the barrier of obstruction against which union activity battered in vain, and looked at from the standpoint of a century of further continuing industrial conflict, they appear to put the judges firmly on the side of the established order, and to render them unresponsive to trade union development.

What had emerged most clearly from the Report of 1869 was the urgent need to get rid of the concept of restraint of trade as the chief ground of illegality, upon which prosecutions of trade unionists were based. This was done in the opening clause of the Trade Union Act 1871, which provided that the objects of a trade union should not be regarded as illegal simply because they were in restraint of trade, so as to render the union members liable to prosecution. It added that no agreement or trust entered into on behalf of the union should be rendered void on that ground. The Act also provided that trade unions might register themselves, and if they did, they would be able to vest their property in trustees, who would be capable of suing and being sued upon all matters touching the 'property, right or claim to property' of the union. In addition, the officers of a registered union were under the obligation to account, and persons dealing improperly with union funds were made liable to criminal prosecution.

Although this Act created new problems in the law of trade unions, it was a very great step forward, and the apprehensions of employers and sections of the public upon the future activities of unions were to some extent allayed by the passing of the Criminal Law Amendment Act in the same year, designed to specify more precisely the conduct of union members which would henceforth be deemed criminal. In addition to intimidation and violence, the Act made criminal any 'molestation or obstruction' of a person, with a view to coerce him, whether he be master or workman. These words were quickly shown to be of wide significance, for in *R v Bunn*,[16] in the year following the passing of the Act, Brett, J, held that an agreement of workmen to control the will of the masters, and an agreement to induce men to break their contracts with a view to securing the reinstatement of a fellow workman, were criminal conspiracies, and further, that the agreement of the workers to control the will of the masters constituted 'molestation and obstruction' under the Criminal Law Amendment Act, 1871. Once again, a court seemed to be extending the interpretation of a statute, thereby diminishing the area of tolerance which the statute had created. Both the Act of 1871 and the decision of Brett, J, in *R v Bunn* were fiercely resented by trade unions, and in 1875, the Conspiracy and Protection of Property Act repealed the Criminal Law Amendment Act, 1871, and provided that an agreement or combination by two or more persons to do, or procure to be done, any act in contemplation or furtherance of a trade dispute should not be a crime if the act would not have been criminal, if committed by one person.

At long last, the legislature had abolished the crime of conspiracy, in as far as it was applicable to union activities. It also regularised peaceful picketing, which thereafter has proved one of the most valuable weapons in the armoury of strikers. After 1875 the teeth of the criminal law had been drawn, so far as trade union activities were concerned.

Unfortunately, the legislation of 1871-5 had at the same time left a major problem unsolved. It plainly recognised the trade union as an entity, or association of persons of a special kind, at any rate if it were registered. But it was not a corporation. The Act of 1871 expressly prohibited a union from incorporation under the Companies Acts. It would not be overstating the matter to say that the Act of 1871 created a novel legal entity, and left it to the courts to work out, as best they could, the extent of the rights and liabilities which accompanied this creation, and many of which were not within the province of the Act at all. This problem is most sharply defined, and is discussed at length, in the speeches of the Law Lords in the *Taff Vale Case,* but before that case arose, the unions had encountered other difficulties in the courts.

These difficulties centred upon the sudden rise to importance of the doctrine of civil conspiracy, especially in connection with breaches of contract by workers. This new development rested upon two elements. In *Lumley v Gye*[17] an impresario had recovered damages against a rival impresario who had induced an opera singer to break her contract to sing at his opera house, thereby establishing that inducing a breach of contract 'maliciously' was a tort. In 1881, this decision had been followed in *Bowen v Hall*,[18] where the contract was again for personal services. Further, a decision of the Court of Common Pleas in 1843 had accepted the proposition that an action lay for conspiracy where the defendants had combined together to prevent the plaintiff from performing as an actor.[19] Jenks says of this case that actual violence was alleged against the defendant, so that the question of law was never really discussed. The 'violence' consisted of hissing and hooting during the plaintiff's performance. It is quite clear that this was at most a tort, whilst all three judges accepted, as not requiring argument, that conspiracy in these circumstances was actionable. On the other hand, the year before its decision in *Temperton v Russell*,[20] the House of Lords had decided in *Mogul SS Co v McGregor, Gow & Co*,[21] that an agreement by a ring of shipowners to undercut rival shipowners and drive them out of business, did not constitute a tort, rejecting the suggestion that the action was in restraint of trade, and also the argument that the agreement constituted actionable conspiracy. It constituted, said their lordships, no more than legitimate commercial competition.

In *Temperton v Russell*[22] in 1893, the plaintiff, a builder, sued the members of the joint committee of three trade unions for inducing by threats of a strike, tradesmen who had contracted to supply him with goods, not to do so, and not to make further contracts with him. For the defendants, it was argued that inducement to break a contract was actionable as a tort only if it were done in respect of a contract for the supply of goods. Further, even in respect of contracts for personal services, inducement was actionable only if it was related to an existing contract. It should not be extended to an inducement not to *enter* into contracts. The Court of Appeal rejected both arguments. Inducement to break, or not to enter into, any contract, they said, was actionable; from which it followed that agreements to achieve these ends were actionable as civil conspiracies. Whilst the authority in support of the first part of this decision may be termed respectable, if thin, there seems to be no authority to support the second part, relating to inducements not to enter contracts, and no reason whatever was offered by the Court of Appeal to explain why, in the *Mogul Case*, agreements to produce such a result were not actionable, whilst in *Temperton v Russell* they were. A conventional, but unsatisfying explanation, doubtless, is that in the *Mogul* case the shipowners were defending their legitimate trade interests, whilst in *Temperton v Russell* the defendants were seeking to compel an employer of labour to comply with their demands.

A series of decisions in the decade following *Temperton v Russell* applied both branches of the decision in that case. In this period, only one reported case, that of *Allen v Flood*,[23] was decided against the employers and that was because there was no evidence of any actual breach of contract by the employees, and no evidence of conspiracy. Against this, in *Quinn v Leathem*,[24] in the eventful year 1901, the House of Lords emphatically reaffirmed the actionability of such agreements to induce breaches of contract, and Lord Halsbury, LC, whose hostility to the advance of trade unionism was notorious, remarked: 'If upon these facts so found the plaintiff could have no remedy against those who had thus injured him, it could hardly be said that our jurisprudence was that of a civilised community.'

By this date Lord Halsbury's lengthy tenure of the Chancellorship had produced an overwhelmingly Conservative bench. There was worse to follow. *Quinn v Leathem* had been argued in May and June, and the House of Lords announced its decision on 5 August. In July, the same tribunal heard the appeal in *Taff Vale Railway v Amalgamated Society of Railway Servants*,[25] probably the most famous of all trade union cases. In it, the House of Lords treated a registered trade union as a quasi-corporate personality and therefore liable for damage caused by its officers and members in the course of a trade dispute. In the language of Lord Brampton: 'A legal entity was created under the Trade Union Act, 1871, by the registration of the society in its present name, in the manner prescribed, and that legal entity so created, though not perhaps in the strict sense a corporation, is nevertheless a newly created corporate body, created by statute, distinct from the unincorporated trade union, consisting of many thousands of separate individuals, which no longer exists under any other name.'

The consequences of this decision were profound, for it exposed the funds of unions to claims of unassertainable magnitude in the event of damage occurring during strikes. That damage need not have been physical. It could be the consequence of actions for civil conspiracy, such as had been developed in the preceding years.

There was of course a legislative aftermath, in the form of the Trades Disputes Act of 1906, which destroyed the doctrine of civil conspiracy in trade disputes, together with the actionability of inducements to commit a breach of contract, if done in furtherance of a trade dispute. This Act also abolished the responsibility of a trade union for the torts of its officials or members, whether committed in furtherance of a trade dispute or not.

It has nevertheless been the experience of trade unions that as soon as one legal fetter has been shed, another has been discovered. For example, in the famous *Osborne* judgement in 1910[26] it was held (1) that a member may restrain a union from applying its funds for purposes beyond its proper objects; and (2) that a member may be protected against expulsion for failure to subscribe to funds so used (ie for political objects). The effect of this judgement was modified by the Trade Union Act 1913 to the extent that it provided for the establishment by the union of a separate political fund.

It is not possible to do more than mention briefly a few subsequent decisions on the trade unions where it has been considered that their activities have been thwarted by the bench. As we have seen, the only British General Strike, in the year 1926, collapsed in consequence of the decision of Astbury, J, in *National Seamen's and Firemen's Union v Reed*.[27] Like so many other decisions in trade union law, the correctness of this decision has been hotly disputed. The essence of the decision was that the strike was not called for the furtherance of a trade dispute. There was not, and could not be, a dispute between the Trade Union Congress and the Government. Accordingly, all participating in it were outside the protection offered by the Trade Disputes Act.

The General Strike was followed by an Act of 1927, restricting the activities of trade unions, and making it clear that a strike for other than industrial purposes was illegal. This Act was always resented by the unions, and on the accession of Labour Government to power in 1945, it was totally repealed. Today, the law is back to the point at which it stood in 1926, and it is not unlikely that in the future, an appellate court will be called upon to consider the correctness of Astbury, J's, judgement.

Still more recently, the courts have been required to consider three other problems of modern trade unionism. The first is the right of expulsion which they exercise, which today may have the effect of denying a worker the right to employ his skill. Of the many modern decisions, the best known is *Bonsor v The Musicians Union.*[28] In that case, in which the House of Lords again discussed the quasi-corporate character of a registered trade union, a member of a registered trade union who had been wrongfully expelled, and had thereby been prevented from being employed as a musician, was held entitled to recover damages from the union for the loss which he had suffered. More recently, in *Edwards v Society of Graphical Trades*,[29] in which the Court of Appeal upheld but reduced an award of damages in similar circumstances, Lord Denning said that no union could give itself by its rules an unfettered discretion to expel a man or withdraw his membership, for a man's right to work was now fully recognised by the law. It is certainly the case that courts are exercising in respect of unions as well as voluntary associations of all kinds, and many other bodies, the right to investigate whether the rules of natural justice have been complied with. In these days when unions in many cases dominate the mode of work in entire industries, they can only expect to secure approval if they show scrupulous regard for the rights of members. The Donovan Commission on trade unions followed the modern trend in this respect by suggesting the establishment of an independent appellate tribunal, but so far, the Trade Union Congress has not responded.

In the meantime, it is plain that questions such as that which the Court of Appeal decided in the *Bonsor* and *Edwards Cases* will arise before the courts with increasing frequency. It is also plain that they involve legal principles of first importance, and that the reaction of the courts to them is not in doubt. In the words of Sachs, LJ, in *Edwards v SOGAT*:

> The courts have always protected a man against any unreasonable restraint on his right to work even if he has bargained that right away; and it matters not whether the bargain is with the employer or with a society.[30] A rule that in these days of closed shops entitles a trade union to withdraw the card of a capable craftsman of good character who for years has been a member, even if styled 'temporary member', for any capricious reason such as (to mix conventional and practical examples) having incurred the personal enmity, for non-union reasons, of a single fellow member, the colour of his hair, the colour of his skin, the accent of his speech, or the holding of a job devised by someone not yet a member is plainly in restraint of trade. At common law it is equally clearly unreasonable so far as the public interest is concerned. Is it then protected by either section 3 or section 4 of the Trade Union Act, 1871? It cannot be said that a rule that enabled such capricious and despotic action is proper to the 'purposes' of this or indeed of any trade union. It is thus not protected by section 3 and is moreover ultra vires. Nor can I find any protection for it in section 4. It is thus void as in restraint of trade.

Two short comments may be made on these observations. The first is that the Common Law is once again providing a shield for personal freedom, as against the organisation. The second is that the necessity to conform to the principles of natural justice is one which now extends to every organisation which exercises such exclusionary functions.

Two other matters on which the courts have been compelled to pronounce, perhaps unwillingly, is (1) the effect in law of collective agreements, and (2) the extent to which a union may interfere with the rights of third parties in pursuing what it considers to be the interests of its members. The second problem arose in acute form in *Torquay Hotel Co v Cousins*,[31] in which officials of a union, in their efforts to organise a branch of the union among the workers in the hotel, intimated to sixty oil companies, with which the hotel had contracts, that deliveries of fuel oil by them to the hotel would be prevented by the refusal of oil tanker drivers (who were members of the same union) to deliver at the hotel. The Court of Appeal held that such acts were not in furtherance of a trade dispute, within the meaning of the Trade Disputes Act, 1906, since the plaintiff hotel was not an employer of members of the defendant union. This case is of first importance, because it emphasises the distinction between the direct interference of a union which procures a breach of contract, and indirect interference. Direct interference preventing the performance of a contract is a violation of a legal right and is therefore actionable. Indirect interference is only unlawful if unlawful means are used to procure such a breach.

Of even greater importance was the decision of the House of Lords in *Rookes v Barnard*[32] in which it was held that where members of a trade union threatened to withdraw their labour, unless a non-union worker was dismissed, this amounted to the sort of intimidation which, the House of Lords decided, could be constituted by threats, not only of criminal or tortuous acts, but also by threats to bring about a collective breach of contract.

The problem of collective bargaining, and the status of agreements arising therefrom, received full consideration in *Ford Motor Company v AEU*.[33] The short point decided in this complex case is that collective agreements are not intended to be legally enforceable, and accordingly there is no legal remedy for their breach. The question whether they should be is one of the most hotly disputed in the whole field of industrial relations today. The Industrial Relations Act, 1971, has made such agreements legally enforceable, unless they otherwise provide, but such agreements can only be construed or enforced in the newly-created Industrial Court.

This brief survey has been made with intention of discovering the judicial attitude towards novel problems, often productive of controversy in a central field of modern life. It can scarcely be challenged that as the nineteenth century drew to a close, the attitude of the courts had hardened against some trade union activities. The bias may not have been conscious, or universally shared, but it was there. So too was the acute discomfort which courts betrayed in expressing the grounds for the decisions taken on these problems. Many American superior judges would have accepted the opportunity to discuss social and economic theories relevant to the problem. In England, since the precedents were frequently defective or ambiguous, some of the logic of the cases appears chopped. At the same time, it must be mentioned that legislation on trade unions could sometimes introduce rules, such as the immunity of a union from liability for the torts of its members or servants, which ran counter to all Common Law thinking. It could also be partial and fragmentary, so that the task of the court was to fill in the extensive lacunae. Moreover it was not open to the court in these cases to speculate upon what the intention of the legislation might have been, for that intention depended upon discovering which party was in power when the legislation was passed. This is not a satisfactory situation, particularly for an English court, and there would be few judges who would regret the removal of large areas of trade union activities from the purview of the courts altogether. This, however, is not in contemplation. Meanwhile, even in the legal sphere, quite apart from the industrial and political spheres, many of the basic problems created by the rise of the unions remain quite unsolved. It is not clear in terms of law or jurisprudence exactly what a trade union is, nor what is or ought to be, the basis of its liability for the acts of its members. The appropriate and permissible sphere of trade union activities is not clearly defined, nor how far these may be permitted to affect adversely the rights of those who are not parties to a dispute. These, and many other problems, have been constantly before the courts, and the appellate courts have at times cautiously attempted the task of establishing principles. These have sometimes proved politically unwelcome, they have frequently provoked adverse criticism, and one or two have been either abolished by legislation or have been quietly abandoned. It may seem obvious today that trade unions, as a special type of association, should have been treated by the courts as organisations *sui generis*, that their functions should have been sympathetically examined, and that their lawful activities should have been treated with the same understanding as those of other distinct bodies, for example merchants, at an earlier date. The conviction that trade unions have not received this treatment has been largely responsible for the tenacity with which the unions today resist any extension of the jurisdiction of the courts in their affairs, and although speculation is hazardous, it may eventually occur that the settlement of trade union problems will have to be undertaken by newer tribunals than the ordinary courts, and that such tribunals function free from Common Law techniques.

A new chapter in the story of attempts to secure judicial control on industrial action began in December, 1971, with the opening of the National Industrial Relations Court, established under the Industrial Relations Act, 1971. In its first president, the court possesses in Sir John Donaldson an experienced and commercial judge who, in his opening statement on first taking his seat, observed that the measure of the court's success would be the frequency with which the court would intervene in labour disputes without going to the lengths of handing down a decision. The omens were not entirely favourable, for the trade unions have been unyielding in their hostility to this bold attempt to confine industrial relations within a legal framework. Further, since the consequences of the *Taff Vale Case* were nullified by the Trade Disputes Act, 1906, the courts have shown the greatest reluctance to enunciate legal principles to govern industrial relations. It has been shown that their activities have been largely confined to the protection of the trade union member against arbitrary action by his union. Now the new court is required by the 1971 Act to promote sound industrial relations in accordance with four general principles: collective bargaining; the maintenance of orderly procedures in industry for the peaceful and expeditious settlement of industrial disputes; the association of workers in independent trade unions and employers associations; and finally, freedom and security for workers, protected by adequate safeguards against unfair industrial practice under the

Redundancy Payments legislation.

Almost at the outset, the court was involved in a major dispute between dockers at Liverpool and firms who packed containers for shipment at depots distant from the docks, by the use of persons who were not dockers. Lorries belonging to such firms were persistently picketed and 'blacked' at the dock gates, and one firm, Heatons, were granted orders against interference, the dockers being unrepresented at the hearing. The most important fact which emerged from this case was that union officials themselves and their union are responsible for the acts of their members, and when the dockers ignored the orders, the Industrial Relations Court imposed fines of £5,000 and £50,000 upon the union and its officials. The union appealed to the Court of Appeal, which set aside the fines, holding that the shop stewards of the union were not its servants, and therefore the union could not be made liable for what they did. This decision was quickly followed by another, in which the Industrial Relations Court held that London dockers and shop stewards were in contempt of orders which it had made, and ought therefore to be imprisoned for contempt. Although the shop stewards themselves did not appeal, the official solicitor surprisingly intervened, and again the Court of Appeal set aside the orders of the National Industrial Relations Court. Whilst these decisions reveal the anxiety of the Court of Appeal to see that the principles of justice completely pervade this new area of judicial activity, they have emphasised the difficulties which the Industrial Relations Court is facing in an area in which judicial decision is inevitably closely linked with executive action.

From the decision of the Court of Appeal Heatons appealed to the House of Lords, who unanimously held that the union was responsible, under the Industrial Relations Act 1971, for the activities of its shop stewards.

Once again, the trade unions have made plain their opposition to any attempt to subordinate industrial disputes to legal process before the courts, and in view of that opposition, it is too early to predict whether this new approach to the solution of industrial problems will find a permanent place in the fabric of English law.

One of the factors affecting this has been the persistent refusal of the unions to recognise, or to appear before the court, in spite of the fact that this has sometimes worked to their detriment. So long as the Industrial Relations Act remains law, there are many questions of major importance for the Industrial Relations Court to decide. For example, in *Langston v AUEW*[34] it decided that where 'unfair industrial practices' are alleged against a union, the complaint could only be brought by the employer, and not by the employee who was adversely affected—in this case, a non-union member.

The Act of 1971 is a comprehensive attempt to establish a legal framework for industrial relations, the absence of which has been for long a peculiarity of English law. It has repealed much of the older trade union law, including the Trade Union Act 1871 and the Trade Disputes Act 1906, and it places collective bargaining on a new legal basis. By s 34 of the Act, agreements between employers and unions are now presumed to be legally enforceable (thus modifying the effect of the *Ford Motor Company* decision in 1969) but no court other than the Industrial Relations Court may hear actions to construe or enforce them. Part II of the Act attempts to define the rights of workers, especially in relation to trade union membership and activities.

Some general restatement of the law governing labour relations was overdue, more particularly since the United Kingdom has become in this sphere steadily more remote from other Western nations. The Act of 1971 differs from an abortive Bill introduced by the Labour Government in 1970 in drawing both on continental and American experience. Hitherto, neither the judiciary nor the legislature has been very successful in their interventions in the sphere of industrial relations. No modern state, however, can afford to leave the problems to which they give rise without an orderly solution.

12

The Struggle for Natural Justice

One of the most significant features of the past two decades in the development of English law by the courts has been the regularity of appeals to 'natural justice', and the consequent extension of the areas in which this concept now may be relevant. Half a century ago, as will be shown later, there was a tendency to minimise its importance, and to suggest that the occasions when natural justice could be successfully introduced in modern law were few and exceptional. It is quite otherwise today. There is an increasing concern over the activities of decision-making bodies of all kinds. There is an uneasy feeling that the idea of 'fair play' which underlies 'natural justice' may be in danger of being ignored in response to the increasing pressures to which the individual is constantly being subjected. At bottom, the frequent appeals to 'natural justice' are an assertion of individual freedom in an increasingly collectivist society. It is seen, in fact, as a shield against oppressive action by groups or bodies of many kinds.

First, it must be stated that 'natural justice' is not a substitute for the ordinary processes of the courts. In *Semtex v Gladstone*[1] Finnemore, J, remarked: 'I hope the law of this country and natural justice will approximate always as closely as possible, but all claims and legal defences have to be grounded in law, and not according to somebody's idea of natural justice, not even that of the judge who may hear the case.'

In the context of that case the reminder was a useful one, for the report shows that an attempt had been made to suggest that although an employee had been found liable for causing damage to a third party, it was contrary to the principles of natural justice that he should make any contribution to the damages awarded. As Finnemore, J, pointed out, such a principle was unacceptable, and he added: 'I find that justice, as we conceive justice in these courts, says that the person who caused the damage is the person who must in law be called upon to pay damages resulting therefrom.'[2]

These observations are an echo of the remark of Lord Sumner in *Sinclair v Brougham*[3] that: 'there is now no ground left for suggesting as a recognisable equity the right to recover money *in personam* merely because it would be the right and fair thing that it should be refunded to the payer.'

Natural justice could be a potentially revolutionary concept, unless confined within plainly-defined limits. It could overturn, or remould existing rules of legal obligation, as equity once did. It could permit the re-opening of disputes closed by judicial decision. It could open, on the broadest front, a controversy over the question of fair play, and whether there is any generally accepted criterion of it. If no such criteria can be found we may be in a position where there is no alternative but to declare that fair play is what the judge trying the case says it is. This may lead us back once more to the era when equity (an earlier conception of natural justice) could be described as varying with the length of the Chancellor's foot—an era which closed when post-Restoration Chancellors imported judicial precedent into the Chancery, thereby setting guide-lines for the future development of equity.

In *Law in the Making*, the late Sir Carleton Kemp Allen showed that the ideas of fair play, reason and conscience played a considerable part in shaping, first the Common Law, and later, equity, and in discovering the test of reasonableness for the acceptance as law of a special custom, he draws attention to the fact that in *Day v Savadge*,[4] Hobart, CJ, rejected a custom of the City of London, proved by the certificate of the recorder, as unreasonable, because the corporation was itself an interested party. The decision, says Allen, is one of the leading authorities in our law for the proposition that it is contrary to the principles of natural justice for a man to be judge in his own cause. In Hobart's day, of course, the situation was regarded as plainly contrary to the principles of natural law. Today, no such appeal to a higher law is acceptable, although there is a distinct echo of Allen's approach in Lord Morris's explanation of the origin of natural justice:[5]

> That the conception of natural justice should at all stages guide those who discharge judicial functions is not merely an acceptable but is an essential part of the philosophy of the laws. We often speak of the rules of natural justice. But there is nothing rigid or mechanical about them. What they comprehend has been analysed and described in many authorities. But any analysis must bring into relief rather their spirit and their inspiration than any precision of definition or precision as to application. We do not search for prescriptions which will lay down exactly what must, in various divergent situations, be done. The principles and procedures are to be applied which, in any particular situation or set of circumstances, are right and just and fair. Natural justice, it has been said, is only 'fair play in action'. Nor do we wait for directions from Parliament. The Common Law has abundant riches; there we may find what Byles J, called 'the justice of the common law'.[6]

1 *The Conflict of Laws*

The manner in which the modern judiciary has handled the increasingly frequent appeals to natural justice calls for close examination. One interesting place where this process may be studied is in the conflict of laws, where it has long been settled law that a foreign judgement which offends the principles of natural justice will not be enforced by the English courts. Such a principle, if broadly interpreted, would open the door to the reconsideration of wide classes of foreign judgements, for a variety of reasons. In fact, however, a foreign judgement will not be invalidated by an English court simply because that court considers the foreign judgement to be unjust either in the abstract, or in relation to the principles of English law. One illustration of this is the case of *Scarpetta v Lowenfeld*,[7] where it was held that the judgement of a foreign court was not opposed to natural justice because the foreign court had declined to admit evidence of a party which would be admissible by an English court. Nor is it open to contend in an English court that the foreign judgement is incorrect from the standpoint of the foreign law. As Channell, J, said in *Robinson v Fenner*:[8]

> Whatever the expression 'contrary to natural justice', which is used in so many cases, means (and there really is very little authority indeed as to what it does mean), I think it is not enough to say that a decision is very wrong, any more than it is merely to say it is wrong. It is not enough, therefore, to say that the result works injustice in this particular case, because a wrong decision always does.

It may be true, as Channell, J, says, that few English judges have attempted a general definition of natural justice in this context. They have nevertheless been ready to emphasise that its significance is primarily procedural. It is concerned exclusively with the question whether either party has had full opportunity to present his case, and has received proper notice of the steps taken by his opponent. As Hamilton, LJ, pointed out in his judgement in *Arlidge's Case* in the Court of Appeal,[9] formerly the courts tended to take a bolder view. At one time, natural justice was regarded as setting up for foreign jurisdictions a standard of judicial correctness upon the pattern of our Common Law courts, and he illustrates this by reference to the decision of Lord Ellenborough in *Buchanan v Rucker*[10] where the ground of invalidity of a colonial judgement was the practice of summoning a defendant who had never been within the jurisdiction by nailing a writ on the door of the court house. Lord Ellenborough described this as 'contrary to the first principles of reason and justice'. On this Hamilton, LJ, comments:

> Nevertheless, this weighty opinion, which having regard to the circumstances, seems, I must say, to be very temperately expressed, was coldly dismissed as 'declamation' by the Court of Queen's Bench in *Schibsby v Westenholz.*[11]

These were settled times, in which the comity of nations seemed to have rapidly developed and with it, standards of justice. Accordingly, whatever might have been the position at the beginning of the nineteenth century, Baron Bramwell's opinion in *Crawley v Isaacs* in 1867[12] was that the term 'natural justice' which has been used in reference to foreign judgements refers rather to the form of procedure than to the events of the particular case. . . If the proceedings be in accordance with the practice of the foreign court, but that practice is not in accordance with natural justice, this court will not allow itself to be concluded by them.

Six years later Mellish, LJ, was even more explicit. He said:

It was always held that a foreign judgment could be impeached at law as contrary to the principles of natural justice, as, for instance on the ground of the defendant having had no notice of the foreign action, as not having been summoned, or of want of jurisdiction or that the judgment was fraudulently obtained.[13]

The modern cases are simply illustrations of the very restricted orbit of natural justice, and Dicey observes that there would appear to be no case where the defence of denial of natural justice has been successfully raised upon the basis of anything other than absence of notice of the proceedings or inadequate opportunity to plead.[14] Even proceedings obviously tainted with unfairness will not be regarded as invalid, provided these two conditions have been observed, and absence of notice may not be decisive if the foreign law makes it unnecessary. Amongst the older cases illustrative of this is *Messina v Petrococchino*.[15] In this case the Privy Council, in an appeal from the Court of Appeal in Malta, held that a judgement of the Greek Royal Commercial Chancery at Constantinople (a court exercising consular jurisdiction) was not impeachable on the ground of natural justice, although the Greek court, without communication or any attempt at communication with the cargo owner in Malta, had appointed a stranger to be curator of the cargo, when the vessel was disabled from proceeding to Malta. It had further directed the curator to borrow money on the security of a bottomry bond as a payment for the cost of trans-shipping and forwarding the cargo to Malta. Here, it will be seen, the Greek court had in fact decided important matters of law between the parties without giving the cargo owner an opportunity to appear, but since this was in accordance with the procedure of a competent court, the Privy Council declined to interfere.

A more recent, and probably better known illustration of the same point is *Jacobson v Frachon.*[16] In that case A, a London firm, contracted to buy silk from B, a Lyons firm. A brought an action in a Lyons court for cancellation of the contract, and damages, alleging that the deliveries were short, and the material of inferior quality. The Lyons court appointed as expert to examine the material in London a person who was a relative of B. The person made no proper examination, and refused to hear the evidence of A, and their witnesses. The result was that A's action failed, and Roche, J, in the English court, found that the expert's report was biased. When, however, A brought an action against B in an English court, B pleaded the French judgement, and the Court of Appeal held that the French judgement could not be said to be contrary to natural justice, since the requirements of French procedure had been observed, and A had not been prevented from presenting their case in a French court. On the other hand, the English courts have shown themselves alert to the necessity for the parties to receive adequate notice of judicial proceedings affecting them, since they regard the maxim *audi alterum partem* as a principle common to the law of all civilised nations. The form of notice required is such as will comply with the requisites of the foreign system, but if the foreign system dispenses entirely with notice, the English court may inquire whether this requirement of natural justice has been satisfied. In *Rudd v Rudd*[17] Horridge, J, refused to recognise an American decree of divorce, which had been instituted by a husband, where the petition had never been served on the wife, nor had proper steps been taken to bring the proceedings to the wife's notice. More recently, in *Kunstler v Kunstler*,[18] a Polish officer, serving in the Polish army in Egypt during the war of 1939–45, divorced his wife, whom he had married in Poland in 1929, and who was still living in Poland. Later, he remarried in Egypt. After the war, the husband and his second wife settled in England, and in 1969 a question of the validity of the second marriage arose. This depended upon the validity of the Egyptian decree of divorce which, though valid in Egypt, was not recognised in Poland. The English court held that it would be contrary to natural justice to make a declaration upon the validity of notice and marriage without the first wife having had opportunity to put forward any case which she might wish to make.

It has already been mentioned that the foreign law may expressly provide that there would be no service of the proceedings upon one of the parties. Thus, in *Igra v Igra*[19] the court refused to invalidate a German decree of divorce, where the proceedings were probably coloured by racial bias, and where no notice had been served on the respondent husband, because German law had provided that decrees obtained in these circumstances were valid. Pearce, J, said: 'As there is a discretion in our own court to dispense with service, we should be slow to brand a foreign decree as contrary to natural justice (particularly when it is made in time of war) merely because notice did not in fact reach the applicant.' Nothing appears to have been said on this point in *Kunstler v Kunstler*.

Finally, if the defendant expressly or by implication agrees to dispense with notice, he cannot subsequently upset the foreign judgement in England on this ground.

It will therefore appear that 'natural justice' is not today (whatever it may once have been) a ground for attacking the quality of justice meted out by foreign courts. It takes cognisance only of want of jurisdiction or failure to comply with procedural requirements. The limitations of its applicability to foreign judgements was based upon a nineteenth-century assumption that standards of justice among civilised nations were substantially similar. Today this is less evident, and it may be that in the future English courts will have to contemplate a return to earlier practices. In this, they may perhaps be influenced by their reconsideration of the function of natural justice in respect of an increasing number of domestic problems. In the conflict of laws, as it exists today, it may be that although the forms of procedure of a foreign legal system have been scrupulously followed, they have been used in such a way as to bring about, in substance, a denial of justice. If such should be the case, the English courts, in pursuance of their present practice, are unable to assist the litigant. He must then rely upon the ponderous machinery of international law, and through the intervention of the Foreign Office, he must seek redress for a denial of justice. Here again, however, the redress available is by no means complete, for, as the arbitrators in the Salem case in 1932 (between Egypt and the United States) pointed out, international law has from the beginning conceived, under the notion of 'denial of justice', only exorbitant cases of judicial injustice. 'Absolute denial of justice; inexcusable delay of proceedings; obvious discriminations of foreigners against natives; palpable and malicious iniquity of a judgement—these are the cases which, one after another, have been included under the notion of "denial of Justice".'[20]

A good many cases of great hardship may nevertheless slip unredressed through the broad meshes of this sieve.

2 *Administrative Tribunals and Proceedings*

It has been thought useful to begin this discussion of 'natural justice' in English law with an exposition of the position in the English conflict of laws because it supplies clues to the treatment of this concept in other branches of English law. Indeed, the acute mind of Hamilton, LJ (later Lord Sumner), in his judgement in *Arlidge's Case* in the Court of Appeal, pointed out that the ideas underlying the concept were the same, whether what was being considered was the judgement of a foreign court or the proceedings of an administrative tribunal. So far as administrative tribunals are concerned, since these operate under statutes, the question whether the requirements of natural justice have been met often turns upon the question of whether the procedure followed has complied with statutory requirements, not upon whether some standard of abstract justice has been satisfied. This appears very clearly from the decision of the divisional court in *R v Brighton Rent Tribunal*.[21] In that case a rent tribunal set up under the Landlord and Tenant (Rent Control) Act, 1949, had decided upon the reduction of rents, not upon evidence put before them, but upon their own personal knowledge. The result was that the rents had been reduced to figures constituting a hardship to the landlord, having regard to the price paid for the property, the cost of repairs, and similar matters. For the landlords, it was strongly urged that the procedure followed by the tribunal was in conflict with the principles of natural justice, and therefore the King's Bench had power to control them by certiorari or mandamus. To these the Attorney-General, Sir Hartley Shawcross, replied that the term 'natural justice' had little value in law. The divisional court held that the procedure followed by the tribunal was within the wide terms of the Act of 1949, and therefore the divisional court had no power to interfere. Lord Goddard, CJ, observed:[22] 'The real complaint made here is that the tribunal, it is alleged, disregarded what are called the principles of "natural justice".' But he goes on to point out that the requirements of the Act of 1949 had been satisfied, even though the result was to permit rent tribunals to dispense with many things which are considered essential in the proceedings of a court of justice; and he continues:

> That these proceedings have not been conducted in a way which would be tolerated in an ordinary court of law there is no doubt; but the ordinary courts of law are not governed by statutes like this of 1949, which permits these tribunals to act on their own knowledge and without any evidence. Here . . . the formalities prescribed by the Act were observed.[23]

The result was that the landlords were left without a remedy. When a statute dispenses with the need for incidents of procedure which are usually considered to be the hall marks of 'natural justice', the courts will not write such requirements into the act. Parliament, being sovereign, can authorise administrative courts to act in a way which, but for this statute, would be regarded as in violation of the principles of natural justice, and there is nothing which the ordinary courts can do to redress the situation.

There was nothing very novel in this decision, for the situation had been made clear thirty-five years before in the classic case of *Local Government Board v Arlidge*,[24] and it is valuable to compare and contrast the views of the Court of Appeal and the House of Lords on this question. Before doing so, it should first be noticed that four years before this appeal reached the House of Lords, the same court had decided another appeal, *Board of Education v Rice*,[25] in which the principal question was the manner in which the Board of Education had decided certain questions under the Education Act, 1902. In his speech in that case, Lord Loreburn, LC, explained the functions of an administrative body in making such decisions in the following terms:

> Comparatively recent statutes have extended, if they have not originated, the practice of imposing upon departments or officers of state the duty of deciding or determining questions of various kinds. In the present instance, as in many others, what comes for determination is sometimes a matter for discretion, involving no law. It will, I suppose, usually be of an administrative kind; but sometimes it will involve matters of law as well as matter of fact, or even depend upon matter of law alone. In such cases the Board of Education will have to ascertain the facts. I need not add that in doing either they must act in good faith and fairly listen to both sides, for it is a duty lying upon everyone who decides anything. But I do not think they are bound to treat such a question as though it were a trial. They have no power to administer the oath, and need not examine witnesses. They can obtain information in any way they think best, always giving a fair opportunity to those who are parties in the controversy for correcting or contradicting any relevant statement prejudicial to their view. Provided this is done, there is no appeal from the determination of the Board under section 7, subsection 3 of this Act. The Board have, of course, no jurisdiction to decide abstract questions of law, but only to determine actual concrete differences that may arise,

and as they arise, between the managers and the local education authority. The Board are in the nature of the arbitral tribunal, and a court of law has no jurisdiction to hear appeals from their determination either upon law or upon fact. But if this court is satisfied either that the board have not acted judicially in the way I have described, or have not determined the questions they are required by the Act to determine, then there is a remedy by *mandamus* and *certiorari*.

In one way or another, these observations influenced all thinking upon administrative tribunals until the Franks Report. Lord Loreburn's statement of their function was not exhaustive, for there are many decisions which emphasise that in addition to the duty to act fairly, and to hear both sides, the tribunal should be free from bias, and also from an interest in the matter to be decided.

In *Local Government Board v Arlidge*,[26] Arlidge was a sufferer under various closing orders of the old Local Government Board in respect of several houses in Hampstead owned by him. The board had acted under the Housing and Town Planning Act, 1909, section 3 9(1), which empowered the board to make rules governing its procedure in respect of appeals from such orders. The procedure it had established was contained in the Local Government Board Rules, which had been complied with in this case. One condition specified in the section was that a public inquiry should be held. Such an inquiry was held in this case, by an inspector appointed by the board. The inspector made his report to the board, but neither the nature nor the contents of the report was disclosed to Arlidge, who thereupon applied to the divisional court for a writ of certiorari to bring up and quash the order. It was argued on behalf of Arlidge that the procedure followed by the board violated the principles of natural justice in three respects: (1) he was not informed what was the composition of the appellate body of the board which decided his case; (2) he had not been allowed to present his case orally to the tribunal (although it should be noticed that the board gave him the opportunity to make further representations in writing, of which he did not avail himself); (3) knowledge of the nature and content of the inspector's report (obviously the key-point of the inquiry) was denied to him.

The conflict of judicial opinion upon this problem is interesting. The divisional court (Ridley, Coleridge and Bankes, JJ) held that the appeal had been properly conducted, since it conformed to the 1909 Act and the rules. There was therefore nothing contrary to natural justice in the board's procedure. The Court of Appeal by a majority reversed this decision, Vaughan Williams and Buckley, LJJ, being of the opinion that the requirements of natural justice had not been satisfied. Hamilton, LJ, thought that natural justice was 'an expression sadly lacking in precision', and that its requirements could not be written into a procedure which conformed with the Act and the rules. All four members of the House of Lords (Lord Haldane, LC, and Lords Shaw, Moulton, and Parmoor) agreed with Hamilton, LJ. Even so, this weight of judicial opinion is a little surprising. There was authority in 1915 to support the contention of Arlidge's counsel that as soon as a

> closing order is made and disputed there is a *lis* between the owner and the local authority. The respondent is in the position of a man fighting for his property, with a right of appeal to a particular tribunal, and he is entitled to an opportunity of appearing before that tribunal and hearing the case of the other side. . . In the application of the Act to Scotland the appeal is to the Sheriff, who is a judicial officer, which shows that the proceeding is judicial, and the ordinary principles of justice and rules of evidence should be applied to it.[27]

Such a view reflects the principle embodied in Article 39 of Magna Carta that no one shall be disseised except by lawful judgement in accordance with the law of the land. In 1915, administrative encroachment was still carried out with circumspection, and it did not seem remarkable to hold that if administrative departments exercised judicial functions in respect of dispossessions of property, they should conduct their proceedings in accordance with principles observed over the centuries by the ordinary courts. As an illustration of this, Buckley, LJ, remarked at the end of his judgement:

> In my judgment it would as matter of public policy be very inexpedient for a Department of the Government in whom powers such as these are vested by statute to refuse an appellant an oral hearing if he requests it. It is not expedient that a party should be sent away with a grievance. It is desirable that the decision of a Government Department, equally with that of a Court of Justice, should be arrived at and pronounced in full publicity and in such a manner as to satisfy the public conscience that the case has been heard and a decision pronounced with full opportunity given to the party to make and sustain his case.[28]

This expression of opinion was often ignored in later developments of administrative practice.

The judgement of Vaughan Williams, LJ, squarely faces the issues of principle which are involved in the case. He points out that the Housing and Town Planning Act, 1909, does not deal with the requirements of natural justice as applied to administrative tribunals, although he is quite clear that an appeal by a houseowner against a closing order is a *lis inter partes*, where the board must ascertain both the law and the facts, and the 'Board acting in good faith and fairly listening to both sides, must disclose all the evidence of fact placed before them, and also the conclusions in law adopted by them as the basis of their decision'.[29] He also stresses that where Parliament commits judicial functions to a government department, then, unless the act expressly permits it to dispense with the requirements of natural justice, these requirements must be read into the procedure for the hearing. That being the case, in the opinion of Vaughan Williams, LJ, the non-production of the inspector's report was a violation of these principles, which invalidated the board's decision. As the learned Lord Justice pointed out, what the board was claiming was to be a judge and a party to the appeal, and at the same time to deny to the other party the right to see the report on which the order has been made, on the grounds that it was confidential.

Later in his judgement, Vaughan Williams, LJ, makes a second point, which in recent years has acquired a fresh importance. Arlidge had asked for particulars of those members of the board who had actually made the decision. On this the learned Lord Justice commented: [30]

> I am not sure that there is not an obligation on the Local Government Board when showing cause to make it plain that in fact the decision was arrived at by an act of decision done by a member of the Local Government Board or some other duly qualified person or officer. This the affidavit of Sir Horace Monro does not express, and I am sure that one would not be justified in saying the deponent avoids expressing. I doubt if it is a case which is properly met by any legal presumption that the Board in fact complied with the statutory obligation. The obvious reason why the appellant wishes to know who in fact decided or was deputised to decide the matters arising on the appeal was to discover whether the person deciding had jurisdiction.

Buckley, LJ, was equally clear that the procedural rules of the Local Government Board must conform to the requirements of natural justice, and that in this instance they did not do so. He says: [31]

> For instance, the Board could not make a rule—first, that neither the appellant nor the local authority should be heard orally or in writing or in any manner whatsoever; nor secondly, that each should be heard only in the absence of the other; nor, thirdly, that neither should be informed of the facts alleged or arguments advanced by the other. These would each and all be contrary to natural justice. I think and will assume that, fourthly, a rule could be made that each should be heard originally, not orally but in writing; but, fifthly, I greatly doubt whether a rule would be valid that a party who having sub-

mitted his case in writing desired to be heard orally should not be so heard.

The necessity for compliance with the requirements set out by the learned Lord Justice is illustrated by the decision of the divisional court in *R v Deputy Industrial Injuries Commission; Ex parte Jones.*[32] The applicant claimed industrial injuries benefit in respect of rheumatoid arthritis, which he stated was the consequence of an injury from an accident arising out of and in the course of his employment. The local insurance officer refused his claim, and on appeal, the deputy commissioner, after an oral hearing, received expert evidence from specialists in rheumatology, without informing the parties. He then gave his written decision, allowing the appeal, and referring to the advice given by the specialist. The divisional court quashed the decision, on the ground that this procedure infringed the rules of natural justice. In the words of Lord Parker:

> Here was a quasi-judicial tribunal, namely the deputy commissioner, deciding a case *inter partes* and required to arrive at his decision after an oral hearing. According to well-known principles, such a tribunal is not entitled, apart from express provision, to continue privately to obtain evidence between the end of the oral hearing and its decision without notifying the parties thereafter of the advice or information received, so as to give the parties an opportunity of having a further hearing if need be, or, at any rate, commenting on the information and making their final submissions thereon.

Hamilton, LJ, in *Arlidge's Case*, thought the term 'natural justice' vague, although Buckley, LJ, had given a precise content to it, and he thought the question of an oral presentation of a case unimportant. He also found nothing exceptionable in the practice of treating the report of the inspectors as confidential. It would not be unfair to say that Hamilton, LJ, gave an extremely restricted meaning to 'natural justice', and found nothing to which to object in the practice of the administrative tribunal. Although the passage of time has shown this view to be over optimistic and the courts have found it necessary to pay increasing attention to the requirements mentioned by Buckley, LJ, Hamilton, LJ's view was adopted in all essentials by the House of Lords. Lord Haldane, LC, neatly summarised the conflicting views in the Court of Appeal:[33]

> It is obvious [he said] that two of the judges there based their conclusions on the principle that in the absence of a direction to the contrary, which they could not find in the statute, the analogy of this procedure in a court of justice must guide them. Lord Justice Hamilton, on the contrary, thought that he found in the statute a scheme of procedure which excluded the analogy.

Later he adds:[34]

> When the duty of deciding an appeal is imposed [on an administrative body], those whose duty it is to decide it must act judicially. They must deal with the question referred to them without bias, and they must give to each of the parties the opportunity of presenting adequately the case made. The decision must be come to in the spirit and with the sense of responsibility of a tribunal whose duty it is to mete out justice. But it does not follow that the procedure of every tribunal must be the same. In the case of a court of law, tradition in this country has prescribed certain principles to which in the main the procedure must conform. But what that procedure is to be in detail must depend on the nature of the tribunal.

Lord Haldane does not attempt to discuss what, in this context, are matters of principle and what are matters of detail. Lord Shaw is even less precise. He says:[35]

> The words 'natural justice' occur in arguments and sometimes in judicial pronouncements in such cases. When a central administrative board deals with an appeal from a local authority

it must do its best to act justly, and to reach just ends by just means. If a statute prescribes the means it must employ them. If it is left without express guidance it must still act honestly and by honest means. In regard to these, certain ways and methods of judicial procedure may very like be imitated; and lawyer-like methods may find especial favour from lawyers. But that the judiciary should presume to impose its own methods on administrative or executive officers is a usurpation and the assumption that the methods of natural justice are *ex necessitate* those of courts of justice is wholly unfounded. This is expressly applicable to slips of procedure or forms of pleading. In so far as the term 'natural justice' means that a result or process should be just, it is harmless though it may be a high-sounding expression; in so far as it attempts to reflect the old *jus naturale* it is a confused and unwarranted transfer into the ethical sphere of a term employed for other distinctions; and, in so far as it is resorted to for other purposes, it is vacuous.

So natural justice, according to Lord Shaw, has nothing to do with steps in procedure or with forms of pleading. It is an unwarranted transfer into the ethical sphere of a term employed for other distinctions. What then, if anything, does it mean? Nothing of value, says Lord Shaw; and after showing undue humility concerning the functions of courts of justice, he abdicates in favour of the executive. Lord Moulton goes even further, if this is possible. He says that the question whether the procedure adopted in confirming the closing order was contrary to natural justice could not possibly be considered by the courts: 'Such a question would be unmeaning in such a connection.'[36] Finally, Lord Parmoor avoids the term 'natural justice' altogether. He asks whether the procedure is in accordance with the principles of substantial justice, but omits any attempt to define the term, and it is therefore not altogether surprising to find that he is of opinion that those undefined principles have been followed by the board in this case.

A student of jurisprudence will find much to puzzle him in these speeches in the House of Lords in this appeal. Terms are used in different senses, and without definition, to establish a conclusion which the law lords would seem to desire for other reasons. The decision has been productive of much subsequent difficulty, more especially as administrative jurisdiction has developed beyond anything thought to be possible in 1915. It has only been in recent years that the necessity of establishing some objective standard of decision for public authorities and tribunals of many kinds has been effectively suggested.

Fundamentally, natural justice does not establish any special kind of procedure, and, as *Arlidge's Case* makes plain, it certainly does not introduce into the proceedings of these varied authorities the stricter forms and rules of evidence of the ordinary courts. It does little more than ensure that parties adversely affected have an opportunity to be heard, that a decision is reached without the intervention of interest or bias, and that the authority or tribunal has a legal power to do what is contemplated. The last requirement is in any event protected by the *ultra vires* rule. These are the minimum elementary conditions for the protection of private rights in an age of incessant encroachment by state organs, whether central or local. A very large number of cases in recent times have been concerned with their maintenance.[37] One illustration will sufficiently demonstrate the need for continuing watchfulness. In *Urban Housing Co v Oxford City Council*[38] the Oxford City Council forcibly pulled down two walls which a housing company erected across private roads in its land, claiming that they acted under the Public Health Act, 1875, and the Private Street Works Act, 1892. In fact, the Court of Appeal held that the Public Health Act, 1875, had nothing to do with the demolition, and the corporation had adopted the Private Street Works Act, 1892, after the walls had been built. Sir Wilfrid Greene, MR, also pointed out that even when a local authority exercises a power of demolition lawfully, it

> is acting in a quasi-judicial capacity and must give the person concerned either a notice that they intend to take this matter into their consideration with a view to coming to a decision, or if they have come to a decision, that they propose to act upon

it, and give him an opportunity of showing cause why such steps should not be taken.

3 *Natural Justice and Trade Union Membership*

From very early times, the Common Law courts asserted the right to test expulsions of members from municipal and other corporations by the principles of natural justice which, as Lord Shaw pointed out in *Arlidge's Case*, were derived from the *jus naturale*. Later, courts of equity applied similar principles to the consideration of expulsions from clubs and voluntary associations of many kinds.[39] Once again, the basis of this supervision was stated to be the observance of the principles of natural justice. In applying them, nevertheless, the courts were careful to preserve the autonomy of the association. Thus in *Dawkins v Antrobus*[40] Brett, LJ, said:

> The only question which a Court can properly consider is whether the members of the club, under such circumstances, have acted *ultra vires* or not, and it seems to me, the only questions which a court can properly entertain for that purpose are, whether anything has been done which is contrary to natural justice, although it is within the rules of the club.

Dawkins v Antrobus was a club case. One of its rules provided that if the conduct of a member was, in the opinion of the committee, injurious to the character and interest of the club, he could be expelled. The Court of Appeal, being satisfied that there had been no violation of the principles of natural justice, and that the committee had acted in good faith, and in accordance with the rule, concluded that they could not examine the matter further.

A series of later decisions have spelled out what is meant by this. Although it is not clear whether a committee, in expelling a member, need give reasons for its decision (in the absence of any provision in the rules), if a reason is given, it must be the true reason. The hearing must be a fair one, and free from bias. This means particularly that a committee-member may not be both prosecutor and judge. All members of the committee must be summoned. The person whose expulsion is under consideration must be given notice of the charge against him, and he must have a proper opportunity of being heard. Failure to summon every member, and failure to state with reasonable clearness the purpose for which the meeting was summoned, invalidated the decision of the club committee in *Young v Ladies Imperial Club*,[41] but Lord Justice Scrutton remarked:

> In view of the very common practice of including rules by which the committee may expel members in the rules of club, I think it is desirable that it should be clearly understood that this court is not a court of appeal from the decisions of committees of clubs, provided the committees are properly constituted and properly summoned and deal with the matter in a way not contrary to the principles of natural justice.

With the growth in power and numbers of members of some associations (eg trade unions, the General Medical Council and the Law Society), the proceedings of tribunals or committees established by them to decide questions of membership and expulsions have acquired very great importance, since a decision to expel may deprive a person of his capacity to follow his calling or profession. Where statutory powers are given, the courts have scrutinised the proceedings of these tribunals minutely. Thus, in *General Medical Council v Spackman*[42] the House of Lords, in sharp contrast with its policy of trusting the executive, as demonstrated in *Arlidge's Case*, decided that the General Medical Council, in carrying out its statutory duty of determining whether a practitioner should be struck off the register after 'due inquiry', would not discharge that duty if it relied upon a decision of the divorce court, in which a doctor had been found guilty of adultery with a woman patient. In such cases, said the House of Lords, the council must give the doctor an opportunity to state his case, and exculpate himself, and Lord Wright said:[43]

> In *Arlidge's Case*, Hamilton, LJ, described the phrase 'contrary to natural justice' as 'an expression sadly lacking in precision'.

So it may be, and perhaps it is not desirable to attempt to force it into any procrustian bed. But the statements which I have quoted may at least be taken to emphasise the essential requirements that the tribunal should be impartial and that the medical practitioner who is impugned should be given a full and fair opportunity of being heard. These are conditions of the validity of any decision enunciated by the council... If the principles of natural justice are violated in respect of any decision, it is indeed immaterial whether the same decision would have been arrived at in the absence of the departure from the essential principles of justice. The decision must be declared to be no decision.

Since trade unions have the power, by expulsion, to prohibit a man from following his calling, their activities must be considered apart from those of clubs or other voluntary associations. Unless the rules of the union confer upon its officers or committee an arbitrary power of expulsion, the principles of natural justice must be observed.

For many years the fullest discussion of these in respect of expulsion from a trade union was to be found in the judgement of Maugham, J, in *Maclean v Workers' Union.*[44] Maclean had been expelled from the union, in accordance with the rules, and the court decided that it had no power to interfere, provided the committee had acted in good faith. In the course of his judgement, Maugham, J, said:

The jurisdiction of the courts in regard to domestic tribunals—a phrase which may conveniently be used to include the committees or the councils or the members of trade unions, of members' clubs, and of professional bodies established by statute or Royal Charter while acting in a quasi-judicial capacity—is clearly of a limited nature. Parenthetically I may observe that I am not confident that precisely the same principles will apply in all these cases; for it may be that a body entrusted with important duties by an Act of Parliament is not in the same position as, for example, the executive committee in the present case. Speaking generally, it is useful to bear in mind the very wide differences between the principles applicable to courts of justice and those applicable to domestic tribunals. In the former the accused is entitled to be tried by the Judge according to the evidence legally adduced and has a right to be represented by a skilled legal advocate. All the procedure of a modern trial, including the examination and cross-examination of the witnesses and the summing-up, if any, is based on these two circumstances. A domestic tribunal is in general a tribunal composed of laymen. It has no power to administer an oath, and—a circumstance which is perhaps of greater importance—no party has the power to compel the attendance of witnesses. It is not bound by the rules of evidence; it is indeed probably ignorant of them. It may act, and it sometimes must act, on mere hearsay, and in many cases the members present or some of them—like a British jury in ancient days—are themselves both witnesses and judges. Before such a tribunal, counsel have no right of audience and there are no effective means for testing by cross-examination the truth of the statements that may be made. The members of the tribunal may have been discussing the matter for weeks with persons not present at the hearing, and there is no one even to warn them of the danger of acting on pre-conceived views. It is apparent, and it is well settled by authority, that the decision of such a tribunal cannot be attacked on the ground that it is against the weight of evidence, since evidence in the proper sense there is none and since the decisions of the tribunal are not open to any sort of appeal unless the rules provide for one. There is perhaps a question whether the decision can be attached on the ground that there is no evidence—a word used presumably in the popular sense—upon which the tribunal could possibly come to such a conclusion. . .[45]

A person who joins an association governed by rules under which he may be expelled . . . has, in my judgment, no legal right of redress, if he be expelled according to the rules, however unfair and unjust the rules or the action of the expelling tribunal may be, provided that it acts in good faith. It is impossible to doubt that, if the rules postulate an inquiry, the accused must be given a reasonable opportunity of being heard. The phrase 'the principles of natural justice' can only mean in this connection the principles of fair play so deeply rooted in the minds of modern Englishmen that a provision for an inquiry necessarily imparts that the accused should be given his chance of defence and explanation. On that point there is no difficulty. Nor do I doubt that in most cases it is a reasonable inference from the rules that if there is anything of the nature of a *lis* between two persons, neither of them should sit on the tribunal. But when it is sought to lay down elaborate rules, taken from decisions as to courts of law, and to apply them in such a case as the present, I think it is prudent to remember that these more or less artificial principles have no application, except so far as they can be derived from a fair construction of the rules, and that the implications can only be made if it is clear that the parties, who are laymen and not lawyers, must have intended it.

These observations, rooted in optimism, appeared to concede the same abdication of judicial control of domestic tribunals as had been conceded to administrative tribunals by *Arlidge's Case*. More recent decisions have shown a consistent reassertion of judicial control.

In *Maclean's Case*, Maugham, J, evidently thought that if the rules of an association give an absolute power of exclusion, there could be no basis for an inquiry by the court whether the principles of natural justice had been observed. In some cases, the judges have been of opinion that rules giving such an arbitrary power are fully binding, particularly in cases where the controlling body of a sport have excluded a participant. For example, in *Russell v Duke of Norfolk and Others*,[46] a racehorse trainer was disqualified and warned off the turf, and his licence to train horses was withdrawn by the Jockey Club, which had power to take these steps in their absolute discretion. The trainer contended that the procedure adopted by the stewards was contrary to natural justice. At first instance Lord Goddard, basing his decision on the observations of Maugham, J, in *Maclean v The Workers' Union*,[47] decided that the Jockey Club, like the trade union, could dispense with the requirements of natural justice between members and others in contractual relations with them. The Court of Appeal preferred to avoid this important issue, by holding that the rules of the Jockey Club do require the stewards to hold an inquiry in conformity with the principles of natural justice before withdrawing a licence, and the procedure had been followed in this case. Once again the lords justices found the term 'natural justice' vague and unsatisfactory, and varied views were expressed by them on its relevance in cases such as this. Tucker, LJ, was of opinion that to import it into cases of this kind contradicted the unfettered discretion which the stewards were entitled to under the rules. Asquith, LJ, thought that there was an implied obligation, express or implied, under the contract, to conduct an inquiry in conformity with natural justice, where the withdrawal of a licence was under consideration. Finally, Denning, LJ, distinguished between withdrawing a licence as a matter of discretion, without inflicting a penalty, and withdrawing a licence as a penalty for misconduct. Only in the latter case was an inquiry, satisfying the requirement of natural justice, necessary.

Professor Robson, in the third edition of his *Justice and Administrative Law*, written shortly after this decision, expresses concern at the assumptions underlying it. As he points out, if Lord Goddard's argument is correct, voluntary associations of great power, unless expressly restrained by statute, may adopt articles and rules giving an arbitrary power to fine, expel or otherwise punish a member, and he adds:

> When we consider the weakness of the position in which an individual jockey, compositor, railway employee, shipyard worker, motor-car distributor, retail newsagent and all kinds of other persons so placed in the modern world, when they confront a powerful trade union, vocational organ or trade association to which they must belong if they are able to carry on their occupation, it is obvious that there are inumerable opportunities for injustice.[48]

He also pointed out that in this case the Court of Appeal had been, at best, tepid in its statement of the requirements of natural justice. It emerges most clearly in the judgement of Tucker, LJ. Commenting on the inquiry held by the stewards, he said:

> A layman at an inquiry of this kind is, of course, at a grave disadvantage compared with a trained advocate, but that is a necessary result of these domestic tribunals which proceed in a somewhat informal manner. Counsel for the plaintiff, in the course of his forceful argument on this point, again and again said: 'What would be said of local justices who acted in this way?' With all due respect, the position is totally different. The matter is not to be judged by the standards applicable to local justices. Domestic tribunals of this kind are entitled to act in a way which would not be permissible on the part of local justices sitting as a court of law. The conclusion I have reached on this aspect of the case is that there is no material on which a jury could have arrived at a conclusion that the inquiry was conducted in a way contrary to the principles of natural justice. If, as I think is the better view, it really was a matter of law for the decision of the judge, I should unhesitatingly hold that there was nothing here which was contrary to the principles of natural justice as laid down in the various authorities which have been brought to our notice. There are, in my view, no words which are of universal application to every kind of enquiry and every kind of domestic tribunal. The requirements of natural justice must depend on the circumstances of the case, the nature of the inquiry, the rules under which the tribunal is acting, the subject-matter that is being dealt with, and so forth.

These last two sentences debase the conception of natural justice even further than Maugham, J's, observations in *Maclean's Case,* and Tucker, LJ's, view was adopted by Pilcher, J, as the foundation for his own in *Davis v Carew Pole,*[49] a case in which a livery-stable keeper was required to attend an inquiry held by the stewards of the National Hunt Committee, to answer allegations that he had trained a horse contrary to the National Hunt Rules. In an action by him against the stewards, following his disqualification, it was held that he had no cause for complaint in respect of the way in which the inquiry was conducted, although Pilcher, J, held on other grounds, that the stewards were not entitled to declare the plaintiff a disqualified person.

Although there still seems to be a distinct tenderness towards inquiries of this kind, there has been an evident hardening of attitude towards the conduct of expulsion proceedings by committees of trade unions, and similar bodies. The principal reason for this is that expressed by Denning, LJ, in *Russell v Duke of Norfolk,* ie that the Jockey Club had a monopoly in an important field of human activity. With its great powers were corresponding liabilities to ensure that justice was done to those who came before its stewards. In other words, the recent tendency has been to bring the proceedings by bodies possessing such powers more closely into line with those of professional bodies such as the General Medical Council and the Law Society, whose disciplinary powers are conferred by statute.

This approach was developed by all the judges of the Court of Appeal, but most fully by Denning, LJ, again, in their impressive judgement in *Lee v The Showmen's Guild of Great Britain.*[50] Lee was a member of a trade union of travelling showmen. He had been allowed a particular site at the fairground by the local corporation. The area committee of the union had given the site to another member, who had used it before the war. Lee refused to accept the ruling of the committee, claiming the benefit of a by-law of the regional section. The rival claimant therefore complained to the committee, alleging unfair competition by Lee, prohibited by the rules. The committee heard the dispute and decided against Lee, imposing a fine on him. This he refused to pay, whereupon the committee expelled him for non-payment of the fine—a decision which had the effect of depriving him of his right to earn his living on fairgrounds in the United Kingdom, controlled by the union.

Lee sued the union, challenging the validity of the committee's decision, and seeking an injunction to prevent the union from expelling him. Ormerod, J, decided that Lee had done nothing which amounted to unfair competition, and that the committee's decision was wrong in law, *ultra vires* and void. The Court of Appeal unanimously affirmed this decision, and in their judgement, they examined fully the nature and extent of the court's jurisdiction in respect of decisions of domestic tribunals. It was based on contract, to which all union members were parties, and being a contract, it was for the law to construe its terms, like any other contract. This was of major importance, for it had been argued on behalf of the union that the decision of the committee on the construction of the rules was final.

Denning, LJ, in his exhaustive examination of the jurisdiction of the court in these matters, pointed out that although this jurisdiction of domestic tribunals was founded on contract, the parties were not free to make any contracts they liked. There are limitations imposed by public policy. These are:

1 The tribunal must observe the principles of natural justice.
2 The parties may not oust the jurisdiction of the ordinary courts.

> They can, of course, agree to leave questions of law, as well as questions of fact, to the decision of the domestic tribunal. They can, indeed, make the tribunal the final arbiter of questions of fact, but they cannot make it the final arbiter on questions of law. They cannot prevent its decisions being examined by the courts. If parties should seek by agreement, to take the law out of the hands of the courts and put it into the hands of the private tribunal, without any recourse at all to the courts in case of error of law, then the agreement is to that extent contrary to public policy.

Denning, LJ, then pointed out that the answer to the question of the extent to which the courts would examine the decisions of domestic tribunals was not to be found in the club cases. In the case of social club, the rules usually empower the committee to expel a member who, in their opinion, has been guilty of conduct detrimental to the club. That is, however, purely a matter of opinion, with which the court will not interfere, so long as the rules of fair play have been observed, and the procedure prescribed by the rules has been followed.

> It is very different with domestic tribunals which sit in judgement on the members of a trade or profession. They wield powers as great as, if not greater than, any exercised by the courts of law. They can deprive a man of his livelihood. They can ban him from the trade in which he has spent his life and which is the only trade he knows. They are usually empowered to do this for any breach of their rules, which, be it noted, are rules which they impose and which he has no real opportunity of accepting or rejecting. In theory their powers are based on contract. The man is supposed to have contracted to give them these great powers, but in practice he has no choice in the matter. If he is to engage in the trade, he has to submit to the rules promulgated by the committee. Is such a tribunal to be treated by these courts on the same footing as a social club? I say no. A man's right to work is just as important to him as, if not more important than, his rights of property. These courts intervene every day to protect rights of property. They must also intervene to protect the right to work.

Lord Denning then explained that the courts will always examine the decision of a domestic tribunal to ensure that it has observed the law. This includes the correct interpretation of the rules. Thus, in the actual case, the court may construe 'unfair competition', and correct a wrong interpretation, for it is the province of the court, *and no one else*, to decide what the true construction of the contract is.

> The rules are the contract between the members. The committee cannot extend their jurisdiction by giving a wrong interpretation to the contract, no matter how honest they may be. They have only such jurisdiction as the contract on its true interpretation confers on them, not what they think it confers. The scope of their jurisdiction is a matter for the courts, and not for the parties, let alone for one of them. This is how the

House of Lords approached the problem in the *Carpenters' Case*,[51] and I think we should follow their example.

This judgement establishes a clear principle upon a very difficult question, and for the first time repaired the damage done by Maugham, J's, judgement in *Maclean v The Workers' Union* by separating the club cases from cases relating to the exclusionary powers of trade unions, professional associations and similar bodies. It also stressed the major public interest in such proceedings, in what Lord Denning termed 'the right to work'. It is directly linked with the decisions of the Court of Appeal and the House of Lords in *Bonsor v Musicians' Union*,[52] which is discussed elsewhere.[53] In that case the House of Lords decided that the worker who had suffered by the wrongful acts of the committee of a trade union could obtain damages, as well as an injunction, after he had been deprived of his occupation by expulsion.

Unfortunately not all decisions on these matters show the same breadth of vision as was shown by the lords justices in *Lee's Case*. In *Breen v Amalgamated Engineering Union*,[54] decided by the Court of Appeal in January 1971, Breen, a former shop steward of the union, had been, in the words of Edmund Davies, LJ, 'pursued with venom over a period of years' by the district secretary, who, with the district committee, refused to reappoint him as shop steward. Cusack, J, held that although the committee's decision was not bound to be based on reasons which would commend themselves to honest people, he could not disturb it, and a majority of the Court of Appeal, whilst doubting that their decision would serve the ends of justice, nevertheless felt unable to reverse it. Edmund Davies, LJ, added: 'That is, to say the least, a most regrettable situation for any judge, but I see no escape from it. Its effect is to turn away, empty-handed, from this court an appellant who, on any view, has been grossly abused. It is, therefore, a judgement which it gives no satisfaction to deliver.'

From this negative conclusion, Lord Denning, MR, strongly dissented. Cusack, J, and the majority of the Court of Appeal had thought that they were debarred from reviewing the decision of the district committee, because that body, in dealing with Breen, were not exercising a judicial or quasi-judicial function. They were simply exercising a discretion, which could only be upset in the absence of bad faith. From this view Lord Denning dissented, pointing out that in the last twenty-two years there had been developed a system of administrative law, which had greatly extended the range of judicial review of decisions, not only of statutory bodies, but of domestic bodies. He continues:

> Take first statutory bodies. It is now well settled that a statutory body which is entrusted by statute with a discretion, must act fairly. It does not matter whether its functions are described as judicial or quasi-judicial on the one hand, or as administrative on the other hand, or what you will. Still it must act fairly. It must, in a proper case, give a party a chance to be heard; see *In re H.K. (an infant)*[55] by Lord Parker, CJ, in relation to immigration officers, and *Reg v Gaming Board for Great Britain, Ex parte Benaim and Khaida*[56] by us in relation to the gaming board. The discretion of a statutory body is never unfettered. It is a discretion which is to be exercised according to law. That means at least this: the statutory body must be guided by relevant considerations and not be irrelevant. If its decision is influenced by extraneous considerations which it ought not to have taken into account, then the decision cannot stand. No matter that the statutory body may have acted in good faith; nevertheless the decision will be set aside. That is established by *Padfield v Minister of Agriculture, Fisheries and Food*,[57] which is a landmark in modern administrative law.
>
> Does all this apply also to a domestic body? I think it does, at any rate when it is a body set up by one of the powerful associations which we see nowadays. Instances are readily to be found in the books, notably the Stock Exchange, the Jockey Club, the Football Association, and innumerable trade unions. All these delegate powers to committees. These committees are domestic bodies which control the destinies of thousands. They have quite as much power as the statutory bodies of

which I have been speaking. They can make or mar a man by their decisions, not only by expelling him from membership, but also by refusing to admit him as a member; or, it may be, by a refusal to grant a licence or to give their approval. Often their rules are formed so as to give them a discretion. They then claim that it is an 'unfettered' discretion with which the courts have no right to interfere. They go too far. They claim too much. The Minister made the same claim in the *Padfield Case* and was soundly rebuked by the House of Lords for his impertinence. So should we treat this claim by trade unions. They are not above the law, but subject to it. Their rules are said to be a contract between the members and the unions. So be it. If they are a contract, then it is an implied term that the discretion should be exercised fairly. But the rules are in reality more than a contract. They are a legislative code laid down by the Council of the Union to be obeyed by the members. This code should be subject to control by the courts just as much as a code laid down by Parliament itself. If the rules set up a domestic body and give it a discretion, it is to be implied that the body must exercise its discretion fairly. Even though its functions are not judicial or quasi-judicial, but only administrative, still it must act fairly. Should it not do so, the courts can review its decision, just as it can review the decision of a statutory body. The courts cannot grant the prerogative writs such as certiorari and mandamus against domestic bodies, but they can grant declaration and injunction, which are the modern machinery for enforcing administrative law.

Lord Denning went on to consider whether these bodies, statutory or domestic, should give reasons for their decisions, and give the person a chance of being heard. On this, he said it depended on the circumstances:

If a man seeks a privilege to which he has no particular claim —such as an appointment to some post or other—then he can be hurried away without a word. He need not be heard, and no reason need be given for his rejection.[58]. . . But if he is a man whose property is at stake, or who is being deprived of his livelihood, then reasons should be given why he is being turned down, and he should be given a chance to be heard. I go further. If he is a man who has some right or interest, or some legitimate expectation, of which it would not be fair to deprive him without a hearing or reason given, then these should be afforded him, according as the case may demand. The giving of reasons is one of the fundamentals of good administration. Again take *Padfield's Case*.[59] The dairy farmers had no right to have their complaint referred to a committee of investigation, but they had a legitimate expectation that it would be. The House made it clear that if the Minister rejected their request without reason, the court might infer that he had no good reason, and, that if he gave a bad reason, it might vitiate his decision.

Many will agree that these observations represent the true role of the Common Law (and also the judicial function) in bringing administrative and domestic bodies into harmony with principles of fairness and justice. By coincidence, an almost contemporaneous decision of Pennycuick, VC, in *Glynn v Keele University*,[60] affirmed the same principle. The Vice-Chancellor of Keele University suspended and fined a student who had been seen naked in the precincts of the university, without giving the student a hearing, at the same time informing him of the penalties and of his right of appeal. Pennycuick, VC, held that the Vice-Chancellor was acting in a quasi-judicial capacity, and that the student therefore had a right to be heard before penalties were imposed. The decision follows the plain indication given by the House of Lords in *Ridge v Baldwin*[61] of the present scope of remedies for a denial of natural justice. In that case the House of Lords decided the statutory power of a watch committee to dismiss a police constable could only be exercised in accordance with the requirements of natural justice, and Lord Reid, together with other law lords, was of the opinion that the principles of natural justice should be applied in an increasing number of matters, many of which involved the personal status of the complainant. Nevertheless, whilst much ground has been recovered by the courts in recent years, it is apparent that the struggle for natural justice, especially in domestic tribunals, intimately bound up as it often is with employment and the right to personal freedom, is as yet by no means won.

13

The Modern Law of Torts and Contracts

Most people, and not only the legal profession, would concur in the view that the role of the judiciary today is very different from what it was a century ago. The judges are different, and so are the problems which they face. In the settled days of the nineteenth century certain principles underlying human behaviour were axiomatic. We cannot say that today. Again, the institution of property was not yet under attack. There was a generally accepted code of public behaviour and the limits of the state's intrusion into the affairs of the individual were clearly defined and generally accepted. In such an environment the Common Law appeared to be a settled system, based on principles derived from earlier ages, still capable of systematic development, but strongly resistant to violent change. To give only one or two examples; the law of contract reflected at once the classic principle of individual freedom and the economic doctrine of *laisser faire*. A contract required a true union of wills, expressed in the term *consensus ad idem*, and because of that freedom, it protected the contracting parties against fraud, oppression or misrepresentation, but it was not concerned with the adequacy of bargains. Here the maxim was *caveat emptor*. Above all, contract was a realm in which the parties were supreme. This stands in sharp contrast to the modern view that the state and the general public have a direct interest in such matters as the price, quality and fitness of wide classes of goods, and even, as in hire-purchase, the conditions of sale—an interest which it manifests both by legislation and by administrative regulation. The courts in their interpretation of individual bargains have necessarily reflected this changed outlook. For example, the courts and draftsmen have fought a prolonged battle over clauses in contracts, purporting to exclude 'all implied conditions and warranties', and almost at the moment when the skill of the draftsmen appeared to have prevailed against the policy of the courts to prevent abuses of contractual freedom,[1] the courts returned to the attack with the doctrine of the fundamental term and the fundamental breach. Though the doctrine is not new to the Common Law, it has been applied with a great deal of flexibility in numerous modern cases. In essence it implied that if the purchaser gets something different from what the contract specified he should get, the contract may be rescinded, or damages may be obtained. Obviously, if A contracts to buy one thing and is offered a different one, this is not performance of the contract, but the complexities increase when the question is, not whether a second-hand motor car is of a specified make or not, but whether it is 'sound', or 'roadworthy', or 'in good running order'. Decisions upon the doctrine of the fundamental term are something more than exercises in linguistics. They are examples of a changed social outlook, as reflected in the opinions of judges. They emphasise that judges, in applying the law, do so in a context of policy, and not as a logical exercise. Long ago, Mr Justice Holmes, in a celebrated aphorism, explained that the life of the law was not logic, but experience. The quality of a judge can often be measured by the ability which he shows in interpreting and assessing the principal trends in the social philosophy of his age, and in expressing his interpretation in terms of legal principle. One of the best known illustrations of this quality is to be found in Lord Atkin's speech in *Donaghue v Stevenson*,[2] when he says:

> In English law there must be and is some general conception of relations giving rise to a duty of care of which the particular cases found in the books are but instances. The liability for negligence, whether you style it such or treat it as in other systems as a species of 'culpa', is no doubt based upon a general public sentiment of moral wrongdoing for which the offender must pay. But acts or omissions which any moral code would

> censure cannot in a practical world be treated so as to give a right to every person injured by them to demand relief. In this way rules of law arise which limit the range of complainants and the extent of their remedy. The rule that you are to love your neighbour becomes in law you must not injure your neighbour, and the question who is my neighbour receives a restricted reply. You must take reasonable care to avoid acts or omissions which you can reasonably foresee would be likely to injure your neighbour. Who then in law is my neighbour? The answer seems to be persons who are so closely and directly affected by any act that I ought reasonably to have them in contemplation as being so affected when I am directing my mind to acts or omissions which are called in question.

In the actual case, the House of Lords was called upon to decide whether a manufacturer of ginger beer was liable to the ultimate consumer who had suffered injury through the negligent introduction of deleterious substances in the bottle. This was recognised by the majority of the House of Lords as an extension of liability for negligence, but on this Lord Atkin commented: 'I do not think so ill of our jurisprudence as to suppose that its principles are so remote from the ordinary needs of civilised society and the ordinary claims it makes upon its members as to deny a legal remedy when there is so obviously a social wrong.' Rarely has the judicial function in law-making been so concisely explained, and in the same case Lord Macmillan discussed that function in rather different terms. He said:

> The categories of negligence are never closed. The cardinal principle of liability is that the party complained of should owe to the party complaining a duty to take care and that the party complaining should be able to prove that he has suffered damage in consequence of a breach of that duty. Where there is room for diversity of view is in determining what circumstances will establish such a relationship between the parties as to give rise on the one side, to a duty to take care and on the other side to a right to have care taken.

In the determination of those circumstances there is plainly scope, not only for judicial law-making, but for the application of social policy in the development of rules of law. The creation and progressive extensions of the law of negligence in modern times, almost entirely as a result of judicial law-making, is an impressive illustration of Lord Atkin's observations, and setting boundaries to the action for negligence has involved the consideration of problems, not all of which are as yet satisfactorily solved. So long as the forms of action exercised an influence upon the development of the law of torts, it would have been difficult to think of negligence as an independent tort, although it could be an element in many torts. There could be liability for damage intentionally inflicted and in many cases, too, there could be liability for similar damage negligently committed, but for many years the basis of liability was the commission of some pre-existing tort; for example—trespass to the person. But negligence is a term which lawyers and others find exceedingly difficult to define in the abstract. Perusal of the decisions and of statutory definitions shows that, wherever possible, it is related to particular situations, and that its meaning is variable. For example, in *Andrews v Director of Public Prosecutions*[3] (a criminal case of homicide by negligence), Lord Atkin said:

> The principle to be observed is that cases of manslaughter in driving motor-cars are but instances of a general rule applicable to all charges of homicide by negligence. Simple lack of care such as will constitute civil liability is not enough; for purposes of the criminal law there are degrees of negligence, and a very high degree of negligence is required to be proved before the felony is established. Probably of all the epithets that can be applied, 'reckless' most nearly covers the case. It is difficult to visualise a case of death caused by 'reckless' driving in the connotation of that term in ordinary speech which would not justify a conviction for manslaughter; but it is probably not all-embracing, for 'reckless' suggests an indifference to risk, whereas the accused may have appreciated the risk and intended to avoid it and yet shown such a high degree of negli-

gence in the means adopted to avoid the risk as would justify a conviction.

These observations are of value in stressing the difference between civil liability for negligence (now a separate and very comprehensive tort) and responsibility in the criminal law, where negligence as such is not a ground of liability. Certain harmful acts, such as homicide, if committed negligently, may involve criminal liability, and as Lord Atkin points out, there may be degrees, and even different kinds of negligence in this context. Even in civil law, the concept itself is difficult to identify with precision. For example in *Nance v British Columbia Electric Railway*[4] Lord Simon said: 'It is, perhaps, unfortunate that the phrase "contributory negligence" uses the word "negligence" in a sense somewhat different from that which the latter word would bear when negligence is the cause of action.'

Faced with these, and many connected difficulties, the courts in the nineteenth century adopted the course of allying the development of the tort of negligence with the concept of the duty of care. In this way, it was possible to associate it with the idea that there was no liability, even in civil law, apart from the duty of care, and in a striking section of his *Jurisprudence*,[5] Paton has shown how well this harmonised with prevailing individualist and *laisser-faire* theories, and consequently, how much of a shock to these theories was the decision of *Rylands v Fletcher* in 1868,[6] with its acceptance of strict liability. In more recent times the scope of strict liability has extended, and it affords, in Paton's phrase, 'an interesting illustration of the adaptation of case law to new situations and new social philosophies'. Thus, one may detect, in some modern decisions, a steady shift from the conception of fault to that of *risque crée* as a basis of tortious liability. Such a substitution has been strongly urged, not only by some American writers, but also in a number of American decisions. Their views, and the fundamental questions underlying such a proposed transfer, were discussed by all the members of the House of Lords in one of the most interesting modern decisions in the law of torts, *Read v J. Lyons & Co Ltd.*[7] The facts of that case were extremely simple, and not in dispute. The plaintiff was employed by the defendants in a munitions factory where shells were filled with high explosives. She was injured in the course of her duties by an explosion on 31 August 1942. There was no allegation of negligence on the part of the defendants, so that the question was whether, by virtue of the dangerous nature of the occupation, the liability of the defendants was strict, on the principle on *Rylands v Fletcher*.[8] All the members of the House of Lords were of opinion that, in the absence of negligence, the plaintiff had no cause of action, and in reaching this conclusion, they expressed the opinion that *Rylands v Fletcher* was not a principle of general application, but should be confined within its accepted limits, ie to cases in which there is escape from land of something likely to do mischief arising out of a non-natural use of the land. Whether this will be the final answer to this question of major principle remains to be seen, but in the meantime, the views of the members of the House of Lords are instructive. Lord Simon cited with approval an observation of Lindley, LJ (given before the end of the nineteenth century),[9] that if *Rylands v Fletcher* were extended as far as strict logic might require, it would be a very oppressive decision. Lord Macmillan emphatically reaffirmed the fault principle. He says:

> In my opinion, the plaintiff's statement of claim discloses no ground of action against the defendants. The action is one of damages for personal injuries. Whatever may have been the law of England in early times, I am of opinion that as the law now stands an allegation of negligence is, in general, essential to the relevancy of an action of reparation for personal injuries.[10] The gradual development of the law in the matter of civil liability is discussed and traced by the late Sir William Holdsworth with ample learning and lucidity in the eighth volume of his *History of English Law* (pp 446 et seqq), and need not here be rehearsed. Suffice it to say that the process of evolution has been from the principle that every man acts at his peril, and is liable for all the consequences of his acts, to the principle that a man's freedom of action is subject only to the obligation not

to infringe any duty or care which he owes to others. The emphasis formerly was on the injury sustained, and the question was whether the case fell within one of the accepted classes of common law actions; the emphasis now is on the conduct of the person whose act has occasioned the injury, and the question is whether it can be characterised as negligent.

In order to determine this, of course, it must first be established that the defendant owed a duty of care, and if he did, a jury must decide whether he has shown that degree of care that a reasonable man would show in the circumstances—unless a statute has prescribed the extent of the duty of care required, as has been done in respect of an increasing number of industrial situations.

The hesitations which eminent judges have in accepting the principle of *Rylands v Fletcher* as capable of extension, even to the extent that the principle of *Donaghue v Stevenson* has been extended, are apparent from Lord Porter's speech in this case. In making this contrast we may perhaps point out that the extensions of the *Donaghue v Stevenson* principle, being within the sphere of negligence, but ultimately founded on fault, are therefore reconcilable with personal responsibility for acts done, whilst extensions of the principle of *Rylands v Fletcher* manifestly are not. Lord Porter, after discussing the limitations in *Rylands v Fletcher* involved in escapes of substances arising from non-natural use of land, continues:

> Manifestly these requirements must give difficulty in applying the rule in individual cases, and necessitate at least a decision as to what can be dangerous and what is a non-natural use. Indeed, there is a considerable body of case-law dealing with these questions, and a series of findings and assumptions as to what is sufficient to establish their existence. Amongst dangerous objects which have been held to be dangerous are included gas, explosive substances, electricity, oil, fumes, rusty wire, poisonous vegetation, vibrations, a flag pole, and even dwellers in caravans. Furthermore, in *Musgrove v Pandelis*,[11] it was held that a motor-car brought into a garage with full tanks was

a dangerous object, a conclusion which as Romer, LJ, pointed out in *Collingwood v Home and Colonial Stores*,[12] involves the propositions that a motor-car is a dangerous thing to bring into a garage, and keeping a motor car there is not an ordinary or proper use of the land.

> If these questions ever come directly before this House it may become necessary to lay down principles for their determination. For the present I need only say that each seems to be a question of fact subject to a ruling of the Judge as to whether the particular object can be dangerous or the particular use can be non-natural, and in deciding the question I think that all the circumstances of the time and place and practice of mankind must be taken into consideration so that what might be regarded as dangerous, or non-natural may vary according to those circumstances.

The resistance to any inclination to lay down any broad propositions relating to social policy is plainly apparent in Lord Porter's remarks, and it would not usually be shared by an American or by a French judge. Possibly an English judge is more conscious of the cramping effects of such pronouncements, especially in a system whose development is conditioned by the doctrine of judicial precedent. At any rate, this survey of judicial attitudes in a highly interesting case may end with an observation of Lord Simonds. After pointing out that two theories had long been in conflict—the first, that a man acts at his peril, and the second, 'that a man is not liable unless he is to blame'—Lord Simonds concludes:

> There is not one principle only which is to be applied with rigid logic to all cases. To this result both the infinite complexity of human affairs and the historical development of the forms of action contribute.

Nevertheless, the sturdy individualism of the majority of our most eminent judges still tilts the balance in favour of liability for fault—a principle which is at least as old as Bracton.

The illustrations already mentioned are no more than isolated examples of a comprehensive process of judicial law-making which has decisively shaped the form of modern English society —a process which has been beset by difficulties of many kinds, and in which judicial successes have vastly outnumbered judicial failures. The Common Law in its earliest phase, when still constricted by the forms of action, defined in terms of civil law the nature of social relationships, and the extent of the legal responsibility of the individual to respect of these social relationships. This was an area into which legislators rarely ventured. Accordingly, it became the inescapable task of the judges to define in accordance with prevailing notions of social and political conduct, the effect of the impact of one individual's action upon another. One wide area of this—the area of negligence involving legal liability—was described centuries later by Lord Atkin in *Donaghue v Stevenson*[13] in terms which have already been mentioned, though there were many others. So long as the forms of action remained a reality, the duty of the judges was to follow well-trodden paths, and accordingly, some bases of civil liability at Common Law—for example, fraud—remained confined within surprisingly narrow limits until the nineteenth century. Remedies were most certain when there was a violation of property rights, whether by trespass, nuisance or some allied tort, for these violations of the rights of another had been well understood, and continuously litigated in the time of the Year Books. It was only when the law of torts began to emancipate itself from the forms of action in response to the far reaching social changes of the first half of the nineteenth century that it began to assume a recognisably modern form.

Not all developments were happy ones. In *Priestley v Fowler*,[14] decided by Lord Abinger in the year 1840, the doctrine of common employment was created, without the support of any authority.

The consequences of the decision were disastrous, and very different from those which Lord Abinger had described. With the development of large-scale industry, with its corporate organisation it became the means of frustrating the claims of innumerable employees for injuries suffered as a consequence either of unsafe conditions or of the negligence of a fellow-employee. The doctrine of common employment was disliked by the majority of later judges, who sought to restrict its operation by defining 'common employment' with some strictures, but they were unable to rid the law of it. The doctrine was applied to persons in many different kinds of employment, for example, a mining engineer, or even a manager. The basis of the rule was that the servant, in accepting employment, had also accepted the risk of injury caused by the negligence of the fellow-servant,[15] a manifest fiction. The doctrine was so unfair to the ordinary workman that it was severely restricted in operation by the Employers Liability Act, 1880, and by various Workmen's Compensation Acts, which provided for compensation for industrial injury quite independently of it. Outside these areas the doctrine still worked injustice, although some of the later decisions sought to find grounds for holding that persons were not in common employment. For example in *Radcliffe v Ribble Motor Services Ltd*,[16] the House of Lords held by a majority that motor-coach drivers employed by the same firm were not in common employment when they were driving on the streets, and the House also held, in *Wilsons and Clyde Coal Co v English*,[17] that the employer is under a duty at Common Law to provide a proper staff of competent men, adequate material, a proper system of work and effective supervision—an attitude to employment which must surely have caused Lord Abinger to stir restlessly in his grave. At last, by the Law Reform (Personal Injuries) Act, 1948, Parliament abolished a doctrine whose birth had been regretted by most of the judiciary for over half a century.

Few judicial excursions into the law of torts have been as infelicitous as this one. For the most part the courts have been preoccupied with tracing the lines between lawful and unlawful conduct, drawing extensively upon the mythical concept of the 'ordinary, reasonable man'. Out of necessity they have been compelled to grapple, although with evident reluctance, with such concepts as proximate cause, *causa causans*, *novus actus inter-*

veniens, measure of damages, and foreseeable consequences. They have also, again with hesitation, accepted the conception of nervous shock as a ground of legal liability. Here, even today, the legislature can be of little direct assistance.

The approach of the courts in modern times to the problem of nervous shock and emotional distress caused by the actions of another has been highly interesting, for it has involved them in a consideration of such diverse elements as duty, the standard of care, remoteness of damage, and the nature of the injury in respect of which damages are claimed. It was at one time thought that damages could be recovered only for actual physical injury, but that view is now discarded, although it may be that even today there is no redress for mere mental suffering, unaccompanied by other injury. However, as Lord Macmillan pointed out in *Bourhill v Young*:[18]

> The crude view that the law takes cognisance only of physical injury resulting from actual impact has been discarded and it is now well recognised that an action will lie for injury by shock sustained through the medium of the eye or ear without direct contact. The distinction between mental shock and bodily injury was never a scientific one, for mental shock is presumably in all cases the result of, or at least accompanied by, some physical disturbance in the sufferer's system.

This is most clearly seen in the frequent cases in which some frightening episode has produced a miscarriage in a pregnant woman who observed it.

In many instances, the injury is caused by the negligence of another, but it can be deliberately caused. Thus, in *Wilkinson v Downton*,[19] the defendant, by way of a practical joke, told the plaintiff that her husband was lying seriously injured in a public house in Leytonstone. This produced such a shock to the plaintiff's nervous system that there were serious and permanent physical consequences for which the defendant was held liable.

Many nervous shock cases arise out of the negligence of another, leading either to an apprehension of danger to the plaintiff, or of danger to a third party, which is witnessed by the plaintiff. The first example poses fewer problems than the second. In *Duliea v White and Sons*,[20] the defendant's servant negligently drove a van into the front of a public house, where the plaintiff was standing behind the bar. She suffered a severe shock and resultant illness, for which she recovered damages. So did the plaintiff in *Hambrook v Stokes*,[21] when the defendant's lorry was negligently allowed to run away down a steep hill, at the bottom of which, and beyond the corner, were the plaintiff's children. The plaintiff's wife suffered such extreme anxiety for the safety of her children that she became ill, and subsequently died. This case, however, introduced the problems of remoteness of damage and the duty of care. If the plaintiff's wife had not seen the run-away lorry, but the episode had been related to her by a neighbour, would the damage have been too remote? Further, to whom does the driver of a vehicle on the road owe a duty of care? The answer as framed by the courts would seem to be that he owes it to all those who can reasonably be regarded as within his contemplation, ie who are either drivers or pedestrians within his range of vision.

This evident anxiety of the courts not to give the action for nervous shock too wide a range is illustrated by the decision of the House of Lords in *Bourhill v Young*.[22] The plaintiff (a pregnant woman) heard (but did not see) an accident in which a motor-cyclist was killed, whilst she was getting her basket off the far side of a stationary tramcar, from which she had just alighted, and which was approximately fifty feet from the accident. She suffered severe shock and subsequent illness, but the House of Lords held that she was not entitled to damages since the motor-cyclist (whose negligence had caused the accident) could not reasonably have anticipated that anyone in her position would be affected by his negligence. Accordingly, he owed no legal duty to her. Lord Wright, in his speech in that case, also stressed that the duty of care, even when it exists, is owed to normal persons, not to persons with an idiosyncratic disability. He says:

The present case, like many others of this type, may however, raise the different question whether the appellant's illness was not due to her peculiar susceptibility. She was eight months gone in pregnancy. Can it be said, apart from anything else, that it was likely that a person of normal nervous strength would have been affected in the circumstances by illness as the appellant was? Does the criterion of reasonable foresight extend beyond people of ordinary health or susceptibility, or does it take into account the peculiar susceptibilities or infirmities of those affected, which the defendant neither knew nor could reasonably be taken to have foreseen? Must the manner of conduct adapt itself to such special individual peculiarities? If extreme cases are taken, the answer appears to be fairly clear, unless indeed there is knowledge of the extraordinary risk. One who suffers from the terrible tendency to bleed on slight contact, which is denoted by the term 'a bleeder', cannot complain if he mixes with the crowd and suffers severely, perhaps fatally, from being merely rushed against. There is no wrong done there. A blind or deaf man who crossed the traffic on a busy street cannot complain if he is run over by a careful driver who does not know of and could not be expected to observe and guard against the man's infirmity.

In the case of a blind man, nevertheless, the possession of a white stick by him may be held to give knowledge to the driver of extraordinary risk. There are, indeed, many problems in this area as yet unresolved, as the two decisions of the Privy Council in the *Wagon Mound* will illustrate. In 1921, the Court of Appeal in *Re Polemis and Furness Withy*[23] rejected the supposed rule that a wrongdoer is responsible only for the natural and probable consequences of his act, and decided that once it had been established that the defendant had been negligent, he was liable for all the direct consequences of that negligent act, whether probable (or apparently, foreseeable) or not. The *Thrasyvoulis*, on charter, carried a cargo of benzine and petrol in tins contained in cases. There was a leakage from the cans into the hold, and at a port of call, whilst some cases were being shifted by the charterers' servants, a board was negligently knocked down into the hold, as a result of which there was an explosion and fire, in which the vessel was completely destroyed. The Court of Appeal held the charterers completely liable for the loss. The real difficulty in deciding the appeal arose from the fact that there was prior judicial authority which appeared to support both views. These were discussed by the three lord justices, but their view is most clearly expressed by Scrutton, LJ, in the following way:

> The second defence is that the damage is too remote from the negligence, as it could not be reasonably foreseen as a consequence. On this head we were referred to a number of well known cases in which vague language, which I cannot think to be really helpful, has been used to attempt to define the point at which damage becomes too remote from, or not sufficiently directly caused by the breach of duty, which is the original cause of action, to be recoverable. For instance, I cannot think it useful to say the damage must be the natural and probable result. This suggests that there are results which are probable but not natural. I am not sure what either adjective means in this connection; if they mean the same thing, two need not be used; if they mean different things, the difference between them should be defined. And as to many cases of fact in which the distinction has been drawn, it is difficult to see why one case should be decided one way and one another. Perhaps the House of Lords will one day explain why, if a cheque is negligently filled up, it is a direct effect of the negligence that someone finding the cheque should commit forgery,[24] while if someone negligently leaves a libellous letter about, it is not a direct effect of the negligence that the finder should show the letter to the person libelled.[25] In this case, however, the problem is simpler. To determine whether an act is negligent, it is relevant to determine whether any reasonable person would foresee that the act would cause damage. The fact that the damage it in fact causes is not the exact kind of damage one would expect is immaterial, so long as the damage is in fact caused sufficiently directed by the negligent act, and not by the operation of independent causes having no connection with the negligent

> act, except that they could not avoid its results. Once the act is negligent, the fact that its exact operation was not foreseen is immaterial... In the present case it was negligent in discharging cargo to knock down the planks of the temporary staging, for they might easily cause some damage either to workmen, or to cargo, or the ship. The fact that they did directly produce an unexpected result, a spark in an atmosphere of petrol vapour which caused a fire, does not relieve the person who was negligent from the damage which his negligent act indirectly caused.

In the half-century which has elapsed since the decision was given, it has been repeatedly discussed, criticised and, upon occasion, approved. It is clear affirmation of responsibility for fault, and its implications may become clearer, if the question is asked: Supposing that the Court of Appeal in the *Polemis Case* had decided that the charterers were not liable for the loss the ship caused by the negligence of their servant, on whom would the loss have fallen, and for what reason?

A decisive rejection of this conception of the extent of liability for a negligent act was given by the Privy Council in the *Wagon Mound*[26] in 1961, after an exhaustive review of the earlier decisions. In view of the unusually impressive array of talent for this appeal (the committee included Viscount Simonds, Lord Reid, Lord Radcliffe, Lord Tucker and Lord Morris), and the fact that only one opinion is delivered in this court, one can only conclude that it was intended to give a judgement as authoritative in England as it would be in Australia. It is worth noting, as their lordships in this case noted, that the *Polemis* rule had never been applied in Scotland, and in explaining the Scottish law in *Glasgow Corporation v Muir*[27] Lord Macmillan had said: 'It is still left to the judge to decide what, in the circumstances of the particular case, the reasonable man would have had in contemplation, and what, accordingly, the party sought to be made liable ought to have foreseen.'

It scarcely needs stating that different judges, dealing with differing circumstances, may take different views of the extent of the foreseeability of the reasonable man who is, in any case, no more than a notional being. However the current is now strongly set in favour of this test, and in *The Wagon Mound*, the court even attempted a moral justification of it. After saying that the *Polemis Case* ought no longer to be regarded as good law, Viscount Simonds added:

> It does not seem consonant with current ideas of justice or morality that for an act of negligence, however slight or venial, which results in some trivial foreseeable damage, the actor should be liable for all the consequences however unforeseeable and however grave, so long as they can be said to be 'direct'. It is a principle of civil liability, subject only to qualifications which have no present relevance, that a man must be considered to be responsible for the probable consequences of his act. To demand more of him is too harsh a rule, to demand less is to ignore that civilized order requires the observance of a minimum standard of behaviour.

However it is regarded, the decision in *The Wagon Mound* represents a sharp retreat from the standards implicit in the *Polemis Case,* possibly as a concession to the increasing industrialisation of the second half of the twentieth century. The facts of *The Wagon Mound Case* in themselves throw this contrast in the two views of liability into sharp relief. An oil-burning vessel, of which the appellants were the charterers, was taking in oil in Sydney Harbour when through the carelessness of the appellants' servants, a large quantity of it was allowed to spill into the harbour. It was carried by wind and tide beneath a wharf belonging to the respondents (who were ship builders and ship repairers) at which a vessel they were refitting was lying. Some cotton waste on a piece of debris floating on the oil underneath the wharf was set on fire, and a conflagration developed which seriously damaged the wharf and its equipment. As a result of the Privy Council's decision, the wharfowners were unable to recover; but the owners of the two vessels under repair at the wharf, which were also damaged by the fire,[28] were more successful, when they brought a claim based on nuisance. The Privy Council said that foreseeability is also a condition for liability in nuisance, as much as in negligence, but a vigilant ship's engineer, noticing the leak, should have foreseen that there was a risk that the oil on the water could be ignited. Accordingly, the charterers of the ship were held responsible; but it will be observed that on different claims, arising out of the same default, two different views of foreseeability were taken, and the wharf-owners may be regarded as distinctly unlucky.

It may be conjectured that the 'foreseeability' test is likely to create as many, or possibly more, problems than it solves. For example, in March 1967, the *Torrey Canyon*, a tanker carrying over 100,000 tons of oil, grounded off the Scilly Isles, through negligent navigation, and eventually broke up. Much of the oil was dispersed into the sea, polluting over one hundred miles of the south west coast of England, and, following a change of the wind, some drifted to the French coast, threatening considerably more damage. As a direct result of this negligence, the British and French governments and a number of English local authorities incurred heavy expenses in their efforts to minimise the loss, and many fishermen and hotel proprietors suffered loss in their livelihoods. Compensation was eventually secured through the energetic efforts of the British Government, but had litigation ensued, foreseeability would have been of major importance. In discussing the *Torrey Canyon* affair in 1968,[29] the present author wrote:

> It cannot be disputed that the foreseeability test, now applicable to both negligence and nuisance, has a particular relevance to cases arising from oil pollution, out of one such case the test itself was constructed. Is it foreseeable, for example, that an error in navigation, committed by the captain of a tanker on the high seas, will cause damage to the holiday industry in one or several countries some distance away?
>
> If not, what remains of the rights of redress of those who suffer in this way? How, for example, is the French claim in respect of damage caused by the wreck of the *Torrey Canyon*

affected by the foreseeability test, having regard to the fact that the damage was the result of change in the wind diverting oil from the Cornish to the Breton beaches?

Parenthetically one may perhaps add that considerations such as these make the appeal to justice and morality in *The Wagon Mound* decision somewhat speculative.

Other illustrations of the readiness of the courts to limit the area of redress for tortious acts exist. One of them began with the decision in *Flint v Lovell.*[30] An active man aged sixty-nine was knocked down by the defendant's motor-car, and in the ensuing proceedings his doctor stated that he could now look forward only to a year of life as an invalid. Substantial damages were therefore awarded for shortened expectation of life, and the Court of Appeal upheld the decision. At the time of the decision this was regarded as a new head of liability in the calculation of damages, although in earlier cases it had certainly been taken into account when deciding the amount of damages for pain and suffering. The new practice received the approval of the House of Lords in 1937 in *Rose v Ford,*[31] when damages were recovered in respect of injuries suffered by a girl who was seriously injured in a motor-car accident caused by the defendant's negligence. She died four days afterwards, and her father as administrator of her estate brought an action under the Law Reform (Miscellaneous Provisions) Act, 1934. The House of Lords held that since a living person could claim damages for loss of expectation of life, this right passed under the Act of 1934 to her personal representative. The members of the House of Lords were aware that their decision would be productive of problems for the courts, and on this Lord Roche said:

> I would add that I confess to some apprehension lest this element of damage may now assume a frequency and a prominence in litigation far greater than is warranted in fact and by becoming common form may result in the inflation of damages in undeserving cases or more probably perhaps may become stale and ridiculous to the detriment of real and deserving

> cases, such as the present. But the abatement of these possible evils may be left to the good sense of judges and juries, and I may be permitted to express the hope that the assistance of a jury—in my judgement a most admirable tribunal for such a purpose—may be not seldom availed of in the future.

Unfortunately, Lord Roche's optimism proved ill-founded and a chaos of awards followed. Accordingly, the House of Lords, in *Benham v Gambling*, decided in 1941,[32] hastily retreated from its former liberality. It reduced an award of £1,200 in favour of a child aged two and a half, to £200 on this head, and it fell to Lord Simon, then Lord Chancellor, to explain the reasons for this precipitate retreat only four years after *Rose v Ford*. He reviewed the varying opinions which had been expressed by judges and legal writers upon the proper principles to be applied in fixing the amount of damages. Lord Simon's speech was directed (with the concurrence of the other law lords) towards establishing firm principles for the future. Since these have reduced claims under this head to very moderate proportions, they merit reproduction, as a notable exercise of the judicial technique:

> In the first place, I am of opinion that the right conclusion is not to be reached by applying what may be called the statistical or actuarial test. Figures, calculated to represent the expectation of human life at various ages, are averages arrived at from a vast mass of vital statistics; the figure is not necessarily one which can properly be attributed to a given individual. And in any case the thing to be valued is not the prospect of length of days, but the prospect of a predominantly happy life. The age of the individual may, in some cases, be a relevant factor: for example, in extreme old age the brevity of what life may be left may be relevant, but, as it seems to me, arithmetical calculations are to be avoided, if only for the reason that it is of no assistance to know how many years may have been lost, unless one knows how to put a value on the years. It would be fallacious to assume, for this purpose, that all human life is continuously an enjoyable thing, so that the shortening of it

calls for compensation, to be paid to the deceased's estate on a quantitative basis. The ups and downs of life, its pains and sorrows, as well as its joys and pleasures—all that makes up 'Life's fitful fever'—have to be allowed for in the estimate. In assessing damages for the shortening of life, therefore, such damages should not be calculated solely, or even mainly, on the basis of the length of life that is lost. Asquith, J, appreciated this view, as his judgement shows, but I think that, in the light of the large amounts awarded in some previous cases in respect of quite young children, the figure he arrived at was unduly swollen by the consideration that the child might otherwise have had many years of life before it.

The question thus resolves itself into that of fixing a reasonable figure to be paid by way of damages for the loss of a measure of prospective happiness. Such a problem might seem more suitable for discussion in an essay on Aristotelian ethics than in the judgement of a court of law, but in view of the earlier authorities we must do our best to contribute to its solution. The learned judge observed that the earlier decisions quoted to him assured 'that human life is, on the whole, good'.[33] I would rather say that, before damages are awarded in respect of the shortened life of a given individual under this head, it is necessary for the court to be satisfied that the circumstances of the individual life were calculated to lead, on balance, to a positive measure of happiness, of which the victim has been deprived by the defendant's negligence. If the character or habits of the individual were calculated to bind him to a future of unhappiness or despondency, that would be a circumstance justifying a smaller award.[34] It is significant that, at any rate in one case of which we were informed, the jury refused to award any damages under this head at all. As Lord Wright said in *Rose v Ford*, special cases suggest themselves where the termination of a life of constant pain and suffering cannot be regarded as inflicting injury, or at any rate as inflicting the same injury as in more normal cases. I would further lay it down that, in assessing damages for this purpose, the question is not whether the deceased had the capacity or ability to appreciate that his further life on earth would bring him happiness; the test is not subjective and the right sum to award depends on an objective estimate of what kind of future on earth the victim might have enjoyed, whether he had justly estimated that future or not. Of course, no regard must be had to financial losses or gains during the period of which the victim has been deprived. The damages are in respect of loss of life, not the loss of future pecuniary prospects.

The main reason, I think, why the appropriate figure of damages should be reduced in the case of a very young child is that there is necessarily so much uncertainty about the child's future that no confident estimate of prospective happiness can be made. When an individual has reached an age to have settled prospects or having passed the risks and uncertainties of childhood and having in some degree attained to an established character and to firmer hopes—his or her future becomes more definite, and the extent to which good fortune may probably attend him at any rate becomes less incalculable. I would add that, in the case of a child, as in the case of an adult, I see no reason why the proper sum to be awarded should be greater because the social position or prospects of worldly possessions are greater in one case than another. Lawyers and judges may here join hands with moralists and philosophers and declare that the degree of happiness to be attained by a human being does not depend on wealth or status.

It remains to observe, as Goddard, LJ, pointed out, that stripped of technicalities, the compensation is not being given to the person who was injured at all, for the person who was injured is dead. The truth, of course, is that in putting a money value on the prospective balance of happiness in years that the deceased might otherwise have lived, the jury or judge of fact is attempting to equate incommensurables. Damages which would be proper for a disabling injury may well be much greater than for deprivation of life. These considerations lead me to the conclusion that in assessing damages under this head, whether in the case of a child or an adult, very moderate figures should be chosen. My noble and learned friend Lord Roche was well advised when he pointed out in *Rose v Ford* the danger of this head of claim becoming unduly prominent and leading to inflation of damages in cases which do not really justify a large award.

This decision was intended to be, and has proved to be, a striking example of judicial legislation, for thereafter awards of damages under this head have dwindled into insignificance. It contained directives based upon assumptions, especially relating to the uncertainties of infant life, which are somewhat less than convincing, but supporting a policy already decided on. In retrospect, possibly Lord Goddard's robuster statement may seem more acceptable. Since the problems arising from the test of legal liability, including those of direct and foreseeable consequences, proximate cause, and remoteness of damage have produced a literature, vast in bulk, and much of it of the highest quality, it may be of interest to conclude this brief survey, of necessity touching upon only a few of the modern problems awaiting solution in the law of torts, with a slightly exasperated remark of du Parcq, LJ (as he then was), in *Smith v Harris*: [35]

> The Common Law of this country has been built up, not by the writings of logicians or learned jurists, but by the summings-up of judges of experience to juries consisting of plain men, not usually students of logic, not accustomed to subtle reasoning, but endowed, so far as my experience goes, as a general rule, with great common sense, and if an argument has to be put in terms which only a school-man could understand, then I am always very doubtful whether it can possibly be expressing the Common Law.

Sir Edward Coke would not have agreed, but these observations have a good deal of modern judicial authority to support them. It is, perhaps, a late echo of Chief Justice Holmes's remark 'the life of the law has not been logic, but experience'.

14

Administrative Law and Common Law

For eight centuries the Common Law steadily expanded its province and increased its authority at the expense of all rivals. On at least two occasions (the last in the sixteenth century) a possible threat of a reception of Roman law passed away in face of the strongly-voiced hostility of the common lawyers. At the Reformation the independence of the church courts was removed, and thereafter they steadily lost jurisdiction to the Common Law courts and the Court of Chancery. At a somewhat later date, the Common Law proved sufficiently flexible to absorb the rules of mercantile law, thereby making the continued existence of a special system of mercantile law unnecessary. An important part of the history of the Common Law (which in this context includes equity) had been the history of its progressive expansion to absorb new bodies of law, thus removing any threat to its supremacy over all persons and all causes. For a time in the seventeenth century it seemed that the challenge of the prerogative courts, and especially of the Star Chamber, closely linked as it was with the assertion of the royal prerogative in the political sphere, might succeed when earlier challenges had failed. Thanks to the learning and courage of Coke, and of other Common Law judges who thought as he did, the challenge was faced, and clear limits were set to this early experiment in administrative jurisdiction. With the emphatic assertion of the supremacy of Parliament and the Common Law in 1688, the threat disappeared, apparently for ever. Thereafter the supremacy of Parliament existed side by side with the supremacy of the Common Law in the legal sphere. Since all, even ministers of the Crown, were accountable for their actions before the ordinary courts, there was need neither for a special body of administrative law, nor for special courts in which such a law could be applied.

Such a state of affairs, it is now apparent, was appropriate for a nation in which the functions of government were consciously restricted, and in which the chief role of the courts in civil matters was to define and enforce private rights. By the last quarter of the nineteenth century newer theories of governmental function were modifying the technique of government. There were many reasons for this. The change from an agricultural to an urban civilisation was already well advanced, rendering inevitable the development of theories of mutual interdependence and of the social responsibilities of governmental bodies. The spread of literacy and the steady movement towards universal adult suffrage implied that increasing attention must be paid to the welfare of the community as a whole, and not of any particular class. To give practical effect to the new social philosophy, it was necessary for the state to exercise ever widening powers of control, and for public interest to override private right with increasing frequency. The central problem of the modern state has therefore been, and remains, the establishment of a just balance between the claims of the community and those of the individual, especially those of the individual as a property owner.

For the achievement of these aims the appropriate instrument has been legislation, not judicial decision. Since it is the primary purpose of the courts to enforce rights and to redress wrongs, they can take little account of new conceptions of social relationships, nor can they give effect to aspirations not yet recognised as conferring legal rights. As far as the Common Law is concerned, the claim of the community is worth little when weighed in the balance against a well-founded private right. It is aptly illustrated by the story of the landowner, who, on being informed that a new railway had been planned, which passed not only through his land, but also through a large barn of considerable antiquity, flatly refused to enter into any negotiations with the railway company, on the ground that neither he nor any of his employees was prepared to open and shut the doors of his barn on Sundays.

Today, of course, such attitudes are held up to derision as obstructive of progress and the common good. In the first half of the nineteenth century, it was by no means an unreasonable action on the part of a landowner, and until statutes began to impinge with increasing boldness upon his rights of property, it is one which would have received full support from the Common Law courts.

Nevertheless, such attitudes could not continue to prevail against the legislation of Parliaments which were elected by an increasingly comprehensive electorate, and now social legislation progressively became the hall mark of vigorous 'progressive' government. The increasing regulation of private rights which was its necessary consequence was embodied, not in statutes, but in the orders and regulations which statutes gave ever-expanding government departments the power to make. This was in reality a reversion to an old practice, for the Tudors and Stuarts, to go no further back, had legislated by proclamation, and one of the matters in issue between the Stuarts and Parliament was the asserted right of the Crown to legislate independently of Parliament. The successful assertion of the sovereignty of Parliament after 1688 had ended this claim. When legislation by the departments of state became a common practice in the second half of the nineteenth century, it was always under the authority of an enabling statute, and before long a number of government departments employed staffs of lawyers, one of whose tasks has been to prepare and draft such delegated legislation.

Although this development did not pass unremarked, it was viewed for the most part without anxiety, and frequently with complacency. In 1877 Lord Thring, who was possibly the greatest of all parliamentary counsel, had stated in his book *Practical Legislation*:

> The adoption of the system of confining the attention of Parliament to material provisions only, and leaving details to be settled departmentally, is probably the only mode in which Parliamentary Government can, in respect to its legislative functions, be satisfactorily carried on. The province of Parlia-

ment is to decide material questions affecting the public interest, and the more procedure and subordinate matters can be withdrawn from their cognisance, the greater will be the time afforded for the consideration of the more serious questions involved in legislation.

He added that there was no likelihood that the departments would acquire excessive powers, since Parliament would always be vigilant to check them.

Lord Thring was followed by many others who expressed similar views, and this climate of opinion probably influenced Dicey, causing him to fail to perceive the deep-rooted threat to constitutional propriety and the Common Law which it presented. The threat was contained, not in the legislation itself, for delegated and subordinate legislation of various kinds has existed at all stages of our constitutional history, but in the ever increasing extent of the powers delegated, and in the consistent attempts of departments to withdraw their activities under this legislation from the control of the ordinary courts.

In the two decades which preceded the war of 1914–1918, numerous judges sounded a note of alarm, and in *Dyson v AG*[1] Farwell, LJ, observed:

The convenience in the public interest is all in favour of providing a speedy and early access to the courts for any of His Majesty's subjects who have any real cause of complaint against the exercise of statutory powers by government departments and government officials, having regard to their growing tendency to claim the right to act without regard to legal principles and without appeal to any court.

Pronouncements such as these were no more than an overture to the chorus of judicial protest which was to follow the war of 1914–1918, in which, for well-understood reasons of national security, administrative powers had been allowed a much wider orbit than had been thought tolerable before. For example, in *R v Halliday ex parte Zadig*[2] the House of Lords declared the courts powerless to intervene when the Home Secretary, acting under Regulation 14B of the Defence of the Realm regulations, interned without trial a person whom he declared to be of 'hostile origin or associations'. He was, in fact, a naturalised British subject, of German origin. The decision nevertheless included a vigorous dissenting opinion from Lord Shaw, who was deeply disturbed not only by the effect of it, but of its constitutional implications. He said:

> The form in modern times, of using the Privy Council as the channel executive for statutory power is measured, and must be measured strictly, by the ambit of the legislative pronouncement, and that channel itself, seeing that under the constitution His Majesty acts only through his ministers, is simply the Government of the day. The author of the power is Parliament: the wielder of it is the Government. Whether the Government has exceeded its statutory mandate is a question of *ultra* or *intra vires*, such as that which is now being tried. In so far as the mandate has been exceeded, there lurk the elements of a transition to arbitrary government, and therein of grave constitutional and public danger. The increasing crush of legislative efforts, and the convenience to the executive of a refuge in the device of Orders in Council would increase that danger tenfold were the judiciary to approach any such action of the Government in a spirit of compliance rather than of independent scrutiny. That way also would lead to public unrest and public peril.

For the time being Lord Shaw's speech was a warning, which passed almost unheard in the middle of a war in which survival was paramount. It was to be echoed many times in the inter-war period when, although the extremely comprehensive war-time regulations, and the wide executive powers by virtue of which they were promulgated, were largely abandoned, the departments of state devised new techniques for circumventing both Parliament and the courts. All departmental legislation, being technically subordinate to statute law, was subject to the *ultra vires* rule, as Lord Shaw had pointed out in *Zadig's Case*. During the inter-war period, therefore, the courts and the departments conducted a war of manoeuvre in respect of the extending activities of the departments. The departments themselves have from time to time shown considerable ingenuity in drafting clauses designed to nullify or limit the effects of the *ultra vires* rule. For example, there has not infrequently been inserted into the enabling act a power to repeal or amend statute law, including the enabling act itself. If pursued to its logical conclusion, this could obviously have enabled the department to get out of the limitations imposed by the original act altogether. An even more audacious device, now abandoned after prolonged protest, and of adverse criticism in the courts, was the famous 'Henry VIII' clause, by virtue of which the department was given power to amend, not only the original act, but *any other act* with the object of bringing the original act fully into operation. Possibly the most common device has been the insertion of a provision that an order made under an act, if confirmed by the department, shall take effect as if originally written into the act itself.

In a series of decisions in the inter-war period, the courts grappled with the problem presented by these wide delegations. Clearly there was little that could be done when an order was confirmed under a statute under a clause of the type last mentioned. In such cases, it was necessary to concentrate upon the procedure which the departments, and those authorities which acted under them, had followed. A number of these cases arose from schemes prepared by local authorities, and were brought with the object of testing the extent of the powers conferred by these acts, and their relation to the purposes for which the acts were passed. One well-known decision was that the Court of Appeal in *R v Minister of Health; ex parte Davis.*[3] The Derby Corporation had prepared a scheme purporting to be under Part II of the Housing Act 1925, providing that a certain area should be cleared of houses, and when cleared should 'be sold, leased, or otherwise disposed of as the local authority may think fit'. The Court of Appeal held that the powers given under Part II were exercisable only when a scheme providing accommodation as required by the Act had been prepared, and the powers of sale and leasing were ancillary to the execution of such a scheme. In the words of Lawrence, J:

> Having regard to the provisions in Part II of the Act as a whole I have come to the conclusion that the legislature did not confer upon local authorities the power compulsorily to acquire large areas of land in towns on the representation of their medical officer, and then, after having cleared such areas, to deal with the land so acquired at their will and pleasure.

In this case, the Court of Appeal had acted by way of prohibition to the Minister of Health, prohibiting him from proceeding further in the confirmation of the scheme, since it was outside the scope of the Act. In the divisional court below, Lord Hewart, CJ, had taken the view that the court could act because the Minister had not confirmed the scheme, but if he had, it would have been too late, because the Act provides that the Minister's order takes effect as if enacted in the Act itself. This, as Lord Herschell had suggested in *Institute of Patent Agents v Lockwood*,[4] appeared to mean that if the Minister had confirmed the scheme, no court could interfere, since the order would then be on the same footing as the statute, and no question of *ultra vires* could arise. This was the major problem in *R v Minister of Health; ex parte Yaffé*.[5] In that case, the Liverpool Corporation had prepared a similar scheme to that which had been considered in *Davis's Case*, and this the Minister confirmed with important modifications. Yaffé sought to have the order quashed by certiorari. In the divisional court, Lord Hewart and Talbot, J (Swift, J, dissenting) held that the provision in the Act, giving a confirmed order the effect 'as if enacted in the Act', deprived Yaffé of any chance of redress in the courts. The Court of Appeal, also by a majority, reversed their decision, holding that the Minister could not validate *ex post facto* a scheme which diverged from the objects of the Act. The House of Lords (Lord Russell of Killowen dissenting) held that the scheme, as modified by the Minister, was a valid one, so that the question of *ultra vires* did not arise. At the same time the anxieties of some law lords to restrict the wide interpretation of Lord Herschell's observations were clearly apparent. Lord Dunedin, after a consideration of *Lockwood's Case*, said:

> The confirmation makes the scheme speak as if it was contained in the Act of Parliament but the Act of Parliament in which it is contained is the Act which provides for the framing of the scheme, not a subsequent Act. If therefore the scheme, as made, conflicts with the Act, it will have to give way to the Act. The mere confirmation will not save it. It would be otherwise if the scheme had been *per se* embodied in a subsequent Act, for then the maxim to be applied would have been *posteriorà derogant prioribus*. But as it is, if one can find that the scheme is inconsistent with the provisions of the Act which authorises the scheme, the scheme will be bad, and that can only be gone into by way of proceedings in *certiorari*.

This assertion of judicial control of ministers' powers was, in essence, a substantial limitation of Lord Herschell's opinion, but it was by no means generally accepted by the judiciary, and the position remained uncertain.

Nevertheless, the frequency of judicial criticisms of the amplitude of powers of legislation conferred on government departments, coupled with growing public awareness of the dangers inherent in the practice, was about to produce tangible results. The anxieties frequently voiced by judges and legal writers, and more especially by Lord Hewart in his challenging book *The New Despotism*, led to the establishment of the committee on ministers' powers, which reported in 1932. This surveyed the existing practice of parliamentary delegation of legislative powers to the departments, and suggested a number of modifications. It also dealt with another, and even more complex problem—that of the exercise of powers of judicial or quasi-judicial decision by departments, and the distinction between them and purely administrative decisions, ie decisions upon policy which, though they certainly affect the rights of the members of the public, do not arise as a direct consequence of an existing dispute.

So far as the courts are concerned, the question of the greatest importance is the extent to which any of these decisions, reached by tribunals or administrative bodies of many kinds, established by one of a number of departments of state, are subject to the scrutiny of the courts by way of judicial review of their decisions. Although the classification of decisions contained in the report has been regarded by both legal writers and judges as unsatisfactory, there was for a time a disposition on the part of the courts to adopt them for the purposes of defining the limits of possible intervention by the courts. For example, in one of the most celebrated of the early post-war cases, *Franklin v Minister of Town and Country Planning*,[6] the House of Lords held that in considering the report of a public local enquiry, held under the New Towns Act, 1946, the Minister has no judicial or quasi-judicial duty imposed on him, so that the question of bias on the part of the Minister was irrelevant, the only question so far as the courts were concerned being whether he had genuinely considered the report and the objections raised at the inquiry. It followed from this decision that natural justice had no application to decisions of this type, which therefore remained free from any kind of judicial scrutiny.

The case itself illustrated some of the difficulties surrounding the subject. Wynn Parry, J, at first instance had regarded the Minister's power to confirm the report as quasi-judicial, and therefore subject to the usual requirement of natural justice. The House of Lords regarded it as an administrative act, and therefore immune from such controlling conditions. The whole area of administrative law, as Professor de Smith shows in the opening chapter of *Judicial Review of Administrative Action*, is one of great variety and complexity, especially as decisions which are predominantly judicial in character are given by a great variety of administrative tribunals and agencies. During the last forty years there has been an increasing desire on the part of persons affected by their decisions to explore the extent to which the courts can control them, and when the first applications were made, decisions such as *Franklin v The Minister of Town and Country Planning* emphasised how much territory had already been lost.

One of the earliest decisions to manifest a greater resolution on the part of the courts was *R v Northumberland Compensation Appeal Tribunal.*[7] This was an application for a writ of certiorari to the divisional court of the King's Bench division, asking that a decision of the Northumberland Compensation Appeal Tribunal should be quashed. Shaw had been employed by two local authorities, and lost his employment in 1949. The tribunal awarded him compensation in respect of only one of his employments, and Shaw contended that this decision was wrong in law. The tribunal, in dismissing the appeal, set out the facts, the contentions raised by the local council, and the manner in which the council had arrived at the sum, and also the fact that the tribunal agreed with the council's figures. The divisional court held that where a tribunal includes reasons in its order (so that it becomes what is termed a 'speaking order') and the reasons are bad in law, the divisional court may examine the reasons, and if they are bad, quash the order. Previously, it had been assumed that certiorari was a remedy which was available only where the inferior tribunal had acted without jurisdiction or in excess of it. Lord Goddard, in a notable judgement, traced the history of the remedy in order to show that the suggested limitation was ill-founded.

This redress, it will be perceived, was available only where the tribunal stated the reasons on which the decision was founded. If it did not, then the courts could not interfere. This defect, however, was remedied by the Tribunals and Inquiries Act, 1958, which provided for a right of appeal by way of case stated for the opinion of the High Court, or alternatively, by imposing on the tribunal or the Minister a duty to give a written statement of reasons for the decision.

To this requirement there were one or two exceptions preserved by the Act. One of them was contained in Section 4(4) of the Foreign Compensation Act, 1950, which states: 'The determination by the commission of any application made by them under this Act shall not be called in question in any court of law.'

In *Anisminic v Foreign Compensation Commission,*[8] the plaintiffs claimed that they were entitled to participate in the Egyptian Compensation Fund in respect of property owned by them and sequestrated by the Egyptian government. The commission made a provisional determination that their claim failed. The company brought an action against the commission for a declaration that the provisional determination was a nullity and that they were entitled to receive compensation from the fund. The House of Lords, by a majority, decided that it had jurisdiction. Discussing this decision Lord Diplock has written:

> The technique adopted by the House of Lords was to analyse the matters into which the commission was directed to inquire upon the application made to it for compensation, so as to identify what facts an applicant had to establish in order to justify his claim. As a result of misconstruing the expression 'successor in title' the commission had inquired into the existence of facts which the applicant was not required to establish. It had thus entered into an inquiry which it was not authorised to make. Its action in doing so was classified as acting outside its jurisdiction and the error of law which led it to do so was classified as one which entitled the court to review the commission's decision.[9]

It will be evident that this decision represents a bold assertion of control over an administrative tribunal which the statute, on the face of it, appeared to have exempted from such control. Whatever its implications, it represents a very great change in the attitude of the courts to such questions during the past half century—a change which has coincided with the progressive extensions of administrative activity. The courts, it will be evident, are now aware that they represent the only defence of the ordinary citizen against the progressive extension of administrative control. A further major step forward in the judicial review of administrative decisions, in order to ensure their conformity with general principles of law, was taken by the House of Lords in their decision in *Padfield v Minister of Agriculture, Fisheries and Food*[10]—a decision which Lord Denning, MR, in

Breen v Amalgamated Engineering Union[11] described as a landmark in the development of English administrative law. *Padfield's Case* arose from the decision of the Minister under the Agricultural Marketing Act 1958, which contained the provisions of the milk marketing scheme, under which producers had to sell their milk to the Milk Marketing Board, which fixed the different prices paid in each of the eleven regions of England and Wales. The difference in prices paid reflected the varying costs of transporting the milk from the producers to the consumers. The South Eastern Region producers contended that the differential between it and the South West Region should be altered in a way which would also have affected other regions. Since the Milk Marketing Board consisted largely of members elected by the separate regions, it was impossible for the south eastern producers to obtain a majority in support of their proposals. They therefore asked the Minister to appoint a committee of investigation under Section 19(3) of the Act, which provided that a committee of investigation should be charged with the duty, if the Minister so directed, of considering and reporting to the Minister as to the operation of any scheme which could not be considered by the consumer's committee. Section 19(6) then provides:

> If a committee of investigation reports to the Minister that any provision of a scheme or any act or omission of a board administering a scheme is contrary to the interests of consumers of the regulated products, or is contrary to the interest of any persons affected by the scheme and is not in the public interest, the Minister, if he thinks fit to do so after considering the report—
>
> (a) may by order make such amendments in the scheme as he considers necessary or expedient for the purpose of rectifying the matter;
>
> (b) may by order revoke the scheme;
>
> (c) in the event of the matter being one which it is within the power of the board to rectify, may by order direct the board to take such steps to rectify the matter as may be specified in the order.

The Minister refused the request of the south eastern producers to appoint a committee of investigation. In the course of the discussions, which were followed by his refusal, the Minister said that the complaint was one which raised 'wide issues going beyond the immediate concern' of the south eastern producers. On his behalf, it was also stated that, if a complaint was referred to a committee of investigation, and the committee upheld it, he would in turn be expected to make a statutory order to give effect to the committee's recommendation. On this Lord Denning, in a dissenting judgement in the Court of Appeal, commented scathingly:

> The one reason disclosed by that letter is that, if the committee were to uphold the complaint, the Minister would be expected to give effect to the committee's recommendations, and that he was unwilling to do. By whom would he be expected? I presume he means by Parliament or, at any rate, by public opinion. See what this comes to! The Minister does not want an inquiry lest Parliament, or the public, would expect him to act on the report. It means this: Even though the complaint was justified on the merits, and even though the committee recommended that it be rectified, the Minister was not prepared to rectify it.
>
> I do not think that was a proper approach to the complaint. The Minister ought not to make up his mind in advance. He could not tell what evidence the committee might have before them, or what reasons might lead to their recommendations. He ought at best to be prepared to consider their report with an open mind. He ought not to shut down an investigation simply because he might be expected to act on such recommendations.

The proceedings in the courts originated in a request in the divisional court for a mandamus, to the Minister to set up a committee. The divisional court made the order, but the Court of Appeal (Lord Denning dissenting) set it aside. The House of Lords by a majority of four to one (Lord Morris dissenting), reversed this decision, and held that the order should be made.

The House, whilst recognising that the Minister had a discretion, nevertheless emphasised that it was a discretion that could only be exercised according to law. On behalf of the Minister, it had been argued that his discretion to grant or refuse an application for a reference to a committee was 'unfettered'. On this, Lord Upjohn commented:

> My Lords, I believe that the introduction of the adjective 'unfettered' and (his) reliance thereon as an answer to the appellants' claim is one of the fundamental matters confounding the Minister's attitude, bona fide though it be. First, the adjective nowhere appears in section 19, it is an unauthorised gloss by the Minister. Secondly, even if the section did contain that adjective I doubt if it would make any difference in law to his powers, save to emphasise what he has already, namely that acting lawfully he has a power of decision which cannot be controlled by the courts; it is unfettered. But the use of that adjective, even in an Act of Parliament, can do nothing to unfetter the control which the judiciary have over the executive, namely that in exercising their powers the latter must act lawfully and that is a matter to be determined by looking at the Act and its scope and object in conferring a discretion upon the Minister rather than by the use of adjectives.

The determination whether a minister is acting lawfully or not can only be a matter for the courts. Lord Parker in the divisional court, in language that was adopted by Lord Upjohn in the House of Lords, classified unlawful behaviour as being: (a) an outright refusal to consider the relevant matters, or (b) the Minister misdirecting himself in point of law, or (c) taking into account some wholly irrelevant or extraneous consideration, or (d) wholly omitting to take into account a relevant consideration.

In *Padfield's Case*, the evidence showed that the Minister had acted unlawfully under (c). It was argued on behalf of the Minister that the reasons given by him ought not to be considered too closely, since he did not need to give any reason for refusing. To this Lord Hodson replied that when, as in the present case, the circumstances indicate a genuine complaint for which the statute provides an appropriate remedy, the Minister cannot escape from the possibility of judicial control by refusing a remedy without explanation. With this Lord Reid agreed.

The result of this most important case, therefore, is to establish beyond doubt that in the exercise of their discretions, ministers are subject to the scrutiny and control of the courts, in order to establish that they are acting lawfully. This, in the last resort, means that they remain subject to the control of Parliament, for, as Lord Reid pointed out:

> Parliament must have conferred the discretion with the intention that it should be used to promote the policy and objects of the Act; the policy and objects of the Act must be determined by construing the Act as a whole and construction is always a matter of law for the court. In a matter of this kind it is not possible to draw a hard and fast line, but if the Minister, by reason of his having misconstrued the Act or for any other reason, so uses his discretion as to thwart or run counter to the policy and objects of the Act, then our law would be very defective if persons aggrieved were not entitled to the protection of the court.

This implicit identity of interest between the courts and Parliament against an ever-powerful executive recalls, in the context of the twentieth century, that earlier alliance between the common lawyers and Parliament which provided the effective opposition to the royal executive in the time of the first two Stuarts. Even so, the protection which the courts afford to the citizen is as yet by no means complete. For example, in *Cummings v Birkenhead Corporation*[12] the defendant corporation sent circulars to parents stating that children educated at Roman Catholic primary schools would be eligible for secondary education places only at Roman Catholic schools. The applicants sought a declaration that this was a breach of statutory duty imposed by Sections 8 and 76 of the Education Act, 1944. They also contended that the decision was *ultra vires* for unreasonableness and was invalid on the grounds of public policy, being an act of religious discrimination. Ungoed Thomas, J, held that even if it was a breach of a statutory duty, or an unreasonable exercise of power, there was an adequate statutory remedy by way of complaint to the Minister, under the Act of 1944.

On the particular allegation that the corporation had acted *ultra vires* and unlawfully, the judge referred to the judgement of Lord Greene, MR, in *Associated Provincial Picture Houses v Wednesbury Corporation.*[13] In this case, the statute provided no remedy, and the claim was for a declaration that the local authority, in exercising its statutory power to grant licences for cinematograph performances 'subject to such conditions as the authority think fit to impose' had in imposing one condition acted *ultra vires* and unreasonably. Lord Greene, in his judgement, pointed out that the court would interfere if it were shown that the local authority had acted unreasonably in taking into account what ought not to be taken into account, or in coming to a conclusion that no reasonable authority could have reached. In the present case, however, Ungoed Thomas, J, said that although the local authority might have been injudicious, they had not considered improper factors, and their decision was not so injudicious that no reasonable authority could have reached it.

It is curious that in the case no reference seems to have been made to the implications of the *Padfield Case*, so far as the exercise of discretionary powers by public authorities is concerned. This later case may have to be considered in the near future since, as it stands, it seems to set limits to the judicial review of administrative misconduct which are at variance with those set in earlier decisions. It serves as a reminder of the need for constant vigilance. This is particularly the case as far as ratepayers and local authorities are concerned. The path of the ratepayer in pursuit of a remedy is beset with pitfalls. Thus in *Cummings v Birkenhead Corporation*, Ungoed Thomas, J, said:

> I come now to the plaintiffs' claim founded on their being ratepayers. There is not in the statement of claim any claim formulated in terms that—either expressly or necessarily im-

plied by—appears as a claim by ratepayers. There is no allegation or suggestion in the statement of claim that the defendants had wasted or misspent ratepayers' money or discriminated financially in any way between ratepayers. The submission made before me was that, by limiting the expression of parents' choice of schools, the defendants discriminated unfairly as between different classes of ratepayers; but as appears from an intervention of junior counsel for plaintiffs during reply, this was rightly sought to be framed as applying rates on such services unreasonably, that is, with discrimination as between ratepayers. But no unreasonable or discriminatory application of rates appeared at all, nor—what is natural—was it alleged. Ratepayers pay rates and the local authority hold the rate fund in a fiduciary capacity to apply impartially to the services to which it is applicable. . . The plaintiffs' submission appears to me to confuse the discriminatory applications of rates to or within school services (there being no such discrimination in our case) with discrimination, not in the application of rates to or within school services at all, but in the course of acting as the local education authority in exercising statutory duties and powers under the Education Act. The discrimination alleged in our case is no breach of fiduciary duty on which rates are held but is as between classes of parents and children, independently of the application of the rates.

This decision must be considered in association with *R v Hereford Corporation*,[14] decided by the divisional court shortly before. The applicants were electrical contractors in Hereford, and they alleged that the corporation was in breach of its statutory duty under Section 266(2) of the Local Government Act, 1933, in failing to request tenders from local firms, in connection with an undertaking, in spite of the provision in its standing orders that tenders should be invited from a reasonable number of persons.

The applicants had asked for a mandamus, and the divisional court held that it was necessary for a person asking for a mandamus to show 'an interest' in the performance of the statutory duty. The divisional court held that 'an interest' means the possession of a legal right—a decision which obviously puts mandamus beyond the reach of all persons hoping to tender unless, as in this case, they were also ratepayers. Lord Parker said:

> It has always been recognised that there is quite a different criterion of interest which would justify an application for certiorari and one which would justify an application for mandamus. It is said that a far more stringent test applies in the case of mandamus and that an applicant must have, as it is put, a specific legal right. The mere fact that these applicants were electrical contractors does not, in my judgment, of itself give them a sufficient right, but if, as I understand, they or some of them are ratepayers as well, then, as it seems to me, there would be a sufficient right to enable them to apply for mandamus.

One last example of the changed attitude of the courts towards administrative action may be given, and once again the judge primarily responsible for it was Lord Denning. In *Ashbridge Investments Ltd v Minister of Housing and Local Government*,[15] he said in the Court of Appeal:

> The court can interfere with the Minister's decision if he has acted on no evidence; or if he has come to a conclusion to which on the evidence he could not possibly come; or if he has given a wrong interpretation to the words of the statute; or if he has taken into consideration matters which he ought not to have taken into account, or vice versa; or has otherwise gone wrong in law. It is identical with the position where the court has power to interfere with the decision of a lower tribunal which has erred in point of law.

This strong claim of judicial control of administrative action was directly illustrated by the decision in *Coleen Ltd v Minister of Housing*.[16] A local authority declared two rows of houses in bad condition in two streets to be clearance areas under Part III of the Housing Act, 1957. At the corner where the two streets met there stood a modern building, which was included by the local authority in the compulsory purchase order. The owners objected, and at the public local inquiry on behalf of the Ministry, the council called no evidence as to the need to acquire the building. The Minister's inspector reported that it was in first-class condition, and that its acquisition was not reasonably necessary for the satisfactory development of the area as required by Section 43(2) of the Housing Act, 1957. He therefore recommended that it should be excluded from the purchase. The Ministry rejected the recommendations and confirmed the purchase order, and Lyell, J, dismissed the application of the owners to quash the order. The Court of Appeal reversed his decision, on the ground that there was no evidence before the Minister, upon which he could reach a decision to override the inspector's recommendation. Moreover, the Minister cannot, as against the subject, rely upon expert evidence within the Ministry, unless he gives the owner thereby affected the opportunity to deal with it. In the words of Sachs, LJ, in this appeal:

> When seeking to deprive a subject of his property and cause him to move himself, his belongings and perhaps his business to another area, the onus is squarely on the local authority to show by clear and unambiguous evidence that the order sought for should be granted.

One or two general conclusions may be suggested from the consideration of these illustrative cases. The first is that the courts today are a good deal more watchful in considering the activities of administrative agencies than they were half a century ago, and their predominant attitude is to construe statutes giving powers restrictively. To achieve this, and to protect individual rights, the courts have refurbished the weapons of certiorari, mandamus and an action for a declaration, and have given them additional offensive power. Secondly, even administrative powers and discretions must be exercised in accordance with generally understood principles of fair dealing. Finally, there remain gaps in the network of judicial control, but they have greatly diminished since the Tribunals Act, 1958. In this sphere, the courts have done much to build a system of administrative law in harmony with the traditional principles and presumptions of the Common Law.

15

The Criminal Law

Unlike the civil law, criminal law has at all periods been linked with the preservation of public order, and the state has therefore had a direct interest in its enforcement. Its administration has included two elements of great importance—the jury, and the lay magistracy. Formerly, there was a third—the grand jury, which presented persons accused of crime before the king's judges, when the assize assembled. Because the practice of holding a preliminary examination of persons accused of serious crimes before lay magistrates, sitting in petty sessions, had been so greatly extended in the nineteenth century, grand juries were abolished in 1933. The jury and the lay magistracy remain as methods of public participation in the criminal process. During critical periods in English history, this participation has been of great importance, although it should not be assumed that it has always been beneficial. For several centuries, the lay justices were drawn from the landowning class, and their outlook was dominated by the views of their class. This was particularly evident in their treatment of offenders under the Game Laws. In addition to class bias, there were also the problems of age and lack of knowledge of the law. A Royal Commission which reported in the inter-war period found a number of benches of magistrates which included members of over eighty, and exceptionally over ninety, as well as persons who were totally deaf or partially blind. Today, magistrates must cease to try cases when they reach the age of seventy, and all property qualifications have been abolished. In making appointments today, the Lord Chancellor is at pains to ensure that the magistracy is fairly representative of the community from which it is selected.

Until recently the charge that justices of the peace were not legally-trained was usually met by the reply that they looked to the clerk of the court (who was almost always a solicitor) to advise them on matters of law, to which there was frequently added the suggestion that the bulk of the magistrate's work was simply a matter of common sense. In the second half of the twentieth century, much of the law administered by magistrates in police courts and quarter sessions has become increasingly technical. Today, therefore, no person nominated for the magistracy may sit until he has attended a course of classes upon the law and practice of magistrates' courts, and as a magistrate he is expected to attend regular conferences and refresher courses. Finally, it should be mentioned that in cities and a substantial number of large towns, the work of the justices in petty sessions may be discharged by stipendiary magistrates, who are professional lawyers, and that in courts of quarter session the bench of lay magistrates may be replaced by a recorder who is a practising barrister of some seniority, and who is for this purpose a part-time judge. Even in less populous areas, where the work of quarter sessions may be expected to be less exacting, there is a growing practice of appointing paid chairmen, who are practising lawyers.

All these things have adapted to modern conditions, more or less satisfactorily, an institution which has existed since the reign of Edward III at the latest. It has survived frequent criticism and periodic ridicule, and, since lay magistrates receive no payment for what they do, it has proved a remarkably economical way of administering justice in respect of the host of lesser infractions of law which are classed, for want of a better word, as crimes. In the twentieth century the jurisdiction of the magistracy has acquired an added importance from the fact that it is in a magistrates' court that most motoring offences are disposed of. Thus, an entire cross-section of the community has been made directly aware of the work which justices of the peace do. A further development has been that special courts have been established in which children charged with offences may be treated informally and without publicity.

At all times in their long history, magistrates' courts have been subject to the supervisory jurisdiction of the Queen's Bench Division, and its predecessor, the Court of King's Bench. This jurisdiction is wider than a simple provision for an appeal on a question of law or fact. It can comprehend the mode of conducting the trial and questions of procedure. It is the existence of this control, ensuring that the strict requirements of criminal justice have been complied with, which has prevented the intrusion of serious abuses into our magisterial system.

The second lay element in the administration of criminal justice—the trial jury (sometimes known as the petty jury)—has a long, and at times, troubled history. It is an institution around which legends have gathered, one of them being that it is the bulwark of the subject's liberty against arbitrary power, and so it was at one time. At others, however, it has been the shield of the rogue and the scoundrel. Juries function best in stable societies, under settled conditions. In times of social upheaval, they not unnaturally reflect the prejudices of the communities from which they have been drawn. Juries have hanged witches, punished the innocent, and have permitted scoundrels and persons guilty of sedition to go free. No doubt in doing so, they have acted under the direction of the trial judge, but they have reached a unanimous verdict nevertheless. On the other hand, they have sometimes proved wiser than the judges under whom they sat. When, in the desperate struggle with the forces of Revolutionary France, the administration of William Pitt sought to suppress all manifestations of popular opinion, juries refused to convict, in spite of admonitions from the bench. On these trials, a nineteenth-century biographer of Pitt commented:

> Considering calmly these prosecutions, they appear in every point of view to have been unfortunate, not to say unwise... It was desirable to frustrate the schemes of desperate innovators; but the British public, who had ever been accustomed to meet, to associate, to proclaim their political opinions and predilections, to devise means and to recommend measures for removal of their grievances, and improvement of their social conditions, viewed with anxiety and alarm those measures

> which tended to plunge individuals into the dreadful gulf of high treason, when they had unintentionally, perhaps, exceeded the bounds which an exact knowledge of the laws and a timid prudence would have prescribed.[1]

The history of the criminal jury is intimately bound up with the evolution of the criminal law, and with the law of evidence, which was until modern times very largely the creation of the judges. It was introduced in the thirteenth century as an alternative to the ordeals which, as appeals for divine decision, had been administered by the clergy, and which a papal bull had forbidden the clergy to administer. Early juries, however, were a long way from acting as judges of fact. They were selected from neighbours, and they decided, presumably by repute, since at that time the process of eliciting evidence for their consideration had not been evolved. Persons accused of crime frequently showed great reluctance to plead to a jury or, as it was termed, to 'put themselves upon their country', since if they were of bad repute a jury was likely to condemn them on that ground. Rather than plead to a jury, some persons accused of serious crime preferred to be pressed to death by the *peine forte et dure*, since if they died under this variety of legalised torture, they were technically unconvicted, and their families were not reduced to destitution by the forfeiture of all their goods, as occurred when felons were convicted.

For some centuries the activities of jurors were strictly controlled. If they delivered what the judge considered to be a perverse verdict, they could be attainted. Their verdict was submitted to a second jury of twenty-four, which reconsidered the first trial and the findings of the first jury. If the second jury decided that the first had given a perverse verdict, the first jurors could be committed to prison, their goods confiscated, and their houses destroyed. By the reign of Elizabeth I, attaints had fallen into disuse, but jurors could still be fined and imprisoned for perverse verdicts. This occurred, for example, on the acquittal of Sir Nicholas Throckmorton, in the first year of Queen Mary's reign. He had been accused of high treason, and there was no doubt that he had taken a prominent part in Sir Thomas Wyatt's rebellion. Throckmorton, however, was the Protestant hero of the London citizens, and a London jury refused to convict him.

Political sympathies have often swayed juries, but in the later Middle Ages, bribery and intimidation frequently influenced verdicts, and it was not unknown even later. Nevertheless, opinion was steadily swinging in favour of the independence of juries, and in 1670 Chief Justice Vaughan, in *Bushel's Case*, delivered a famous judgement, and affirmed this independence. Bushel was a member of the jury which had acquitted William Penn and others of unlawful assembly by preaching in Gracechurch Street, London, against the directions of the court. The recorder fined Bushel and the members of the jury for contempt, and as they refused to pay, they were committed to Newgate Prison. Bushel applied for a writ of *habeas corpus*, and Vaughan's judgement was delivered on this application. It affirmed the right of the jury to decide against the judge's directions on matters of fact. As Vaughan pointed out, if they were not to have this freedom, their presence in court was useless, and juries might just as well be abolished. If they were free to decide of themselves, then in his view they could not be punished for it, although he conceded that it was still possible to attaint a jury. In fact, however, this cumbrous weapon was almost obsolete.

Whilst this decision has been properly regarded as a landmark in the history of the jury, and also of constitutional freedom, the years which followed were to abound with examples of its dangers. The London mob, whipped up to a frenzy by the impudent inventions of Titus Oates and others of a mythical 'Popish Plot', intimidated juries into condemning innocent Roman Catholics to the scaffold, whilst the judges made no attempt to prevent these miscarriages of justice. When this fury had spent itself, juries were browbeaten by Jeffreys, Jones, and other Royalist judges into bringing in verdicts of 'guilty' against Whigs accused of complicity in the 'Rye House Plot', and finally, at the opening of James II's reign, against those who had been involved in Monmouth's rebellion.

At the time of its introduction, the jury in criminal trials had been seen simply as a substitute for the ordeals. As the procedure of the Common Law courts developed, more particularly from the standpoint of the production of evidence through the instrumentality of witnesses, the juries progressively approached their modern function of judges of fact. One result of this was that courts gradually became concerned to regulate the testimony which was placed before them, and particularly the evidence offered orally by witnesses. Prior to the seventeenth century, not even the outlines of a general law of evidence are discernible, although there were isolated rules relating to documents under seal, to the production of the instruments by which a crime had been committed, and to the position of the accused himself. In charges of felony the accused could not be legally represented, although he could be professionally advised beforehand. He was allowed to make statements in court, although since they were not made upon oath they would not carry as much weight as that of the witnesses. He could examine the witnesses, although his examination of them could scarcely be comparable with the examination of him by counsel for the Crown. Finally, his defence would at all points be handicapped by the statements which he had already made, during a searching preliminary examination before magistrates. It has often been stated that so long as these handicaps existed, it was the function of the judge to supplement the prisoner's efforts, but the records of pre-Revolution trials show that although judges participated in trials much more extensively than they do today, by examination of witnesses and of the prisoner himself, it rarely operated in the prisoner's favour. In a number of cases, it sealed his fate.

Even before the Revolution of 1688, the absence of a systematic body of rules governing the admission of evidence was already being deplored by some judges, and it is noteworthy that Jeffreys was among the foremost in rejecting hearsay, because of its possible inaccuracy, and also because it could have an influence upon the jury altogether disproportionate to its true worth. In the more enlightened years of the eighteenth century, this lacuna in the law was progressively filled, and in a characteristically English Common Law fashion. The law of evidence of many continental countries is largely concerned with the establishment of certainty, the process of proof, and the weight of testimony. Possibly this is also linked with the fact that in most continental systems, criminal procedure is investigatory, and in theory counsel and judges are allied for the purpose of eliciting the true facts which are relevant to the crime. The English law of evidence was shaped to function in a different legal environment and for a different purpose. A criminal trial is, in essence, a judicial combat, which starts with the premise that the prisoner is innocent. It is therefore for the Crown to establish his guilt, and for the defence to rebut the Crown's case. Both conduct the combat in accordance with strict rules, and before a jury which in theory is ignorant of everything relating to the crime except what the two sides present to it. Since the jury are laymen, and may be swayed unduly by certain types of evidence, these are excluded by the rules of the combat. The English law of evidence therefore consists, as to one extremely important part, of exclusionary rules; and because so much has been excluded, and because it is the function of the judge to guide the jury on these matters, it has little to say about the *weight* of the evidence which either side offers. It is also concerned with the competency of witnesses, and with the extent to which they can be compelled to give evidence. For some time, the Common Law courts adhered to the view that evidence offered by a witness who was related to an accused, either by family connection or by employment, was likely to be biased testimony, and therefore this testimony should not be admitted. Naturally, this view applied with greatest force to the testimony of the accused himself, and therefore his testimony was rejected, although he was allowed to make a statement not under oath.

The courts also developed the rules of procedure by which trials are conducted. These involved the regulation of the mode of presenting a case—by each of the parties in turn, by means of an opening statement by counsel, the production of evidence through the testimony of witnesses, whose evidence was given on oath, and who when examined, first 'in chief' by counsel introducing the evidence, then by cross-examination on behalf of the defence, and finally, by re-examination by counsel introducing the witness. The prime purpose of cross-examination is to shake the evidence given 'in chief', or to elicit additional facts which may compel the modification of conclusions drawn from it. In re-examination, counsel producing the witness seeks to repair the damage done in cross-examination, and to place the evidence which has already been given in a favourable context. So long as legal representation was denied to the prisoner accused of felony, the prisoner himself conducted, often imperfectly, the cross-examination of the Crown's witnesses.

Thus, the whole process of trial, whether civil or criminal, has been moulded at all stages by the judiciary with the object of eliciting the truth in accordance with judicial conceptions of fair play. This is strikingly illustrated by the application of the first rule of criminal procedure, embodied in the maxim that everyone is presumed to be innocent until proved to be guilty—proved, that is, by properly-adduced and tested evidence. In every criminal trial, the onus of proof is initially with the Crown as prosecutor. It is for the Crown to bring forward evidence from which the guilt of the prisoner is inferred. Only then is the prisoner under an obligation to bring forward, if he can, evidence which either contradicts the Crown's case, or which places it in a different context (eg by showing that the accused acted under compulsion, or fear of physical harm offered by a third party, or that he suffered from some mental infirmity sufficient to relieve him, either wholly or partially, from criminal liability).

The judges also introduced another salutary rule into criminal trials. In a civil trial the court—whether judge or jury—must decide on the balance of the evidence offered. In a criminal trial, the Crown must prove its case beyond reasonable doubt. This does not mean 'beyond possible doubt'. A court is free to reject hypotheses which are so slender that they would not weigh with any reasonable person; but unless the Crown's case links the accused firmly by an unbroken chain of evidence with the crime which has been committed, then the accused must go free.

In theory, there is only one law of evidence, common to civil and criminal trials, and it is a fact that the basic rules are equally applicable to both; but questions of evidence arise much more frequently in criminal trials, where the court is vigilant to ensure that the rules are strictly adhered to. For this reason, the Crown may not always offer all the evidence which it may consider to be admissible, since even if it is admitted at the trial, it may be decided on appeal that the evidence should not have been admitted, and that its admission unfairly prejudiced the accused, who must therefore be released. At all stages of the trial the Crown is attempting to establish the person's guilt by the adduction of evidence and by the application of reasoning and persuasion to the evidence so produced. The court, therefore, in applying the rules of evidence, is ensuring that only those matters are placed before a jury from which they may be able to reach an unbiased conclusion. Another group of rules of evidence therefore defines the area of *facts* which are admissible. These are known as the facts in issue, and the rules of evidence exclude much that the layman might consider to be relevant. Naturally they include everything which can throw light on the commission of the crime, but they exclude evidence of other crimes which the accused has committed, and for which he has been convicted, unless these can be connected with the crime now charged against him, for example, by showing a system or series of operations of a similar nature, of which the crime for which he is now being charged is the latest example. The English courts will never entertain an allegation that the prisoner's record is so bad that it is likely, or probable, that he committed the act charged.

Although most of the principal rules of evidence are of considerable antiquity, and there are frequent references to them in the Year Books, their systematic development by the courts was undertaken in the century which followed the Restoration of Charles II in 1660. Even in the time of Lord Mansfield's Chief Justiceship, the rules were regarded as still fluid, and a century earlier judges had still considered themselves free to apply or reject them at discretion. This is particularly evident in the development of the hearsay rule. It was already suspect at the beginning of the seventeenth century, and Sir Edward Coke says in the *Institutes*: 'One eyewitness is worth ten by hearsay.'[2] Nevertheless, it was not infrequently admitted in the state trials of the time, and both Archbishop Laud and Lord William Russell protested against its admission against them. In admitting hearsay evidence, the judges of the period conceived that they were securing the safety of the state. Even so, a number of judges of Charles II's reign, including Atkins, Chief Justice Scroggs (who presided at the 'Popish Plot' treason trials) and Chief Justice Jeffreys himself, all at various times either refused to admit hearsay evidence, or warned the jury against placing reliance upon it. In general, however, there was no legal bar to its admission, and Phillipps, the author of one of the early treatises on the law of evidence, sums up the position prior to the Revolution as follows:[3]

> Throughout the State trials before the time of the Commonwealth the worst species of hearsay was constantly received; such as the examinations of persons who might have been produced as witnesses, or who had been convicted of capital offences, or who had signed confessions in the presence only of the officers of government, and under the torture of the rack... On the trials for the Popish Plot, the evidence consisted principally of a narrative of the transactions of the supposed conspirators in various countries, collected during a long period of time from a multitude of letters, the contents of which were given from recollection, – the witnesses not having taken a note of any part of the letters at the time of reading, nor having read them for a great number of years, nor having been required in reading to notice their contents, and not producing one of the letters, or a copy, or even an extract.

It was only after 1688 that the rules of evidence came to be regarded as binding, and that the decisions of courts upon them became precedents in the same way as decisions upon points of substantive law. Gradually, too, some parts of the law of evidence received statutory force. Once legal representation for persons accused of serious crime became possible, the way was open to the judicial combat between the Crown and the accused, which has continued to the present day, with steadily increasing solicitude on the part of the court for the protection of the rights of the accused. One outstanding illustration of this has been the elaboration of what are known as the 'Judges' Rules' for the interrogation of prisoners by the police before a person is charged. These rules, devised by the judges, and applied by them in all criminal charges, govern the admissibility of statements made to a police officer. They include the requirement to caution a person 'whenever a police officer has made up his mind to charge' him, and they provide that the statement should be voluntary. It is also a settled rule of practice that a statement by an accused person is inadmissible if any inducement or threat has been offered to obtain it; and finally, if a person taken into custody, who is resolved to remain silent, makes no reply to questions put to him, the police have no means, other than by reiterated questioning, to compel him to talk. Increasingly at the present day it is felt by police officers and others that the extent to which these rules protect an accused makes it frequently possible for a guilty man to treat the efforts of the police with indifference, and to be assured, when he comes into court, that his counsel will diligently scrutinise all that has happened since he was detained, for the purpose of placing any irregularity before the court.

Because the modern criminal is so much more resourceful than his predecessors, the Criminal Law Revision Committee, in an impressive report, published in June 1972 after eight years of study, have proposed far-reaching changes in procedure and evidence in criminal trials with the object of curtailing the protection which an accused now enjoys. These, the committee concludes, may have been necessary in the past as a protection against injustices, but today they may operate to enable the guilty to escape.

> In fact [the report says] they are frequently used at present by highly sophisticated and skilful professional criminals in order to avoid conviction—for example by refusing to answer questions put by the police and by the elaborate manufacture of false evidence.

The report also stresses that it is the guilty, and not the

innocent, who would lose by a relaxation of rules of evidence which today tend to be too favourable to them. Trials must be fair, but fairness means

> that the law should be such as will secure as far as possible that the result of the trial is the right one. That is to say the accused should be convicted if the evidence proves beyond reasonable doubt that he is guilty, but otherwise not.

Possibly the most significant feature of the report is that it condemns the firmly-entrenched notion that a criminal trial is a species of game or combat with fixed rules, in which a guilty person is entitled to go free if he can get the advantage of a legal technicality arising from a strict application of the rules. Over and over again, judges have been compelled to reject evidence which would certainly have been valuable, and which could not possibly have caused injustice, because as a result of earlier decisions it was inadmissible. Similarly, appellate courts have often quashed convictions, because evidence has, upon the authorities, been wrongly admitted at the trial. The committee might have gone a step further. Fear of a possible adverse decision on appeal has frequently impelled counsel for the Crown to omit relevant evidence from the Crown's case from the outset.

A number of important changes are therefore recommended. One of them is designed to overcome the persistent silence of an accused person under interrogation. If at such a time the accused fails to mention a fact on which he afterwards relies at the trial, this may be mentioned, and the court or jury will be free to draw inferences from it. It is also suggested that the Judges' Rules should be modified in a number of ways. For example, the police caution that an accused need not say anything unless he wishes should be replaced by a written notice advising him to mention any fact on which he intends to rely in his defence, and warning him that if he holds it back until the trial, it may have an adverse effect. Perhaps the most striking recommendation is that the Judges' Rules should be entirely replaced by Home Office directives to the police.

At the present time, an accused may not be compelled to give evidence, and if he does not, the prosecution may not comment on it. On the other hand, he may make an unsworn statement at the trial, and if he elects to do so, he may not be cross-examined on it. This, the committee concludes, is far too favourable to the accused, and it is of the opinion that when a *prima facie* case has been made out against him, he should be required to give evidence in all ordinary cases, and his right to make an unsworn statement should be abolished.

Two other major recommenations are (1) that the rule excluding statements made by the prisoner, if made as a result of threats or inducement, however slight, should be relaxed; and (2) that if the defence introduces evidence with a view to establishing directly or by implication the previous good character or reputation of the accused, the prosecution may introduce evidence to the contrary, including evidence of previous convictions.

Clearly this last recommendation, if adopted, will pose a question of extreme difficulty for the defence in many criminal trials, but it is simply one of many which are advanced in the belief, after careful and prolonged study, that the protection for the accused, which the judiciary has developed in the past century and a half, has not infrequently permitted the guilty to escape, and that with the spread of organised crime, and the increasing skill of criminals, it is a luxury which can no longer be afforded.

In the sphere of the substantive criminal law, the influence of the judiciary, though somewhat less apparent, has nevertheless been considerable and continuing. It has been less apparent because crime, as a threat to the security and well-being of the community, has been from earliest times the subject of legislation. This has been particularly marked in respect of serious crimes. A glance at recent volumes of the statute-book will show that they include a comprehensive Theft Act, a Homicide Act, an Act legalising abortion under certain conditions, an Act permitting homosexual behaviour between consenting adults, and an Act abolishing capital punishment. These are only a few examples, but together they reflect some important changes in the attitude of society towards criminal behaviour and its treatment. They raise, directly or indirectly, some fundamental questions, of which the two most important are: (1) Why are certain kinds of behaviour regarded as criminal, so that the appropriate correction is undertaken by the state, rather than the individual, and (2) What is the object of criminal proceedings—is it corrective, retributive, reformative, or is it a kind of vicarious revenge by society for the injury inflicted by the accused? Debate upon these and allied topics is unceasing, and while some solutions—not necessarily permanent ones—are embodied in legislation, it is the task of the judiciary to assess the dominant ideas held by the community in any age, and to interpret the law, as far as is appropriate, in accordance with them. Two examples from the history of the criminal law may serve as illustrations. In the reign of Edward III, there was passed in 1351 the Statute of Treasons. Its primary intention was to define the limits of this most serious crime, since a very wide variety of offences had been punished under this head. In essence, the Statute defined the crime as a breach of the feudal bond which bound the subject to his sovereign. For this reason, an alien who had never been resident within the realm could never be guilty of treason. If, however, the alien comes within the realm, he owes a temporary allegiance, and so may be proceeded against. The Statute of 1351 is still the basis of the law of treason, although today it is regarded as an offence against the security of the state, and not as a breach of a personal feudal bond. This transformation has occurred through judicial interpretation over a period of six hundred years, and it was described by a great authority upon the criminal law, Professor Kenny,[4] in memorable terms:

> The historical development of our nation tended steadily, century after century, to make a consciousness of the stability of public order—rather than the feudal feeling of more personal loyalty to a prince—become the binding force of the body politic. This new conception of civil duty rendered necessary new provisions for its legal enforcement. The criminal law had to begin to take cognizance of politicians who, whilst devoted

to the reigning King, were nevertheless disturbing the order of the realm; though possibly only by assailing those institutions whereby the constitution had set a check upon the King's powers. It is a remarkable instance of the activity of judicial legislation that the important legal development, thus rendered necessary, was effected not by Parliament, but by the judges. They transformed the feudal conception of treason, as a breach of personal faith into the modern one, which regards it as 'armed resistance, made on political grounds, to the public order of the realm'.

To this, it may be added by way of postscript, that where the security of the state is threatened, the judiciary even today will make their interpretation sufficiently comprehensive. At the end of World War II, William Joyce, who had broadcast from Germany on behalf of Hitler's Reich, was tried, condemned and executed for treason, because, although he had exchanged his British nationality for German nationality at the outbreak of war, he had retained his British passport.

On the other hand, the enlightened attitude of the judiciary at the beginning of the nineteenth century very greatly mitigated the severity of the criminal law. Until the reforms of Sir Robert Peel, when Home Secretary, over two hundred crimes might involve the death penalty. Faced with brutality of such an indiscriminating criminal law, juries were encouraged to acquit, or to make findings by virtue of which the accused might escape the extreme penalty. This was most evident in respect of one of the commonest crimes, ie larceny. If an accused was convicted of stealing goods valued at more than a shilling, he could be hanged. Accordingly, juries were encouraged to bring verdicts that goods demonstrably worth much more than a shilling, which were alleged to have been stolen by the accused, could be valued at sixpence or some similar amount. In this humanitarian activity, consistently pursued, the courts anticipated the action of the legislature by many years.

There are, however, even more fundamental characteristics of the criminal law which owe their existence to judicial activity. The great principle that every man is presumed innocent until the contrary is proved to the satisfaction of the court, is to be found in no statute. It is judge-made law, and it is the root of all criminal justice. Distinct from it, yet closely allied, is the other basic principle that for a crime to exist, there must not only be a wrongful, and harmful act, but also a guilty intent, or *mens rea*. It is this characteristic which distinguishes a mature from an early system of criminal law. The latter frequently attributes criminal liability without proof of intention, and it is possibly in this development that English criminal law shows, in its evolution, its association with medieval Christian philosophy, and from which is derived the conception, now in process of abandonment, that a crime also involves an offence against current morality. This concept of *mens rea*, however, is applicable only to the more serious criminal offences. One of the characteristics of the vastly increased activity of the state during the past half-century has been the readiness of the legislature to introduce conformity to its policies by the establishment of a very large number of offences of absolute liability; this is to say, of offences in which the intention, or in some cases even the knowledge, of the accused, is irrelevant. French law distinguishes these from crimes in the strict sense by terming them *contraventions*. As yet, English law has given them no general description, although they are generally known as statutory offences. Where the legislative intention is that infractions of the rule should involve a direct application of the penalty, the courts are powerless, but they have shown anxiety lest the habit of excluding the necessity for *mens rea* be spread too widely.

It cannot be too strongly emphasised that the degree of respect accorded to the administration of the criminal law is an index of the health of the community in which it operates. The anxiety of the courts of criminal justice to preserve that respect is therefore increasing. A great criminal advocate, Sir Harry Poland, once said: 'Criminal law is an essentially fluctuating thing, since our judges rightly interpret it in accordance with the spirit of the age.' In doing so, however, they must carefully tread a path between undue flexibility and resistance to new theories from outside the law. In an extremely dynamic age, this exercise is an extremely difficult one.

It is not made easier by an unresolved problem on which judges of the highest eminence have differed. Something has already been said about the flexible concept of criminal conspiracy, in its application to trade unions. This, however, is only one application, and there may be conspiracies of many different kinds—for example, to commit torts, or even to violate standards of public decency. In addition, there has existed in the judiciary from early times, a power to punish criminally acts designed to cause a public mischief. This, too, is a wide, and vague concept, and in *R v Manley*[5] a woman was convicted of this offence for making false statements to the police that she had been attacked and robbed, thereby causing the police to waste their time in investigating her allegations. In this case, Lord Chief Justice Hewart reaffirmed a statement in an earlier decision that 'all offences of a public nature, that is all such acts or attempts as tend to the prejudice of the community, are indictable'. This decision, with others which have followed it, has been consistently discussed, and in *R v Newland*[6] another Lord Chief Justice, Goddard, suggested that one day the House of Lords might wish to consider whether the courts still possessed a Common Law jurisdiction to create crimes of such broad extent. This opportunity was afforded in 1961, in the celebrated appeal in *Shaw v Director of Public Prosecutions*.[7] The appellant had published the *Ladies' Directory*, which was in fact a list of names and addresses of prostitutes, in some cases stating their availability for sexual perversions. Shaw was charged with conspiring with the prostitutes to corrupt public morals. The House of Lords held that he was rightly convicted, and in so doing, discussed at length the power of the courts to recognise such offences, independently of any statute. In expressing the view of the majority, Viscount Simonds said, bluntly:

> In the sphere of criminal law I entertain no doubt that there remains in the courts of law a residual power to enforce the supreme and fundamental purpose of the law, to conserve not only the safety and order but also the moral welfare of the state, and that it is their duty to guard it against attacks which

may be the more insidious because they are novel and unprepared for.

There are numerous earlier decisions affirming this principle, but Lord Reid, after an historical survey, doubted whether this function of the judiciary still survived. In reaching this conclusion, he adopted the observations of Lord Goddard in *R v Newland*, that the days are gone in which judges can create new crimes. This is now the function of the legislature. Although *Shaw's Case* appeared to have settled the question so far as the application of the law in the courts is concerned, the decision provoked much discussion, and in *Knuller v Director of Public Prosecutions*,[8] a case on somewhat similar facts to those in *Shaw's Case*, the members of the House of Lords were in agreement that today the courts do not have the power to create new offences or to widen existing offences, so as to make punishable conduct of a kind not previously subject to punishment.

16

The Modern Judicial Contribution

In recent years a small number of distinguished judges have discussed the part played by the judges in the making of modern English law. Among them are Lord Devlin, a former Lord of Appeal in Ordinary, and Lord Diplock, a present Lord of Appeal. Both have expressed the view that the judicial function today is not so extensive as it used to be, and both, by inference or in the case of Lord Diplock, by actual statement, have concluded that modern English judges are not the equals of their predecessors. Lord Devlin writes:

> The work done by the Judges of England is not now as glorious as it was. Their opportunities are not what they used to be nor are they the equal of those which judges have seized in other countries administering the Common Law. There are no great constitutional questions for English judges to decide such as still have to be considered by the Supreme Court of a Federation or such as may arise under the Canadian Bill of Rights. They have no such exciting task in front of them as awaits the Courts of India and Nigeria, that of fusing English law with the indigenous law.[1]

In the last chapter of the book from which this quotation is taken, Lord Devlin discusses how far the decline in their importance is due to their supersession by the legislature, and how much more to their recoil from the impact of any new ideas in the law. In that chapter, he reaches the pessimistic conclusion that during the past half-century, the Common Law, as expounded by the judges, has been retreating, and not expanding, and that this has been in part forced upon them by the ever-expanding claims of the executive, but in important part also, it is due to a voluntary retreat of the judiciary from the determination of broad questions of social policy.

It is true that there are many decisions (some of them discussed by Lord Devlin) which give support to this view. Before the omnipotence of Parliament and the ever extending activities of the executive, the Common Law appears to offer only a frail barrier. We have moved a very long way away from the affirmation of Holt, CJ, in *City of London v Wood*: 'When an Act of Parliament is against common right and reason, the Common Law will control it and adjudge such Act to be void.'[2]

No English judge, and no English court, could possibly make such an affirmation today. On the contrary, in a presidential address on the *Independence of the Judges* at the Holdsworth Club of Birmingham University, on 16 June 1956, Lord Denning recalled that the then Attorney-General had recently said in the House of Commons that it was a most important principle of our constitutional practice that judges do not comment on the policy of Parliament, but administer the law, good or bad, as they find it. That is the point of doctrine on which the independence of the judiciary rests.

The claim may have been extreme, but it expresses clearly enough the attitude of the executive to the work of the courts. It explains the expressions of powerlessness uttered by members of the House of Lords (with the very notable exception of Lord Atkin) in *Liversidge v Anderson*,[3] or again, of the immunity of public documents from production in court, in the case of *Duncan v Cammell, Laird*[4] decided by the House of Lords in the same year.

The retreat of the judiciary, especially from the areas of public policy and social change, was also emphasised by Lord Diplock in an address, *The Courts as Legislators*, delivered to the Holdsworth Club of Birmingham University in 1965. Discussing the criticism that by reason of their temperament and training, judges are too averse to change to be entrusted with the development of legal rules in a society where social and economic conditions are changing so rapidly, he said:

> At first it was not always so. Where do you find the sources of the Common Law today? In the bold, imaginative judgments delivered by a great generation of judges between the sixties and the nineties of the last century. It was these, rather than the activities of Parliament, which transformed man's duty towards his neighbour as he emerged from a static, agricultural and aristocratic society to a dynamic, industrial and democratic one. True they made some errors. The doctrine of common employment dates from this period. True these changes reflected the current social and economic philosophy of the nineteenth century which is no longer representative of majority thought today. But had the same attitude survived into the twentieth century, the same process of change would have continued to adopt the Common Law to the needs of contemporary society without the need for intervention by Parliament. Yet somehow, at the turn of the century, the courts seemed to have lost their courage. In the clash between precedent and flexibility, precedent seemed to win that day. What in the nineteenth century was done by judges to adapt the Common Law and equity to the needs of contemporary society has in the last thirty years had to be done by the Law Reform Committee, upon whose reports nearly a score of Law Reform Acts have been added to the other judge-made rules of Common Law and equity. Each of these Acts announces the twentieth century failure of the judges, to show courage and imagination.

Lord Devlin, in the address already mentioned, did not attribute the diminished role of the courts to their timidity in the face of advances by the executive, 'But rather to voluntary withdrawal in the field of public policy as a whole. There are two reasons for this recession. The first is that in it the Common Law is obeying the law of its own nature and the second is the increase of parliamentary activity.'

This increase has now reached the proportions of a flood, and a comparison of any volume of the Law Reports today with a nineteenth-century volume will show how much judicial activity is now concentrated upon legislation, and relatively how little is devoted to the establishment of private rights at Common Law. A comparison of a modern volume of statutes with one for a year of the eighteenth century is even more illuminating. The range and variety of matters in respect of which there has been parliamentary intervention is incomparably wider, and it becomes even more comprehensive if there is included ministerial regulations, Orders in Council, subordinate regulations and by-laws, all with compulsory force.

These developments have been part of a complex social process, which has transferred the initiative in law-making from the courts to Parliament. It has been shown how, in the thirteenth and fourteenth centuries, the judiciary of the Common Law courts evolved from the royal administration, and only gradually acquired independence from it, mainly through the development of an independent legal profession, which secured a monopoly of judicial appointments. Even in Stuart times, the Crown still looked on the judiciary as a branch, though an autonomous branch, of the royal administration. The final disappearance of any such theory was one of the consequences of the Revolution of 1688, and the constitution which evolved from it rested upon the twin-pillars of parliamentary sovereignty and judicial independence. That independence has never been more freely exercised than during the eighteenth century, when government impinged as little as possible upon personal freedom, and when legislation, infrequent in incidence, was not seen as a vehicle for reform. Any such view was, in fact, untenable until Parliament itself was reformed, and this was delayed by the long conflict with the French Revolution and Napoleon. It was not until 1832 that the great Reform Act of that year swept away many ancient abuses, reformed the system of parliamentary representation, and took a first cautious step along the road which has led to universal suffrage of both sexes at the age of eighteen.

Many other changes have accompanied these progressive extensions of the franchise. They include the successive reductions in the power of the House of Lords, and its change of function to that of a revising chamber; the assumption of almost dictatorial powers by the government, which can ensure the achievement of its policies by its control, or manipulation, of its majority in the House of Commons; and finally, the general acceptance of the principle that in the interests of the national welfare, of which the government of the day is the judge, government may direct the execution of sweeping policies of social change, and that it is legitimate, or even praiseworthy to do so. This makes ever-increasing demands upon the citizens' purses for the money which is needed to carry them out.

This, in turn, has led to a great increase in the volume and comprehensiveness of legislation. Bentham, Austin and other jurists explained that this was desirable, because legislation was the expression of the will of the people through its chosen organ, Parliament. Equally, they disliked the technique of judicial precedent, which they regarded as cumbrous, dilatory and, ultimately, inadequate to express the popular will. Although the legal philosophy of Bentham and Austin is no longer fashionable, their criticisms of legal development through the instrumentality of case law, together with some additional criticism, can still be heard today. For this reason, the judiciary now treads with greater caution, and it has retreated completely from the field of public policy.

The successive stages of this retreat have been indicated with clarity in the address which has already been mentioned. Lord Devlin also stressed the fact that the power of the executive over Parliament is now such that, although members can still make themselves felt on questions of principle, the detail of legislation is almost entirely the work of the ministers. To this should be added the fact that the initiative for legislation comes almost entirely from the same source. The Government decides questions of policy. Where this involves legislation, the appropriate department prepares it. Because of the incessant growth in power of the executive, Lord Devlin argues, the Common Law can no longer keep it under proper control. The responsibility for this rests with

Parliament, which can (a) keep a close watch upon the powers given to the executive, and (b) can control the way in which the powers given are used. He concludes: 'Since that cannot be effectively done under the law as it stands, there must be created a new body of law of the sort that has come to be called administrative law.'[5]

These views, it would appear, are shared by other leading members of the judiciary. They received very clear definitions by Lord Denning in *Breen v Amalgamated Engineering Union*[6] and they underlay the opinions expressed by four members of the House of Lords in *Padfield v Minister of Agriculture, Fisheries and Food.*[7] Administrative law, in the assertion of judicial control over administrative action, already exists, and is being developed. The extent of that development has been discussed elsewhere.

At an earlier point in his address, Lord Devlin considered the respective merits of statute law and judge-made law. 'Judge made law [he said] has the advantage that the judges feel their way step by step and so this law is tested empirically while it is being formed. But that has the disadvantage that all the steps are not always in the same direction and there may be prolonged periods of uncertainty while the course is being plotted. Sometimes the process ends up in a muddle that can only be cured by the legislature.'

His conclusion was that probably the best solution was the statutory formulation of the Common Law when fully developed, although this raises the question, at what point can a branch of the Common Law be regarded as ready for codification? Some good examples will be considered later in this chapter, but Lord Devlin drew attention to an address by Lord Evershed,[8] which illustrated the extent of the task of the courts in extracting from a growing body of legislation workable principles of law, suitable for incorporation into the general body of English law. Statutory interpretation has produced its own particular problems, and the process of interpretation is frequently a difficult one.

Before discussing how far the somewhat pessimistic views of Lord Devlin and Lord Diplock reflect the position generally, something should be said of the change in structure and outlook of the judiciary during the past century, during which the far-reaching changes just described have been taking place, and which may ultimately be traced to the changes introduced by the Judicature Acts 1873–5. These introduced comprehensive changes into the substance of English law, particularly in the provision that all branches of the High Court should henceforth have full jurisdiction in law and equity. They also brought a number of courts with special jurisdictions into a Supreme Court of Judicature, with two divisions: (1) a Court of Appeal, to hear appeals from superior courts in all civil cases; and (2) the High Court of Justice, whose jurisdiction absorbed those of the old courts of Common Law, the Chancery, the Courts for Probate, Admiralty and Matrimonial Causes, the Court of Pleas at Durham, the Court of Common Pleas at Lancaster, and finally the courts created by the Commissioners of Oyer and Terminer, Gaol Delivery and Assize. In the years immediately following the Judicature Acts, the High Court sat in five divisions: (1) the Chancery Division; (2) the Probate, Divorce and Admiralty Division; (3) the King's (Queen's) Bench Division; (4) the Common Pleas Division; and (5) the Exchequer Division. The last three, inheriting the traditional jurisdictions of the Common Law courts which they replaced, were merged into a single Queen's Bench Division in 1881.

The Court of Appeal also inherited the jurisdictions of a number of Courts of Appeal with limited jurisdiction existing before the Judicature Acts. Of these, the principal were the Court of Exchequer Chamber, the Court of Appeal in Chancery, the Judicial Committee of the Privy Council in appeals in lunacy and from Courts of Admiralty (except in prize cases), and the Court of Appeal from Lancaster.

In the original scheme for the re-organisation of the judiciary, which was embodied in the Judicature Act, 1873, it was provided that the ultimate appellate jurisdiction of the House of Lords should be abolished. There were sound reasons for this since, quite apart from the association of legislation with political functions, the House had frequently failed to achieve the distinction which should belong to a final Court of Appeal. At the end of the eighteenth century, the House of Lords, as the final Court of Appeal, on some occasions comprised only the Lord Chancellor together with two lay lords. In the first half of the nineteenth century, there were instances of decisions in which it was necessary to seek the presence of lay lords to make up the court, and even when ex-Lord Chancellors assisted the Lord Chancellor, they were sometimes so aged that their suitability might be questioned. Sometimes, too, the House took advantage of an old device—consultation of the entire body of Common Law judges, to inform themselves of the legal rules involved in the appeal. In an effort to overcome this difficulty, the government of Lord Palmerston in 1856 procured the conferment of a life peerage on Baron Parke (a baron of the Exchequer) with the object of strengthening the House in the exercise of its appellate functions. The House regarded this as a dangerous precedent, which might in the future lead to creations to increase the strength of the government in the Lords, and therefore they declined to admit the new peer,[9] whereupon Baron Parke was created a hereditary peer, with the title of Lord Wensleydale.

The provision for the abolition of the appellate functions of the House of Lords, contained in the Act of 1873, was removed by the Judicature Act 1875, but to meet the criticisms of the House which had been made, the Appellate Jurisdiction Act 1876 provided that there should be in any appeal, a quorum of at least three members, and in order to ensure this, the Act also provided for the appointment of two Lords of Appeal in ordinary (now increased to nine) who should be life peers, but who, so long as they held office, should be paid salaries for the judicial work which they discharged. In addition, it was enacted that members of the House, in its judicial capacity, should include ex-Lord Chancellors, and any peer who has held high judicial office. So strengthened, the House hears appeals, not only from English Courts of Appeal, but also from those of Scotland and Northern Ireland.

The judicial re-organisation undertaken at this period also extended to the judicial committee of the Privy Council, and by successive acts, its membership has been strengthened to include the members of the House of Lords as a final Court of Appeal, together with a number of eminent judges from the Commonwealth, and finally, the Lords Justices of Appeal. In this way the Privy Council was made a strong court with a special function as a final Court of Appeal for the Commonwealth (a function today which is greatly restricted by virtue of the abolition of the right of appeal to it in many Commonwealth nations), which also, by virtue of its composition, would play a major role in interpreting the Common Law as applied in the Commonwealth nations in harmony with its interpretation in English courts. One consequence of this has been that Privy Council decisions, although not technically binding on English courts, have nevertheless been treated with highest respect by them.

The Judicature Acts have had a profound effect upon the development of English law, and upon the relations of Common Law and equity. So far as the latter is concerned, it has frequently been stated that the Acts did not fuse law and equity, but only the administration of them, making both applicable in any proceedings in any court. This is true, but there has nevertheless been a deep change in outlook in consequence. Before the Act, practitioners and judges were trained in one system only—the system which they saw in operation daily in the courts. Each system therefore remained distinct. Since the Acts, practitioners and judges have been trained in a single system—English law. In some areas, the distinction between law and equity has ceased to be of importance—for example, in the law of mistake in contract, or in the land law (where the old Common Law and equitable rules have now been largely overlaid or superseded by statutory rules). In other areas, the distinction between law and equity is still of importance—for example, in the law of trusts and those rules which determine the effect of fiduciary relationships. There is, however, a subtle change of approach even in these areas, arising from the position of the judge as an administrator of both systems. In some decisions, the line between law and equity has become indefinite, as in *Hurst v Picture Theatres.*[10] In others, eg *Central London Property Trust v High Trees Ltd,*[11] rules have been introduced in the name of equity, for which there was no precedent before 1873. It is difficult to resist the conclusion that, although fusion is not yet here, it cannot be long delayed. Recently, Lord Denning has urged the need for a new equity, as an instrument of law reform,[12] but such an equity, if it should come into existence, would be something which would permeate the entire legal system. It could not operate, as the pre-1873 equity did, as a supplement to the Common Law.

One great change introduced by the Judicature Acts has attracted little comment, although its effects are apparent in successive volumes of the law reports. Particularly at the appellate level, a small body of distinguished judges transformed the nature and spirit of English law in the forty years between the Judicature Acts and the outbreak of World War I. It became a long and progressive adaptation to the needs of a rapidly changing society. Writing shortly after the Judicature Acts, and with reference primarily to the law of torts, Maitland wrote in *The Forms of Action*: 'The forms of action we have buried, but they rule us from their graves.' Nothing of the forms of action remains today, and the law of torts has escaped from the bonds which the forms of action imposed upon it. Most of the decisive steps to this end had been taken before 1914. Elsewhere in the law, judges constantly reminded themselves that they now administered both law and equity, and as the distance from the Judicature Acts grew, most of them did not look too closely at the ancestry of the rules they applied, although this exercise was common in the first fifteen years after 1875. Even Common Law judges made themselves acquainted with the unfamiliar material of the Chancery reports, and did not hesitate to make full use of their new freedom. For example in *Re Carey*,[13] in an appeal from a decision of the divisional court upon the custody of an illegitimate infant, Jessel, MR, said: 'Moreover, now that all the Courts are courts of law and equity, the question does not depend upon the mere legal rights, upon *habeas corpus*, but upon equitable doctrines.'

And with this the other two members of the Court of Appeal were in agreement.

Even a cursory glance at the Queen's Bench Reports for 1883 will show how much the judicial outlook had broadened since the

Judicature Acts. For example, in *Maddison v Alderson*[14] the House of Lords was free to make a complete review of the relation of law to equity in respect of the part performance of oral contracts to leave property by will. Much of the discussion in the House of Lords related to the sufficiency of evidence of facts needed to prove an oral contract, and on that point Lord Blackburn observed significantly:

> There are many rules laid down as to what should guide a judge, determining for himself what the facts are, in thinking the proof of a contract sufficient. I see great difficulty, now that equity is to be administered by a court which has the facts found by a jury; but that is a question not raised now.

Happily, the difficulties mentioned by Lord Blackburn did not develop to the extent which he feared; and now the jury itself has been largely abandoned in many civil actions. Nevertheless, an appellate judge, surveying the scene in the eighties, could not have failed to be conscious of them. It is also quite evident that Common Law judges were taking great pains to accommodate themselves to equitable principles. For example, shortly before *Maddison v Alderson* was decided by the House of Lords, the Court of Appeal, on appeal from Manisty, J, in the Queen's Bench Division, was also considering part performance of an oral contract, this time in respect of the purchase of a farm, in *Humphreys v Green*.[15]

Another major decision of the House of Lords in the same year is again an excellent illustration of the development of a new outlook which was taking place. In *Goodman v The Mayor of Saltash*,[16] the incorporated borough had enjoyed a seasonal oyster fishery by usage from time immemorial, for the free inhabitants of the borough. The corporation claimed a several fishery free of this usage. The House of Lords upheld the right of the free inhabitants, presuming a grant to the corporation, subject to a condition or charitable trust in their favour. In the judgements of the House of Lords, there was much learning upon the various points of law which had been argued and in which both legal and equitable arguments had been put forward. Lord Blackburn, as a very distinguished common lawyer, was quite plainly uncertain about the interaction of law and equity in a problem such as this. He said:

> It was argued that at all events such a grant in favour of a fluctuating body might be worked out by treating the corporation as a trustee, and the intervention of the Court of Chancery. I speak with diffidence on a subject with which I am not very conversant, but I believe the rule against perpetuities which is founded on nearly the same reason as that of *Gateward's Case*,[17] applies to all trusts, except those in which the sovereign has the power, as being the ultimate trustee for charitable uses, of altering them. And although there are many cases to the effect that a trust for public purposes, or confined to the poor, may be considered charitable for many purposes, I do not know of any that say that such a trust as is now supposed would be taken out of the rule against perpetuities; and *Carne v Long*[18] seems rather against it. As, however, the noble Earl [Earl Cairns][19] agrees with the Lord Chancellor[20] that such a trust would not be held void in equity as being against the rule against perpetuities, I do not venture to differ from them.

The search for the origins of legal rules is again illustrated in *Kendall's Trustee v Marshall & Co*,[21] a notable decision of the Court of Appeal, in which the law of stoppage *in transitu* was traced and defined. After discussing the difference between the Common Law and the custom of the merchants on this point, Bowen, LJ, added:

> This difference existing between the custom of the merchants and the English law as to the passing of the property, the courts of equity in 1690,[22] and the courts of Common Law shortly afterwards, grafted this just indulgence upon the English law; and this rule of merchants is now accepted by English law.

In the *North London Ry Co v The GNR*[23] the Court of Appeal examined the principles applicable to the award of an injunction after the Judicature Acts. Discussing Section 25 (8) of the Act of 1873, Cotton, LJ, said:

> In my opinion all that was done by this section was to give to the High Court, comprising what was formerly the Court of Chancery and the courts of Common Law, power to act where some of these courts did act before, and to exercise all the powers of the divisions of which the court had previously consisted, and to give a remedy which they formerly would not in that particular case have given, but only a remedy in defence of or to enforce rights which, according to law previously existed, were capable of being enforced in some or one of the different courts, which no longer exist, but which are now all united in the High Court. But it is the High Court which amalgamates or unites in itself all the jurisdictions which have previously existed, and undoubtedly in that sense a new jurisdiction is given to the Chancery Division now in matters with which the Court of Chancery never could have dealt, but which were dealt with by the Courts of Common Law dealing with legal rights where the Court of Chancery had no jurisdiction to interfere. In my opinion the general intention of the Judicature Act is this, that where there is a legal right capable of being enforced by action in the High Court either at law or in equity, then, whatever may have been the previous practice, the High Court may interfere to protect that legal or equitable right which, independently of the Act, could be made the subject of an action either at law or in equity.

But the fact that the common lawyers were taking pains to become familiar with equity is perhaps best illustrated by the *Attorney-General v Hubbuck*,[24] a decision upon an action filed by the Attorney-General, to determine the status for probate duty of land forming part of the share of a deceased partner. In this decision, three Common Law judges (Pollock and Huddleston, BB, and North, J) exhaustively considered the development of the rules of equity relating to partnership property, explaining why real property bought and held for partnership purposes was deemed to be held upon trust for sale, so that in this case, the deceased partner's share was deemed to be personal property.

These are no more than a few illustrations from the decisions of a single year, which originated in the Queen's Bench Division. Almost every other volume of the Law Reports at this period would yield its quota of comparable decisions. The impression is gained that the judges both of the Court of Appeal and the House of Lords were consciously freeing themselves of pre-1873 limitations, and were continuously examining, defining and broadening the principles from which the modern law was derived. In both appellate courts, the law could be surveyed as a whole, and full advantage was taken of the opportunity which was offered.

The list of names of outstanding judges who made important contributions at this period is long, and it is not possible to mention them all. Sitting in the Court of Appeal in the first years after the Judicature Acts there were Sir George Jessel, as Master of the Rolls; Bramwell (who as Lord Bramwell, also later made a notable contribution to the judicial work of the House of Lords); Brett (later Lord Esher and Jessel's successor as Master of the Rolls); Cotton; Lindley (later Lord Lindley); and, a little later, Bowen, Fry, Romer and Farwell. Bramwell had been a leading member of the commission whose report was the foundation of the Companies Act, and he was also a member of the commission, whose report was the basis of the Judicature Act, 1873. His reputation in the last quarter of the nineteenth century was extremely high and his judgements not infrequently have a rugged individuality which reflected his uncompromising support of individual freedom, and often a touch of humour or irony; as when, in *Weir v Bell*,[25] he somewhat mischievously expressed his inability to understand the term legal fraud.

> To make a man liable for fraud [he said] moral fraud must be proved against him. I do not understand legal fraud. To my mind it has no more meaning than legal heat or legal cold, legal light or legal shade.

This was a deep-rooted conviction. It is evidenced again in his speech in *Derry v Peek*,[26] which quite plainly influenced all the other members in the House except Lord Herschell.

Like Jessel, he believed implicity in *laisser-faire* theories of freedom of contract, and he regretted the tendency to restrict it by statutes such as the Employers Liability Act. It led him in one of his last judgements, in *Salt v Marquess of Northampton*,[27] to regret the development of the equitable rules relating to clogs on the equity of redemption.

In the House of Lords during the first years of the new system, the Lord Chancellor, the Earl of Selborne, had a commanding place, and the list of notable judgements by him is a very long one. So also is the list of these of his Liberal predecessor, Lord Cairns. They are remarkable not only for their lucid expositions of principle, but for their sparing citation of authority. It may be, nevertheless, that the most commanding figure in the House during the early years after the re-organisation was that of Lord Blackburn, who died in 1896. His treatise on sale, first published in 1845, was notable for the knowledge which it showed, not only of the Year Books, but also of French law, more particularly the works of Pothier and Domat. Lord Campbell appointed Blackburn, whilst still a junior, to be a judge of the King's Bench in 1859, at the age of forty-six. As Blackburn, like Campbell, was a Scot, the appointment evoked both surprise and criticism, but it proved to be an extremely good one—so good, in fact, that Blackburn was the obvious choice as one of the first two Lords of Appeal in Ordinary. His acknowledged mastery of both Common Law and commercial law was an evident source of strength to the reconstituted House of Lords. It is seen to great advantage in decisions such as those of the House of Lords in *Burdick v Sewell*[28] and *Capital and Counties Bank v Henty*,[29] but unlike Bramwell, Blackburn took pains to elucidate the rules of equity, where these required consideration on the appeals before him. The quality of his learning can be appreciated by perusing speeches such as that which he delivered in *Dalton v Angus*.[30] The case had produced a great deal of learning and some considerable variation of opinion in the court, below, and on further appeal, the House of Lords consulted the judges. There were two principal questions, the first being the nature of prescription in relation to an easement of lateral support; and the second, the liability of a principal for the negligence of an independent contractor. Among the judges whose opinions appear in the report are Lindley, Bowen, Fry and Pollock, and among members of the House of Lords, Lord Selborne once again delivered a speech of great acuteness. Nevertheless, it is overshadowed by Blackburn's masterly survey of the law of prescription, not only in English, but also in Scottish, Roman and French law—a survey in which comparative law joined forces with European legal history. By any standards, it is an outstanding judgement, and after its massive learning, Lord Watson was able to state, with evident relief, that it was unnecessary for him to make any lengthy observations on the case.

As Lord Blackburn dominated the earlier decade after the Judicature Acts, Lord Macnaghten dominated over two decades round the turn of the century. His influence is apparent, and some of his judgements—for example, in *Pemsel's Case*[31]—have become part of the normal reading for entrants to the legal profession. One of them, delivered in *Van Grutten v Foxwell*,[32] is one of the classics of judicial literature. Its elegance of form is matched by its erudition, and this is the more noteworthy since it was evoked by such unpromising material as *The Rule in Shelley's Case*, an old chestnut in the law of real property, upon which judges and legal writers alike had expended much industry and learning, and had produced an impressive array of varying opinions.

Since those formative years, the House of Lords has continued to include a number of great intellects, although it would be wrong to assume that there have been no judicial failures in that august assembly. On the other hand, the list of these who have made major contributions to the fabric of English law is an ever-lengthening one, and in our century there have been judges such as Lord Wright, Lord Atkin and others who are fully able to stand alongside the greatest of their predecessors. Sitting as they do in the quietude of the upper chamber, they have the opportunity, within the limits set by judicial precedent, to shape the continuing development of the law in the framework of a rapidly changing social context, re-interpreting the past in the light of the present. It is not open to question that, whilst in face of the legislative omnipotence of Parliament, and the constantly mounting pretensions of the executive, there have been, as the two law lords already mentioned have pointed out, significant retreats, but in other areas less attractive to legislators and bureaucrats, there have also been important gains. For example, in their insistence upon the necessity for natural justice in a steadily extending range of transactions, the courts have performed a valuable service in protecting the individual against arbitrary acts whether it proceeds from an organ of government or from powerful associations.

In some areas, it is not open to question that the balance between judge-made law and legislation has tilted decisively in favour of legislation. For example, the Property Legislation of 1925 virtually ended the creation of the land law by the judges. In this area their function is now one of statutory interpretation. This is by no means a mechanical function, whatever branch of law is under consideration. It is as much a product of judicial ingenuity as the Common Law itself, and beneath the highly technical body of rules governing the interpretation of statutes there are a number of general principles which define the judicial function, and its relation to the legislature.

The first of these is that the judge will approach the construction of a statute through prior decisions upon that part of it which is being construed. That is to say, the doctrine of judicial precedent applies to statutory interpretation just as much as to the Common Law. This is a rule of long standing, and is illustrated by the very large body of case-law which served as a gloss upon section 4 of the Statute of Frauds, 1677. A similar, though not as yet so extensive an apparatus has been created in respect of the Sale of Goods Act, 1893.

Similarly, the case-law upon sections 1 and 2 of the Finance Act, 1894, have gradually given a specialised meaning to these sections, and there are numerous sections of the Property Legislation of 1925 which cannot be correctly understood without consideration of the cases which have been decided on them. Perhaps the best illustrations of all are to be found in decisions upon the Wills Act, 1837 and the Wills Act Amendment Act, 1852, relating to the position of the testator's signature.

As a further development of this principle, if the courts construe a section of a statute in a particular way, and a later act incorporates the section, then it will be assumed that the later act must be construed in the same way, unless the earlier decisions are plainly erroneous, or unless the later act contains a contrary intention.[33]

There is, of course, a possibility that a long line of decisions may extend the terms of a statute or vary its purpose in a way different from what the legislature contemplated. This, indeed, probably happened in the judicial treatment of section 4 of the Statute of Frauds. In such a case, it is for the legislature to provide a remedy. It is not open to English courts to do what Lord Sankey, in a Privy Council decision upon the construction of the Canadian Constitution, suggested might be done—viz return to the act and look at it with a fresh eye, remembering the purpose for which the Constitution was enacted.[34] The Privy Council is not bound, as English courts are, to follow precedents so strictly, and the Canadian Constitution is not simply a statute. It is the fundamental law of Canada. Possibly here Lord Sankey was remembering that the American Supreme Court has always construed the American Constitution in a different way from other legal instruments. In the words of Cardozo:[35] 'A constitution states or ought to state, not rules for the passing hour, but principles for the expanding future.'

In the main, the judges of the American Supreme Court have consistently adhered to this view, and in so doing, they have adapted the constitution of a scantily populated and overwhelmingly agricultural community along the Atlantic seaboard, organised in thirteen states, to the needs of a great transcontinental industrial republic of fifty states.

Lord Sankey's opinion in the Aeronautics Appeal represented a change in the outlook of the Privy Council, brought about by the Statute of Westminster in 1931 and by the growing feeling of national identity in Canada. At an earlier period, the Privy Council, largely influenced by Lord Watson, who was a Lord of Appeal in Ordinary from 1880 to 1899, had construed the key sections 91 and 92 of the British North America Act, 1867, generally in a sense favourable to the rights of the provincial governments, at the expense of those of the dominion government. After the passing of the Statute of Westminster, there was a change in outlook, although this did not prevent the Privy Council, in a series of decisions, from invalidating much of the 'new deal' legislation of the dominion government, in a manner strikingly similar to that of the American Supreme Court in respect of President Roosevelt's *New Deal* legislation in the United States. In the long run, this probably was an important contributory factor in inducing the Canadian Parliament in 1949 to abolish all Canadian appeals to the Privy Council.

The Canadian appeals, especially those upon Canada's *New Deal*, involved a succession of distinguished English law lords in pronouncements upon the constitutionality of Canadian legislation—an exercise familiar to American courts, but not possible in the United Kingdom, in so far as parliamentary legislation is concerned. It is for that reason that the judicial function in interpreting it is so important. Courts may express their views upon the effects of a statute, upon its inadequacies, or even upon its faulty drafting, but they can never refuse to give effect to it. This total divorce from the legislative process has influenced the attitude of the courts in other ways. The courts will not investigate the origin and purpose of a statute as revealed in its parliamentary history, in reports of committees or commissions on which the legislation is based. Lip service is often paid to the intent of the legislature in the course of delivering judgement, but the cases have repeatedly emphasised that the intent is to be discovered from the words used in the statute, not from extraneous sources. One of the clearest expositions of this is to be found in the speech of Lord Watson in the well-known case of *Salomon v Salomon & Co*[36] in the House of Lords. Salomon had incorporated himself as a 'one-man' company under the Companies Act, 1862, and had taken a debenture over the company's assets as security for the purchase price. The Court of Appeal thought that this violated the intent of the Companies Act, 1862, but the House of Lords reversed their decision, holding that Salomon had completely fulfilled the provisions of the Act. Lord Watson said:

> 'Intention of the Legislature' is a common but very slippery phrase, which, popularly understood, may signify anything from intention embodied in positive enactment to speculative opinion as to what the Legislature probably would have meant, although there has been an omission to enact it. In a court of law or equity, what the Legislature intended to be done or not to be done can only be legitimately ascertained from that which it has chosen to enact, either in express words or by reasonable and necessary implication.

Some judges have not always been content to regard their function so narrowly, and in *Mayor and St Mellow's RDC v Newport Corporation*,[37] Denning, LJ, said:

> We sit here to find out the intention of Parliament and of Ministers and carry it out, and we do so the better by filling up the gaps and making sense of the enactment than by opening it up to destructive analysis.

This earned a strong rebuke from Lord Simonds, on appeal, in the House of Lords.[38] Commenting upon this extract from Denning, LJ's, judgement, he said:

> The first part of this passage appears to be an echo of what was said in *Heydon's Case*[39] three hundred years ago, and, so regarded, is not objectionable. But the way in which the learned Lord Justice summarizes the broad rules laid down by Sir Edward Coke in that case may well induce grave misconception of the function of the court. The part which is played in the judicial interpretation of a statute by reference to the circumstances of its passing is too well known to need restatement; it is sufficient to say that the general proposition that it is the

duty of the court to find out the intention of Parliament—and not only of Parliament but of Ministers also—cannot by any means be supported. The duty of the court is to interpret the words that the legislature has used; these words may be ambiguous, but, even if they are, the power and duty of the court to travel outside them is a voyage of discovery that are strictly limited; see, for instance, *Assam Railways & Trading Co Ltd v IRC*,[40] and particularly the observations of Lord Wright.

The second part of the passage that I have cited from the judgment of the learned Lord Justice is no doubt the logical sequel of the first. The court, having discovered the intention of Parliament and of Ministers too, must proceed to fill in the gaps. What the legislature has not written, the court must write. This proposition, which restates in a new form the view expressed by the Lord Justice in the earlier case of *Seaford Court Estates Ltd v Asher*[41] (to which the Lord Justice himself refers), cannot be supported. It appears to me to be a naked usurpation of the legislative function under the then disguise of interpretation. And it is the less justifiable when it is guess-work with what material the legislature would, if it had discovered the gap, have filled it in. If a gap is disclosed, the remedy lies in an amending Act.

So the court will not rescue the legislature, if by any chance the draftsman has slipped. One other aspect of this same problem is that there is no such thing as the 'equity of a statute'. Whenever the court is applying a judicial precedent, it will search for the *ratio decidendi*, and it will seek to apply it whenever the underlying principle would appear to be applicable, but whenever a statute is being applied, it must be shown that the case under consideration falls within its actual words. In his rebuke of Lord Denning, Lord Simonds was in reality saying no more than Lord Sumner had said in *Guardians of Salford Union v Dewhurst*:[42]

Personally, I think it not an unwholesome rule of construction (and construction is the whole of our task) to say that just as we are bound by language of the legislature, so we must abstain from putting upon the legislature anything which is not clearly what it has said, for this very good reason, that it is so expressly apt to make judicial ideas as to what is good for the public or within the vague confines of public policy do duty, instead of a literal and unimaginative interpretation of the legislature's words.

This attitude is in turn derived from another general principle, underlying the interpretation of statutes. It is that every statute is a derogation from pre-existing Common Law. For this reason, although a Common Law precedent declares what the law has always been, the construction of a statute defines the extent to which the statute has modified the law for the future. This can be perceived most plainly in the construction of statutes which impose taxation. Where the Crown claims that a tax is leviable, the onus is upon the Crown to show that the case under consideration falls within the actual provisions of the statute. This is, in essence, simply one application of the principle that there is a presumption against taking away rights conferred by the Common Law. Thus in *Leach v R*[43] the House of Lords was called on to construe section 4 of the Criminal Evidence Act, 1898, which had made a wife a competent witness in cases in which her husband was accused of crime. The question to be decided was whether she was also compellable. The House of Lords decided that she was not, and Lord Atkinson said:

> The principle that a wife is not to be compelled to give evidence against her husband is deep-seated in the common law of this country, and I think if it is to be overturned, it must be overturned by a clear, definite and positive enactment, not by an ambiguous one such as the section relied upon in this case.

So far as taxing-statutes are concerned, Lord Sumner put the position succinctly—'The Crown does not tax an analogy, but by statute.'[44] The same point was made with great force by Lord Tomlin and other law lords in *IRC v Duke of Westminster*.[45] It had been argued on behalf of the Revenue that although certain deeds executed by the duke, containing covenants to pay annual sums, were not within the terms of the Income Tax Act, 1918, they were nevertheless taxable because the substance of the transactions was, in substance, the payment of wages to employees. On this, Lord Tomlin said:

> It is said that in revenue cases there is a doctrine that the court may ignore the legal position and regard what is called 'the substance of the matter', and that here the substance of the matter is that the annuitant was serving the Duke for something equal to his former salary or wages, and that therefore while he is so serving the annuity must be treated as salary or wages. This supposed doctrine—upon which the Commissioners apparently acted—seems to rest for its support upon a misunderstanding of language used in some earlier cases. The sooner this misunderstanding is dispelled and the supposed doctrine given its quietus the better it will be for all concerned, for the doctrine seems to involve substituting 'the uncertain and crooked cord of discretion' for 'the golden and straight mete wand of the law'.[46]
>
> Every man is entitled if he can to order his affairs so that the tax attaching under the appropriate Acts is less than it otherwise would be. If he succeeds in ordering them so as to secure this result, then, however unappreciative the Commissioners of Inland Revenue or his fellow taxpayers may be of his ingenuity, he cannot be compelled to pay an increased tax. This so called doctrine of 'the substance' seems to me to be nothing more than an attempt to make a man pay notwithstanding that he has so ordered his affairs that the amount of tax sought from him is not legally claimable.

It was formerly believed that taxing statutes, like penal statutes, were construed strictly, but today the position is that they are construed like any other statutes, ie in accordance with the meaning to be attributed to the words used. It is for the Crown to establish that a case falls within the scope of the actual language used, and there is no general principle or intent to be extracted from that language. One of the clearest illustrations of this rule of construction is the case of *Ormond Investment Co v Betts*,[47] in which the Court of Appeal had applied a rule applicable to the trading profits of a company to the receipt of dividends from foreign securities, this being regarded as an analogous situation. The decision of the Court of Appeal was reversed by the House of Lords, and Lord Sumner commented acidly:

> In its express terms this rule applies to trading profits. The contention is that by analogy it can be applied to foreign shares, which are not in themselves stock in trade and the dividends of which are not trading profits. I cannot accept this. The analogy between the date of starting a trade, which is the aggregate of many operations, and the date when an investor buys a stock to hold, is too remote to be applicable, and in any case the Crown does not tax by analogy but by statute, and there is nothing in the Act which says what is here contended for.

By a similar rule of construction, in the absence of fraud, the language of dispositions which are affected by tax is taken at its face value. To cite Lord Sumner again in another tax appeal, *Levene v Inland Revenue Commissioners*:

> It is trite law that His Majesty's subjects are free if they can to make their own arrangements so that their cases may fall outside the scope of the taxing Acts. They incur no legal penalties and strictly speaking, no moral censure if, having considered the lines drawn by the legislature for the imposition of taxes, they make it their business to walk outside them.

This principle has been repeatedly re-affirmed by other eminent judges, and its major importance, from the standpoint of personal freedom, cannot be exaggerated, more especially having regard to the extent and severity of modern taxation. It is the foundation of all modern estate planning, and without it, the last bastion of private property in a collectivist society would have been destroyed.

The contest between the taxpayer and the Revenue is one conducted in accordance with strict rules, of which the courts are the guardians. The legislature is at liberty to alter the rules at any time, and has frequently done so to make taxable dispositions which had previously been free under the rules existing when they were made. In the words of Lord Greene, MR:[48]

> For years a battle of manoeuvre has been waged between the legislature and those who are minded to throw the burden of taxation off their own shoulders on to those of their fellow-subjects. In that battle the legislature has often been worsted by the skill, determination and resourcefulness of its opponents of whom the present appellant has not been the least successful. It would not shock us in the least to find that the legislature has determined to put an end to the struggle by imposing the severest penalties. It scarcely lies in the mouth of the taxpayer who plays with fire to complain of burnt fingers.

Perhaps so, but it still remains the function of the court to decide whether the words a section actually have achieved the desired end. In *Vestey's Executors v IRC*[49] Lord Simonds said:

> The determination of these appeals involves a consideration of certain sections of two Acts of Parliament (Finance Acts, 1936, S 18, and Finance Act, 1938, S 38) which are designed to bring within the ambit of taxation to income tax and surtax, income which would otherwise escape that burden. For that reason and because the ways of those who would avoid liability to tax are often devious and obscure, the sections are framed in language of the widest, most general scope, and in the case of one of the Acts (I refer to the Finance Act, 1936, S 18(4)) the operative subsections are reinforced by a provision which appears to exhort the assessing authority, and presumably the court, to let the balance, wherever possible, be weighed against

the taxpayer. But, this notwithstanding, I think it remains the taxpayer's privilege to claim exemption from tax unless his case is fairly brought within the words of the taxing section.

Judges are well aware of the major importance of their function in taxation cases. In his address to the Holdsworth Club, *The Courts as Legislators*, Lord Diplock (then Diplock, LJ) said:

> Every revenue appeal that comes before the court—generally after any dispute of fact there may have been has already been decided by the Commissioners—involves a dispute as to whether a particular kind of gain is taxable, whether a particular kind of document attracts stamp duty. Whenever the court decides that kind of dispute it legislates about taxation. It makes a law taxing all gains of the same kind or all documents of the same kind. Do not let us deceive ourselves with the legal fiction that the court is only ascertaining and giving effect to what Parliament meant. Anyone who has decided tax appeals knows that most of them concern transactions which members of Parliament and the draftsmen of the Act had not anticipated, about which they had never thought at all. Some of the transactions are of a kind which had never taken place before the Act was passed: they were devised as a result of it. The court may describe what it is doing in tax appeals as interpretation. So did the priestess of the Delphi oracle. But whoever has final authority to explain what Parliament meant by the words that it used makes law as much as if the explanation it has given were contained in a new Act of Parliament. It will need a new Act of Parliament to reverse it.[50]

Whilst the courts have been able to preserve the essential rights of the citizen against the Crown in matters of taxation, and the right to know precisely the rules governing its imposition upon him, they have fought a prolonged battle with the executive on the broader front of judicial review of administrative adjudications, arising from the proliferation of administrative tribunals, the chief stages of which have already been discussed. The principal lesson to be learned from it is that so long as departments of state are able to shelter behind the smoke-screen of parliamentary sovereignty the power of the courts to intervene is confined within narrow limits.

Although not hesitant in the protection of the subject's property rights as against the ever-more comprehensive demands of the revenue, the courts have occasionally shown themselves reluctant to avail themselves of powers which they undoubtedly possess in order to assist the subject to diminish his burdens. Such problems have again arisen in the field of estate planning. Here, settlors were faced with a dilemma. If a power of revocation and modification were included in a settlement, the settlor was held not to have completely divested himself of the property settled, and accordingly, he still remained liable for tax upon it. If he completely transferred the property to the trustees, the settlement could only be subsequently modified in the unlikely event that everyone entitled to a beneficial interest, whether present or future, vested or contingent, were *sui juris*, and could therefore give an effective consent when modifications were desired. Such a situation could rarely, if ever, exist. On the other hand, a court of equity possessed an inherent jurisdiction to sanction transactions for the benefit of infants or unborn persons. The broad question of policy to be settled was whether a court of equity would exercise its discretionary jurisdiction on behalf of such persons of defective capacity, when modifications in a settlement were desired for minimising the burden of taxation, where all the persons of full capacity were in favour of the change. The incidence of taxation, it should be added, might change very greatly during the existence of a modern trust. This was the policy question which the Court of Appeal and the House of Lords were called upon to decide in *Chapman v Chapman*[51] and both courts thought that the jurisdiction could not be exercised in favour of a modification of trust interests primarily to reduce taxation. In the Court of Appeal, Lord Denning (who dissented) said that where the court had doubted that it should exercise a discretion which it had jurisdiction to exercise, such a restrictive decision had not infrequently been followed by a statute conferring it in plain terms, but this view did not commend itself either to his colleagues or to the members of the House of Lords. The policy question was most clearly put in the speech of Lord Morton in the following terms:

> If the court had power to approve, and did approve, schemes such as the present scheme, the way would be open for a most undignified game of chess between the Chancery Division and the legislature. The alteration of one settlement for the purposes of avoiding taxation already imposed might well be followed by scores of successful applications for a similar purpose by beneficiaries under other settlements. The legislature might then counter this move by imposing fresh taxation upon the settlement as thus altered. The beneficiaries would then troop back to the Chancery Division and say, 'Please alter the trusts again. You have the power, the adults desire it, and it is for the benefit of the infants to avoid this fresh taxation. The legislature may not move again.' So the game might go on, if the judges of the Chancery Division had the power which the appellants claim for them, and if they thought it right to make the first move.

This undue judicial timidity in face of the Revenue evoked a prompt response from a legislature which apparently remained quite unimpressed by the undignified game of chess which Lord Morton foresaw. The Variation of Trusts Act, 1958, expressly conferred on the court a power to vary trust provisions in very wide terms, and modifications primarily for the diminution of the burden of tax are now approved with very great frequency. So in this instance Lord Denning was a more accurate prophet than Lord Morton; but the case clearly shows the discomfort of some of our most eminent judges in facing social problems of this importance.

It is not open to question that many modern judges regard their function as a good deal more limited than that of their predecessors, and are somewhat pessimistic about its future.

Even so, it would be quite wrong to regard the attitude of the present-day judiciary as defeatist. New principles are constantly making their appearance, and old principles are being constantly re-examined, and, if socially valuable, are being extended. Some have already been mentioned, but one or two additional ones may be given. It used to be accepted law that the court would never award specific performance of a contract of personal service. Since the recent decision of *Hill v Parsons*[52] this may no longer be an absolute rule. In the sphere of trade union law, the courts have steadily extended their protection of a member against arbitrary action by his union or its committee. In the law of contract, important new principles relating to frustration and to the 'fundamental term' (this latter doctrine operating as a protection of the purchaser or hirer in contracts relating to the sale or hire of motor vehicles) have won acceptance. It is perhaps in the law of torts, and particularly in the law of negligence, that the activity of the judiciary can be observed on the widest front. The important extension of liability in negligence of a manufacturer of goods to the ultimate consumer or user, independently of any contract, in *Donaghue v Stevenson*[53] (the 'snail in the Ginger Beer Bottle Case') has already been noticed in an earlier chapter. Later decisions defined the extent of that principle, but in so doing they excluded situations involving the owners or builders of real property. A changing social outlook made that exclusion anomalous, and accordingly, in *Dutton v Bognor Regis Council*[54] the Court of Appeal took this further step forward in a decision which is notable in several ways. Besides its extension of the principle in *Donaghue v Stevenson* to real property, it also made liable to the original owner for negligence a local authority whose inspector had executed his statutory duty negligently, thereby involving the owner in loss. Again, the decision is notable because Lord Denning, in another impressive judgement, discussed frankly the matters of social policy which have so often failed in the past to obtain expression in English judgements. It will be interesting to see how far this practice, so familiar in American judgements, is followed in the future.

To sum up: there have been retreats in the exercise of the judicial function, as Lords Devlin and Diplock have pointed out;

there has been a change of function, a consequence of the great extensions of statute law; but finally, there have been notable advances, in areas in which, as yet, the legislature shows only occasional interest. Today, therefore, English law still draws extensively upon the work of the judiciary in the past, but that material itself is in process of continuous transformation. Although the province of the modern judge is more restricted than that of his predecessors, the part which he plays in the development of the law, and his assessment of the extent and direction of social change make his task no less exacting than theirs.

Nevertheless, there remain some major problems for the future, which must be briefly mentioned. The apparent association of the judiciary with the legislature, which is evidenced by the membership of the law lords in the House of Lords as a second Chamber, and the participation in government and in the Cabinet by the Lord Chancellor, have been frequently commented upon. In general, the law lords have not strayed far beyond the area of law reform in their participation in the legislative work of the House, and on the whole, this association today is not of major importance. Nevertheless, a final separation might please the constitutional purist. The presence of the Lord Chancellor in the government is, historically, a survival, and today a Lord Chancellor, whilst in office, has little time for the decision of cases in court. His continued existence as a cabinet minister has, in reality, prevented the evolution of a Department of Justice, presided over by someone who is not necessarily a lawyer. The creation of such an office has always been strongly resisted by the legal profession, but it may not be indefinitely shelved. There are also other major questions. One is the narrow area from which the higher judiciary is selected. Recently, the claim of solicitors to break the monopoly which the Bar has retained for so long has been strongly pressed. In the United States, the area of selection is wider. It includes leading academic lawyers, and there has been a two-way traffic between bench and university, to the benefit of both.

In one respect there are already signs that English judges are taking pains to make explicit the social implications of the decisions which they deliver. This is apparent, for example, in the decision of the Court of Appeal in *Dutton v Bognor Regis Council*. Such expositions have for some time been a feature of major American decisions, under the collective name of 'the Brandeis brief', from the Supreme Court Judge who first gave form to them. One may anticipate that, under present conditions, this practice will spread in English courts.

Over and above all these questions, however, there remains the issue of personal liberty in the modern state. It has been shown that judges have already expressed anxiety on this question, and that their efforts have been directed towards controlling the power, not only of the executive, with its ever-more comprehensive regulation of every aspect of modern life, but also against mighty organisations, whether trade unions or bodies controlling other aspects of social life. Their activities, however, are at all points limited by the fact that no English court has power to pronounce upon the validity of Acts of Parliament. They do not have, as American courts have, an independent constitutional position. In the last resort, therefore, the success of their efforts must continually depend upon the extent to which they are supported by an enlightened public opinion which is aware of the limitations under which they function.

Notes and References

CHAPTER 1

1 H. Cam. *Selected Historical Essays of F. W. Maitland* (1957)
2 Ibid, xi
3 Tout. *The Place of the Reign of Edward II in English History* (2nd ed), 79
4 Ibid, 79-80
5 Maitland. *The Constitutional History of England*, 142-3
6 Richardson and Sayles. *The Governance of Mediaeval England From The Conquest to Magna Carta* (1963), 62
7 Ibid, chapter 3, note 6
8 Ibid, 50
9 Stenton. *Saxon England*, 473
10 Ibid, 362, note 12
11 Ibid, 362
12 Ibid, 636

CHAPTER 2

1 They are considered in Bigelow's *History of English Legal Procedure* (1880)
2 Stenton, op cit, 644, note 12
3 Book I, chapter 2
4 Pollock and Maitland. *The History of English Law Before the Time of Edward I*, 252-3

CHAPTER 3

1 [1953] 1 Ch, 149
2 Ibid, 162
3 *Current Legal Problems* (1949), 116
4 Richardson and Sayles, op cit, 157
5 It has been suggested that it was really written by Glanvill's nephew, Hubert Walter. See Plucknett. *Concise History of the Common Law* (1956), 18
6 Stubbs. *Constitutional History*, 326
7 Richardson and Sayles, op cit, 175-88
8 Ibid, 182
9 Ibid, 197-8
10 Plucknett, op cit, 110
11 Pollock and Maitland, op cit, 143

12 Richardson and Sayles, op cit, 205
13 Pollock and Maitland, op cit, 138

CHAPTER 4

1 There is an extensive literature on these trials. See particularly M. M. Bigelow. *Placita Anglo–Normannica* (1879); G. B. Adams. *Councils and Courts in Anglo–Norman England* (1926)
2 See particularly *The Governance of Mediaeval England*
3 Pp178-80
4 Richardson and Sayles, op cit, 152
5 Ibid, 245
6 Ibid, 384-6
7 YB 32, 33 Edw I (Rolls Series), 429
8 YB 33 and 35 Edw I (Rolls Series), 82
9 *Belyng v Anon* (1312), YB 5 Edw II (SS 31), 177
10 *Statutes and Their Interpretation*, 70
11 William Latimer, the Plaintiff
12 The Bishop of Bath and Wells, then Lord Chancellor
13 Eyre of Kent III (SS vol 29), 53
14 Tout. *The Place of the Reign of Edward II in English History*, 51, note 3
15 Tout, op cit, 50
16 *Concise History of the Common Law* (8th ed), 259
17 *History of English Law*, II, 286
18 SS vol 85, xxxvi-xc
19 SS vol 53
20 *The Eyre Rolls of Lincolnshire and Worcestershire*, xix
21 *The Place of Edward II*, 328
22 SS vol 22, xxi

CHAPTER 5

1 Holdsworth, op cit, II, 313
2 *Concise History of the Common Law*, 224
3 Holdsworth, op cit, II, 573
4 YB 33-5 Edw I (RS), 83
5 Ibid, 584
6 Holdsworth, op cit, II, 308
7 [1901] AC 446
8 [1898] AC 1
9 *Concise History of the Common Law* (5th ed), 25-9
10 Holdsworth, op cit, II, 554-6
11 *English Law and the Renaissance in Historical Essays*, 140
12 *Concise History of the Common Law* (5th ed), 627
13 (1602) 4 Reps 92b
14 [1941] AC 1
15 Ie he could declare under oath that he was not indebted, and thus escape liability to pay
16 Ie the judge
17 Op cit, 461
18 Op cit, 459

CHAPTER 6

1 (1880) 13 Ch D 696
2 This comparison of the Chancellor with the Praetor is highly interesting
3 Cited in Holdsworth, HEL, op cit, XII, 262
4 (1676) 3 Swanst 600
5 Dr Yale in his edition of *Lord Nottingham's Cases* (p368) notices that Nottingham's implied trusts are really constructive trusts and his presumptive trusts are implied trusts
6 *Essays in Legal History*, 294
7 *Lord Nottingham's Cases*, introduction, xvii-xx
8 (1683) 1 Vern, 163
9 (1684) 1 Vern, 273
10 (1683) 1 Vern, 220
11 (1682) 1 Vern, 135
12 (1750) 1 Ves Sen, 444
13 Eg *Hollis v Edwards* (1683), 1 Vern, 159
14 [1947] Ch 716
15 (1669) 1 Ch Cas, 135
16 Ibid, 148
17 (1675) 1 Ch Cas, 256
18 (1682) 1 Vern, 96
19 [1948] Ch 465, 485
20 Dr Yale has an admirable discussion of them. *Lord Nottingham's Cases*, II, 195-207
21 (1683) 1 Vern, 162
22 [1951] AC 251
23 [1953] Ch 218
24 [1901] 2 Ch 534
25 Pp 269-70
26 (1686) 1 Vern, 438
27 [1954] AC 429
28 (1688) 2 Vern, 50
29 (1684) 1 Vern, 296. See further, Keeton. *Lord Chancellor Jeffreys*, ch 13
30 [1970] 2 WLR 1110
31 (1673) Fin 53
32 (1694) Free, Ch 198
33 Holdsworth, op cit, VIII, 193-237
34 (1719) 1 P Wms, 570
35 (1726) Cas t King, 61
36 (1750) 1 Ves Sen, 444
37 Holdsworth, op cit, XII, 216
38 Ibid, 256
39 (1750) 2 Ves Sen, 250
40 [1934] 1 KB, 380
41 [1889] 14 App Cas, 337
42 [1914] AC 932
43 (1789) 3 Term Rep, 51
44 (1863) 1 De GJ & S, 185
45 [1903] 1 Ch 211
46 (1681) 1 Vern, 33
47 *Barter v Manning* (1684) 1 Vern, 244; *Shuttleworth v Leywick* (1684) 1 Vern, 245

48 (1750) 2 Ves Sen, 190
49 *Hulme v Tenant* (1778) 1 Bro CC, 16
50 (1791) 3 Bro CC, 340
51 (1811) 18 Ves, 429, 434

CHAPTER 7

1 3 St Tr, 825
2 12 Co Rep, 74
3 (1615) 1 Ch Rep, 1
4 Moore, 898
5 11 St Tr, 1165
6 Holdsworth, op cit, 510-11
7 (1868) LR 3 Ex, 223
8 *The Supreme Court in the American System of Government*, 9-27

CHAPTER 8

1 [1923] 1 Ch, 258, 266, upheld in the House of Lords *sub nom.* *AG v National Provincial Bank* [1924], AC 262
2 *Morice v Bishop of Durham* (1804), 9 Ves, 399, 405
3 [1891] AC 531
4 (1805) 10 Ves, 522
5 P532
6 [1891] AC 531
7 [1941] Ch 308, 310
8 [1944] AC 341
9 Ibid
10 *Re Diplock* [1948] Ch 988
11 [1959] AC 457
12 (1862) 31 Beav 14, 19
13 See the *Myth of Superstitious Uses*. Keeton. *The Modern Law of Charities*, Ch III
14 [1919] AC 815
15 [1949] AC 426
16 [1949] AC 426
17 [1953] 1 WLR 725
18 (1669) Cas in Ch 134
19 [1948] 2 All ER 842
20 [1907] 1 Ch 382 following *Thornber v Wilson*, Drew 350 and *Re Delaney* [1902] 2 Ch Ch 642
21 [1912] AC 197
22 [1931] 1 Ch 197
23 [1939] AC 430
24 [1907] 1 Ch 382 following *Thornber v Wilson*, Drew 350 and *Re Delaney* [1902] 2 Ch Ch 642
25 [1948] Ch 257
26 [1945] Ch 123
27 [1955] AC 572
28 *Oppenheim v Tobacco Securities Trust* [1951], AC 297
29 (1952) Cmnd 8710
30 [1910] 2 Ch 124
31 (1859) 27 Beav 107, 111

32 (1835) 2 Beav 317a
33 See Keeton. *The Modern Law of Charities*, pp121 et seq
34 P632
35 *Nathan Report*, p83

CHAPTER 9

1 (1875) 44 LJ Ex 157, 162
2 2 Lut 1582
3 Holdsworth, op cit, pp526 et seq
4 *Luke v Lyde* (1759) 2 Burr 887
5 Gross. *Select Cases in the Law Merchant*, introduction, xvii
6 Ibid, xviii
7 Eyre of London (ed H. Cern), II, 184
8 Holdsworth, op cit, I, 542
9 Ibid, 531
10 On the Rhodian Sea Law, see Ashburner. *The Rhodian Sea Law* (1909); and L. Pleionis, 'The Influence of the Rhodian Sea Law', in *Revue Hellenique* (1967), 171
11 (1875) LR 10 Ex 76; 337 (affirmed by HL 1 App Ca 476)
12 (1846) 12 Cl & F 805
13 [1898] 2 QB 658
14 Holdsworth, op cit, 146
15 Vol 1, 247
16 (1875) LR 10 Ex 76
17 [1898] 2 QB 658
18 Third ed, p23
19 Carr. *Select Charters of Trading Companies*, 70-1
20 *Morse v Slew* (1671), 3 Keb 72, 1121, 135
21 *Select Pleas in the Court of Admiralty*, 9, xxx
22 (1951) 67 LQR 230
23 (1701) Cas t Holt 495
24 (1771) 26 St Tr 1
25 (1704) 2 *Ler* Raym 909
26 *Lives of the Chief Justices*, II, 137
27 (1700) 1 Ld Raym 574
28 (1702) 2 Ld Raym 757
29 Holdsworth, op cit, VI, 522
30 Atk 40, 47
31 1 Sch & Lef 152
32 Cowper 161
33 *Lives of the Chief Justices*, II, 407
34 (1810) 12 East 648
35 [1921] 2 AC 41
36 2 TR 62
37 Holdsworth, op cit, XII, 138
38 *R v Wilkes* (1770) 4 Burr 2549
39 Holdsworth, op cit, XII, 477

CHAPTER 10

1 [1939] AC 356, 364
2 [1924] AC 797

3 [1970] 3 WLR 934
4 [1969] 1 AC 645
5 (1868) 7 Wallace 700, 733
6 (1779) 21 St Tr 1045
7 (1876) LR 2 Ex D 63
8 [1905] 2 KB 401-2
9 [1890] 24 QBD 368
10 Ca t Talb 281
11 3 Burr 1478
12 4 Burr 2015
13 Holdsworth, op cit, XII, 694
14 Lord Stowell in DNB (cited in Holdsworth, op cit, XIII, 679)
15 (1799) 1 C Rob 349
16 Eg in *The Maria*
17 [1916] 2 AC 77
18 Holdsworth, op cit, XIII, 689
19 (1827) 2 Hagg Adm 94
20 (1811) 2 Hagg Con 54, 161
21 (1688) 2 Vern, 48
22 6 Co Rep 48 (a)
23 (1765) 3 Burr 1664, 1672
24 A. N. Seck. 'Conflicts of Laws in the History of English Law', *Law: A Century of Progress,* III, 3, 4, 5
25 (1760) 2W Bl 234
26 (1774) 1 Cowp 161
27 (1775) 1 Cowp 341, 344
28 (1752) 2 Hagg Con 395
29 (1811) 2 Hagg Con 54

CHAPTER 11

1 [1967] 2 All ER 367, 377
2 *Edwards v SOGAT* [1970], 3 WLR 713, 720
3 [1909] 1 KB 901
4 (1796) 6 Term Rep 619, 636
5 Holdsworth, op cit, 500
6 (1855) 6 E & B 47
7 6 Term R 619
8 [1867] LR 2 QB 153
9 [1869] LR 4 QB 602
10 (1837) 3 M & W 1
11 (1847) 5 Cox 495
12 (1851) 5 Cox 436
13 (1867) 10 Cox 600
14 [1915] AC 829
15 Holdsworth, op cit, XV, 71-3
16 (1872) 12 Cox 316
17 (1853) 2 E & B 224
18 (1881) 6 QBD 333
19 *Gregory v Duke of Brunswick* (1843), 13 LJC, 34
20 (1893) 1 QB 715
21 [1892] AC 25

22 (1893) 1 QB 715
23 [1898] AC 1
24 [1901] AC 495
25 [1901] AC 426
26 *Amalgamated Society v Osborne* [1910], AC 87
27 [1926] 85 LJ Ch 192
28 [1956] AC 104
29 [1970] 3 WLR 713
30 *Dickson v Pharmaceutical Society* [1970], AC 403
31 [1969] 2 WLR 289
32 [1964] AC 1129
33 [1969] 2 QB 303
34 [1973] 1 WLR 521

CHAPTER 12

1 [1954] 1 WLR 945
2 Ibid, 953
3 [1914] AC 398, 456
4 (1615) Hob 85
5 *Wiseman v Borneman* [1969] 3 AE ER 275, 278
6 *Cooper v Wandsworth Board of Works* (1863), 14 CBNS 180, 194
7 (1911) 27 LT 509
8 [1913] 3 KB 835, 842
9 [1914] 1 KB 160, 199
10 (1807) Camp 63
11 [1870] 40 LJ QB 73 75
12 (1867) 16 LT 529
13 *Ochsenbein v Papelier* (1873) LR 8 Ch 695, 700
14 *Conflict of Laws* (7th ed), 1011
15 (1872) LR 4 PC 144
16 (1928) 138 LTR 386
17 [1924] 72
18 [1969] 1 WLR 1506
19 [1951] P404
20 Schwarzenberger. *International Law as Applied by International Courts* (3rd ed), 620
21 [1950] 2 KB 410
22 [1950] 2 KB 417
23 Ibid, 421
24 [1913] 1 KB 463; [1914] 1 KB 160; [1915] AC 120
25 [1911] AC 179
26 [1913] 1 KB 463; [1914] 1 KB 160; [1915] AC 120
27 [1915] 84 LJ KB 72, 75
28 [1914] 1 KB 160, 190
29 [1914] 1 KB 160, 175
30 Ibid, 179
31 [1914] 1 KB 160, 185
32 [1962] 2 QB 677
33 [1915] AC 120, 130
34 Ibid, 132

35 Ibid, 138
36 [1915] AC 120, 150
37 For examples, see de Smith. *Judicial Review of Administrative Action*, Ch 4 and 5
38 [1940] Ch 70
39 Lloyd. *Unincorporated Associations and the Law*, 127
40 (1881) 17 Ch D 615
41 [1920] 2 KB 523
42 [1943] AC 627
43 Ibid, 644
44 [1929] 1 Ch 602
45 This is discussed by the Court of Appeal in *Leeson v General Council of Medical Education* [1889] 43 Ch D 366 and *Atkinson v General Council of Medical Education* [1894] 1 QB 750
46 [1949] 1 All ER 109
47 [1929] 1 Ch 602
48 Third ed, 331
49 [1956] 1 WLR 833
50 [1952] 2 QB 329
51 *Amalgamated Society of Carpenters, Cabinet Makers and Joiners v Braithwaite* [1922] 2 AC 440
52 [1956] AC 104
53 Chapter XI
54 [1971] 2 WLR 742
55 [1967] 2 QB 617, 630
56 [1970] 2 QB 417, 430
57 [1968] AC 997
58 Cf cases cited in *Schmidt v Secretary of State for Home Affairs* [1969] 2 Ch 149, 170-1
59 [1968] AC 997
60 [1971] 1 WLR 534
61 [1964] AC 46

CHAPTER 13

1 Eg as in *L'Estrange v Graucob* [1934] 2 KB 394
2 [1932] AC 562
3 [1937] AC 576, 583
4 [1951] AC 601
5 Section 103
6 (1868) LR 3 HL 330
7 [1949] AC 156
8 (1868) 3 HL 330
9 *Green v Chelsea Waterworks Co* (1894) 70 LT 54
10 Presumably as an alternative to an allegation of wilful harm
11 [1919] 2 KB 43
12 (1936) 155 LT 550
13 [1932] AC 562
14 (1837) 2 M & W 1
15 *Hutchinson v York Railway Co* (1850) 5 EX 351
16 [1939] AC 215
17 [1938] AC 57
18 [1943] AC 81, 103

19 [1897] 2 QB 57
20 [1901] 2 KB 669
21 [1925] 1 KB 141
22 [1943] AC 92
23 [1921] 3 KB 560
24 *London Joint Stock Bank v Macmillan* [1918] AC 777
25 *Weld-Blundell v Stephens* [1920] AC 956
26 [1961] AC 388
27 [1943] AC 448
28 *The Wagon Mound* (No 2) [1967] AC 617
29 *The Lessons of the Torrey Canyon in Current Legal Problems* (1968), 94-112
30 [1935] 1 KB 354
31 [1937] AC 826
32 [1941] AC 157
33 Gilbert, in fact, put it very neatly in *The Mikado*:

Is life a boon?
Why then it must befall
That death whene'er he call,
Must call too soon.

34 This is difficult to follow. The award is for the loss of *expectation* of life, not for loss of expectation of *enjoyment*
35 [1939] 3 All ER 960, 967

CHAPTER 14

1 [1910] 1 KB 410
2 [1917] AC 260
3 [1929] 1 KB 619
4 [1894] AC 347
5 [1931] AC 494
6 [1948] AC 87
7 [1951] 1 KB 711
8 [1969] 2 WLR 163
9 'Judicial Control of the Administrative Process' in *Current Legal Problems* (1971), 13
10 [1968] 2 WLR 924
11 [1971] 2 WLR 742
12 [1970] 3 WLR 871
13 [1948] 1 KB 223
14 [1970] 1 WLR 1424
15 [1965] 1 WLR 1320, 1326
16 [1971] 1 WLR 433

CHAPTER 15

1 Adolphus. *Pitt*, VI, 71 (cited in Campbell. *Lives of the Chancellors*, VI, 494)
2 4 Inst 279
3 *Evidence* (10th ed), 166
4 *Criminal Law* (14th ed), 278-9
5 [1933] 1 KB 529
6 [1954] 1 QB 158

7 [1962] AC 220
8 [1972] 3 WLR 143

CHAPTER 16

1 *Samples of Law Making*, 6
2 (1708) 12 Mod 669, 687
3 [1942] AC 206
4 [1942] AC 624
5 P119
6 [1971] 2QB 175
7 [1968] AC 997
8 In *Government in Post-War England* [1956] 72 LQR 42
9 *The Wensleydale Peerage Case*, 5 HLC 958
10 [1915] 1 KB 1
11 [1947] KB 130
12 *Law Reform and Law Making*
13 (1883) 52 LJ QB 442
14 (1883) 52 LJ QB 737
15 (1883) 52 LJ QB 140
16 (1883) 52 LJ QB 193
17 6 Rep 596
18 29 LJ Ch 503
19 A former Lord Chancellor
20 The Earl of Selborne
21 (1883) 52 LJ QB 313
22 *Wiseman v Vanderput* 2 Vern 203
23 (1883) 52 LJ KB 380
24 (1883) 52 LJ QB 464
25 (1878) 3 Ex D 243
26 (1889) AC 337
27 [1892] AC 18
28 (1884) 10 AC 90
29 (1882) 7 AC 769
30 (1881) 6 AC 808
31 [1891] AC 531
32 [1897] AC
33 *Lancashire & Yorkshire Railway v Bury Corporation* (1889) 14 App Cas 417
34 *Re Aeronautics in Canada* [1932] AC 54
35 *Nature of the Judicial Process* p83
36 [1897] AC 22
37 [1950] 2 All ER 1226, 1236
38 [1952] AC 189, 190-1
39 (1583) 3 Co Rep 7a
40 [1935] AC 445
41 [1949] 2 KB 481, 498-9
42 [1926] AC 619, 633
43 [1912] AC 305
44 *Ormand Investment Co v Betts* [1928] AC 143, 158
45 [1936] AC 1
46 These terms are used by Coke 4 Inst 41
47 [1928] AC 143

48 *Lord Howard de Walden v IRC* [1942] 1 KB 389, 397
49 [1949] 1 All ER 1108, 112-13
50 [1928] AC 217
51 [1954] AC 429
52 [1971] 3 WLR 995
53 [1932] AC 562
54 [1972] 2 WLR 299

Index